Trumpets of Jubilee

CONSTANCE ROURKE

TRUMPETS OF JUBILEE

Henry Ward Beecher
Harriet Beecher Stowe
Lyman Beecher
Horace Greeley
P. T. Barnum

WITH AN INTRODUCTION
BY KENNETH S. LYNN

A Harbinger Book
Harcourt, Brace & World, Inc.
NEW YORK AND BURLINGAME

For MY MOTHER

First Harbinger Books edition 1963
LIBRARY OF CONGRESS CATALOG CARD NUMBER: 63-20973

Printed in the United States of America

Contents

Foreword

IT *is a habit in these days to scorn popularity, and to measure success-*
ful leaders by their product, which may not be always exquisite.
But popularity is a large gauge and a lively symbol; the popular leader
is nothing less than the vicarious crowd, registering much that is essential and otherwise obscure in social history, hopes and joys and conflicts
and aspirations which may be crude and transitory, but none the less
are the stuff out of which the foundations of social life are made. At
certain times and in certain places popularity becomes a highly dramatic
mode of expression. One of the places, surely, is our own country; one
of the times that middle period of our history when at last the great experiment in voicing the popular will was fairly launched. As the new
century rolled into amplitude a chosen people moved forward; the surge
into the wilderness brought strange new hopes companioned by antique
memories and despairs; not an easy triumph took place, but an immense
conflict of the human spirit. In this era of shattering change, many shrill
or stentorian voices were lifted; orators appeared on every platform;
with their babel arose an equal babel of print; perhaps there never was
such a noisy chorus or so fervid a response. Words—the popular mind
was intoxicated by words; speech might have provided liberation; sheer
articulation apparently became a boon. A public which was not yet a
civilization, which much less composed a society, might have been seeking a common legend or sign manual.

Out of that large and stirring confusion arose a few orphic figures:
Emerson, Whitman, Melville, Thoreau, possibly Hawthorne, and in another arena, Lincoln; but we shall be concerned with these only as they
oddly mix with the multitude or clash with it, or cross the paths of our
popular characters. In the expectancy of considerable rewards we shall
fix our gaze upon success; we shall choose figures who have commanded
superlatives, in the numbers which they drew to themselves, in the
praises which they received, in the huge tumultuous reverberations

which they produced in the public situation. Harriet Beecher Stowe, Henry Ward Beecher, Horace Greeley: each of these attained the utmost degree of popularity. Who indeed outstripped them in their time? Mrs. Stowe's great novel was read by millions around the world. Beecher took the Rocky Mountains as his soundingboard. Greeley founded the most popular newspaper of the century, and maintained during an entire era a stormy personal eminence which has most often been accorded to public leaders briefly in times of conflict.

Into this numbered company steps another character, or rather crowds his way, as indeed from the briefest acquaintance one might guess that he would do: the rusty, antiquated figure of Lyman Beecher, fabled in his time as the father of more brains than any man in America. He claims our attention first because of his famous son and daughter; but he stoutly holds his ground by virtue of a tenacious character and an extended public influence. Even with his far narrower public in small villages of the older New England, in a circumscribed Boston, in a thinly populated Ohio valley, Lyman Beecher matched his better-known offspring in timely ascendancy. He had a singular gift for encountering major movements in his period—for crashing into them, glancing past them, or riding them as a skilled swimmer rides a wave. His ardent temperament concentrated popular influences which reached forward even as his own long and eager life reached forward.

These characters had a unity beyond that created by their vast popularity. They sprang from the soil of New England, "the seed-bed of the great American Republic," as one of them grandly observed, "and all that is likely to come of it." Even in the matter of time the younger group was closely bound together; they were born in successive years, 1811, 1812, 1813. With Lyman Beecher as a forerunner or a disputant of their choices they bring together certain high contrasts and progressions and even climaxes. And, through time and place and popularity, they evoke still another figure, who at first glance might seem to belong to quite a different gallery, the rotund and Rabelaisian Barnum. Born in 1810, he was their exact contemporary. He too hailed from New England, and was agog with movements. He crammed them into his many-sided spectacles by instinct or intention; he used the popular medium of language in superabundance; he was a writer, an orator, a bally-hoo shouter, and perhaps the great plastic artist of his time. With a sweep of powerful fancy he reached back into the era of Lyman Beecher; by an elastic stride he kept pace with the younger group, touched the same aggregations, encountered the same influences—and gave these his own powerful twist.

Popular authority is hardly a simple affair; between the leader and his audience innumerable relationships can exist, with odd inversions and unexpected rôles. Public life is lived on many levels, is reached by many circuitous paths, is the result of obscure personal impulses or imperative inner struggles. Within the public drama passes another, which may be intricate or shadowy, but is always dominant. There they were, in the midst of their crowds, those public figures, solitary like the rest of us. What were their inner motives and goals? What went on behind the showy admired front of their public fame? Within the hidden channels of their lives, what did it come to, this immense living in public? Such secrets are difficult; these figures have come down to us even from so recent a past with a thick mantle of legend upon them.

In their train comes others. With Lyman Beecher appear his three wives, his eleven less famous children, and certain figures of an older period by whom he was influenced or with whom he did battle. He dragged many in his train; they all did, or were swept into the concentered circles of other existences. Here we must begin, in the peopled region of a smaller world. We need not speculate whether characters are more important than epochs. "The times are a masquerade of the eternities," said Emerson. We may come to believe that the social panorama is transcendent; and surely the secrets of an era are as deeply buried as those of an individual. But character remains an inexhaustible matrix; so, aware of the task, we shall consider these five popular figures and the men and women by whom they were intimately surrounded. If something of their guise and gait can appear, or even their obscurer fancies, then perhaps a little of the singular life of the mid-century may crowd through, with its constricted spaciousness, its stirring trouble, and loud laughter.

Introduction to the
Harbinger Edition

Kenneth S. Lynn

Thronging. It was one of Constance Rourke's favorite words. She loved, as Whitman did, the sense of being a part of the American crowd, and the best of her books make us feel the throb of a collective excitement. While her literary attention centered on individuals—in whose personal eccentricities she clearly rejoiced—the One was always taken to be the symbol of the Many. As she wrote in the foreward to *Trumpets of Jubilee,* her first book, popular leaders like Lyman Beecher, Harriet Beecher Stowe, Henry Ward Beecher, Horace Greeley, and P. T. Barnum were "nothing less than the vicarious crowd, registering much that is essential and otherwise obscure in social history, hopes and joys and conflicts and aspirations which may be crude and transitory, but none the less are the stuff out of which the foundations of social life are made"; even when she went on to deal with writers like Nathaniel Hawthorne and Emily Dickinson—who could scarcely be described as having the popular touch of a Barnum or a Beecher—she nevertheless conceived of them in a social way: as interpreters of a people's quest for national identity.

When *Trumpets of Jubilee* appeared in 1927, Constance Rourke's insistence on the vital connection between the American artist and his society was a lonely position indeed; as for dealing sympathetically with popular leaders, "it is a habit in these days to scorn popularity." Ever since the Civil War, so she was to acknowledge in *American Humor* (1931), American critics had been carrying on what one of Henry James's characters had called the "wretched business" of quarreling with their country. The masterworks of post–Civil War writing had all voiced in their various ways the alienation of their authors from the accepted values of the Gilded Age. In the artistic generation to which Constance Rourke belonged—that truly remarkable group of poets, painters, literary critics, and social commentators who were born between the end of the 1870's and the mid-1890's and who came of age in the first decade and a half of the twentieth century (Miss Rourke was twenty-one in 1906)—the attitude of the American artist toward his society became even more intransigent. Where Henry Adams, Henry James, and Mark Twain had been deeply troubled by their inability to feel at home in their society, the iconoclasts of the new generation gloried in their separateness. The word of the day was *new,* and contempt for the conventional was vast. Gaily vying with one another as to how best to offend American proprieties, the young image-smashers adopted cubism, Nietzscheanism, Freudianism, Bergsonism, and Marxism. At Mabel Dodge Luhan's fabulous salon on Fifth Avenue in New York, representatives of these rebellions gathered together and discussed even more outrageous schemes for upsetting "the old order of things." Recalling the period 1911–16, Malcolm Cowley has suggested that subversive conspiracies were everywhere in these years: "Everywhere new institutions were being founded—magazines, clubs, little theatres, art or free-love or single-tax colonies, experimental schools, picture galleries. Everywhere was a sense of secret comradeship and immense potentialities for change." A group of young radicals, among them Walter Lippmann, dreamed of a "new republic" and founded a magazine of that name. Harriet Monroe's new magazine, *Poetry,* spoke for a New Poetry. Joel Spingarn called for a New Criticism. Ezra Pound's critical exhortation was "make it new," and Pound further foresaw an "American Risorgimento" that would "make the Italian Renaissance look like a tempest in a teapot." For scores of young painters, the famous New York Armory Show of 1913 represented the dawn of a Renaissance in American painting. That reincarnation of the Renaissance woman, Isadora Duncan, cast off conventional dance patterns and conventional sex morality with equal abandon; Amy Lowell wrote free verse and smoked Havana cigars; and neither woman cared when the editorial writers of America screamed in pietistic protest. Alfred Stieglitz, the famous photographer, expressed the contempt that the young iconoclasts in all the arts felt for the middle class's disapproval of their activities when he placed on a framed picture of the rear view of a horse the title, "Spiritual America."

In literary criticism, the focal point of the new generation's quarrel with their society was "Puritanism." Different as they were from one another in some respects, Randolph Bourne, H. L. Mencken, Van Wyck Brooks, Waldo Frank, and Lewis Mumford were united in their belief that the cultural legacy of Massachusetts Bay had proved to be a first-class disaster to a later America. Although Brooks derived a certain number of ideas on the subject from Bourne's striking essays and his even more striking conversation ("I shall never forget my first meeting with him," Brooks later wrote in tribute to Bourne's unforgettable personality, "that odd little apparition with his vibrant eyes, his quick, birdlike steps and the long black student's cape he had brought back with him from Paris"), Brooks's own essays constituted the most formidable case against the Puritan tradition put forward by any critic of his time; certainly this was Constance Rourke's view. (Mencken may have had more readers, but in her opinion his scoffing humor was a narrow and "methodical hilarity"—whereas she honored Brooks's opinions as important, even when she disagreed with them.) In *The Wine of the Puritans* (1908), Brooks contended that the Puritans had disapproved of the desire for beauty and pleasure and had saddled upon our society a worship of "things." The result was moral blindness as well as aesthetic stupidity. America was not without ideals, he went on to say in his famous manifesto, *America's Coming-of-Age* (1915), but these ideals were formless and juiceless and bore little relation to life. Constantly in danger of being ground to a powder between the upper and nether millstones of a vapid idealism and a "catchpenny opportunism," was it any wonder that American culture was thin?

"Attracted to failure"—a phrase that almost surely was resounding in Constance Rourke's mind when she wrote in her first book that "in the expectancy of considerable rewards we shall fix our gaze upon success" —Brooks next turned his attention to the lives of Mark Twain and Henry James, both of whom he depicted as victims of American life. Thus in *The Ordeal of Mark Twain,* which next to *Main Street* was the literary sensation of 1920 (and which makes some of the same assumptions about American small towns as does Lewis's novel), Brooks described the post–Civil War era as "a horde-life, a herd-life, an epoch without sun or stars, the twilight of a human spirit that had nothing upon which to feed but the living waters of Camden and the dried manna of Concord." "There is no denying," Brooks wrote the following year, "that for half a century the American writer as a type has gone down to defeat." The reasons advanced for this defeat were not only sociological but psychological, for like his friend Sherwood Anderson and many of their contemporaries Brooks had been deeply influenced by Freud. "Puritanism," as the intellectuals of the teens and twenties used the term, was not only the symbol of a suffocating environment, it pointed to an inner repression as well. *Winesburg, Ohio* (1918) had painted a nightmare-picture of sexual guilt, frustration, and fear, and Brook's version of Mark Twain's Hannibal was only slightly less chimerical. The religious intensity of Puritanism had once proved a mighty weapon in the battle to subdue the wilderness, as Brooks freely admitted, but in 1920 it was three hundred years since the landing at Plymouth. What had once been grand had long since become debased. The traditional Protestant culture of the country was not just a corrupter of institutions, not merely the font of a crass materialism, it was a form of psychic cancer that was rotting the American personality from within. Clearly, if modern American culture was to have a chance for significance, it would have to make a break with its past.

Yet at the same time that the young iconoclasts were endeavoring to make a fresh start, they became keenly conscious of the need for continuity. "I can connect/Nothing with nothing" was the piteous cry of the young woman on Margate Sands in *The Waste Land,* a poem published in the same year—1922—that Willa Cather said the whole world "broke in two" for her; the comments of both women were expressive of a hunger for connection with some external order that was felt by an entire generation. If Freud reinforced rebellions against repressive customs, the "Cambridge School" of anthropology lent support to the idea that individual artists derived both reassurance and inspiration from collective myths. Jane Harrison, whose work meant a great deal to Constance Rourke—and whose ideas T. S. Eliot encountered via Jessie Weston's *From Ritual to Romance*—had uncovered, along with F. M. Cornford, A. B. Cook, and Gilbert Murray of Oxford, the ritualistic basis underlying the art, religion, and philosophy of ancient Greece. To Constance Rourke, their findings confirmed Herder's theories about the connection between folk art and the fine arts. To T. S. Eliot, they gave a resonance to his own thinking about the relationship between the individual talent and the Western cultural tradition. To Van Wyck Brooks, they underscored the necessity for linking the modern American artist to a "usable past." To artists like Scott Fitzgerald and Eugene O'Neill, who had read little or no cultural anthropology but who felt with particular sensitivity the needs of their generation, the quest for the Holy Grail of belief in some self-transcendent myth of the past became the subject of their most compelling works. The lonely and depressed professor in Willa Cather's *The Professor's House* (1925), whose imagination is uplifted by this vision of a primitive but culturally harmonious Indian village in the American Southwest, was the intellectual symbol of an era.

Eliot, however, an expatriate living in London, was more interested in establishing a bridge between himself and the poets and dramatists of Elizabethan and Jacobean England than he was in aligning himself with a specifically American tradition. And Brooks, despite his acknowledgment that the regeneration of American literature could be accomplished only by writers who had a proud sense of who their predecessors were and what their achievements had been, was too busily engaged in demolition work to say anything very affirmative about the American past. (Even his portrait of Emerson in *Emerson and Others* (1927), while it lacked the devastating irony of his assessments of Twain and James, nevertheless had the effect of diminishing Emerson's claim on our admiration.) Lewis Mumford and Waldo Frank also delved into our cultural past, but their primary purpose in doing so was to enlist history on their side in the battle against their *bêtes noirs*, the American megalopolis and the American business culture. Like Vernon Louis Parrington, whose monumental *Main Currents in American Thought* appeared in the same year as did Constance Rourke's *Trumpets of Jubilee,* Mumford and Frank were myth-makers who re-created the American heritage in the image of their own preoccupations.

The unique achievement of Constance Rourke's first book is that she alone, among all the members of her generation who were bent on exploring the cultural resources of the country, was willing to honor the spokesmen of an older America for their own sake as well as for the sake of present and future American artists. Yet she was no more a pious antiquarian, who approached the past hat in hand, so to speak, than she was a debunker or a myth-maker. At once sympathetic and objective, she was a superb cultural historian; by her quiet but compelling example, she has had a continuing influence on writers concerned with the American past for more than thirty-five years.

II

Born in Cleveland, Ohio, in 1885, a graduate of Vassar in 1907, a student at the Sorbonne for a brief period, she began her career as a teacher. For several years, beginning in 1910, she was an instructor in literature at Vassar. Then in 1915—the year of Brooks's famous announcement that America had at last reached an age when it could begin properly to evaluate its past—she resigned from her alma mater in order to devote more time to research and writing. Whether consciously or coincidentally, she had answered Brooks's call to the intellectuals to regenerate America by rediscovering it, and her later career continued to be curiously intertwined with his. 1927 not only witnessed the publication of *Trumpets of Jubilee,* but it was the year that Brooks gave personal illustration to his thesis that the American writer was the victim of a morbid psychology by suffering a severe mental breakdown, an event which decisively terminated the first phase of his literary life. When he emerged from the darkness in 1932, he began to publish a series of books that revealed a drastic change in emphasis. Under the impact of Constance Rourke's and Bernard DeVoto's scholarship, he recanted his assertion in *The Ordeal of Mark Twain* that America had no indigenous folk art, and his own illustrations of our native folk tradition drew heavily on their work. It was altogether fitting, then, that in 1942, a year after Constance Rourke's untimely death, Van Wyck Brooks should have written the preface to *The Roots of American Culture,* a collection of her essays which were to have been part of a three-volume history of American culture that she had been planning and preparing to write for thirty years.

Yet if Brooks's *Makers and Finders* series was a massive accomplishment in cultural rediscovery, it did not supersede Constance's Rourke's more slender achievement. Brooks changed his ideas about American folk art, and about the literary importance of Mark Twain's humor, but he never really freed himself from the false notion that Henry James's stories were not in the American grain—even though Constance Rourke's brilliant chapter on James in *American Humor* had demonstrated otherwise. Brooks persisted, too, in the animus against the Puritans that was typical of his generation. (Significantly, the *Makers and Finders* series begins the story of the writer in America in the year 1800, whereas *Trumpets of Jubilee* opens with a brief sketch of Calvinism in Connecticut in the eighteenth century and then pursues, via the lives of Lyman Beecher and his remarkable children, the Calvinist tradition in nineteenth-century America.) But the main point of comparison lies in the blandness of the later Brooks. When he finally turned to an affirmation of the national past, he saw everything through an Indian-summer haze that softened and rounded the harsh outlines of many an American tragedy. Constance Rourke, by contrast, was never tempted into lobotomizing our cultural history, for she had never exaggerated its more dismal aspects and therefore had no need to compensate. First and last, she took a balanced view; as she wrote in the foreword to *Trumpets of Jubilee,* her aim was to let "a little of the singular life of the . . . [past] . . . crowd through, with its constricted spaciousness, its stirring trouble, and loud laughter." Except for Barnum, all the major figures in *Trumpets of Jubilee* endure a public trial and humiliation in one form or another: Lyman Beecher was tried for heresy by the Presbyterian General Assembly; his daughter Harriet Beecher Stowe's attack on Lord Byron's sexual mores brought down on her head the vilification of thousands of readers who had once worshipped her as the author of *Uncle Tom's Cabin;* his son Henry Ward Beecher, in one of the most sensational legal battles of American history, was tried for adultery with the wife of one of his parishioners; Horace Greeley's Presidential ambitions led him to a downfall that was literally mortifying.

Laughter, however, as well as trouble, is given its due. Constance Rourke's appreciation of Yankee wit, which is more fully manifested in *American Humor,* seasons her treatment of Lyman Beecher and immensely humanizes him; in a decade when the term *Puritan* became a synonym, in Charles Beard's phrase, for anything that interfered with "the new freedom, free verse, psychoanalysis, or even the double entendre," Constance Rourke insisted on the sly humor, the homely ways, and the boisterous passion of Lyman Beecher. With her folk-detective's instinct for finding older forms beneath newer ones, she conceived of Beecher's sermons—and those of his son Henry even more so—as a kind of theatrical performance that ranged from high tragedy to low comedy. Indeed, she conceived of all the *dramatis personae* of *Trumpets of Jubilee* as theatrical performers, for she adored the theater, as Whitman did, as the most social of all the arts—the place where the One and the Many confronted one another most directly. The theater had the "constricted spaciousness" that she felt was the key to American culture, and therefore all things theatrical became a primary source of her metaphors. The very title, *Trumpets of Jubilee,* leads us to anticipate a circus—with cosmic overtones. In her second book, *Troupers of the Gold Coast, or The Rise of Lotta Crabtree* (1928), she indulged her delight in theatricality in less oblique terms,* but whomever she wrote about, whether *Davy Crockett* (1934) or *Audubon* (1936), the gaudy theatricality of her subject's imagination was the quality that most stirred her own. In her own way she was Barnumesque, and the reader comes away from her studies of American life with the feeling that he has just witnessed the Greatest Show on Earth.

* Constance Rourke was also drawn to Lotta Crabtree's career because of the touching, lifelong intimacy between an artistic daughter who never married and her mother, a relationship that bears a strong similarity to Constance Rourke's relationship with her mother. Both *Trumpets of Jubilee* and *American Humor* are dedicated to the author's mother, to whom Constance Rourke was utterly devoted. When she wrote that "the bond between Lotta and her mother was close —too close, too confining, even mysterious, some observers said—but there was no sign that it chafed," she might have been describing her own situation.

Which is not to say that she was not discriminating or that she lacked standards—quite the contrary. Unlike many students of the popular arts, Constance Rourke was equally at home in discussing the fine arts. If her study of *Charles Sheeler: Artist in the American Tradition* (1938) is valuable for the connections it establishes between an individual artist's practice and the aesthetic expression of a communal group (in this case the Shakers), the book is also important for what it says about the intrinsic merits of Sheeler's work. To state the case in literary terms, Constance Rourke was a critic of texts as well as of contexts, and when she undertook to defend some of the masterpieces of an earlier America against the jeering sophisticates of the 1920's, she did so with an authority that only those who have read the best of what has been thought and said can command. Take, for example, her defense, in *Trumpets of Jubilee,* of *Uncle Tom's Cabin:*

It has become the custom to belittle *Uncle Tom's Cabin* as a work which was always over-colored, which never had a place outside the turbid sphere of propaganda, and is now outdated. But propaganda sole and simple it is not; it declares no platform, and is unconcerned with measures; what it offers is a sweeping picture and an outcry. Battered though it has become through the overplus of excitement which has attended its career, defective though it is in certain essentials, it still has qualities which lift it above its contemporary position as a tract, qualities which should dismiss the easy, usual charge of exaggeration. Obviously the book lacks a genuine realism; but perhaps it should not be judged as realism at all. Obviously it lacks the hardiness and purity of view which belong to great writing; its emotion is never free, but intensive, indrawn, morbid, sentimental if one chooses, running an unchecked course which seemed created by hysteria. But the unbroken force of that emotion produced breadth; in its expansions and uncalculating balances, its flowing absorption in large sequences of action and its loose combinations of interwoven fates, the story at least brings to mind what is meant by the epical scale. . . .

Writing with that combination of descriptive specificity and visionary sweep which constituted her personal signature, Constance Rourke helped bring us to an awareness of a tradition that, as she wrote in *American Humor,* was "various, subtle, sinewy, scant at times but not poor."

Trumpets of Jubilee

Lyman Beecher

ONE • *According to family legend, one of the remoter grand-*
fathers of Harriet Beecher Stowe could lift a barrel of
cider and drink from the bung-hole. His son could lift a full barrel into
a cart. His grandson, David Beecher, could carry a full barrel into the
cellar. They came of English stock, with a Welsh and a Scotch strain
through women of the family, and sprang from the Puritan soil of Guilford in Connecticut, the home of the Beechers from the time of the
Davenport settlement. They were all blacksmiths.

Life had its hazards in the family of David Beecher. He was five times
married, and of his fourteen children only four lived to maturity. Lyman, one of these, entered the world in stirring times, in 1775, a feeble
seven months' infant whose mother died at his birth; he was wrapped in
a towel and laid aside as negligible by the village women tending
Esther Beecher in her last moments; his rescue was a casual after-
thought. The heroic tradition appeared to be broken. But was it? At the
outset the infant Lyman confounded the prophets and clung to life.
When he was given to an uncle and aunt Benton to grow up on their
farm near Guilford—or more likely to die—he became hardy, compact,
and muscular, and helped Lot Benton wring from a stubborn soil the
most that it would yield, raising oats and corn, cutting salt hay from the
marshes, pulling flax. When he became inexpressibly bored in that quiet
place, he escaped from the tedium which afflicted him; he eagerly
hunted and fished. Once he ran down the shallows of a stream on all
fours after a perch that had dropped from his hook.

By way of thrill or change great thunderstorms came rolling up over
the Connecticut hills, throwing down their floods and racing by. "When
I used to be out hoeing corn and saw two thunderclouds rising, my
nerves braced up," Lyman exclaimed, "and as it grew darker the excitement increased till finally when the thunder burst it was like the effect
of a strong glass of wine!" One night the Aurora Borealis broke in a

blood-red arch from the horizon to the zenith, and it was light enough to read out of doors. Some one spoke of the Last Judgment, saying no man could tell when it might come, whether at midnight or cockcrowing. Lyman thought that it *had* come, and wept in an ecstasy of terror and dismay. "I knew what fire was, and what forever was," he cried. "What emotion I had, thinking *No end! No end!*" But this episode came to little enough. In a fit of rage a few years before, Uncle Lot had departed from the Puritan faith and had become an invincibly mild Episcopalian; questions of eternal destiny were not diligently pursued in his household; and Lyman was left to his flax and his corn.

At last, when a new strip of woodland was being cleared, he fell into prolonged daydreams; and his team kept leaving the furrow; Lot Benton was obliged to follow him and draw back the horses. Again Lyman was lost, and again; these lapses became periodic. Finally he grazed the wheel of the ox-cart against the plow. At this there was a stormy crisis; to Lot Benton his plow was a sign of ingenuity, thrift, and fortune. Most men had wooden plows; his was of iron; he had forged the monstrous instrument himself, and had repeatedly welded pieces of old metal against its sides to ensure its preservation. "There, there, Lyman," he burst out in a peppery fever, "you've run all over that plow and broke it all to pieces!" In the wrangle which followed he withdrew his promise to make Lyman his heir. But it was Uncle Lot's habit to offer with one hand what he had just denied with the other. "Shan't have no candle," he would declare when he discovered that Lyman, as usual, had forgotten to blow out his candle at night. The next evening he would quietly hand him a fresh tallowdip. When a farmer came to borrow a hoe, Uncle Lot would say, "Why don't ye have hoes o' your own? What d'ye want to hang onto your neighbors for?" Then in a moment, "Here, come back! Take the hoe, can't ye? You'll break it, I s'ppose." Uncle Lot soon recovered from his dismay over the episode of the plow; and Lyman persisted in the habit of revery. Presently he became strange indeed. He was seen walking alone over Toket Hill wrapped in a tempest of somber thought, and calling to the oxen as though he were driving them. Uncle Lot gave it up; he decided that his nephew must possess the attribute spoken of with peculiar emphasis in that locality as *mind*. Making a slender offer in the matter of clothes, he cajoled David Beecher into sending his son to Yale College. As it happened, young Lyman had no literary tastes, and no choice between the two professions open to him, the ministry and the bar; but he had gained what he wanted; he was to leave the farm. He dutifully studied simple subjects with a neighboring parson the following winter, and in 1793 went to New Haven, clad in Aunt Benton's homespun.

TWO • *In the final decade of the eighteenth century Yale College* was a cluster of three or four plain buildings, and owned a small collection of books, a telescope, a great rusty orrery, and a quaint medley of relics assembled in the name of literature and science by its venerable president, Dr. Ezra Stiles—or Dr. Magpie, as he was called by a satirical New York gazette.

Brisk and bright-eyed, exquisitely trim in black and white clericals, with a hooded wig, and an amazingly long, thin, sharp nose, Dr. Stiles darted about on innumerable errands of acquisition and inquiry. He sought and hoarded for the College a leaf from the tomb of Virgil, a stuffed two-headed calf, and an enormous tooth discovered near the Chemaung River, at a point whose latitude and longitude and exact relation to an Indian fort and an English settlement he scrupulously noted. He delved into the Rosicrucian mysteries, spent hours at the telescope, traced endless genealogies, was vocal and voluble in English, Latin, Greek, and Hebrew. And at the end of each day he hid the record of his ardent pursuits and certain notable happenings within the pages of his great diary. He even set down the passage which called him Dr. Magpie.

The lampoon, in fact, was neat; yet after all it failed of its main point. Using the familiar English aspersion, the gazette had meant to ridicule Dr. Stiles as a diplomatist of the Puritan church and state. He was nothing of a diplomatist in any relation; and his allegiance to the faith of the fathers had been changeable. As a young tutor at Yale he had renounced it, and had left its ministry when a wave of deistic sentiment swept over the College. He had accepted the hard canon of Calvinism again at last, but during the long turmoil of his doubt he seems to have developed another, perhaps rather more inclusive principle—a passion, indeed, which wreaked itself as passions will. This was nothing less than a passion for truth; and it soon became manifest in relation to Yale College.

Deism had arisen at Yale as result of the reading of books given to the College by Bishop Berkeley. From this circumstance Rector Clap had learned a lesson as to the perilous seductions of books. The College had been founded as a stronghold of the Puritan orthodoxy, a School of the Church, and so Rector Clap intended it should remain. Somewhat later, when a similar collection was offered by a gentleman of Newport, Rector Clap declined the gift. But the episode did not close quietly. Young Mr. Stiles wrote in eager remonstrance. "Deism has got such a Head in this age of Licentious Liberty," he declared, "that it would be vain to try to stop it by hiding deistical writings; and the only way left to Conquer and Demolish it is to come forth in the open Field and Dispute the matter on an even Footing. . . . Truth, and this alone, being in fact our Aim, open, frank, and generous, we shall avoid the very Appearance of Evil. It is true that with this Liberty Error may be introduced; but turn the Tables, the propagation of Truth may be extinguished." Rector Clap was unmoved by these arguments; and young Mr. Stiles was undaunted by his failure in the issue. "I hold it beneath the dignity of a philosopher to suppress his sentiments," he declared.

Young Mr. Stiles suppressed nothing; he was always voicing new speculations, always appearing in doubtful places. His tolerance of the scarcely recognized minor sects became notorious; during his ministry at Newport he consorted with a Romish priest, and all but inhabited the Jewish Synagogue in his eagerness to peruse the scrolls. Meantime his learning grew apace. He carried on a tireless Latin correspondence with scholars all over the world, and made the first electrical experiments in New England. Franklin became his friend, and procured for him a coveted degree from Edinburgh. So, when Rector Clap announced his impending resignation, Dr. Stiles seemed an obvious candidate for the presidency of Yale. But the Corporation hesitated. Candid little Dr. Stiles was amazed by the delay; he wondered whether his temper constituted a disability; he could indeed easily splinter a cane with rage, and his turn for invective was surpassingly vivid. Presently he alluded to another, perhaps more troublesome handicap. "I conceive it as infinitely difficult for the Governor of a Province, or the President of a College, to be conversant with, and prudently to adjust himself to, a great variety of contrary views, dispositions, tempers, and characters, many of them very important, and not endanger the firmness of the moral principle."

At last he issued a defense of his orthodoxy. But the honor—and he loved honors—continued to dangle before him like a ripe and luscious fruit. It dangled for eleven years; a temporary provision was made for the presidency. Dr. Stiles poured out his disillusion and his pride in a long passage in his diary. "I never was *particular & exclusive* enough for a cordial & close union with any sect, not even my own," he declared bitterly. "And when I first set out in Life I had a much better opinion of Mankind & of the different Sects as to *Sincerity and Virtue* than I now have. To love a whole Character, or a whole Church, or any Fraternity, whether literary, religious, or politic, I do not find within me . . . I shall never cordially & externally unite with Mankind in any of their Affairs, Enterprizes, & Revolutions . . . & am, perhaps, more than any man of extensive Acquaintance & Correspondence—ALONE—and unconnected in the World . . . I expect no great Felicity from fellowship & open Communication with Mankind, but intend to become more and more the Recluse—waiting for the Rest of Paradise, where I foresee that my soul will unite with Perfection & Acquiesce in eternal universal Harmony."

But after all Dr. Stiles was unable to maintain his studied seclusion. In 1777, blown perhaps by the stormy winds of the Revolution, the great prize fell; he became the president of Yale, and soon with bright incaution was dipping and sallying among many affairs, enterprises, and revolutions. Twice he listened to the discourses of the astonishing Jemima Wilkinson, the Public Universal Friend, who was about to lead a band of her disciples into the wilderness to found the New Jerusalem. Presently he granted the Yale students permission to frequent a newly opened dancing school, considering that this institution might cultivate polite manners. "A great Combustion about the Dancing School," he briefly noted in his diary. "A great Noise about the Dancing School; Meeting of Select Men & Civil Authority," he subsequently observed. And finally: "Violent Proceedings about the Dancing Master—to leave the Town tomorrow." Portions of plays had sometimes been given by the students in their rooms; presently several of these were performed at full length in public; and when this experiment was terminated by a vigilant civil authority, certain "gay, jovial, tumultuous young Men," as Dr. Stiles called them, strolled forth and gave their exhibitions in neighboring towns. He seemed unperturbed by these adventures. He was now eagerly cultivating the French language and literature; he forthwith introduced *L'Esprit des Lois* as a text in the College, and conducted debates on doubtful subjects like the advisability of considering agriculture a classical subject—a theme obviously drawn from the insidious French naturalist philosophy. He read Mary Wollstonecraft's *Vindication of the Rights of Women,* and began to study the whole crew of English revolutionaries. By the time Lyman Beecher entered Yale the inevitable had occurred. Yale was a hotbed of the most dangerous radicalism of the day; again deism was abroad in the College, this time in a new and virulent form.

Many of the farmer lads who came to New Haven had kept a volume of Tom Paine in their pockets as they thrashed their wheat or hatcheled their flax; some of them had discovered Godwin's *Political Justice.* Now, without any apparent let or hindrance, they were calling each other by great French names—Voltaire, Rousseau, Turgot, d'Alembert; they were denying the Puritan Jehovah and most of his works; they had found a new subject for homage—Man! They believed that a remote deity had created the universe and had left it to run itself, or rather had committed its proper governance to human hands; and how marvelously was the human creature equipped for his task with the great faculty of reason and the majestic will! A bright picture sprang up in the youthful fancy of the race in an irresistible onward movement; surely nothing short of perfection was its goal; perfection was to be reached by easily measurable stages, and was in fact discernible down a radiant pathway. Once more reason was enshrined at Yale, but now the stern countenance of that elusive goddess was all but obscured by a shining nimbus of hope.

Hope was not the sustaining emotion of the Puritan faith; in the Puritan view a dream of perfection, of a world plastic in human hands was nothing short of blasphemous. Orthodox Connecticut was aghast as these wild prophecies floated out from the School of the Church—aghast, and sharply pricked by fear. These were the ideas which had loosed the recent red terror of the French Revolution—and still another specter, now horridly stalking the American shore under the name of Democracy, "a troubled spirit, fated never to rest, and whose dreams, if it sleeps, present only visions of Hell," as Fisher Ames had mournfully observed. Alas! as the anxious orthodox eye scanned the Connecticut horizon, it perceived a multitude of other ominous straws floating down the wind. All sorts of people, new, unlocalized people, deists, atheists, infidels, small farmers, tradesmen, were clamoring to be made freemen, whether or not they possessed the property or the moral character required by law. The minor sects had pushed forward to the point of legal recognition; and the rosiest of these were actually becoming popular: Methodism, with its promises of a frequent descent of the Holy Spirit, and Universalism with its infamous assurance of ultimate universal salvation. Many of the orthodox had themselves grown lighter-hearted since the disruptive years of the Revolution, less deeply absorbed in those terrible problems of eternal destiny which had been the staple of existence for their fathers. Undoubtedly, wastrel hope was in the air. Nor was this all. Orthodoxy was the basis of government in Connecticut. The Standing Order, as it was appropriately called, was a replica of the divine system, with the orthodox as the elect, its ministry at the seat of power, and the solid rock of Federalism mixed in its foundations. If a reckless insurgency became preponderant, the government of the Puritans must undoubtedly topple and crash.

With righteous anger, and with a prime respect for the force of ideas, orthodox attention was fixed upon Yale. At this point Dr. Stiles achieved the single diplomatic act of his ruffled career. In 1795 he quickly and quietly, though no doubt reluctantly, died. It was indeed high time; deism was not the only desperate outcome of his adventures in the realm of thought. In his latter years he had become an enthusiast for immigration—in a state which was vigorously repelling the settlement of foreigners. "This fermentation and communion of nations will doubtless produce something very new, singular, and glorious," he had irrepressibly declared. Under his presidency Yale had granted a degree to Thomas Jefferson, who was the favored playfellow of the devil in the fancy of New England. And in the stronghold of Federalism Dr. Stiles had elevated a rank republican to the principal professorship.

His death closed an era at Yale. In truth, it seemed that the year 1795 brought to an end something of an interlude in New England, and perhaps elsewhere. Out of the mid-eighteenth century had briefly come a delicate and charming worldliness, even in the Puritan stronghold, which was figured forth in the exquisitely curled wig of Dr. Stiles, and in his insistence upon polite manners in the College. That exploratory freedom in which he had indulged was not uncommon; his alliance with Franklin was a token. But at the close of the eighteenth century the fabric of American existence, so mixed and many-hued, was torn and shaken. Those insurgents who had appeared overnight in Connecticut seemed suddenly to increase in strength and numbers. Stiff alignments took place, with new defenses and a drastic insistence upon ancient principles. At this great point of change Yale College played a part both far-reaching and profound.

Dr. Stiles was succeeded by Timothy Dwight, who quickly discovered a distant post for the rank republican as president of the newly founded University of Georgia, and who gave the Magpie's little medley of relics to an early example of the dime museum. He swept aside the system of fagging, and opened courses in logic, rhetoric, and moral philosophy. He intended that Yale students should be equipped for leadership, and he had a precise notion of the movement which they were to inaugurate. What Dwight proposed at this crisis in Connecticut affairs was nothing short of a vigorous renascence of the Puritan mode, method, and spirit. "Government, since the days of Mr. Locke," he scornfully declared, "has extensively been supposed *to be founded upon the Social Compact*. No opinion is more groundless than this. . . . The foundation of all government is, undoubtedly, the will of God"—as revealed by the Saybrook Platform, as embodied in the institutions of primordial Connecticut. In truth, Dwight fairly *was* primordial Connecticut. "Old Pope Dwight" he was called by the loose-banded opposition in the state; and apostolic honors were thick upon him. He was a dictator in the regnant clerical party; he was related by birth or marriage to the few dynastic families of Connecticut; and within or above these distinctions he possessed another, which was quite special. He was a grandson of Jonathan Edwards, and though he lacked the metaphysical insight of the great New England saint, upon his commanding figure the evangelical cloak had richly fallen.

Tall, bland, and terrible, he launched the batteries of a pitiless revivalism against those young men disporting themselves under French names, and brought the revival once more into play in New England as an engine of the faith. Revivals had scarcely existed in burning strength since the era of the Great Awakening, sixty years before; the racking method was new to the younger generation; Dwight's intimate portrayal of sin was new. Sin! He preached a race dead in sin, and passed far beyond the colorless remarks of contemporary divines into bold discussions of lying, idleness, fraud, gaming, prodigality, and traffic with the "strange woman." "The pleasures of men, their darling and customary pleasures, have ever seemed to me an affecting proof of the extreme depravity of our nature," he declared. He banned pleasure, banned idleness, and in his discourse on lewdness called into question the appeal of all the arts. "The numbers of the Poet, the delightful melody of Song, the fascination of the Chisel, the spell of the Pencil, have all been volunteered in the service of Satan, for the moral destruction of unhappy man." Providing a complete and reasoned code of prohibitory ethics, playing upon that "agonized conscience" which was the ample heritage of his young hearers, he set forth his doctrine with a calm radiance which seemed only to grow brighter as its terrible implications were unfolded. Righteousness must be tirelessly pursued, yet righteousness counted for nothing. In consequence of the great initial fault, divine wrath was to be exercised without stint against the greater portion of the race; every act was evil unless accomplished in a state of grace—and grace might or might not be bestowed, according to the divine will.

But—was it humane feeling, or had Dwight himself been blown upon by soft insidious winds from France? As he posed the great Edwardean paradox Dwight gave a slightly new and added emphasis to the possibilities of human freedom within the fixed eternal scheme; in his arguments on the will and on human "ability" his audience might perhaps have found a touchstone to evoke some of the imaginings they had so recently enjoyed. But these young men were unskilled in dialectic, and Dwight quickly turned his slight glimmering of hope into a blacker despair. If the will was free, the greater was man's anguished responsibility; there remained for him only a stripping away of the pride of the flesh, the greater pride of the spirit; in the desperate issue between himself and God, he could only yield; through submission might come at last the ineffable miracle of the re-birth. Submission, submission—power! power! The sound and the intention of power rang with something like grandeur as Dwight swept onward into a rhetoric which fell into broad and searching rhythms, and made resonantly clear the unresting state into which the Calvinistic believer must fall—never secure in his hope, always exultant in his worship.

The *Philosophes,* bold as they had been, were the same persons who wore their black calico gowns on the streets of New Haven with simple pride, and followed a ritual in the wearing and doffing of hats, and were watched at Commons from elevated platforms by wary tutors. That is, they were young; they lacked leadership, and craved it. Dr. Stiles had only permitted them to go their own gait. Timothy Dwight carried the College with him.

"Oh, how I loved him," cried Lyman Beecher more than fifty years later. "I loved him as my own soul, and he loved me as a son!" There may be a question as to the completeness of this relation; Dwight was abysmally reserved for all the sweetness of his smile; but certainly Beecher was enraptured. In the loose and airy speculations of the later deism this young rustic had discovered nothing to which he responded; like his blacksmith ancestors he demanded solid mass and resistant form; and he found them in the bold, uncompromising drama of the Puritan faith. He leapt to Dwight's resounding note, sank almost joyfully into an abyss of terror at his bidding, wondered desperately whether he could "charm" God, and suffered an interval of shattered nerves. At last, out of his rushing acceptance of absolute power came a strange, mixed peace; out of his painful, turbulent effort arose that mysterious sense of renewal which seemed a beneficent sign. In the swelling, thrilling forces of revivalism he had at last discovered something to which he answered. Ah, that profound sense of increase given to whole peoples! The case of man might be hopeless, yet surely—surely multitudes could be pushed through the gates of the New Jerusalem.

In a whirlwind of exhilaration he prepared for the ministry, and wooed Roxana Foote of Nutplains, near Guilford, sought her so ardently that she feared lest his sentiment might not endure. Roxana possessed a delicate reticence, and came of a finer strain than the Beechers. "She shone preëminent!" cried Beecher. She had been permitted to cultivate a taste for the sciences, mathematics, physics, and chemistry; she also practiced exquisite feminine arts like painting on ivory, and tied French books to her distaff as she spun. She had once remarked that she would never marry until she found a Sir Charles Grandison. "Presume she thought she had," said Beecher ironically. But Roxana, with her clear detachment, may have taken a more realistic view of her crude young lover. At the time of his ordination in 1799 he looked the ultimate Puritan in his shrouding cape and broad hat; his narrow, swart face and scornful under-lip seemed to revive the severities of an early type. Noting his pointed eyebrows, the close smile which sometimes drew in his cheeks, and the suppleness of his stocky figure, another might perhaps have wondered whether he would prove the perfect apostle of any order. But Roxana, at least, seems to have had no doubts. At his bidding she gave up her own faith, the Episcopalian, and followed him to the scene of his first labors, at East Hampton on Long Island, an offshoot of early Connecticut, which had kept its primitive character almost intact, as if this had been preserved in isolation by the salt sea air.

THREE • East Hampton lay at the foot of the Shinnecock Hills on a wild white shore, its plain unpainted wooden houses facing each other in two even rows across a single, immensely wide roadway. An elm tree stood at one end of the village, a windmill at the other; there was a small, steepled Presbyterian church. On the broad shimmer of ocean the sails of a few fishermen might be seen. At long intervals were heard the shrill notes of the weft, or signal that whales had been sighted. The rest was silence, except for the stir of weekly and Sabbath meetings.

Even Timothy Dwight found as excess of sobriety in East Hampton. In his famous *Travels in New-England and New-York* he observed that "the inhabitants appear in no peculiar degree subject to any disease, except the Hypocondria."

"Write me all the news," begged Roxana's lovely and vivacious sister, Mary Hubbard, writing to a friend during a visit at the Beechers'. "Here we are so still, so quiet, so inactive, that we have forgotten but that the world goes the same way; we have forgotten that there are society, and friendship, and intercourse, and social affection, and science, and pleasure, and life, and spirit, and gayety, and good-humor alive still among the sons of earth. We neither laugh nor cry, sing nor dance, nor moan nor lament; but the man that took ten steps yesterday taketh the same today, and sleepeth at night, eating as he is wont to do daily. A kind of torpor and apathy seems to prevail over the face of things; and as standing water begins to turn green, so all the countenances you meet seem to have contracted the expression indicative of the unagitated state in which they live. I wish I could procure some nitrous oxyd for them to inhale once a week; what do you suppose would be the effect?"

"My preaching seems not to move," cried Beecher in desperation. "I speak against a rock. The people continue to watch me as narrowly as a mouse is watched by a cat."

Then, out of this close and somber scrutiny, sprang a sudden caprice. Without effort on Beecher's part, without warning, a revival broke in East Hampton. "Before evening service, one Sabbath, news came to me that two of Deacon Shirrel's sons were under conviction. Oh, how I went down there! Whether walking, or flying, or on tiptoe, I don't know. When I got to the deacon's seat, oh, how I preached! I spilled over." But his people quickly settled back into their first solemn apathy. He tried a bold onslaught to rouse them, and was made to realize his mistake. "Was deficient," he ruefully admitted, "in that wisdom of the serpent which is not incompatible with the harmlessness of the dove." He doubled his visiting in the town, rode about on horseback among the wild highlands and rugged cliffs to the scattered hamlets of his parish, Amaghansett, Three Mile Harbor, Fireplace, Wayunscott, hoping to arouse these outlying groups and so to create a momentum. But in vain: it was as if his congregation had set themselves to match him in a trial of endurance.

Months passed, and began to flow into years; he grew bewildered, pushed his efforts with increasing anxiety, and fell into profound depression and ill-health. He was unable to preach. "Exercise! Go out!" urged one of his deacons. "Run down cellar! Run up garret! Stir around!" Old Mr. Fithian announced that he, for one, wouldn't pay his rates if the minister didn't preach. "What's the reason you ministers are always so hungry for money?" queried old Mr. Fithian. In fact, it was being whispered that the minister's family was *worldly*. Roxana had adorned her wooden chairs with little patterns of silver and gilt; and Beecher had bought a great bale of cotton at an auction, which she had spun, woven, and braided into a carpet, painting bright flowers for a border with colors of her own grinding and mixing. In East Hampton plain chairs and sanded floors were the immemorial custom. When a deacon was urged to enter the Beechers' parlor he answered tartly, "Can't, 'thout stepping on't!" And he put the question: "Think you can have all that, *and Heaven too?"* As if to prove the case, it soon turned out that the minister was in debt on his stipendium of three hundred dollars a year and firewood. Roxana set up a small private school which was attended by daughters of some of the more prosperous inhabitants of the neighboring villages, and boarded some of her pupils in her tiny house; but six children were born to her in as many years—Catherine, William, Edward, George, Mary, and an infant who died; and though she maintained her school almost without interruption her small earnings were quickly consumed. Beecher also tried to teach a school, but found the task unendurable. "It was a perfect torture. It was just like driving Uncle Lot's old plow, only worse, to sit there looking at my watch ten times an hour to see when I could get out!" At last, in reckless despondency and also in the hope of escape, he demanded an increase of salary. His people decided that they could not spare Lyman Beecher. After sufficient deliberation they granted him an additional hundred dollars a year, which made a handsome figure for the time and place; and according to long established tradition, a minister remained in his parish, except in the case of the most pressing need or untoward circumstances, until the release of death.

But young Beecher had determined to end his long prelude to a career. "There was I with my heart burning, and they feeling nothing!" he bitterly exclaimed. Beyond, in the larger world, lay an unaccountable future; at the turn of the century the rankest republican of them all had been elected to the presidency, and Connecticut was now a smoking battleground. In Connecticut and even in New York he began reconnoitering.

At East Hampton, cutting turf fences and hauling seaweed, he recovered his health and a fair measure of his spirits, and began to predict a revival. Still stubborn, his people eyed him doubtfully. "They made me think of hens in the night, when you carry a candle into the hen-roost, how they open first one eye and then the other, half-asleep!" This time, however, they were not permitted to enjoy their indifference. For his climactic endeavor in this archaic battle of the spirit Beecher chose the least acceptable doctrine of the common faith, that of election, and preached it with a cool, remorseless logic, without pity or alleviation, probing, exploring, leaving not a phase of the helpless human condition untouched. Step by reluctant step his people were pushed to the very wall of terror; one of the older members of the congregation fairly begged him to desist. Then—was it triumph, or tactics, or sheer exuberance?—he delivered a discourse which was to remain the sweetest and purest of his utterances, spiraling into the empyrean, all but flinging open a radiant heavenly kingdom. Surely, he argued—by joyous exclamations, by irresistible queries—the number of the elect must be unimaginably vast, crowding and multiplying far beyond the limits of the human imagination! Hope—a rushing, abounding measure of hope—he offered with an assuaging tenderness. His hardy people quavered and yielded; the mystic stir of spirit came at last, running like tidings from one group to another until the whole church was caught in a wave of exultation.

This final discourse, which was called *The Government of God Desirable,* created a little whirlpool of controversy among the older clergy of New England when it was printed; a grave question of Beecher's orthodoxy arose. But it also brought him fame; certain Congregational gentlemen of Litchfield, Connecticut, who were seeking a minister, were agreeably impressed by its moderation of tone. Under the Plan of Union Beecher was equally eligible to preach before Presbyterian Churches and the Congregational Societies of New England. At the earliest intimation of their favor he hastened to Litchfield, preached a trial sermon, received a call, and entered into a series of flinty exchanges with his East Hampton congregation. They rebuked him for a procedure which had in truth been highly irregular, and tried to bind him by a new bargain; but he meant to be off. At last he received his dismissal; and East Hampton turned a stubborn shoulder upon the world. Ministers came, and went; the village settled into its first drastic composure, and was not again to be betrayed into sudden, bright emotions. A few years later an American youth in a Paris attic, swept by affection for the bare little cluster of houses where his family had lived for a brief time during his boyhood, wrote melting words and flowing measures which were quickly to be accepted as something of a national anthem; East Hampton became the lyric inspiration of *Home, Sweet Home.* Probably the village never learned of this tribute, and might have repelled it. There was no quiet home upon this earth! Noisy rumors soon were rising from the boisterous spreading city on the great harbor to the south. Presently even on that narrow fringe of shore were felt the pulse and thrill of the great movement westward, stirring like some natural upheaval. Young men and women steadily left the village, and joined the long tumultuous procession. For the dwindling remaining numbers there was only—tenacity. They sowed and reaped on that spare sandy soil, watched the slow disappearance of the whaling industry and the dubious progress of the oyster trade, and kept their somber original habitudes intact. In the seventies when a railroad crept out on Long Island and the east shore began to bloom with villas, East Hampton was still the relic of a primitive adventure, small and thin and unbroken, like a waveworn shell.

FOUR • *Liberty and equality had become words to make men shudder in Connecticut.* Timothy Dwight, pursuing his great resolve, had announced that an enormous conspiracy was afoot to destroy all the governments of Europe, and probably that of America, with the purpose of "rooting out of the world civil and domestic government, the right of property, marriage, natural affection, chastity, and decency . . . all under the pretense of giving man liberty and equality."

"The truth is, many of our leading political men, during and after the Revolution, were visionary enthusiasts," said Noah Webster, bitterly discoursing on a topic which was to agitate him throughout a long lifetime. "The loose, undefined sense in which the words *free* and *equal* are used in some of the American constitutions has been, and will be, of immense evil to this country. . . . The very principle of admitting everybody to the right of suffrage prostrates the wealth of individuals to the rapaciousness of a merciless gang, who have nothing to lose, and will delight in plundering their neighbors."

After the galvanic shock of Jefferson's election, agitation in New England grew apace. Defensive proposals were whispered. "I have seen many of our friends," wrote Tapping Reeve of the Litchfield Law School, to Senator Tracy in 1804, "and all that I have seen, and most that I have heard from, believe that we must separate, and that this is the most favorable moment." The plan of a limited confederation was postponed, and finally melted away; but no happy solution took its place. Amazing tremors constantly shook a startled society. When manifestoes against Democracy were hurled from First Church pulpit in Litchfield, certain persons became unreasonably incensed, and went over to the small body of Episcopalians, and openly avowed themselves republicans. When Judge Reeve uttered suitable animadversions upon the life, works, and personal character of Thomas Jefferson, he was promptly sued for libel. Soon Litchfield was invaded by Sellick Osborn and another young printer from the region of Danbury, who set up a republican paper, and began a sprightly anti-Federalist campaign. They were quickly sued, tried, and imprisoned, but somehow the noise of the case spread; and at the next annual election two republican candidates were found to have wedged their way into the Litchfield delegation.

Litchfield had seemed quietly impregnable. In the fallow period which had followed the Revolution, Litchfield had basked upon its lovely hill, gazing out over the silver lakes and thickly wooded valleys of its county with an air of leisure, dignity, and elegance. Its spacious mansions opened upon formal gardens and broad courtyards; the word "gentry" still belonged to its vocabulary; the persons thus designated took promenades along the Hill, gave stately balls, welcomed the diversions of strolling players, and even, with decorum, in a gentleman's orchard, enjoyed the mild semblance of a circus—"the Surprizing Performances of the celebrated John Brannan and Wife, of Dublin, in the Curious and Ingenious Art of Dancing on the Slack-Wire." Orthodoxy had sat a little lightly upon this amiable society; quips were merrily fabricated out of the doctrine of total depravity and cast at the entire French nation. As for revivals, the Litchfield tradition had been distinctly against these disturbing outbreaks; the town had been one of only two in Connecticut to repel the crude traveling evangelists who spread the terrible fire during the Great Awakening. But now, with a dark and horrid chasm yawning, perhaps revivals were the very besom needed. Litchfield, storm-stricken, rallied to the support of the Puritan tradition.

Young Mr. Beecher, installed at First Church, began pouring forth a gusty volume of emotion, hammering out souls upon the hard anvil of the common creed with seasoned muscularity, voicing in all this new clangor the most militant tenet of them all, that of an illimitable divine sovereignty with all its most drastic implications, commanding an absolute submission, an absolute worship. If at East Hampton he had at the last wooed his people with comfort, there was nothing calm or assuaging in his doctrine now. "They say everybody knows about God naturally," he said. "A lie. All such ideas are by teaching." Once after a brief absence he returned to find that a powerful but specious impression had been made by a visiting minister. A Mrs. Smith was mistakenly seeking regeneration by "amendment of temper and life." Beecher speedily pointed out to her the danger and the futility of such a proceeding. "Nearly a dozen persons, children and youth, had in my absence begun to hope," he wrote his sister Esther. "I felt alarmed. . . . A few, no doubt, through excessive ignorance, mistook their first impressions for religion, and began to rejoice in *safety,* and not in God. . . . The two Miss Candys have false hopes which I am now going over to destroy if I can." Safety! There was none, with that flying force abroad; Beecher was up—and his family was up—with prayers before sunrise, and he was quickly away on his pastoral errands. "Lectured sometimes nine times a week, besides going to converse with the awakened. If any ministers happened along, I did not want them; did not ask them—not a single one. They would strike forty miles behind. My mind and the mind of my congregation were in such a state that they couldn't come up to us." In winter riding along cattle-paths up to his saddlebags in snow, he soon began what he called "border warfare" in outlying hamlets and beyond, where a prejudice against revivals had developed, or where other faiths were gaining a foothold.

His house, an old spacious farmhouse with a hipped roof and an ell, set a little apart from the town, thrummed with activities. The proud, the lofty, the delicate, and high-minded went in and out on solicitous spiritual errands; all the notabilities—and their fame had spread to Washington and Philadelphia—belonged to his congregation, Judge Reeve among them. Ministers stopped for consultations on their journeys up and down the state as the work of revivalism spread; many of these were Dwight's disciples; among them Beecher formed innumerable alliances, the most ardent and lasting of all a friendship with the Reverend Nathaniel Taylor, an exquisite dialectician and fiery revivalist with whom he argued steadily during visits and by letter, and against whom he pitted his skill in raising early cucumbers. Beecher's house was crowded, his own household almost a congregation. A few pupils from the Law School and from the Young Ladies' Seminary were taken as boarders when his salary, which at first had seemed munificent, began to shrink under the pressure of many demands. Three more children were born in rapid succession, Harriet, Henry Ward, and Charles; there was now a noisy, lusty flock of eight. Beecher romped with them at hasty intervals, yearned over them far more tenderly than did Roxana, who seems to have looked upon all the stirring life about her from a quiet distance, and punished them on occasion with unmitigated harshness. When she was a little girl he once tipped Catherine's head into a tub of water to see what she would do. He kept them all steadily at work, and waged a ceaseless revivalism among them. Sometimes as a reward for their labors in stacking wood or picking up stones in the garden, he would lead them all on a nutting expedition, which became a stage for his own exploits. Once he climbed a great chestnut tree that grew at a slant fifty feet without branches over a precipice, and whirling himself over the abyss, shook down nuts for the admiring band below.

Occasionally, for the diversion of the entire household, came Roxana's seafaring brother, Captain Samuel Foote, who sailed his own square-rigged bark to Spain, Mogadore, and Peru. Captain Foote had known Miss Edgeworth, and had been well received in Dublin for his wit and handsome person. With a flamboyant touch he told stories of shipwreck, and strangely contended that Turks were more honest than Christians, and that he had known Catholic priests who were both learned and pious. Then he would unload from his great chest Moorish slippers, ingots of silver, implements which he said were taken from the tombs of the Incas, and packets of new English books, which included recent volumes of Scott and Byron.

Already Byron was a sign and symbol of utter wickedness in this country, even in remote American hamlets where his works were never seen; the children were forbidden to read Byron. Yet Beecher himself fell under the spell of those swirling lines and that legendary personality. "Byron is dead—gone!" he exclaimed with dismay some years later, as though he had sustained a personal loss; and he was deeply moved by the fate of a character after whom he felt Byron to be modeled. As he read aloud the long passage in *Paradise Lost* describing the fallen angels and Satan's tears and scorn when he addressed them, he himself burst into tears, and put the book aside. There was no question as to his final judgment on Satan or Byron; and poetry on any theme was a rare diversion for the Beechers. Novels were forbidden, though a shattered fragment of *Don Quixote* and a larger portion of the *Arabian Nights*— perhaps purveyed by Captain Foote—had been discovered in a dusty recess by the children. Yet in the end, Scott's novels with their color and their information proved irresistible to Lyman Beecher. "I'll tell you what will make the evening go off," he would exclaim as the whole family sat around the great kitchen fireplace in autumn, peeling baskets of apples and quinces for the great barrel of cider apple-sauce which was to be frozen and put away for the winter. "We'll see who can tell the most out of Scott," and the young Beechers would recite entire scenes out of *The Black Dwarf* or *The Bride of Lammermoor*.

As for the Turks and the priests recommended by Captain Foote, Beecher had his own flow of argumentative bravura. After a long tilt— or the more arduous toil of the Sabbath—he would take down an old fiddle and play *Money Musk*, which he never mastered, or *Go to the Devil and Shake Yourself*, which he played with considerable ease, or exhibit certain lively dancing steps which he had picked up, nobody knew where.

But intervals for diversion were brief in this household; and strictures rapidly narrowed. When Catherine, marshaling the others, arranged Miss Edgeworth's *Unknown Friend* as a play, the performance was allowed to proceed to a close, but a repetition of such an experiment was forbidden. If any of the children tried to dance when Beecher played his fiddle he stopped short. The Puritan renascence was now in full swing. The fiddle itself was suspect—an instrument used mainly by idlers, frequenters of taverns, and the like. The older Puritans had approved only the trumpet and jew's-harp; and the judgments of the older Puritans were taking on a fresh validity in New England. Under Dwight's quiet but still potent leadership a Society for the Prevention of Vice and the Promotion of Good Morals had been founded, or the Moral Society, as it was more briefly called, whose purpose it was to revive the older standards and to bring questionable conduct under surveillance and reproof. Branches of the Moral Society were formed in nearly every town and hamlet in Connecticut; and at about the same time a similar organization was founded in Massachusetts.

Beecher clung to his fiddle, but he soon was ranging the fertile fields of moral reform. Alas! in quarters which might have been supposed exemplary he discovered a deplorable state of affairs. "None of the Consociation was drunk," he remarked of a clerical gathering held at Plymouth. "But that there was not, at times, a considerable amount of exhilaration I cannot affirm. . . . A broad sideboard was covered with decanters and pitchers of water, and there we found all the various kinds of liquor then in vogue. The drinking was apparently universal. When the Consociation arrived they all took something to drink; also before the public services, and always on their return. As they couldn't all drink at once, they were obliged to stand and wait as people do when they go to mill. There was a decanter of spirits also on the dinner-table, to help digestion, and gentlemen partook of it through the afternoon and evening as they felt the need, some more and some less; and the sideboard, with the spillings of water, and sugar, and liquor, looked and smelled like a very active grogshop. . . . When they had all done drinking, and had taken their pipes and tobacco, in less than fifteen minutes there was such a smoke you couldn't see; and the noise I cannot describe; it was a maximum of hilarity; they told stories and were at the height of jocose talk. They were not old-fashioned Puritans. . . ."

The convivial ministers were quickly shamed. The temperance movement was on, with Beecher in the lead. Persons were excommunicated from the Litchfield church because of intemperance, or because they had proved stumbling-blocks to purity and order. "I was waked up for the war!" cried Beecher. "I was not headstrong, but I was heartstrong—oh, very, very!" Dwight was obliged to warn his young friend that he might "transcend the sanction of public sentiment." Indeed, the new Puritanism was racing beyond the old. Even in primordial Connecticut slight pleasures had often cropped up between the grave demands of the spirit and the exigencies of a primitive daily life. The older Puritans themselves had recognized "that lawful comfort which God aloweth all men in the use of wine." Their suppressions had tended to be sudden, irregular, and irascible. Wigs would be declared "contrary to truth," or vanity proclaimed in slashed sleeves or "superstitious ribbons." Then for a time such matters would be forgotten. Sleeves, wigs, and ribbons would again become noticeable, and again would come an onset of suppression. But Timothy Dwight, in his great rejoinder to the Yale students, had reached the nadir of definition and denial; he had codified the wicked human digressions completely for the first time in New England; and he had loosed a force which he could not stay. Along with the energy of his own closely packed logic now hurried the livelier emotion of his young disciple, ardently pushing logic to an extreme. Beecher abated his insistences not a jot. Gone in Litchfield were the casual days of balls, strolling players, and slack-wire dancing. Under his glancing touch the ball became a fantasy of wickedness, and the circus was anathema. Joining with other ardent new Puritans—for they seemed to start up on all sides—he condemned all careless gatherings for mere diversion as though through fear that in such assemblages some incalculable power might be set free. Steadily extending its purposes of watch and ward, the Moral Society urged prosecutions for infringement of the laws governing Sabbath observance. "We really broke up Sunday riding!" cried Beecher exultantly. The blue laws were affirmed; legislation prohibiting circuses from entering the state was tightened; and a concerted war was begun on the theater.

Yet at the outset, in urging the benefits of the Moral Society upon certain of his fellow-ministers, Beecher had skimmed rather lightly over problems of conduct. Among the habits, "the old steady habits" which he said must be perpetuated at all costs, was that of permitting the lieutenant-governor to succeed the governor. Presently the republican forces charged that the Society was only a system of thorough-going caucuses, and a means of personal "espial." Certainly the new organization with its extensive branches was admirably adapted to political ends, since the right of suffrage still rested upon guarantees of moral character; and the Puritan clergy were an essential portion of the Standing Order. Into the entire mixed struggle Beecher flung himself with heat, with anger, with perennially flying colors, as if his main intention after all were to destroy the rising political hopes of a new era. Freedom—the rights of man: for a decade he fought the waxing and rancorous issues, took potshots at Jefferson, and furiously rode up and down the state in an effort to save the ancient hierarchy. Toleration became the battle-cry of the opposition: "the Toleration dream," as Beecher scornfully called it, composing a long allegory on the subject. Then, at last, in 1819 came the resistless deluge. "So the Democracy as it arose," said Beecher in wrath, "included all the minor sects, besides the Sabbath breakers, tippling folk, infidels, and ruff-scuff generally, and they made a dead set at us of the Standing Order. . . . They slung us out like a stone from a sling." A Toleration governor was elected, Oliver Wolcott, of Litchfield, who actually was a member of Beecher's own congregation. The new constitution leveled the qualifications for the suffrage; and the church of the fathers was hurled from power.

The day after the election found Beecher in the kitchen of his house at Litchfield, his head drooping on his breast; his depression was extreme, and unalleviated. "It was the worst attack I ever met in my life," he cried. "It was as dark a day as I ever saw. . . . I worked as hard as mortal man could, and at the same time preached for revivals with all my might, and with success. . . ." But presently he was declaring with exuberance that the downfall of the Standing Order was *the best thing that ever happened to Connecticut. . . .* They say ministers have lost their influence; the fact is they had gained!"

But the upheaval was by no means over. These drastic changes were scarcely effected when New England was found to be in the grip of a force even more disruptive than any controlled by radical Republicans or belligerent minor sects. The great movement westward, steadily swelling in volume for two decades, was revealed as a menace to the stable society of the coast; Connecticut was riven. Packing their possessions in Conestoga wagons, great numbers of people, farmers mainly, were leaving a stony soil which was now all but exhausted by nearly two centuries of remorseless agriculture, and were traveling toward the rich lands and bright horizons of the West. Dismay overwhelmed those portions of communities which had chosen to remain. Taxes were reduced on agricultural lands—a measure long overdue. Newspapers entered upon ardently dissuasive campaigns; it was declared to be "the height of madness for men *who have no extraordinary reasons for removal* to leave their homes for the wild lands of the West, and their still wilder states of society." Small siren songs were piped:

> "Let the idle complain
>   And ramble in vain
> An Eden to find in the West—
>   They're grossly deceiv'd,
>   Their hearts sorely griev'd,
> They'll sigh to return to the East."

As if his very life depended upon a continuance of the older Connecticut, Beecher passionately endeavored to stop the outgoing flood. Forgetting the irksome labors of his boyhood, he intoned hymns to agriculture, an idyllic pursuit which he declared could most safely be followed in the settled regions of the East. He was importunate, he seemed panic-stricken. He insisted that a rapid migration was a national evil which demanded a remedy. But no remedy appeared; the great drift continued. Small holdings were put up at auction in Connecticut by the hundreds.

Then the political rebels of Connecticut began to protest against the stringent laws and active surveillance which still remained as a last Puritan heritage. A small vociferous anti-Puritan group flung out broadsides, concocted jokes on the ministry, and told satirical stories about the Pilgrims; Puritan doctrines were declared to be "gloomy, superstitious, severe, irrational, and of a licentious tendency." Again the shout of Toleration was raised; and worst of all, rebellion passed into practice. At apple-bees and corn-huskings young people frequently slipped the rein of authority and gave way to noisy games, drinking, and dancing; the entire social structure which had claimed Beecher's allegiance seemed to be crumbling into dust. Yet at the last, in the essential engagement of the early twenties over the moralities, the Puritan party fought with the big battalions. Defeated in the field, the older order impressed its culture, and became established on its narrow strip of shore as an arbiter of both taste and morals. Circumstance played a timely part. A money panic swept the country, and worldly affairs became dust and ashes. Moreover, the rebels were drawn in the main from the loose populace of taverns and country stores; they lacked cohesion; above all they lacked the nearly invincible weapon of respectability. Among many changes perhaps a stable society seemed to many even of the ruff-scuff something of a refuge; in denial lay safety.

"The tide of Toleration is ebbing," cried Beecher in happy crescendo, and preached a fiery sermon on Lord Byron. Presently he blew the bold salvo of his *Six Sermons on Intemperance,* which found many responses, and brought him fame not only in New England but in the West, and even across the sea. With his energetic collaboration the blue laws were again affirmed. As for the Pilgrim fathers, who still were being disparaged by a small derisive chorus, he raised them to lofty niches as public exemplars, in an election discourse called *The Memory of Our Fathers,* delivered in 1826, twice repeated, and widely circulated as a pamphlet. Claiming that the early Puritans had abolished the monopoly of the soil, had established the rights of conscience, had given to the country the great boon of self-government, he raised them to apotheosis. "The world hath not seen their like, nor will it soon, we fear, again," he cried. "Such models of moral excellence—such apostles of civil and religious liberty

—such shades of the illustrious dead, looking down upon their descendants with approbation or reproof according as they follow or depart from the good way, constitute a censorship only inferior to the eye of God!"

With rapid enthusiasm Beecher was transforming Puritanism into a cult. Yet this discourse presented a singular spectacle. Stormy elements of an era seemed to meet there and mingle. He began properly enough with a sentence which might have adorned the sternest exposition of the older faith; "The history of the world is the history of human nature in ruins." He denounced the "Vandal spirit of innovation." But all at once he forgot the solemn admonitory fathers; the past became a springboard from which he leapt to a new and unimaginably glorious future. *"And He that sat upon the throne said, Behold, I make all things new."* New —new—a new dispensation, a new era—crowding through in thick and breathless utterances, the theme of a transcendent new epoch ran through his speech like fire. The thousand years of predicted happiness was at hand, hastened by the power and the example of the new nation. "The time has come when the experiment is to be made whether the world is to be emancipated and rendered happy, or whether the whole creation shall groan and travail together in pain," he shouted; and celebrating the republican form of government in terms which easily matched those of the Jacksonian era, sweeping onward to consider the condition of France, Italy, Portugal, Greece, the South American states, Asia, and Africa, he proclaimed that the great and joyous change had indeed already begun— to be followed by fortunate revolutions and overturnings throughout the world. "If it had been the design of Heaven to establish a powerful nation in the full enjoyment of civil and religious liberty, where all the energies of man might find full scope and excitement, on purpose to show the world by one great successful experiment of what man is capable, and to shed light on the darkness which should awake the slumbering eye, and rouse the torpid mind, and nerve the palsied arm of millions —where could such an experiment have been made but in this country! . . . The light of such a hemisphere shall go up to Heaven, it will throw its beams beyond the waves; it will shine into the darkness there, and be comprehended,—it will awaken desire, and hope, and effort, and produce revolutions and overturnings until the world is free. . . . Floods have been poured upon the rising flame, but they can no more extinguish it than they can extinguish the fires of Aetna. Still it burns, and still the mountain murmurs; and soon it will explode with voices and thunderings, and great earthquakes. . . . Then will the trumpet of jubilee sound, and earth's debased millions will leap from the dust, and shake off their chains, and cry, 'Hosanna to the Son of David!' "

At a stroke Beecher had caught the emotion arising from the half-broken, half-settled regions of the West. An archetypal expectancy was abroad, running back many years for its origin—Jonathan Edwards had thought that the Millennium was to begin in America—but now surging up with fresh fervor as the nation floated into the sense of a boundless common patrimony. As men blazed trails or made their clearings in the wilderness for homesteads they were saying that a new life, a new civilization had begun such as the world had never known before. Catching the thrilling intimation, Beecher fitted it to a primary pattern. The supreme issue was that of the new birth—on an epic scale. Where—where was he to begin? Perhaps his own dissuasive to immigrants was still ringing in his ears; Beecher did not choose the West. Scanning the lifted horizon he perceived in a flash the critical point from which the vast work should be undertaken—Boston.

"Write instanter on receiving this, that I may know what to depend on," he wrote from Boston to his friend Nathaniel Taylor. "We must have some one on the ground before I leave. Now is the time to strike for all New England and the United States!" From the high eminence of his hope he surveyed the abysmal blackness. In fact, the condition of Boston was a scandal among the orthodox New England clergy. "A thick moral darkness broods over that once favored and exemplary spot," said the Reverend Gardner Spring in a New England Society oration. "From the time Unitarianism began to show itself in the country it was as fire in my bones," cried Beecher. "My mind was all the time heating—heating—heating." He hated "the icy system." His sense of an adversary rapidly mounted. He talked of running off sermons, "each one fresh, like bullets from a mold." "I have been reading the controversy about Cambridge College, and think that the abominations of her secret history are coming to light. . . . The higher classes—the Cambridge College folks—have their spies abroad to see what is going on. . . . The whole influence of Unitarianism is a poisonous bribery." Happily this apostasy was *"one of the last great controversies which were to afflict the church."* The task was to demolish it, shore up the ruins, revive a primitive glory, and make of Boston a great shining, commanding fortress of the faith.

Miraculously, Beecher's vision coincided with opportunity; he received a call from Hanover Church in Boston. He now regarded Litchfield with a disillusioned eye. He saw that his house was falling into disrepair, that his old horse and chaise and his own clothes were shabby, that for years he had lacked money for the most necessary books. He was out of sorts with his congregation, though they had recently made him a gift of three thousand dollars. "I could not get my salary quarterly or half yearly," he afterward told a brother minister. "I could not and did not get a vestry, but held conferences in that old west schoolhouse, dark and dirty, with candles stuck up on the side walls with old forks; and at last we grew so liberal as to buy half a dozen tin things to hang on the wall and put candles in. I cannot revert to the scene without shuddering" He discovered the desperate fact that he had "lost his susceptibilities," and declared that he had spent sixteen of the best years of his life "at a dead lift." And while the matter was under the consideration of his Litchfield church he furiously rode back and forth to Boston.

Roxana Foote had died at the height of the Standing Order controversy. Aloof and serene, she had spun and woven and mended and made carpets and superintended the vast seasonal activities which were part of the New England domestic economy, and had cared for her eight children and her large company of boarders and a host of visitors whose number steadily increased as the warfare in Connecticut grew intense. "Pray save me some pink-seed of your double pink," she had begged one of her sisters in a letter written during her earlier years in Litchfield; "and lay me down some honeysuckle of all sorts that you have, and save me a striped rose; I have never seen one. . . . Mary has, I suppose, told you of the discovery that the fixed alkalies are metallic oxyd. . . ." But her days quickly became too crowded for rose-gardens or chemistry or even for a casual reading of the new books brought to Litchfield by Captain Foote; many times her tasks seemed insuperably difficult. "Would now send you a long letter," she wrote, "were it not for several vexing circumstances, such as weather extremely cold, storm violent, and no wood cut; Mr. Beecher gone; and Sabbath day, with company—a clergyman, a stranger; Catherine sick; George almost so. . . . Mr. Beecher is gone to preach at New Hartford, and did not provide enough wood to last, seeing the weather has grown so exceedingly cold." Riding home with her husband from the country in the bitter chill of a winter's night, she announced her impending death, and floated away in a quick consumption with an entire willingness to die which Lyman Beecher ascribed to her perfect spiritual peace. He mourned her as he had loved her—blindly—he could never mention her name without emotion. Nearly forty years after her death he was so deeply moved by a letter which mentioned her that he could not speak, and was obliged to leave the room. Once he sat alone far into the night pouring out difficulties which seemed to him overwhelming in a letter addressed to Roxana.

But life—the stirring life of Connecticut in midstream—had to go on; his house was without a mainstay, himself without a helpmeet. Within a year he had wooed and married Harriet Porter in Boston, who was tall and elegant and willowy, with auburn curls. Her father, a physician of Portland, was a courtly gentleman, and Harriet was not unaware of her superior birth and breeding. She granted that the society of Litchfield was "singularly good." "It is an immense advantage," she said, "that the people here are decidedly the most religious." But the rough and tumble little Beechers noticed that she seldom laughed; she developed, indeed, a somewhat combative strain. In the early months of her marriage when her husband was reading aloud to her from Jonathan Edwards' *Sinners in the Hands of an Angry God*—a favorite work of his at the time— she arose and swept from the room, exclaiming indignantly, "Why, Mr. Beecher, I will not listen to another word! Why, it is horrible! It is a slander on the character of my Heavenly Father!" And when Mr. Beecher emptied out all the baskets in her linen room to take on a nutting expedition she was distraught: and she was overwhelmed when he stuffed into a missionary box a roll of one hundred dollars which had been collected for a much needed new carpet. Gradually he learned to accommodate himself to her exquisite housekeeping and to certain of her prejudices. He took down his fiddle after she had retired to her room for the night, and removed his shoes when he wished to dance a jig, and enormously enjoyed the disintegration manifest in the soles of the socks she had dutifully knitted for him. Yet, once in stately perversity, when she chanced to hear him playing his fiddle in another part of the house, she lifted her arms with a graceful motion, and rhythmically wheeled about the room.

Harriet Porter had borne him four children, one of whom had died. There were now eleven in all. Seven were sons, and were to enter the ministry, upholding like mighty pillars the structure of the ancient faith. Beecher had been barely able to maintain William and Edward in college; his children constituted a final argument for a release from his charge at Litchfield. Promptly enough, in 1826, he received his dismissal; and he began his new momentous task with elation.

FIVE • *"I never stood in such a place before," Beecher cried,*
"and do not believe that there is, all things considered, such another perhaps on earth!"

Yet almost at the outset in Boston he fell into an abysmal melancholy. "Ah, William, I'm done over! I'm done over!" he mourned after his installation; and tipping a chair for a head-rest upon the kitchen floor he lay down in front of the fire.

"He suffered much from fear, and does still," William wrote to Edward. "I never knew him more cast down. He felt as if his course was finishing." When Mrs. Beecher observed that he had frequently entertained this notion, and in a day or two had been as well as ever, "Yes," he groaned in reply, "but I never was so low as this before. It's all over with me." Indeed, his discouragement was not without foundation. The cool ranks of the Unitarians passed him by without a glance, or were amused by his scholarship and his language; he still said "creetur" and "natur." His own congregation looked doubtfully at his habit of rushing into the church with a satchel full of manuscript after the organ had begun to peal; once he launched into his sermon without preliminaries, forgetting the ritual of hymns and prayer and scripture. He was physically cramped in Boston. He sawed his own wood, but every stick was soon cut and stacked; and though he skirmished through the neighborhood with his saw set to a nicety, and entered into a contest with an old wood-cutter in another street with results which passed into legend, the episode was soon over, and he was again at loose ends. Rusty, untidy, uncouth, he roamed about with an entire disregard for appearances. One morning he rushed along a narrow thoroughfare with arms upraised and outstretched, carrying oysters tied in a handkerchief in one hand and a live lobster in the other; spying two acquaintances coming down the other side, he hailed them for an argument, and pursued it with insistence until a crowd assembled in sober amazement. At a house in Concord where he stopped for a brief errand he grew gesticulatory and noisy. A little boy looked up at him, gravely trotted round to the other side for further inspection, and said, "Sir, I think you must be Apollyon."

Yet a portrait of Lyman Beecher painted after he had spent a few years in Boston shows him as quiet and quizzical and silvery, his head gently turned, though his mouth was still ironic and his shoulders ruggedly squared. Perhaps the look of sobriety was superimposed by the painter; in any case it may have been fleeting. But Beecher seemed incalculably changed after his first desperate period of depression. He had soon discovered that the Bostonians of his faith had dreaded his ministrations; fear lay beneath the armor of aloofness worn by his fastidious people. They understood "that I had been a man of war from my youth, and had shed much blood, and they could scarcely credit their ears when I began to address them in terms of candid instruction and affectionate exhortation." He could still tear a passion to tatters—a favorite phrase —and he sometimes did so, pitched himself in the highest key, used the highest language and the strongest arguments, as he said, though for mere heady violence in preaching or in prayer he now had the contempt of the superior craftsman. " 'Twas soon after he was converted," he remarked of a noisy brother, "and was on his high heels, and he had to mouth when he prayed, and swing his arms. . . . Well," he added drily, "'twas lucky our room was large."

His own approach became increasingly mild. With the skill which made every New England blacksmith an artisan he devised little intricate tools with which to induce a nice self-scrutiny—little keys and locks and chains and tiny compasses; as his people began to yield to a congenial mental discipline he elaborated a whole series of graduated steps adapted to bring the seeking soul to salvation. Then the procedure became play—a great divine sport; he set springes, and loved a logic-trap, and swiftly pursued elusive quarries until they were, as he said, "snared." "No sportsman ever watched a shy bird with more skillful, wary eye than he watched, not to disgust or overburden or displease the soul he was seeking to save," said his daughter Harriet, who was a close observer of his pastoral labors at this time. "His eye, his voice, his whole manner, were modulated with the utmost tact and solicitude. He could tone himself down to the most shy, timid, and fastidious. . . . He excelled most particularly in the conduct of delicate and desponding natures, with whom religious emotion was apt to be complicated by nervous disarrangements. . . ."

"I *struck,* just according to character and state," said Beecher. "It was really amusing to see the rapid changes in language I underwent as I passed from one class to another. . . . They believed what I told them as if it was the Bible—as it was!" He began to speak of his "clinical Theology."

A sharp and zealous gaze was soon fastened upon these flexible new methods by some of the older New England clergy and by certain laymen. One of the few exponents of a rigid orthodoxy in Hanover Church complained in a public letter that Beecher neglected to preach "those parts of Calvinism against which the unsanctified heart revolts. . . . The deep, fixed, inherent aversion of the soul to God and all holiness is kept out of sight. . . . Adult depravity is resolved into a habit of sinning. . . ."

"He plumply denies that the more unregenerate man sees of God the more he hates his character," wrote Dr. Porter of Andover in great agitation to a clerical friend. "The grand danger of Brother Beecher is too much reliance upon means," continued Dr. Porter. Means—around that dry little word was raging an essential controversy. Means were the efforts of the anxious soul to attain a saving faith, and included prayer, repentance, righteous living. But if the human soul, using means, could approach salvation by its own efforts, what became of the doctrine of election, of instantaneous regeneration, of an illimitable divine sovereignty? Dr. Beecher seemed in truth to have given over preaching divine sovereignty altogether. "I objected to him," said Dr. Porter, who had earnestly labored with Beecher on these questions, "that while Calvinism had two legs—the agency of God and the agency of man—he had made it walk on one, and thus had given it the halting gait of Thersites, instead of the majestic march of Achilles."

The more the elder clergy regarded the figure of Calvinism which Beecher was projecting in Boston the more decidedly it seemed to limp, while the little creature Man, running at the side of the disabled hero and presumably under his protection, was gathering under Beecher's glancing touch an unprecedented strength and stature. It was remembered that even in Connecticut Beecher had begun to dwell upon free agency to an alarming extent; questions were revived as to that impetuous discourse delivered long ago at East Hampton, called *The Government of God Desirable,* by which he had successfully produced a revival. Then, as if these vagaries were not enough, Dr. Beecher precipitated a rash and troublesome dispute on the subject of infant damnation. The Unitarians, seeking a vulnerable spot in the heel of the majestic Achilles, had declared that the older faith preached a hell paved with infants' bones; and Beecher had loudly answered that infant damnation was a monstrous doctrine, and "that having passed the age of fifty, and having been conversant with the most approved Calvinistic divines in New England and in the Middle, Southern, and Western states, I must say that I have never seen nor heard of any book which contained such a sentiment, nor man—minister or layman—who believed or taught it." But Calvinistic ministers in New England and in the Middle, Southern, and Western states, reading Beecher's pronouncements as they appeared in print, uprose in numbers to deny the mildness imputed to them. The Unitarians harped on the discrepancy; the older Calvinists labored the point. If infants were not born depraved, just when did the mysterious change take place which rendered them so? What became of the doctrine of imputation if any such transition was made? If infants were *not* depraved, then precisely what was their spiritual state? Were they innocent? Hardly; that would be to repudiate the entire doctrine of the Fall.

In the midst of these speculations came a bold stress upon human powers and human agency from Nathaniel Taylor, now Professor of Didactic Theology at Yale, in his long famous *Concio ad Clerum.* For many years a troubled reverberation had run beneath Taylor's fiery eloquence. Delicate and sensitive, he had been so obsessed by a conviction of sin as a student under Dwight at Yale as almost to lose his reason;

and the generic problem had continued to haunt his nights and days. Why had a God whom he imaged as radiantly benevolent permitted the black and bitter condition of sin to exist? If Adam was created with a propensity for making the terrible choice, then God himself was the author of sin—a thought which Taylor found intolerable. In his *Concio* he cut—or tried to cut—the knot. His God was absolute yet Promethean —unable to control the race to which he had given the great endowment of free will; even the supreme blessing of divine grace was not wholly sovereign. "I do not believe that the grace of God can be said to be truly irresistible," said Taylor. "I do believe that in all cases it may be resisted by man as a free moral agent. . . . It is not man's disposition which is the cause of sin, but his own act, consisting of a free choice of some object other than God." The human tragedy in Taylor's thinking was thus man's own fluctuant tragedy, as the path by which humankind might attain regeneration was one of man's own choosing. Though he took for his text in the *Concio* the harsh phrase, "And are by nature children of wrath," at the same time he declared that man sought God in order to satisfy the profoundest longing of the human heart—the longing for happiness.

With the preaching of the *Concio* clerical agitation in New England became intense, and again swirled around Beecher. Taylor and Beecher were not only old friends and associates in revivalism, but were editing together a new organ called *The Spirit of the Pilgrims*. Were they bent upon a schism, the worst of schisms—a subtle venture in the direction of the Arminian heresy—or Unitarianism itself? Intimate colloquies were held, formal debates, and prolonged conferences, many of them in Beecher's own house in Boston. Sheaves of Calls, Appeals, Reviews, Replies, and Rejoinders were issued. A controversy broke which for ardor and thoroughness fairly matched a more famous movement of the same period in another ecclesiastical body across the sea. Doctrinal dissension spread among the investigating brethren like a fever, passing far beyond the implications either of Beecher or of Taylor. The aroused orthodox clergy themselves began to draw delicate distinctions, to define shades of spiritual feeling. What actually happened in the human mind and heart during the many states involved in the momentous drama of sin and re-birth? Pyramids of logic were built in answer to this question; the "taste" scheme was discussed once more, and the "exercise" scheme, and triangularism; discussion bore closely upon the difficult metaphysical problems of imputation and the extent of the atonement. In the tightly locked argument "direct proof" was adduced by one divine that "God is able to convert more sinners than are actually converted." Another came out "high, dry, and stiff, that God was the author of sin." The controversy eddied, and began sharply to divide into New and Old Schools, with fresh refinements of statement and meaning.

"Connecticut was quiet as a clock," mourned Dr. Porter, recalling the comparatively calm theological condition of that state in the first two decades of the century. "Massachusetts, indeed, has been an exception for a part of that time," he said bitterly. "This state (Massachusetts) was the region of *original geniuses,* every man having his own *psalm,* and his *doctrine,* every man putting forth his *Bible news,* or his book in some form, to show that he was an independent thinker. . . . But our orthodoxy had settled into a solid, tranquil, scriptural state. . . . It were vain now to hope that all this alarm will subside in a few months, and that Unitarians will never learn the secret that we are divided. . . . Our hills will ring with the noise of conflict, our brethren of the South and West will turn away with sighing from this land of the Pilgrims as a region of theological speculation. The Spirit of God will forsake our churches; and Unitarians—aye, UNITARIANS!—what will they say!" In a long letter overflowing with fraternal candor, Dr. Porter charged Beecher with the largest share of responsibility for the dissension, questioned his alliance with Taylor, and begged him to stop before he crossed the Rubicon. "Once in a century or two the Church needs a GREAT REFORMER to arise," said Dr. Porter. "Some of your remarks have seemed to mean (what Brother Beecher ten or twenty years ago would not have dreamed of) that you were born for that end, and that the theology of New England is the theater for operation. . . ."

Dr. Porter was answered by a letter of stormy and ingenuous protest. "Had I gone to sleep in Boston and waked up in Calcutta," wrote Beecher, "I should not have found myself surrounded by more strange and unexpected associations than I was in being called upon by you, in such a tone, for explanations on such topics, to remove from your mind such apprehensions as you express. Never have the emotions of surprise, mirthfulness, and grief held such strange conflict in my mind. . . . To refrain from laughing was impossible, and to refrain from tears equally so. . . . I cannot suppose that you saw all your implications at one view as I have placed them." Perhaps he *had* relaxed certain doctrines in his zeal to secure converts; but with his Boston congregation in so strange and precarious a condition, what else could he do? They had been repelled by the more stringent elements of the older faith; he was obliged to be cautious. *"Caution,* CAUTION," Dr. Porter had roared. "The grand danger of the ministry has always been to modify the Gospel to appease opposition." Yes, Beecher insisted, but caution had been needed. With the Millennium all but breaking on the horizon, with his people "crammed" with false notions of a repellent Calvinism, what could he do but offer them a soft persuasion? Perhaps at times he *had* slipped into unguarded extremes of expression. He humbly admitted that he was given to what Edwards had called "bursts of emphatic displacency." "As to my hyperboles and metaphors, alas! I despair of ever reducing them to logical precision!" But his doctrine was completely and thoroughly orthodox; in fact, in the midst of the reproaches, the moments of surprise, and the considerable number of bursts of emphatic displacency in his long reply to Dr. Porter was embedded a promise that those aspects of Calvinism against which the unsanctified heart revolted should be preached with new vigor at Hanover Church.

As for the "assumed coalition" with Taylor, "for no man's opinions will I consent to be made answerable, by common fame and suspicion, and only as I specifically adopt and profess them." Presently in an impassioned appeal to the members of both the Old and New Schools at a deliberative conference Beecher pled for unity, and pledged the factions to an armistice. Yet during the interval between his letter to Dr. Porter and the meeting of the conference, he had proposed to Taylor that they put down the Old School contingent—"never to peep again or mutter." Calvin Stowe considered that Beecher crippled Taylor at this point.

Then at a sudden blast all the orthodox ministry of New England of whatever school were aroused and overwhelmed by a menace that came out of the West. A new revivalism had arisen which made their most drastic efforts seem dull and prim.

SIX • *The year in which Timothy Dwight had begun his revivals* at Yale had seen a few itinerant preachers of undistinguished talent moving from Virginia and the Carolinas into the scarcely broken Cumberland region of Kentucky and Tennessee, where with an almost casual touch they initiated one of the most extraordinary outbreaks of religious emotion known in modern times—the Scotch-Irish revival, as it was called, of 1800. In the first heat of summer, camp-meetings were created as by a mysterious, whispered summons. Gathering from far-off trails and tiny clearings, men, women, and children came together they hardly knew how or why, leaving their newly planted crops, their tools, their unprotected huts and cabins, and plunged and sank into a welcome common sea of anguished feeling. All the terror of their venture in the wilderness seemed pooled in unison; they courted terror. Death was their crying theme—death, pressing upon them in the unbearable culmination of the Last Judgment, dark and fearful, a destroying mystery like the strange horse of the Apocalypse. Night after night amid the blackness of the forest, their contorted bodies lit by the rude flare of torches or camp-fires, they moaned and wept, danced, jerked, leapt into the air, fell into trances, or even abruptly expired as the terror of the Word was preached. As the dread excitement reached a higher and higher pitch a medley of uncouth sounds rang out; men and women barked and growled like wild creatures, went down on all fours, whined, and snapped their teeth. At last came the requital of hope as the insistent image grew of the blood of the Lamb. The conviction of safety spread like a happy phantasm; with a strange sense of increase and power the crowds melted away into the forest, to gather for the same dark ecstasy and rising hope again in the autumn, and with rhythmic recurrence in the early summer. A climactic emotion had moved outward in waves; by 1803 it had reached the lower areas of the Western Reserve; within a decade it had crept into Michigan. Was it the circuit-riders—rude and heroic and often terrible figures—swinging in larger and larger irregular orbits—who carried the primitive stress of feeling into central New York? Or did the reasoned revivalism of New England, carried by an emigrant ministry, break in wild forms as it reached the frontier? Two churning floods might have met from the violence which followed. Beginning at Palmyra where the prophet Joseph Smith was living as a child, the new revivalism flung central New York into a maelstrom of emotion, and the first blind rage of excitement had hardly slipped into an extreme lassitude when, in the middle twenties, a special portent appeared in the figure of Charles Grandison Finney.

Even in his old age Finney's countenance wore the fierce white glow of steel—not molten, but irrevocably cast. His heavy brow, flat fringe of whisker, and great staring eyes seemed furiously fixed. "When I saw you my heart began to burn and grow hot within me," said a young man who had bitterly opposed Finney, "and instead of feeling as if I wanted to avoid you, I felt so drawn that I came across the street to see you." Walking through a cotton-mill at Utica, Finney noticed two girls at a loom. "I could see they were a great deal agitated, although they both laughed," he said. "I went slowly toward them. They saw me coming and were evidently much excited. One of them was trying to mend a broken thread, and I observed that her hands trembled so that she could not mend it. I approached slowly, looking on each side at the machinery as I passed, but observed that this girl grew more and more agitated, and could not proceed with her work. When I came within eight or ten feet of her, I looked solemnly at her. She observed it, and was quite overcome, and sank down, and burst into tears. The impression caught almost like powder, and in a few minutes nearly all in the room were in tears." When he preached, using a furious intimacy of appeal, within a quarter of an hour men and women began to moan and fall from their seats in trances. "If I had had a sword in my hand I could not have cut them down as fast as they fell," he said. The number of "the slain," as they were called, was prodigious. Whole towns fell under his sway; even the most skeptical were sometimes caught by an involuntary thrill, and admitted that they clasped trees as they left Finney's meetings in an effort to keep from falling.

Gathering a band of fellow-evangelists, Finney moved eastward. He reached Troy; obviously he was headed for New England. Beecher was aghast. Already Finney was descending upon peaceful folds and seizing flocks from their lawful shepherds. The Unitarians were pointing the finger of scorn, for Finney was an ordained Congregational minister; five books had been written on Finney and his methods by Unitarian writers. Beecher wrote a violent letter of protest against the so-called "new measures," which somehow was circulated as a handbill. Still Finney and his band continued to advance. With the purpose of delivering an ultimatum Beecher summoned the free lance revivalists to a conference with certain orthodox ministers at New Lebanon. Surprise attended his efforts. Many of the New England ministers yielded to Finney's spell; after nine days of discussion the conference was about to strike a fraternal note. "Stop," cried Beecher, leaping to his feet, and addressing one of the most notable of his own group. "Brother Hawes, don't be in a hurry, and don't decide too quickly!" He turned in a flash to Finney and the opposition. "Gentlemen, you needn't think you can catch old birds with chaff. It may be true that you don't go personally into ministers' parishes, but in the noise and excitement, one and another of the people in the towns want you to come and preach, and you are mighty reserved, and say, 'Ah, no, we cannot come unless the ministers invite us,' and so you send them back like hounds to compel them to call you. Finney, I know your plan, and you know I do! *You mean to come into Connecticut, and carry the streak of fire to Boston.* But if you attempt it, as the Lord liveth, I'll meet you at the state line, and call out all the artillery, and fight you every inch of the way, and then I'll fight you there."

The meeting broke up in confusion. But Finney advanced into Connecticut, and with the assistance of many of the settled clergy conducted revivals there on an unprecedented scale. New England arose in blind excitement under Finney's violent hand. Beecher's own delicate and fastidious people clamored for Finney. At first he fended them off; but when twenty deacons demanded the revivalist, when Hanover Church united with other orthodox churches in insisting that he be invited to Boston, Beecher yielded, and drew up a covenant among his fellow-ministers, pledging their support. In Boston, though the Unitarians held aloof, Finney was said to have aroused an excitement equal to that of the Great Awakening. Yet he was not altogether satisfied with the results, at least at Hanover Church. When he had reached a tremendous climax of appeal, and paused for a moment of drastic and terrifying silence, Beecher sprang up and re-stated his argument in totally different terms, giving the impression that Finney had stopped in embarrassment; he noted henceforth a faint frigidity in Beecher's congregation. And when one of Finney's band was arranging to take a pulpit in Philadelphia during an important meeting of the General Assembly, Beecher stepped in, and secured the place. "That blocked somebody's wheels," he exclaimed joyfully. "It blocked a good many wheels. That defeated their plans. They failed."

These were sprightly sorties; and Beecher enjoyed their memory to the end of his life. But he had incurred the lasting resentment of the more severely orthodox clergy of New England by his compromise; and in the end Finney seemed unperturbed by minor pricks. Like some tireless and terrible general bent upon harrying the land, he ranged up and down New England, returned to central New York, and again moved eastward. The long and rhythmic progress of Beecher's own more reasoned revivalism might have prepared the ground; in an austere society fear surged up with violence. The new terror spread in widening circles, and broke at last in the great binding emotion of the revival of 1831.

Instead of the restrictive approaches of the older faith there had now arisen a turmoil of tempestuous feeling. Beecher's own children were swayed by it; from the first, it seemed, even in the Litchfield days, they had been moved by feeling. William was "forever hunting after feeling, feeling, *feeling,* when he has so much of it already as to shatter his nerves," said his father bitterly. Step by reasoned step he had tried to lead them all to the great climax of submission; whatever his light excursions in the matter of doctrine with others, among his own children he remitted nothing; but it was as if his own mind had set itself to resist him at the point where conquest should have been easiest. Mary and George, Henry Ward and Charles, the older and the younger alike, had been swept by alternate gusty waves of despair and exaltation; but to Beecher's practiced eye this emotion was without depth or ground of intellectual apprehension; it did not "grapple." "Oh, may the Lord make his way prosperous . . . that I may see at least one child out of danger and in the Ark," he cried in an agony of impatience. "Oh, what knowledge and what stupidity coexist in our family; Oh, Lord, I have heard Thy voice and am afraid!" "My heart overflows with grief and fear, and my eyes with tears," he wrote to Edward, who, in spite of his uncertainties, was studying for the ministry at Yale. *"You must not continue stupid!* . . . A family so numerous as ours is a broad mark for the arrows of death. I feel that one or more of you may die suddenly, and I be called to mourn over you without hope. . . . Oh, my dear son, agonize to enter in. You *must* go to Heaven. You *must not* go to Hell."

Edward had agonized; they all had agonized. Catherine's case had remained the most difficult. Her betrothed, a promising young scholar, had been lost at sea without having experienced the great change, unless it was precariously at the last dreadful moment; in Beecher's view his fate in eternity was only too clear. Her father had permitted no short cut, no substitutes for an entire acceptance of his faith; he softened nothing. "Guard against those seasons when the clouds clear away and present an inviting, smiling world," he admonished Catherine. "I dread such clearings off. Had rather you should walk in darkness and see no light till you trust in the Lord and stay on your God. . . . When you consider the character of man as entirely depraved, when you consult your own cold, selfish heart, if God does not demand immediate spiritual obedience, he does not demand anything. . . . Remember that the most perfect honesty and the most correct morality are nothing. . . ." But Catherine in her grief was unable to feel either Professor Fisher's depravity or her own. Human beings were "formed" as they were, she said; it was "our misfortune and not our fault that we are born with a nature inclined to evil"; and if because of this propensity millions were doomed to an eternity of punishment the whole system seemed to her unbelievably cruel. "When I look at the little Isabella," she wrote to Edward, "it seems to me a pity that she was ever born, and that it would be a mercy if she were taken away. I wonder that Christians who realize the worth of an immortal soul should be willing to give life to immortal minds, to be placed in such a dreadful world." At Hartford where she was conducting a school, she had welcomed the releasing terror of Finney's revivalism. And Edward, whom his father had finally pushed through a theological course and into a Boston pulpit, was one of the ministers who had asked to have Finney brought to Boston; he had grasped at violence as the firmest straw. Edward had wished to accept a professorship at Dartmouth; he was not proving acceptable at Park Street, and was about to leave his Boston charge. "His nervous system falters considerably," said Beecher. In fact, Beecher's purpose to see all his seven sons gloriously preaching the faith now seemed phantasmal. William had entered the ministry, but was undistinguished. Young Henry Ward Beecher was at Amherst, but he was thick of tongue and wavering of purpose. Four other boys were still to be set on their way. Then there were the younger girls; and of these Harriet, who was moody and changeable, had passed an even shorter distance along the road toward salvation than had Catherine.

If Beecher had cast about him a dispassionate glance, he might have read the signs of failure on every side. That heresy which was to be among the last to afflict the Church still serenely flourished. He had molded his style, and had become as much of a Bostonian as his taste and temperament would permit; but he still looked the country minister. If at the outset "the higher classes, the Cambridge College folks" had perhaps regarded him with a faint derision, in the end they never noticed him at all; in scarcely one of their familiar records does he figure even as a phenomenon. By their calm and assured efforts a small mount of vision was arising. The great literary ascendency had begun, with Holmes's first verse and Longfellow's, and the voluminous, premonitory writings of Mrs. Child. That other society, which Beecher had expected to overwhelm, was quietly becoming a super-society, which glanced with negligence at all tumultuous stirrings of the world outside.

SEVEN • *Beecher never had a dispassionate eye; and he had grown oblivious of Boston. His gaze was fixed elsewhere.* At last, in the midst of confusion, he saw the finger of destiny pointing unmistakingly toward the West.

"While in Philadelphia and since, my interest in the majestic West has been greatly excited and increased," he wrote in a fine feather to Catherine shortly after Finney's advent in Boston. "The moral destiny of our nation, and all our institutions and hopes, and the world's hopes turn on the character of the West. I have seriously thought of going over to Cincinnati, the London of the West, to spend the remnant of my days in that great conflict, and in consecrating all my children to God in that region who are willing to go. If we gain the West, all is safe; if we lose it, all is lost. . . . This is not with me a transient flash . . . but a feeling as if the great battle is to be fought in the Valley of the Mississippi, and as if it may be the will of God that I may be employed to arouse and help marshal the host. . . . If I go," he repeated, "it will be part of my plan that *you* go, and another that Edward, and probably all my sons and daughters who are willing to go. . . ."

An inkling had reached him of a new theological seminary to be established in Cincinnati; in a Boston street soon afterward he saw one of its founders talking with a clerical friend. "Now they are going to pitch on me!" he thought. "I went home and ran in, and found Esther" —his sister—"alone in the sitting-room. I was in such a state of excitement I could not speak, and she was frightened. At last I told her. It was the greatest thought that ever entered my soul; it filled it, and displaced everything else." Within a few weeks he was formally offered the presidency of Lane Seminary. There were difficulties; Hanover Church had recently burned. "My jug's broke," he cried, skipping home after viewing the little stone tower, split from top to bottom by the heat; here perhaps was a providential release. But his clerical associates insisted that he could not leave his congregation homeless. Impatiently he remained in Boston for two more years, and at the end of that time was rewarded by another and more urgent call to Lane. At the crux of the decision all his older friends were against the move. Taylor tried to dissuade him, holding out the possibility of a chair at Yale; other ministers added their arguments. The change, indeed, was momentous. Beecher was nearly sixty; he was venturing into an untried region, to assume heavy labors at a new institution; he was to become the senior professor at the Seminary, and he was to preach at Second Church in Cincinnati. Besides, he was to leave the faith of which he had been a part for so many years, and enter the Presbyterian Church once more, at a time when that body was threatened with dissensions, and under a Plan of Union whose dissolution was already being discussed. Brusquely confident, he dismissed objections. Gathering together those of his children who were free to leave—Catherine, Harriet, the other girls, the younger boys—making provision for the rest rapidly to follow, joined by Harriet Porter, to whom the whole enterprise was intensely distasteful, he set out in 1832 for the majestic West.

When the Beechers arrived at Cincinnati the party was halted on the outskirts of the city for days by an epidemic of cholera. Pigs ran in the streets, and the mud on the winding hillsides might have been devised as a torture for man and beast. Famine appeared when the Ohio River grew low. But if Lyman Beecher was aware of these discolorations on the figment of his vision he gave no sign. Scattered over its amphitheater of hills, commanding the wide, rushing *Belle Rivière*, Cincinnati promised magnificence, and magnificence was all he saw. Cincinnati was the Queen City; with a small fling backward he insisted that Cincinnati was already as notable a "literary emporium as Boston." Of the Puritans in the East he began to speak with detachment; New England was diminished.

The West—the West! The exhilarated cry ran through all his talk, his letters, his public utterances. In the West was to begin the glorious thousand years; undoubtedly the evangelization of the world was to start in the West. He issued his famous *Plea for the West*. "The West is destined to be the great central power of the nation. . . . The West is a young empire of mind, and power, and wealth, and free institutions, rushing up to a giant manhood, with a rapidity and a power never before witnessed below the sun. . . . Such an extent of forest never fell before the arm of man, and gave place as by enchantment, to such an empire of cities, and towns, and villages, agriculture, and merchandise, and manufactures, and roads, and rapid navigation, and schools, and colleges, and libraries, and literary enterprise! . . . The later peopled states of New England did by no means come as rapidly to the same state of relative intellectual and moral culture as many portions of the West have already arrived at, in the short period of forty, thirty, even twenty years. . . . No people ever did, in the first generation, so fell the forest, and construct roads, and rear dwellings and public edifices and provide the competent supply of schools and literary institutions. . . . New England did not. . . . The motives which call upon us to coöperate immediately in this glorious work of consummating the institutions of the West, essential to the perpetuity of her greatness and glory, are neither few, nor feeble, nor obscure. The territory is eight thousand miles in circumference, extending from the Alleghany to the Rocky Mountains, and from the Gulf of Mexico to the lakes of the North; and it is the largest territory, and the most beneficent in climate, and soil, and mineral wealth, and commercial facilities ever prepared for the habitation of man, and qualified to sustain in prosperity and happiness the densest population on the globe. . . . All at the West is on a great scale, and the minds and the views of the people correspond with these relative proportions. . . . The West is filling up as by ocean waves, and such is her prospective greatness that the capitals of the East and of Europe hold competition for her acceptance and use, so that in a day she is rising to that high eminence that all other nations have approached progressively through the revolution of centuries. . . . When I first entered the West, its vastness overpowered me with the impression of its uncontrollable greatness, in which all human effort must be lost. But when I perceived the active intercourse between great cities, like the rapid circulation of a giant's blood, and heard merchants speak of just stepping up to Pittsburgh—only six hundred miles—and back again in a few days; and others from New Orleans, or St. Louis, or the Far West; and others going thither; and when I heard my ministerial brethren negotiating exchanges in the near neighborhood—only one hundred miles up or down the river—then did I perceive how God, who seeth the end from the beginning, had prepared the West to be mighty, and still wieldable, that the moral energy of his word and spirit might take it up as a very little thing. . . ."

If only a few years before Beecher had believed that trumpets of jubilee were about to be blown, now he could all but hear their first vibratory notes; all about him were signs, bright, near, and startling, most of all that of the nation raised in a day.

Signs and bold prefigurings—in the fat and favored land, in the new western country, everywhere these were becoming an abundant power, leading men to abandon the habits of a lifetime and to yield themselves to rapturous expectations. In the wake of the terror of the new revivalism had come a fresh outbreak of millenarian hopes. On the fringes of frontiers were being laid the foundations of many an eternal city, or at least for earthly dwellings which were to enshrine a flawless temporal existence. One questing company, setting out from Vermont in search of the Promised Land had been forever lost in the wilderness, but others, undaunted, were making journeys to realize their own securer dreams. The leaders and first followers of a famous hegira to await the Second Coming had already proceeded out of New York into Ohio, guided by the prophet Joseph Smith, with the special designations of golden plates, records of the Lost Tribes, and a buried history which described the new country as chosen for a transcendent destiny from the time of the Flood. Jemima Wilkinson's New Jerusalem prospered, as did the colonies of the Shakers, the Harmonists, the Separatists of Zoar, the schismatic Rappites; new numbers clustered about them, seeking a firm foundation for the eternal life. Robert Owen had been confident of a new social and political era which was to begin in the lush profusion of the new western country; and though his colony at New Harmony had failed, and likewise that at Yellow Springs, a succession of others had been founded on the basis of his pronouncement that "human nature is radically good, and is capable of being trained, educated, and placed from birth in such a manner that all ultimately must become united, good, wise, and happy"—at Allegheny and Blue Springs, Coxsackie, Haverstraw, Nashoba, and half a dozen other points of picturesque and mouth-filling nomenclature.

Lyman Beecher had small patience with these fanciful adventurers. In Owen he discovered one of the scoffers who were to appear in the Last Days; in the brightly tinted expectations of the multifarious others he saw the terrible efficacy of false signs. Any sort of communistic enterprise filled him with loathing. "Naked, ferocious human nature, conglomerate and condensed in respect to all its tendencies to evil" could never be trusted with such schemes. "The entire system is constructed for the accommodation of the most disgusting licentiousness, and produces the most fearful paroxysms of infuriated depravity," he declared in a public invective. His own exultant vision found its climacteric in a great golden doom, in which all those flamboyant little bands would be as nothing, in which the utmost exactions would be demanded of whole peoples and fallen millions, and good and evil be swept apart for all eternity. "He shall rebuke them, and they shall flee far off, and shall be chased as the chaff of the mountains before the wind, and like a rolling thing before the whirlwind. And behold, at eveningtide trouble; and before the morning he is not. . . . For so the Lord said unto me, I will take my rest, and I will consider in my dwelling place like a clear heat upon herbs, and like a cloud of dew in the heat of harvest. For afore the harvest, when the bud is perfect, and the sour grape is ripening in the flower, he shall both cut off the sprigs with pruninghooks, and take away and cut down the branches. They shall be left together unto the fowls of the mountains, and to the beasts of the earth: and the fowls shall summer upon them; and all the beasts of the earth shall winter upon them."

With his desperate purpose hard upon him Beecher began to fortify his own special outpost in eternity amid the tulip trees, walnut trees, beeches, and towering black oaks at Walnut Hills. When he came to Cincinnati the Seminary consisted of two buildings of the plainest construction, a box-like edifice containing classrooms, and a dormitory which to the impartial eye resembled a cotton-factory. Soon a spare little white chapel was built, with a high portico and pillars; a scattering of professor's houses was added among the thickets. Beecher's old carryall ran back and forth between the Seminary and the city on innumerable errands; he preached, argued, lectured, and hurried back to the East for funds. "Rearing of the future ministry of the West . . . is a work of such magnitude as human instrumentality has never before concentrated upon," he declared. In this work—his own work—he was irresistibly, waywardly happy, despite the shuddering abyss which lay for half the world at the end of the enormous journey. Once before his little class of forty students he broke into rhapsody and pictured all the intelligent universe of all time assembled in the great dusk which must have preceded creation. These untold millions were to decide whether with the glorious hope of eternal happiness on the one hand, with irretrievable ruin for countless numbers on the other, with mankind marching toward a vast final upheaval and a triumphant doom—whether the irreparable act of creation should be performed. Create—should God create? Posing the question as himself the Creator, he urged the resistless answer upon his class, and drew forth in that bare little hall a loud exultant response as from far greater numbers, *"Create! Create!"*

Yet even here, in the glorious West, Beecher was pursued by defeat. Beneath the rising thunder of the advancing hosts might be heard the rumble of another conflict. Within a year Lane Seminary was disrupted by the action of its own students as they encountered a many-sided issue of freedom. They were a hardy band, most of them poor, some of them middle-aged, all of them radically in earnest. They had grown up in the half-developed regions of middle New York and in the Great Valley, had worked on little farms or on river-boats to earn their tuition at the Seminary, and had come to Lane largely through the influence of Theodore Weld, who had lately been made the agent for the National Manual Labor Society. In the early thirties manual labor was being philosophized, as inducing health, wealth, clarity of mind, purity of purpose, a sense of brotherhood, and a consciousness of progress. A National Manual Labor Convention had been held; colleges in half a dozen states had been persuaded to combine the fruits of intellectual effort with those of simple toil; a Grand Manual Labor Institution was to be founded near Rochester as a model of its kind. Traveling in the interests of this project, collecting funds, and enlisting the enthusiasm of prospective students, Weld had come to Cincinnati at the time when plans for Lane Seminary were first being formulated, and had been favorably struck by the location at Walnut Hills. The Lane trustees, for their part, were impressed by the advantages of a coalition. Weld threw in his lot and that of his disciples with that of the Seminary, entered as a student, and was promised the chair of Sacred Rhetoric and Oratory when he should have graduated. Beecher had been unapprised of Weld's connection with Lane when he accepted the presidency; the field of sacred rhetoric and oratory was his own; he could hardly enjoy the rise of minor personalities. "They thought he was a god," he remarked bitterly of Weld and of the students. "In the estimation of the class he was president"—of the Seminary. "He took the lead of the whole institution." Indeed, Weld seemed oblivious of Beecher. "I have a fine class," he wrote early in the first academic year as if the Seminary belonged to him, "and have never been placed in circumstances by any means so *imposing*. . . . When I came here matters were getting at loose ends."

Three hours a day of agricultural or mechanical labor became part of the regimen at Lane. With this point established, Weld turned to another cause, which was to occupy him for a lifetime: the cause of antislavery. A fiery speaker and a born iconoclast, he marshaled the Lane students—many of them from the South—for religious and educational enterprises among the free blacks of Cincinnati. But the city—in free Ohio but on the border of Kentucky—was already deeply threatened by the rising issue; opinion had rapidly crystallized there against any open recognition of the slavery question. At the beginning of Weld's activities certain supporters of the Seminary announced that funds would be withdrawn in case Lane became identified with the cause of abolition.

Apart from his annoyance at the ascendency of Weld, Beecher resented the intrusion of the whole vexatious problem. He was profoundly uninterested in the question of slavery. Calvin Stowe, who had known him for some years, and was now a member of the Seminary faculty, said that Beecher had "without being aware of it, not a little of the old Connecticut prejudice against the blacks." Long before, he had preached on the iniquities of the African slave-trade, it was true; but when Garrison came to him for support in Boston at the almost formal beginning of the abolitionist movement, he had replied abruptly, "No, I have too many irons in the fire already." In 1831 in Boston he had publicly sneered at "the few foolish whites" who advocated immediate emancipation, and had casually proposed the deportation of slaves to Africa. The scheme of colonization in any form was always obnoxious to the abolitionists; indeed, they never forgave Beecher for his contempt, or his failure to declare himself inalterably opposed to slavery. Years afterward Oliver Johnson said that in the thirties it required only the example of a strong man like Beecher to rally the churches to the antislavery cause. Johnson went even further. "I verily believe that if Lyman Beecher had been true to Christ and to Liberty in that trying hour, the whole course of American history would have been changed, and the slaves might have been emancipated without the shedding of blood." The charge was extreme; but there was no doubt that Beecher's influence would have given momentum to the cause. He offered nothing. In the interval between his encounter with the abolitionists in Boston and his arrival in Cincinnati, his attitude had grown even more aggressively neutral. Slavery was an evil, Beecher somewhat negligently admitted; but all evil would be cast into a final pit by the oncoming rush of divine righteousness in the Millennium. He had warned his son William, who was preaching in Ohio, against committing himself on either side of the question, and declared bitterly that the abolitionists were "the off-spring of the Oneida denunciatory revivals"—that is, Finney's—"and are made up of vinegar, *aqua fortis,* and oil of vitriol, with brimstone, saltpetre, and charcoal to explode and scatter the corrosive matter." This perhaps was in part a sidewise shot at Weld, who had become a disciple of Finney's at Oneida.

Now in the crisis, upon Weld and the other students he urged moderation—perhaps immoderately—and misgauged their temper. They not only continued their work among the free blacks of Cincinnati, but in spite of Beecher's protests held a nine days' debate on slavery, which resulted in their unanimous vote in favor of immediate abolition, and a flat condemnation of the colonization scheme as inadequate and inhumane.

These events occurred toward the end of the academic year, which closed quietly; but during the summer recess, while Beecher was in the East and the other members of the faculty were absent from the city, the Seminary trustees took action which might have been expressly calculated to dissipate the lull. They passed resolutions instructing the faculty to prohibit public meetings of any sort on the Seminary ground, and to forbid the participation of students in meetings held elsewhere without express permission. The Anti-Slavery Society at the Seminary was ordered disbanded; and expulsion was prescribed as the penalty for students who failed to comply with the new rulings. To make assurance doubly sure, Professor Morgan was dismissed, the only faculty member whose anti-slavery sentiments were known to be strong. The trustees added their justification in a memorandum. "Many of our best citizens were looking upon the Seminary as a nuisance, more to be dreaded than cholera or plague," they declared. "The spirit of insubordination, resistance to law, and of civil commotion which they regarded it as fostering was deprecated in a tone to make one shudder. The scenes of France and of Hayti recur to their imagination. . . ."

A storm broke which foreshadowed many an academic storm to follow, in many a school or college, though the issues have seldom been drawn so boldly as at Lane. At the opening of the Seminary in the autumn the students threatened to withdraw if the offensive mandates were not rescinded. As for Beecher, his authority had been ruthlessly overridden by the trustees; the humiliating fact was publicly noted; the abolition papers insisted that his only proper course was to resign. But the students, too, had overpassed him. If he joined them in their rebellion he could only become a tail for Weld's kite—a rearward position which he was unfitted to assume. The situation was further complicated because, in a burst of anger against the trustees when he learned of their action in New York, Beecher had assured Arthur Tappan that he would never consent to an abridgment of the students' right to discuss the question of slavery. Tappan was president of the National Anti-Slavery Society, and had been a liberal contributor to the Seminary.

Beecher did not resign; nor did he contest the ruling of the trustees. The general issue of free speech he never saw at all; it was as if a blank curtain had dropped before his mind at this point. Gathering all his persuasive warmth, all his unquestioned gift for soft entreaty, he begged the students to disregard the new rulings for a time or to accept them with tolerance, promising that the storm would soon blow over. Unfortunately in the rapid pace of his appeal he argued that true wisdom consisted in advocating a cause only so far as the community would sustain the reformer; and he repeated the counsel. Later he declared that when he reached the Seminary it was too late to alter the situation. It would always have been too late to offer such an argument to that uncompromising band. Under the leadership of Weld they quitted the Seminary —all but three or four—leaving behind them a terse memorial which closed with the hope that the triumph of expediency over right might soon terminate. During the winter they were supported by Tappan in a neighboring village; in the spring they went to Oberlin—another outpost in eternity, where a few years earlier a group from New England had entered the wilderness, hoping to find a way to the perfect life; over their little collection of sheds, tents, and barracks floated a banner bearing a millennial battle-cry. From the first at Oberlin a college had been projected; and for this enterprise the seceding students from Lane were a handsome beginning, the happiest windfall; students were hard to find in the new West. Fairly within striking distance of his own deserted institution, Beecher saw another college enlarging with a well-grounded promise; nor was this the end of irony. Because of an upspringing sentiment in the colony itself, because of the issue at Lane, complete freedom of speech was promised; the doors of the College were opened to applicants regardless of their sex or color. And Tappan persuaded Finney to give up the larger part of his revivalistic labors and become Professor of Didactic, Polemic, and Pastoral Theology at Oberlin. Finney came reluctantly, for he had been preaching with unparalleled success at the Broadway Tabernacle in New York. "I felt great difficulty in giving up that admirable place, where such crowds were gathered within sound of my voice," he said. But he came, and mingling his turbid force with the primitive idealism of the colony, led Oberlin through its first difficult years, and later was made president of the College.

EIGHT • *If Beecher was perturbed by these events he gave no sign.* "You will have troubles, young gentlemen," he would say to his small remaining class—two of them his own sons—"go where you will; but when they come don't dam them up! Let them go down stream, and you'll soon be rid of them." But for himself the flood of disaster was by no means over.

Six weeks after the exodus of students Beecher was formally charged with heresy, and tried, under specifications laid before the Cincinnati Presbytery by the Reverend Joshua L. Wilson, an Old School minister who enjoyed litigation, and who for more than twenty years had preached at the First Presbyterian Church in Cincinnati. In truth, the peace of the great day was not yet at hand; Beecher had become the storm-center of a controversy which was to rend whole communities for a time, and finally to split the Presbyterian Church of the North and the South like a prelude to the violent upheaval of the entire country a generation later. His trial made an enormous stir, not only in the Great Valley but in New England. Reporters were sent from Pittsburgh and even from New York to set down its flow and progress; and a rich collection of matter, both personal and doctrinal, was spread before them.

Wilson had watched Lyman Beecher from afar for many years with a disapproval which had slowly but steadily mounted to the point of combustion. "Alleluia!" he had shouted when he learned that Beecher was coming to Cincinnati, and proceeded to lay his train. His labors must have been prodigious; the heavy, constricted bulk of his charges drew in nearly every phase of Beecher's career. Hypocrisy was the ugly Biblical word upon which Wilson pivoted his preliminary declarations. Hypocrisy, he declared, lay at the root of Beecher's relation to the Presbyterian Church—hypocrisy and ambition. Beecher had first entered the Presbyterian Church to obtain a pulpit at East Hampton: he had lightly left it when a larger opportunity arose at Litchfield, and had come back to it once more to obtain the presidency of Lane Seminary. In Wilson's obstinate picturing Beecher was shown to have sought the presidency of Lane mainly because of difficulties in Boston. This tireless antagonist brought letters, depositions, and printed communications to set forth the desperate tangle of doctrinal controversy in which Beecher had become involved; some of the material came from Beecher's own congregation.

Wilson expounded the affair with Finney in such terms that Beecher's every action appeared equivocal; he announced that Beecher had in the last instance entered the Presbyterian Church by a trick, getting himself accepted by the New York Presbytery, under which he did not reside, without examination, then being passed on, still without doctrinal examination, to the Cincinnati Presbytery—an irregularity of proceeding which was, in fact, never fully explained. And what, Wilson asked, was Beecher's attitude toward the standards which he had thus ambiguously adopted? He drew a credible portrait of Beecher clasping the Westminster Confession to his breast before a large audience, and declaring that it contained the truth, the whole truth, and nothing but the truth. Once Beecher had pronounced it the very word of God. Yet on another occasion he had jocularly remarked that there never was such a document for saying one thing and meaning another; he had frequently cast all the reformers before Edwards "into the shade of ignorance and contempt," thus diminishing the entire conclave of Westminster divines. Not content with such contumelious slander, Beecher had publicly proclaimed that those churches, like Wilson's own, which taught the Presbyterian doctrine of inability, were like Egypt, dark beside the land of Goshen. "Yes, sir," cried Wilson, quoting Beecher's own words to the Moderator in a storm of bitterness, "like Egypt in its midnight darkness, like the mountains of Gilboa without dews of Heaven or fields of offering, or like the valley in Ezekiel's vision, where the bones were *many and dry*—VERY, VERY *DRY!*"

But the damaging pith, Wilson heatedly argued, of Beecher's dissimulation lay in his doctrinal teachings. "Dead in sin and wholly defiled in all faculties of soul and body . . . they are by nature children of wrath and bound slaves of Satan. . . . They have lost all ability of will. . . . No man is able, either of himself or by any grace received in this life, perfectly to keep the commandments of God." In contrast to these fateful avowals certain of Beecher's statements appeared florid indeed. "Look, sir, at the following," cried Wilson to the Moderator. "Man," Beecher had said, "is in possession of such faculties and placed in such circumstances as to render it practicable for him to do whatever God requires. . . . Man is able to do what God commands. . . . So long as the sinner is able and willing to obey there can be no sin." Nothing, then, was simpler than for man to become perfect—man, all whose acts were a corrupt stream proceeding from a corrupt fountain, all whose righteousness was as filthy rags! This was the doctrine of perfectionism, a product of Finney's revivals, hatched in the very shadow of Yale by John Humphrey Noyes, who argued that the Millennium had already begun, that perfection was now attainable, and who was developing his theory in a colony of his own founding at Putney, Vermont. Wilson introduced a letter which had appeared in Noyes' organ, *The Perfectionist,* which argued that Calvanism had been "renovated" by Beecher and Taylor, and now provided an easy stepping-stone to perfectionism; and he buttressed his crowning charge with citations from Beecher's printed discourses on the essential points of total depravity, original sin, and effectual calling. With an excess of caution, perhaps, at the last Dr. Wilson warned the Presbytery against Beecher's ability to mingle false and true in order to make a fair seeming. In fact, he suggested that error was sometimes so subtly compounded with an appearance of truth in Beecher's writings that the Presbytery might well find the task of making the distinction difficult and even dangerous.

There was such a thing as introducing the most deadly poison into the most wholesome aliment; and if *he,* Dr. Wilson, were invited to partake of what appeared to be nutritious food, and, after commencing, found a deposit of arsenic contained within it, he most certainly would stop and eat no more, unless he could be certain of passing over all dangerous portions of the preparation, and of completing his meal with what was not poisonous. He urged—for the safety of the Presbytery—that Beecher's discourses should not be admitted in their entirety into the record. However, the Presbytery decided to risk what Dr. Wilson had evidently survived, and the writings were admitted.

"When Wilson arose to prefer his charges," mused Beecher in happy reminiscence, "I laughed in my sleeve, and said to myself, 'You think you know more of Presbyterian management than I do, but I have as much commonsense as you have, and have attended several ecclesiastical trials in my day, and all those councils and consociations in Connecticut were not for nothing!' ... When the trial came on, I took all my books and references, and sat down on the second stair of the pulpit. It was in my church. I looked so meek and quiet, my students"—his little class of three or four—"were almost afraid I shouldn't come up to the mark." As he began his defense, indeed, there appeared in his look and words a touch of the ingenuous boy; he offered a bit of gentle, halting apology. "I know I am liable to be regarded as a stranger," he declared, "thrust in upon the quiet and comfort of a venerable patriarch who has borne the heat and burden of the day, vexing his soul with my crude and novel heresies. . . ." Wilson was in fact only a year older than Beecher, but under these soft approaches he emerged as debilitated and pitiful; a few added strokes gave him a cramped and niggardly air; and Beecher faintly suggested that Wilson himself had had an eye upon the presidency of

Lane. As for hypocrisy, how did Dr. Wilson explain his signature of the letter of the Presbytery inviting Beecher to come to Cincinnati?

Around the plausible ghost of his accuser Beecher lightly skipped, fresh, youthful, frank, ready to open his heart to the Presbytery—and also exhibiting his strength. By a sudden series of nimble blows he attacked the charge of perfectionism, and raised some interesting questions about his brother Wilson. Would his brother Wilson actually affirm that a man could be held accountable for the mistaken inferences drawn from his teachings by other men? If so, then surely Wilson himself was a heretic. For had not the Shakers claimed him? Had not the New Lights claimed him? Indeed, in their strange vagaries, in their horrid heresies, they had stoutly maintained that they were only taking Dr. Wilson as their guide. Disposing thus of Wilson's "pinching argument" of the letter in *The Perfectionist,* Beecher brought a cloud of witnesses to prove that the doctrines of perfectionism had never been tolerated at Lane; he offered sheaves of letters and depositions to show that his capital of fame was *not* damaged when he had left Boston, that he was in fact at a very apogee. Passing rapidly on, with a broad gesture, a sweep of rhetoric, a bold circling of summary before which his accuser seemed to shrink to an even more halting and diminished stature, he gathered all the charges, of hypocrisy, dissimulation, slander of the Church—yes, Wilson had called it that—and irregular entry, into a careless bundle which he tied with a taut if simple knot; the question was whether the doctrines which he had enunciated were false, under the Confession of Faith. He admitted the doctrines. "My course will be to justify," he announced. "I presume I must have misunderstood my brother Wilson when he said the Confession is not to be explained. That," he calmly stated, "is popery."

If the test was crucial, if Beecher knew that the eyes of all his world were upon him, no one could have guessed this from the triumphant security with which he darted and turned and fluently rolled back argument after argument in his long rejoinder. Gone was the smothered uncertainty of those earlier colloquies in Boston; now at last he was on the happy ground of open controversy. "I knew to a hair's breadth every point between Old and New School, and how to puzzle them with them!" he afterwards exclaimed.

The crux of the matter, the basic question of ability, rested, indeed, upon exquisitely puzzling distinctions. When the Confession spoke of man as being utterly disabled, this might seem to imply a total human inability to fulfill the divine commands; but as a matter of fact the difference between natural ability and moral ability was thoroughly well established. Man was morally disabled but naturally able—oh, fully able to follow in the ways of righteousness, but unwilling because of the Fall; at that crisis Adam, and henceforward his descendants, had lost all ability of will—in the words of the Confession. "Does this mean," queried Beecher, "that in respect to the power of choice he fell into a state of natural inability? Not at all. He had the power of choice as much as ever." In other words, his will was free, or whence the justice of the divine commands? From an abstract discussion of the qualities of justice, from experience, from the character of human aspirations, but less directly perhaps from the Confession of Faith, he argued that man *must* have the ability to obey the divine will; and he hurried on to prove that after all this ability counted for very little—scarcely anything, in fact. Sin could be and ought to be avoided, but it never was avoided.

As for those strange-sounding sentences of his own which Dr. Wilson had made crucial in his indictment—"So long as the sinner is able and willing there can be no sin," and the others—why, it was true that there would be no sin if God rendered the sinner willing. "But," he exultantly cried, *"my sermon nowhere teaches that God does actually render him willing!"* And in support of these nice distinctions he brought a host of authorities. Had he cast the reformers before the time of Edwards into the shade of ignorance and contempt? He poured forth commentaries of patristic writers and theologians from the time of Justin Martyr onward, including Tatian, Irenaeus, Clement of Alexandria, Tertullian, Origen, Cyprian, Lactantius, Eusebius, Cyril of Jerusalem, Hilary, Basil, Gregory of Nazianzen, Gregory of Nyssa, Ambrose, the great Jerome and the great Augustine, advancing to Luther and Calvin, to the Proceedings of the Synod of Dort, to the opinions of Turretin—who was used as a text at Princeton—to those of Tuckney, Owen, Bretschneider, the celebrated Dr. Twiss, Dr. Spring of New York, Dr. Witherspoon of South Carolina, and other impeccably orthodox contemporary divines, and alighting at last dove-like on the solid ark of a volume by Presbyterian ministers of the Mississippi Valley, which contained a discourse by Dr. Wilson himself. From this he quoted a passage on imputation, a subject which he was already rapidly skimming, and declared that his position and Dr. Wilson's were identical—if only Dr. Wilson would see this!

He seemed as fresh at the end of this long flight as at the beginning. In fact, with the exception of the last stroke, he had gathered the whole showy array by an exceedingly simple process. Before the trial he had gone to Calvin Stowe for assistance with his authorities; but when Stowe, who was a scholar, began to take down volume after thick theological volume, Beecher had grown cloudy and irritable, and exclaimed, "Pish! Pshaw! Take your books away, Stowe. They plague me." Undisturbed by niggling questions of scholarship, he had drawn the assortment from a single, highly controversial work.

Higher and higher rose the flood of his rhetoric. With passion and thoroughness, with tears, with illustrations from his own spiritual experience, with a further stream of quotations, he considered original sin, native depravity, the federal headship of Adam, effectual calling, necessity and certainty, and delivered a sudden essay on the common usages of words as supporting his arguments, with a triumphant shower of passages from Burke, Bacon, Dr. Johnson, Shakespeare, Alexander Hamilton, and Justice Story. Leaving this large medley of problems after a view of the good and the bad angels, a few more quotations from patristic writers, and a series of intermediate logical steps, he began to justify his stress upon free agency during his ministry in Boston. Could not the Presbytery see, he demanded with heat, as if the challenge had rankled for long, that his main business was to save sick souls, and that he had used the doctrine of free agency as a physician uses barks and tonics in a crisis? "I hold that we are not to take a whole apothecary's shop and throw it at the people at once, but that we are to administer it judiciously, in measure, according to the state of the pulse." Rapidly changing to another and perhaps more congenial figure, "My people know that I am not always banging their ears with the doctrine of natural ability. . . . I alternate the two edges of the sword, and smite as seems to me good . . . and if I find any among my people who carry the doctrine to an extreme, I put the sword of the Spirit upon them. . . ."

Above the noise of the still rising torrent Dr. Wilson managed to shout that much of this was irrelevant, that there were strange discrepancies between his charges and Beecher's restatement of these, that if Princeton used Turretin as a text, then Princeton was corrupt, and the opinions of most of the patristic writers had been proved noxious. "The versatility of some men is truly surprising," he bitterly exclaimed, "if a man could be surprised at anything in the nineteenth century. . . . All this learned parade about the *usus loquendi,* and the reigning philosophy of former ages, and all this running to Dr. Twiss or to Dr. Any Body Else for the meaning of the Confession of Faith is but casting of dust into men's eyes. . . . Any plain, commonsense elder knows without the help of any scholarly professor that to be 'utterly indisposed, disabled, and made opposite to all good' does not mean 'full ability to do what God requires.' "

Numbers—numbers—numbers—Beecher triumphantly adduced the numbers brought into the Kingdom through his successful revivals. Poor Dr. Wilson was inundated—and worse; he seemed to be magnetized into fulfilling the portrait which Beecher had fluently sketched of him at the outset; he became doddering; he interrupted with wrong points of order, was corrected by the Moderator, and muttered helplessly, "Well, let that pass." In feeble imitation he began to speak of Beecher as aged.

His aged victim was now briskly launching upon a diatribe against sectionalism within the Church, declaring that this body had known quite well what materials it was accepting when it took the New England Congregationalists into its fold; he made the attack upon himself seem a shameful breach of hospitality as well as of good faith. Conjuring up his old dream of a single militant worship, playing upon the dangers of discord, in swelling diapason he pleaded for unity—unity—unity—that the two great churches of a single tradition might sweep onward at this crucial moment in the history of the nation and the world, "as terrible to God's adversaries as an army with banners." He ended his *apologia pro vita sua* with "one word more in respect to my brother Wilson. I love him. . . . I have no prejudice to gratify; and I hope there exists no foolish ambition between us as to which shall be the greater. That day when Dr. Wilson can walk with me and bear with me, he may take with joy, so far as I am concerned, the entire lead. He may be commander-in-chief, and I will consent to be a corporal." But it proved difficult for Dr. Wilson to envisage Beecher in the rôle of corporal; nor could he accept another tender made him in Beecher's peroration. According to Church law the bringer of proceedings for heresy was himself liable to punishment if he failed to prove his case. Beecher had begged the Presbytery to waive this ruling, since there was no proof of malice on either side; he suggested that if Dr. Wilson's friends felt that he was to suffer the issue might become confused. "I am always, I hope, thankful to any one for courtesy and kindness," retorted Wilson; "but I do apprehend that Dr. Beecher's last remarks had that design more toward the speaker than toward myself." And he rancorously remarked that his opponent—never his brother—had been lively, "oh, very lively!"

Beecher was acquitted by the Presbytery; and Wilson carried the case to the Synod. Once more Beecher triumphed. "When the time came, there was a majority against him of ten to one," he cried. "They came round me like bees, some that had been on his side, as cordial as could be."

Risking his life for days and nights on a floating volcano, at great expense, as he said, Wilson went to Pittsburgh and laid his appeal before the General Assembly. But he mysteriously dropped the case at the last moment. "They sent him back with a flea in his ear," said Beecher, who regarded this action as a piece of Old School strategy. Indeed, the battle was by no means ended. Again upon Beecher's every phrase was bent the severe scrutiny of the Old School theologians of New England. It was quickly observed that he had skirted the crucial question of the fate of infants, and that his conclusions on instantaneous regeneration precisely contradicted those which he had offered in Boston on the same subject; and if his discussion of ability was Edwardean, on the linked topic of moral agency he had certainly moved toward the New Haven school, while at many points he had split hairs so finely that it was impossible to be sure of his meaning. What, in lucid language, *was* his final attitude toward the New Haven school—Taylorism, as it was now frequently called? Since the days of the *Concio* Taylor had added here and there a flying buttress to the aspiring structure which he had attempted to rear, still seeking to transform Calvinism into something like Hellenism. In consequence he had been subjected to a desperate onslaught of ridicule and contempt; over him again and again had been flung the harsh and strangling net of the bitterest of all hatreds, the *odium theologicum.* Where, then, did Beecher stand on the question of Taylorism? In the course of the trial he had let fall the remark, "All attempts to identify me with the New Haven school, as that is generally represented, are slander." *"As that is generally represented"*—a loop-hole, plainly! "Is it possible to reconcile that man's whole conduct with a sound, honest, straightforward course?" queried one divine. Still another whispered his fear that "there has been somewhere such a tampering with conscience as will be found to eat like a canker into both character and usefulness."

Suddenly Beecher saw himself and Taylor as the harried defenders of a set of principles which he had always—yes, always maintained. His affection for Taylor flared up, with tenderness and a protective touch. Taylor had nearly perished in the long controversy. Flinging caution to the winds, Beecher burst forth in anger to Dr. Woods during a visit to New England the summer after the heresy trials. "Dr. Woods, I know what you and these gentlemen want. They want me to say what will go to implicate Taylor as heretical, and *I never will do it!* And you may tell them so. I'll never denounce Taylor," he shouted. "To reach Taylor they must pass over my dead body. My bones shall whiten on the battlefield beside Taylor's!" The gesture quickly became public; the charge of hypocrisy against Beecher broke into such a broadside of quotations, letters, damaging instances, and closely wrought arguments as to make Wilson's indictment seem by comparison slight and amiable. If Taylor appeared as a willful heretic, Beecher was now pictured as a subtle liar. "They took burning arrows tipped with gall," Beecher exclaimed with profound emotion. "They rifled the graves of my dead friends, out of their ashes to evoke spectral accusations against me."

These bitter antagonisms spread; heresy trials sprang up in thick abundance in New England and in the West. Somberly resentful, perhaps, of the change of forums, Daniel Webster remarked that the oratory of the nation was now to be heard in Conferences, Presbyteries, Synods, and Assemblies rather than in the halls of Congress. And in these rapidly growing controversies a disquieting tendency was plainly manifest.

"The new spirit," Dr. Porter had declared with melancholy emphasis, "is like the he-goat of Daniel—bold and pushing." The New School doctrines had grown popular; in the communities of middle New York and the Western Reserve where New England settlers were in the majority, they were positively rife. A sharp line of sectional cleavage appeared; New England became theologically suspect in the South, which was solidly of the Old School. Then, into the sufficient tinder of doctrinal differences was flung the firebrand of the slavery question. In the very regions of the new country where New School doctrines were strongest, anti-slavery sentiment was surging up as an aggressive movement of reform. The New School Presbyteries introduced a resolution to disfellowship slaveholders into the Presbyterian General Assembly of 1836. The motion was lost, for the Old School Presbyteries of the South held a majority; but southern resentment at once broke into white heat. "When men contend for *liberty*—an *opinion*—they will *fight like men*," wrote Dr. Witherspoon of South Carolina to Lyman Beecher shortly after the meeting of the Assembly. "But when they contend for *property*, they will fight *like devils*. . . . I have been a slaveholder from my youth, and yet I detest it as the *political and domestic curse* of our Southern country; *yet I would contend to the death* against Northern interference with Southern rights." At the next meeting of the Assembly the Plan of Union was abrogated by pressure from the Old School majority, to prevent further invasions of the radical spirit of Congregationalists from New England; and the following year, at Philadelphia, even more drastic action was taken, with an extensive and fitting panoply.

While a mob raged in the streets against the Anti-Slavery convention being held at the same time, while bells tolled in warning, and Abolition Hall went up in flames, a bitter debate was held in the Assembly for days over that jot of human power which had proved a vexing problem for so many years. Perhaps its exact quantity or even its actual existence was not fully established on that occasion; but the outcome of the debate at least was foreordained. The Old School Synods denied that jot; the New School Synods argued its eternal importance, and were at last put under discipline for heresy. This action automatically deprived them of votes. They were then formally expelled from the Presbyterian Church; and the breach remained unhealed for over thirty years.

Around Lyman Beecher in strewn wreckage lay the hopes and labors of a lifetime. His vision of a single militant faith which should control the destinies of the nation and the world in preparation for the Millennium had now disappeared in the gulf of controversy. By the dissevering acts of the Assemblies he had been cut off from the faith of his origins, cast first into one diminished church and then into another, and identified with a cause in which he was but faintly interested, that of slavery, a cause which had already brought about his humiliation and defeat at the point where his hopes had been highest—at Lane Seminary. Union —his sense of union had sprung from a sense of power, that antique foundation of his dynamic faith; and how he had loved it, like an abstract good, as a warm possession! It was gone: even the much argued term ability which had occupied him for so many years had become worn and debased like an old coin through the ceaseless rubbing of argument. The practical question had long ago been settled. Who could doubt the boundless extent of human power and human will in the face of the spreading conquest of a continent? A new order of thought and feeling had been surging up around him—for how long, indeed?— whose character he had often clairvoyantly felt, whose momentum he had endeavored to catch. Ironically enough, he had never fully accepted the tenets of the New School; he had always brushed over Taylor's exquisite distinctions; he maintained the older doctrines to the end. Yet in the stormy transition Beecher did not hesitate. Breathless, worn, disheveled, he swung into the vanguard, assumed the always attractive rôle of the modern, and sounded with vehemence the magical cry—"new!" At the end of the main session, when the final motion to expel was put, "some were standing on their seats, some on the tops of pews," said a spectator. "Immediately I heard a general yell of '*aye*'! and there was one 'aye' louder than all the rest. It was Dr. Beecher, of Cincinnati, who made the loud yell."

NINE • *Even as Lyman Beecher stood in the stormy, trium-phant attitude of the progressive leader there was* something illusory about his position. He now had scarcely a foothold in public life. The Seminary was still almost empty. Disaster had come on the heels of disaster. The recent schism had cut off a whole area from which new students might be expected—the South. Financial support had been completely withdrawn as result of the severe panic of 1837.

Beecher's drafts had been dishonored in New York; he was without personal resources. Calvin Stowe, in despair, urged that the venture be abandoned, that they all return to the safer vantage of the East; one by one the three or four other members of the faculty had left. Always before when affairs had grown disastrous or even dull, Lyman Beecher had heard the unmistakable signals for a happy change, as if in answer to his need. Now the signals were loud enough; he could catch the scarcely muffled roar of thousands pouring into the farther reaches of the West; the great tide of migration was flooding past the easier channels of the great rivers and valleys across the plains and into the northern forests. Ohio was beginning to be considered well settled. Beyond—again, just beyond, lay the bright horizons. New—new—that cry of his spirit which he had often tried to answer now sounded with more resonance than ever. But for Beecher there was nothing new. He was past sixty; after the suspicions and discords of his recent years nothing was offered him by way of change, or was likely to be offered; and humiliation lay in the fact that his hopes had been publicly staked on Lane Seminary. He was a solitary figure at this juncture. Even his personal life was at loose ends; his household was incomplete and disorderly; Harriet Porter had died in the midst of the heresy trials. She had never become reconciled to Cincinnati; she had hated its crudeness, and had fallen into melancholy which quickly lapsed into incurable disease.

"The meal in the barrel is low, the oil in the cruse has failed," Beecher wrote laconically to a friend in Boston. "Send me a hundred dollars." With this sum or another gained in a like fashion he made one of the rapid journeys to the East which he always seemed able to contrive, wooed and married a Mrs. Lydia Jackson, a capable widow who had belonged to his Hanover congregation, and hastened back to Cincinnati to begin the work of rehabilitating Lane. That summer drouths came; the Ohio River was an open roadbed; crops failed throughout the region; and the fortunes of the Seminary sank to their lowest ebb. No students appeared for the next class. Beecher searched the little towns along the Ohio and the Miami, scoured farms in Indiana, Kentucky, and southern Illinois in vain. Galvanizing himself for a last effort, he traveled to Marietta College, aroused the faculty to a sense of their duty to an older institution, borrowed—and kept—five students. On the trip he met a member of his Boston congregation, a middle-aged man traveling in the West on a prosaic errand. His former disciple was eagerly apprised that he had mistaken his calling, which was the ministry. Said Beecher afterward, "I told him to study, and he did!" On hurried Beecher to Jacksonville, where he had engaged to lecture; there five young men yielded to his ardent persuasions. One of these had expected to become a teacher; he changed his mind. "I got hold of him—excited his interest. I told him, 'Come on, and bring these young men, and I'll support ye.'" When Beecher returned to Cincinnati he found Calvin Stowe in bed, steeped in melancholy. "Stowe," he said, "I've brought ye twelve students. You've got no faith, and I've got nothing but faith. Get up, and wash, and eat bread, and prepare to have a good class."

"Come, Stowe," he would cry, "let's get by this pinch, and then we'll have plain sailing!" Later it was, "Come, Stowe, let's get by this pinch, and then we'll be ready for the next!" The money to support the five young men was to be raised; money was always to be raised, in small sums, dollar by dollar; Beecher begged, borrowed, searched the country for funds as he had searched it for students. Once he gave away his last five dollars, to the dismay of Lydia Jackson, and triumphantly waved a wedding fee before her eyes the same evening. As difficulties multiplied he became gayly irrepressible. On a dark wet night of winter as he was traveling in Kentucky his coach was badly upset; a fellow passenger shouted that he would pick up the scattered bags and bundles since he was wearing boots while Beecher had on thin shoes. "No, I ain't. Lost 'em off long ago!" he cried, dancing about in the deep mud. He would rush into Second Church in Cincinnati with a blotted manuscript in his hand or his hat, and treat his congregation to whatever raillery occurred to him, though they were still deeply vexed and divided by the recent animosities. Once he peered up into the vault of the church through a barrel formed of his two hands, and staring with obvious exertion, announced that it would require a telescope of unusual power to discern the grace of meekness in the constellation of their Christian virtues. Ouster proceedings were instituted against him at Lane by an Old School faction, and a long vexatious civil suit followed. "Vexatious enough they found it," he said brightly. "The fact is, we outwinded them." He also outwinded Finney in a sufficiently important encounter. At a conference of the western colleges held in Cincinnati, the delegates from Oberlin were amazed to find themselves unaccredited; Finney himself was among their number. Rumors were flying that perfectionism in its most dangerous form was being taught at Oberlin; a tangle of technicalities appeared in the matter of credentials. The Oberlin group offered their arguments, but these were strategically met at every point. "Beecher was on the ground," said Finney briefly. After such smart brushes or after the day's hard traveling, Beecher would happily take down his old fiddle, as at Litchfield, and play his favorite *Go to the Devil and Shake Yourself*, or *Merrily O!*

With all his errands and preoccupations he was usually late at the Seminary; but once in the lecture-room he taught with ardor and eagerness—taught nearly every subject in the curriculum except linguistics, which he left to Stowe. "Fill yourselves full of your subject," he used to urge his little class, "then pull out the bung and let nature caper." The admonition was not strictly Calvinistic, nor was another which he sometimes offered. Salvation must be the first object of ministerial endeavor, "not theology, not controversy." He grew restless as this theme expanded, and used to sit in his study with his papers on the table and a cocked gun across his knees, ready to go out for a chance shot at the millions of pigeons flying overhead in spring and autumn with a great whir of wings, darkening the sky. Soon he slipped forth once more for revivalistic labors, skirmishing about on horseback or in his rusty old buggy, lighting the mysterious train in little villages of the Ohio Valley, bearing down upon important points in Kentucky. He looked now like one of those circuit riders of the West whose creed he had always considered inferior. Subtleties had gone from his face. Ruddy, storm-beaten, but erect, his white hair floating out behind as in a perpetual wind, he preached as they preached—urging the coming Millennium in simple rushing terms to gatherings of farmers and mechanics. Once he rode on horseback seventy miles from St. Mary's to Fort Wayne through the Black Swamp. "Besplashed and bespattered," said a friend in reminiscence, "with smoking steed and saddle-bags crusted with mud, he rode in the dusk of evening up to the back gate of Judge M'Culloch's residence, and alighted, weary and stiff, but still hale and hearty, as though horseback rides of seventy miles were everyday occurrences. A hearty welcome, a heartier supper, and a thorough washing, before going to bed, of the whole body in cold water, brought him out the next morning as sound as a nut, and with a step as light and springy as a young man's."

He had made this journey to witness the ordination of Charles, who a few years earlier had plunged into fatalism, had abandoned his theological studies, and had begun a business career in New Orleans. With tears and prayers, by the claim of an urgent affection, Lyman Beecher had at last brought Roxana Foote's youngest child through the crisis, and into the ministry. Thomas, who had a distinguished talent for the natural sciences, had studied these for a time at a western university; then, pleading loneliness, his father had kept this son at his side for a year or two. Thomas was now taking a final divinity year at Yale under Taylor. James was soon to be ordained; George was already preaching. Through the vexing years which had seen the exodus of students from the Seminary and the prolonged battle of his heresy trial, Beecher had maintained unbroken alliances with all of his eleven children, had written to them untiringly when they were absent from home, had stormed and argued and prayed and pleaded with them when they drifted into the household at Walnut Hills. During the trial he had kept young Henry Ward constantly at his side, and afterward had made him a companion during the stormy sessions of the Assembly: now the indifferent lad was preaching in the White Water Valley. He had caressed and cajoled them all; for his older sons he had steadily invoked the memory of Roxana, declaring that she had wished them to be ministers; the younger ones he subjected to a running revivalism and a battery of argument, bestowing a special affection. He knew when to stop, when to grow silent, when to let tears speak for him; he had always known; all their lives his children had been subject to his profound and unchecked emotionalism, to the possessive torrent of his drastic appeal.

Had any of them escaped his tether? The romantic and capricious Harriet was now safely married to Professor Stowe, who was far more straitly orthodox than Lyman Beecher himself; and she still lived fairly under her father's eye at Walnut Hills. Catherine for a time had been a militant and rebellious figure; with her bold, plain features, her heavy frame, and commonsense garments, she looked like one of the protagonists of woman's right—or rather the public vision of them—who were soon to burst upon the American scene. She had published her *Difficulties of Religion* from beneath her father's very roof; and this little brochure, which cast aside the intricacies of theology and urged the force of feeling, had been received with derisive comments on the part of Old School divines, and with apprehension by members of the New School. The daughter of Lyman Beecher? But Catherine, having launched her public diatribe, was already voicing other themes which strangely translated her father's philosophy. Her counsel, repeated over and over, in her essay on slavery and abolition, in her many little pamphlets on domestic economy and the education of women, even in her *Letters to Persons Engaged in Domestic Service,* was the familiar counsel of submission. Miss Beecher declared that reformatory movements *"in all cases"* lay "entirely outside the sphere of female duty." She became the most conspicuous opponent in her generation of the new feminism. Over and again she mentioned "the place which woman is appointed to fill by the dispensation of Heaven. . . . In this arrangement Heaven has appointed to one sex the superior and to the other the subordinate part. . . The moment woman begins to feel the promptings of ambition or the thirst of power, her aegis of defense is gone." To preach woman's acceptance of her inferior place became Miss Beecher's great mission; and this, clearly, was the Puritan mode, which not infrequently appeared in practice, even in Lyman Beecher's practice.

Briefly, most of the younger Beechers had raced off at tangents in matters of belief. They all had moved toward the conviction that love was, or could readily become, the moving spirit of the universe. Hell they tended to reject, or at least to depopulate; and for the militant Calvanistic heaven set high upon splendid battlements they were substituting a mild and beamy paradise. "Have at least one sermon a week which will tax your own intellect and that of your hearers," their father had commanded William; he had always insisted upon the exercise of that function in his family. But they all were increasingly shaken and stirred by that problematical element of feeling which had vexed Lyman Beecher years before. *"Feel, not know,"* was Harriet's perfervid advice to Charles.

Yet there they were, all of them, with the propulsions of a stringent mode of thought and a vigorous personality upon them. Lyman Beecher had marshaled all of his seven sons into the ministry, as he had meant to do; he had drawn all of his children into the West, as he had desired; in a hundred subtle ways he had closely conditioned all their lives. The most talented or the most stubborn—Harriet Beecher Stowe, Henry Ward Beecher, and the youngest, Isabella—were to struggle for inner integrity and freedom with a pertinacity which fairly matched Lyman Beecher's own; but even in these resistant efforts might perhaps be discovered a fulfillment of their father's purposes. His children were born with an assumption of leadership; they were born famous; they were Beechers, and they knew it. They were to fight their personal battles in a hundred vicarious forms, but always in the public eye; they were to achieve their victory or go down to an inner defeat before the vast and swelling numbers of audiences.

Lyman Beecher was briskly indifferent to their digressions and vagaries; his own mind had been rippled over by innumerable currents which ran counter to the main stream of his convictions; yet he had retained something hard, simple, pristine, in spite of these fluctuations; doubtless he expected the same solidity—and pliancy—from his children. He relished their rising fame; was it not in truth his own? And, as they seemed about to supersede him, he swept once more into something like his old celebrity. The students he had brought to the Seminary—neck and crop—seemed to have found there a sustenance which they craved; the classes were gradually increasing, and came now without a headlong suasion. Property values at Walnut Hills had greatly increased with the rushing growth of the city; Lane entered upon an era of moderate prosperity. With the easing of problems at the Seminary, Beecher's revivalism swung into a wider orbit; his name began to resound throughout the Great Valley as it had resounded in New England; he was again Lyman Beecher, the great revivalist and pioneer in moral reform. He lectured on reform, to eager audiences; he lectured on temperance; in 1846 he was invited to become the principal speaker at the first World's Temperance Convention, held in London, and went, spoke many times on the great topic, preached, and even delivered an anti-slavery address as a final feat. With his plain Yankee idiom and simple fire he created something of a furor. Queen Victoria learned of Lyman Beecher at this time, with approbation.

When he relinquished his duties at Lane a few years later, he suddenly looked backward, was thrilled and amazed by the crowded eventfulness of his own career, and settling in Boston to be near Edward, embarked upon the enterprise of writing a history of his life and times. "I am sensible that the fifty years of my active life have been years of unparalleled interest, and of rapid, terrible, and glorious results," he declared. "I perceive, also, that the comprehensive field over which my vision, and prayers, and efforts have traveled, has connected me with a large portion of the great events of the government of God. Such a history, seen from a single point of observation, and running through fifty years, may include facts and instructions . . . which might not otherwise appear on the page of secular or ecclesiastical history, and which, great and significant as these may now appear, will, in the coming ages, when their antiquity shall have magnified them, be eminently worthy of preservation, as exhibiting the image and body of the times."

Beneath the yellow, torn, and mixed accumulation of his papers ran a semblance of order. He had made a copy of every important communication of his own; all his letters, however hastily scrawled, were dated; he had saved the documents of a lifetime. But the task, as he bent to it, seemed endless. So many associations came tiding up, such a flood of memories! He paused over Roxana's letters, and inscribed the little packet in trembling characters, "To Roxana, beloved still." He read and re-read, sorted and re-arranged his vast correspondence with members of the New England clergy. He turned to his discourses; the old controversies became important once more. He would build up the body of his thought on matters of eternal import, would prove himself a mediator; he believed that even now his Select System might bridge the abyss between the two schools; indeed he declared that his discourses "had extensively united the suffrage of evangelical pastors and churches who supposed themselves more widely to differ from one another." The statement was singular in view of the doctrinal tempests which Beecher had encountered; and in the end the elements of the Select System grew knotty under his hand. He puzzled, trimmed, revised, searched, for precise effects of emphasis; but those nice balances upon which he had prided himself, between free agency and divine sovereignty, between natural and moral ability, between necessity and certainty, now seemed to escape him. Perhaps it was because he lacked an audience; perhaps it was because these discourses were old; he had always been cramped, or bored, by his own finished utterances. Once Charles had taken down a sermon as he delivered it, but he had thrown the transcription away with the remark, "No, that's spoilt! Never shall preach it again. It's all fixed and tight—I can't work in it!" He grew restless, hurried out to preach at a little mission, and returned unwillingly to the quiet of his study. At last, with the assistance of Charles, he prepared three volumes of his discourses for publication; three more were to follow, he announced, with his life and the history of his times. But the Select System, so far as this was revealed, proved of faint interest to the public of the early fifties; the abyss, after all, was not bridged. The three narrow black-bound volumes were carried into their slight circulation by the Niagara torrent of *Uncle Tom's Cabin.*

Harriet! His careless daughter, with her tumbled domestic life and six or seven children—he never would have guessed it! He hastened to Brunswick, where the momentous narrative had been written, followed the Stowes to Andover, where they presently settled, and there, in the warm atmosphere of public acclaim, flung aside his project of a written history and launched upon another enterprise, far better suited to his taste. He proposed to tell aloud the story of his life and exploits; all his famous children were to be his audience; he summoned as many as could come, and was at his happiest. In the racy pleasures of recollection he lived again; sparks seemed once more to fly from his wheel. "I pant not for fame," he cried; but he panted for life, and had it, as he poured forth the reminiscences of his many years out of a tenacious memory. As for fame, that stimulating fantasy was by no means absent. Beyond the company of his children he could see larger numbers; Charles was setting down his father's story as he told it, and this was to be published with many selections from his correspondence and from his many papers as an autobiography.

"Curious, now, this thing of personal identity!" he mused. "Here am I now, an old man, telling you this story about a little boy; and yet I feel that I am the same person now that I was then. . . .

"Once, at the saw-mill, I hooked a pickerel without bait; how I whopped him out! . . . Another time I found a school of perch in a hole under the roots of a tree, and took them all out with my hand. . . . Fished all day till dark, and felt sorry when night came. That was my passion.

"Now I am naturally quick, and that old plow was so slow—one furrow a little way, and then another—and the whole fifteen acres three times over, some of it steep as the roof of a house—I became inexpressibly sick of it. . . . Flax-pulling was hard enough to break your back the first day. . . . Uncle Lot had strong feelings, hid under a don't care look, yet spilling over at the corner of his eye. If a neighbor came to borrow a hoe, Uncle Lot would say, 'Why don't ye have hoes o' your own? What d'ye hang onto your neighbors for? . . .'"

A tiny distant picture of Dr. Stiles appeared, briskly saying *notetur,* and a more radiant figure of Timothy Dwight. "Oh, how I loved him! . . .

"From the homage of all about her I perceived that Roxana was of uncommon ability. . . . I had sworn inwardly never to marry a weak woman. I had made up my mind that a woman, to be my wife, must have sense, must possess strength to lean upon. She was such as I had imagined. The whole circle in which she moved was one of uncommon intelligence, vivacity, and wit. . . .

"All the new works that were published at that day were brought out to Nutplains, read, and discussed in the old spinning-mill. When Miss Burney's *Evelina* appeared, Sally Hill rode out on horseback to bring it to Roxana. A great treat they had of it. There was the greatest frolicking in that spinning-mill! Roxana was queen among those girls; they did not pretend to demur to her judgment. . . . Soon after our marriage we were riding together from Sag Harbor. With great good nature we were reconnoitering to find if there were any faults in each other which might be the occasion of trouble. I told her I didn't know as I had any faults—unless one: that I was passionate, quick, and quick over. But if she answered quick we might have trouble. Her face overspread with a glow of emotion, and tears flowed. . . . If she saw I was touched, she never said a word—she appreciated the thing; she entered into my character entirely. . . ."

By an ungracious lapse Beecher now spoke of the children of his second wife as belonging to Roxana. Of Harriet Porter he had little or nothing to say, but he hurried to tell the story of the Standing Order in Connecticut, and of his voluminous campaign in Boston. "It was as finely organized a church as ever trod shoe-leather. I never knew them to make a mistake. . . . Shall never forget how Chaplin heard. He was of quick, strong feeling, and was wide awake to hearken. He made me think of partridge on a dead limb, watching me when I was trying to get a shot at him. . . .

"When Wilson got up and made his speech—the best he ever did make as he misrepresented things—it made the issue look dubious. . . . When my turn came, I went on from one point to another, and by-and-by the tide turned; and when the time came to vote, there was a majority against him of ten to one. . . .

"Scampy concern, that Old School Assembly! . . ."

Free at last from clogging details he skimmed the triumphs of a lifetime, never aware of frustration, never admitting defeat. Triumph—everything was triumph until at last he settled down for the long remainder of his years in a house in Willow Street, Brooklyn, near that of Henry Ward Beecher. He was still physically vigorous; cutting across lots on the way to one of Professor Stowe's classes at Andover he had leapt a five-barred fence rather than stop to open the gate. He had outlived Lydia Jackson. As if determined to belong to his day he had sat, aged and placid, on the platform at one of the preliminary meetings which were heralding the birth of the Republican party. But he soon slipped into a partial twilight of the mind, and was quiet for hours at his window. At times he flashed answers to statements which he had seemed hardly to notice. When one of his daughters remarked that he must have been handsome in his youth, "Am still!" he exclaimed with a quaver of irony. In the thickening quiet it became clear that he was rehearsing an ancient drama. He had forgotten Roxana; but Taylor's name came frequently to his lips. "Part of *me,* part of *me,*" he exclaimed in a less articulate moment, striking his breast when Taylor's name was mentioned. "Bury me beside Taylor," he commanded with a show of his old authority, "and the young men will come . . . and it will do them good." Then began a struggle with a hard question; the dread which had always lain at the heart of his faith arose to overwhelm him. The doctrine of election . . . could he be sure? He who had always thrilled to the note of change, was thrown into turmoil on the brink of the great change. In fragmentary meditation he turned from one anxious query to another, and could find nothing but confusion. "I am sick," he cried in anguish, "because I cannot express the feelings of my heart!" When one of his children tried to comfort him with the thought that in eternity he was to rejoin old friends, he answered desperately, "Ah, there is that to go through first which I cannot contemplate!" In response to other consolation which mentioned the heavenly rest he answered sharply, "Go there if you want to!" But, as might have been expected of Lyman Beecher, he arose at last on a wave of exultation.

"Oh, such scenes as I have been permitted to behold!" he cried at the last during a clear interval. "I did not think I could behold such glory while in the flesh! Until this evening my hope was a conditional one; now it is full, entire, free." His daughter Harriet, who was with him, thought that as he spoke she too had caught a glimpse of the bright eternal battlements. In loud full tones, with a touch of his old astringency, he replied that no doubt she was a pious woman, but in this she was certainly mistaken; the vision had been vouchsafed to himself alone.

Thus still in the pride of life, and with the hope of glory, Lyman Beecher died. The great golden doom which he had so passionately anticipated had not come; instead, outside his tranquil dwelling might be felt the blackness of mortal failure and despair; the year was the heavily freighted year of 1863. But there was fitness in the time as a boundary for the career of Lyman Beecher. He left the world as he had entered it—to the noise of conflict. He had always encountered salient issues; now a desperate crisis shook the nation; and he had spanned an epoch, the first long restless epoch of its history.

Harriet Beecher Stowe

ONE • *Small Hatty Beecher had a temperament which did not permit itself to be ignored.* She was a pretty little girl, with eyes laden with sensibility, arched eyebrows, and thick brown curls; radiance glimmered over her dark little face, glimmered and was lost in the full pouting lips. For her bright willfulness and airy vanity she should have been given a charming niche; but alas! in the rushing Beecher household there were niches for no one.

Harriet was Roxana Foote's seventh child, born in Litchfield in 1811; two boys—Henry Ward and Charles—came tumbling quickly after, and when Roxana died, smiling remotely, and Lyman Beecher married the severe and elegant Harriet Porter, another younger brood began to appear. The old plain farmhouse on the outskirts of the town was always crowded—with children, with boarders and visitors, with the lively presence of Lyman Beecher. "What hard good work have I to do today?" was a question Hatty was expected to learn and answer. She hated hard good works, most of all in the form of long seams and endless knitting. When her father enlisted the enthusiasm of all his children for such tasks as stacking the winter's supply of wood or carrying away the stones that paved the garden lot, Hatty, a sturdy little figure, would toil furiously; and Lyman Beecher once remarked that he wished she were a boy since she worked so well. But this was praise with a sting, for while he was unyieldingly fond of all his children, he was concerned first of all with his sons, who could follow in his own path and become ministers; if he had a favorite among his daughters it was Catherine, his first-born. Sometimes Harriet would scramble with the rest into the old carryall and go off, hugely delighted, fishing or nutting; but as often she was left behind. She tried amusements of her own. "Harriet makes as many wry faces, is just as odd, and loves to be laughed at as much as ever," wrote one of her older brothers. But laughter rang out less frequently in the house than in the lifetime of Roxana Foote; the second

Mrs. Beecher remained a solemn woman. Harriet would saunter over to see her father's sister Esther, who had never married and who lived near by in the wing of an old house. Esther Beecher's rooms were inflexibly neat, with shining andirons and polished cherry tables and chairs; and Aunt Esther herself was a bright, hazel-eyed, trim little enigma who could tell marvelous stories when the children were sick, but who at other times was inclined to regard her turbulent young nephews and nieces with a sharp appraising glance. Harriet would sit for a time in her parlor with chips carefully placed under the heels of her boots, would receive a walnut or a cookie, and would saunter away.

With a stubborn fancy she began to create an illusory world of her own. Dipping into the mild pseudo-classicism of Gesner's *Idylls,* she peopled the green hills which lay about Litchfield with shepherds who played on ivory flutes and shepherdesses who brought leafy garlands to the shrine of Apollo. Though Byron was forbidden in the Beecher household she somehow contrived to read *The Corsair,* and was caught by the magic of the great Byron legend which had swept over the country, and pondered for long a line which seemed strange to her,

"One I never loved enough to hate."

She was twelve when the tidings came of Byron's death; she drifted away to pick strawberries with a basket on her arm, lay down among daisies, as she afterward remembered, looked up at the blue sky, and wondered about Byron's soul. It was a picturesque moment; she enjoyed it, and sought others. Further and further she slipped into daydreams and lapsed into revery—seeing herself where? how? in what charming guises? She became enamored of distances. But out of these soft moods she was rudely awakened. "Revery is a delightful intoxication into which the mind is thrown," declared Lyman Beecher with resounding emphasis. "I once knew a person who was wont to retire into the garden of revery whenever he wished to break the force of an unwelcome truth. I told him he must give up the habit or be damned!" As for Byron, her father preached a discourse on his life and works, taking for a text, "The memory of the wicked shall rot." She soon found herself being swept toward the holy mountain by a passion quite as fervid as any celebrated in *The Corsair.* With a gasp—was it pleasure? was it pain?—she was carried along by the current of her father's will. But soon she arose like a light little shallop. Gazing at the communion table one bright June morning, she felt a sudden soft wish for participation, was aware of a happiness which seemed supernal, and was confident that the great moment of divine approval had come.

Lyman Beecher shed hot tears at her announcement, but he intended that no child of his should be betrayed into a specious hope of everlasting bliss by what, with a considerable acumen, he called "nat'ral" feeling. Marshaling the reasoned elements of the Calvinistic faith, he speedily pointed out her error. Harriet struggled and wept and argued; her father probed and endlessly explained; words were the life of a household like his, language the great indulgence. She was irresistibly drawn by that stormy force; yet after all—why was it?—she could not submit either to God or to Lyman Beecher; she obstinately refused to acknowledge the black impinging condition of her native guilt; she declined to be "snared," in that graphic metaphor of her father's which she herself recorded. A strain of resentment began to develop within her filial devotion. Shut out of the simple paradise which she had begun to create, she became so absent and silent and strange that her father and the others laughed—perhaps hoping that ridicule would arouse her—until, as she wrote to Catherine, she thought that she would go distracted. Then she became preternaturally gay—and met reproof. Presently at Catherine's school in Hartford she began to write a long drama called *Cleon,* in which the element of cruelty played an overwhelming part through the character of Nero. Year slipped into year; she grew listless. "Little things have great power over me, and if I meet with the least thing that crosses my feelings I am often rendered unhappy for days and weeks. I wish I could bring myself to feel perfectly indifferent to the opinions of others," she wrote. "This desire to be loved forms, I fear, the great motive for all my actions." Languidly she followed her father's fiery train to Boston.

She was twenty-one when Lyman Beecher migrated to Cincinnati, singing *Jubilee* along the hard route over the Alleghanies and preaching revivals. Suddenly she was lifted to a high bouyancy; now at last in the lush new western country, amid spreading scenes, encircled by far horizons, every moment would be touched with glamor. But upon her as upon her sisters and their melancholy stepmother the hardships of cold, uncomfortable, poorly built houses, of cholera and famine, bore heavily; they drudged; they hated the West. Cincinnati was scant and bare for all its ranging heights and the beautiful rush of the river. Lyman Beecher's radiant outpost in eternity at Walnut Hills appeared to them for what it was—a thin spare little cluster of buildings on a ragged slope, surrounded by all but impassable muddy roads; if the Great Day was at hand, the evidences were hardly obvious; and misfortunes had come, first of all with the exodus of the first body of students from the Seminary, then with the storm of the heresy trial, and the impoverished years which followed. And for Harriet the old dizzy questions remained, haunting her every hour. Across every threshold stood Lyman Beecher, bright and tireless, insisting upon the fact of sin and the need of submission. During this hard confusion she joined in the work of a new school which Catherine had established in Cincinnati. At odd moments she began to write little pieces for those western annuals which, like albums, enclosed faint small literary flowers of the new region. Presently she read *Corinne,* like many other young women in the country of the period, and drifted on those long flowing periods, drifted into pictures of a great, versatile, sparkling society, where the arts were exalted, where learning was a commonplace, where conversation had a subtle worldliness. How entrancing was the character of Corinne! "Her fancy was changeful; talent, especially in a woman, creates a zest for variety that the deepest passion cannot entirely supply. A monotonous life, even in the bosom of content, dismays a mind so constituted. . . ."

"Hold!" said Corinne to Oswald, "you know me not. Of all my faculties the most powerful is that of suffering. I was formed for happiness; my nature is confiding and animated; but sorrow excites me to a degree which threatens my reason—nay, my life. Be careful of me! My gay versatility serves me but in appearance; within my soul is an abyss of despair which I can only avoid by preserving myself from love. . . ."

There were other fascinating revelations in this book, and matters for meditation. "However distinguished a man may be, he rarely feels unqualified pleasure in the superiority of a woman. . . ." Indeed, the story presented a novel and stirring controversy. "Women were made to manage their husbands' houses and to watch over the health of their children," flatly declared Lady Edgarmond, who considered feminine accomplishments dangerous. Oswald likewise clung to the domestic tradition; genius suffered restraint. Corinne—ah, the lovely, sensitive heroine!—died after long interchanges of romantic letters with Oswald, and a final outpouring of poetry. It was only too apparent that woman's life, the life of a woman of talent, was baffling and complex.

Harriet was transported by this suave and spacious tragedy. Quite in the modern manner she began to speak of repression; and she sounded an uncommon note of social criticism. "Recently I have been reading the life of Mme. de Staël, and *Corinne,*" she wrote to a school friend in Hartford. "I have felt an intense sympathy with many parts of that book, with many parts of her character. But in America feelings vehement and absorbing like hers become still more deep, morbid, and impassioned by the habits of self-government which the rigid forms of our society demand. They are repressed, and they burn inwardly till they burn the very soul, leaving only dust and ashes. . . . It seems to me that the intensity with which my mind has thought and felt on every subject presented to it has had this effect. It has withered and exhausted it, and though young I have no sympathy with the feelings of youth. . . ."

"Thought, intense, emotional thought, has been my disease," she explained at another point. "All that is enthusiastic, all that is impassioned in admiration of nature, of writing, of character, in devotional thought and emotion, or in emotions of affection, I have felt with vehement and absorbing intensity—felt till my mind is exhausted and seems to be sinking into deadness. About half my time I am scarcely alive, and a great part of the rest I am the slave and sport of morbid feeling and unreasonable prejudice. . . . How much good it might do me to be where I could not but be thoughtless!"

In a maze of perturbed feeling she pondered, she wept, she still viewed the terrible problems of eternity; and at last, following the lead of her bold sister Catherine, she rejected the harsher elements in her father's faith, and with tired rapture slipped into the new gospel of love, which now, in the early thirties, was timidly abroad in the new West. Harriet talked and wrote endlessly of this mild sweet belief, too fluently, indeed, with an air of striving lip-service, as if her avowals came from the formal upper levels of her mind. At the same time, urged by her brother Henry, she contemplated marriage with Calvin Stowe, then a professor—indeed the only professor—at Lane Seminary.

Carried along by high hopes of a swiftly oncoming Millennium, swept off his feet by Beecher's unflagging zeal, Professor Stowe had relinquished a position at Dartmouth to throw in his fortunes with those of Lane Seminary, bringing with him to Cincinnati as a bride a beautiful and talented young woman named Eliza Tyler. She had died within a year during one of the periodic outbreaks of cholera; and he had mourned her with vehemence, he was still inconsolable; as affairs at the Seminary went from bad to worse he had dropped into an abyss of melancholy where he helplessly floundered. From time to time he would be pulled out by a sardonic commentary of Lyman Beecher; but back he would slip; he wept and took to his bed; he wanted to leave Cincinnati; but he was continually restrained by that unremitting will. Shaken by many of the same forces—she too had known and loved Eliza—Harriet flung about Calvin Stowe the graceful garlands of her pity. The gesture was charming, and perhaps . . . perhaps . . . here was learning . . . she had talent. . . . What might she not do? . . . Another Corinne. . . . She might conquer. . . . She was a little breathless. She ran rapidly up the flowing scale of sensibility and down again into something like emotional anesthesia.

"Well, my dear G.," she wrote to a school friend on the morning of her marriage, "about half an hour more, and your old friend, companion, schoolmate, sister, etc., will cease to be Hatty Beecher and change into nobody knows who. My dear, you are engaged, and pledged in a year or two to take a similar step; and do you wish to know how you shall feel? Well, my dear, I have been dreading and dreading the time, and lying awake all last week wondering how I should live through this overwhelming crisis, and lo! it has come, and I feel *nothing at all.*"

TWO • *Calvin Stowe seemed hardly a suitable subject for romance.* Even as a child there must have been about him something antiquated. At the time of his marriage to Harriet Beecher he appeared as a contemporary of her father's rather than her own, though there was scarcely ten years' difference between their ages; she was twenty-four, and he was thirty-three. Fussy and helpless, already growing bald, with thick curly side-locks, a tight, turbulent mouth, and a broad, inquisitive, and stubborn nose, he devoted himself to the pursuits of the general scholar, setting down the minutiae of theological and Biblical lore on endless sheets of paper in a script which resembled Arabic. As if these occupations were not sufficiently remote, he entertained phantoms—his visions, as he called them. Since his earliest childhood they had appeared before him, emerging from the unlikely background of the homely Puritan village of Natick, Massachusetts, where he was born. It had been years before he had realized that they were not as tangible as the persons about him; and he saw them with pride and pleasure to the end of his life. Their talk, which was silent, shook him profoundly, as did the playing of their musical instruments, which he always heard. They came into view through the walls or the furniture; lovely landscapes often lay about them; they enacted little dramas over and over again, without variation, in a thrilling rhythm. Indians were among their number, who played viols and fiddles; there was a tiny figure of a woman who danced and was followed in her long retreat by a little hopping dwarf. Most of these ghostly visitants had no counterparts in life; but occasionally men and women whom he detested would swim before him in pleasant guises, while persons whom he loved would be terribly torn, blackened or shriveled by tunnel-shaped clouds. Once as a child he had awakened to discover in his bed an ashy-blue skeleton which seemed to him entirely palpable.

Whatever inner stress these strange figments bodied forth, there was small doubt that in his complex seclusion Calvin Stowe was fairly contented alone. After his marriage he continued to mourn Eliza, to regard his visions, to steep himself in a remorseless scholarship, and to consider with satisfaction the close logic of Calvinism; his faith was even more solid and uncompromising in its orthodoxy than that of Lyman Beecher. As if by a blind instinct Harriet had placed herself in a situation almost precisely like that which had been her lot under the sway of her father; against each of those absorbed, impervious, masculine minds she could raise her cry for recognition in vain; she was not truly a center of imaginative regard for either of them. Calvin Stowe expected much of her, yet he ignored her; when tried by interruptions he was likely to give way to a peppery temper or to dissolve into floods of tears. Their house was set down at the edge of a half-broken road at Walnut Hills; they were always without money; Professor Stowe's salary was never paid in full, seldom in considerable part, one or two years not at all. Children came in rapid succession, first twin girls—named Harriet and Eliza—fifteen months later another child, within a brief space another, and then another. Once Mrs. Stowe nearly died of cholera. With passionate irregular energy and a spasmodic courage she struggled with her situation, but she hated the domestic routine. She tried to write; with an air of determined renascence she began composing little tales and sketches, never of the West, but of the New England life which she had left behind, using materials which she thriftily drew from her husband's reminiscences; for this homely mystic could—when he liked—emerge from his strange inner sphere to sum up certain aspects of the New England character in a style as close and flavorsome as a nut; his mimicry was incomparable.

In the great laying on of local color which was about to begin Mrs. Stowe thus became a dashing pioneer, writing in the midst of gingerbread and baked beans in the kitchen, with tins and unmixed ingredients on a dresser at her side, and a baby in a clothesbasket at her feet. These episodes became part of a legend which was many times repeated—not, so far as one knows, by Calvin Stowe, but by members of Mrs. Stowe's own family, by her friends, and most of all by herself. At this juncture she became deeply interested in the business of self-portraiture; she wrote long letters in the descriptive style, of awaking at half past four in the morning, with breakfast at six, of interminable sweeping and dusting and tending the children, and cutting out little dresses, and sending Professor Stowe to market, and a dozen other trying tasks. "Indeed, my dear," she wrote to her friend Georgeanna May, "I am but a mere drudge. . . . I hope I shall grow young again one of these days. . . ." Sadly she considered her lost youth. Yet—this new literary exercise had its fascinations; she practiced it with gusto, and emerged in her little pictures resourceful and wise, rippling and laughing, in truth with a fine good temper and a steady good sense in the midst of numberless cares and trying interruptions—and always saving the financial day by writing a story! Out of her descriptions emerged likewise the figure of Professor Stowe—clumsy, middle-aged, and absurdly incapable of meeting the tedious and sometimes tragic episodes of their common life, and quite unfitted to care for his family. At last in a sketch called *A Scholar's Adventures in the Country* Mrs. Stowe lifted her husband's helplessness to a pointed little apogee. The scholar and his wife lived in an embowered cottage which was surely not a replica of the Stowes' plain dwelling; their gay and easy interchanges surely did not mirror the Stowes' relationship; but undoubtedly the object of the sketch was to picture the scholar's wholly visionary mind and simple follies, his ridiculously impractical schemes and futile ineffectiveness in maintaining a household. It was the scholar's wife who assumed the real responsibilities. With a small, decided hand Mrs. Stowe hammered the point; and oddly enough, this sketch was published with Professor Stowe's foreknowledge.

These were sparring gestures, offered with a touch of sharp and sprightly fancy; but after all the authority which Mrs. Stowe had achieved was hardly immense. Writing of any sort she found difficult; in her noisy, busy household she always lacked privacy. "All last winter I felt the need of some place where I could go and be quiet and satisfied," she told her husband with candor. "If I came into the parlor where you were, I felt as if I were interrupting you, and you know you thought so, too." At times she was flatly rebellious. "It is a dark, sloppy, muddy, disagreeable day," she wrote Professor Stowe during one of his absences from Cincinnati, "and I have been working hard, washing dishes, looking into closets, and seeing a great deal of the dark side of domestic life. . . . I am sick of the smell of sour milk, and sour meat, and sour everything, and then the clothes *will* not dry, and no wet thing does, and everything smells moldy; and altogether I feel as if I never wanted to eat again. . . ." "The absence and wandering of mind that so often vexes you is a physical infirmity with me," she continued in another letter. "It is the failing of a mind not calculated to endure great pressure of care," she insisted during another of his absences. In spite of the iron Beecher constitution she was often ill, but she also cultivated an hospitable feminine convention of her time, that of extreme fragility. Yes, she languished, and picked up the melancholy theme in many of her little tales or sketches. "Borne down by the tide of her agony, she leaned her head upon her hands, the tears streamed through her fingers, and her whole frame shook with convulsive sobs. . . . 'I have borne up under all that tries a woman,' she said. . . ." Thus ran a passage in one of her brief stories. "As to my health it gives me very little solicitude, although I am bad enough, and daily growing worse," she wrote to her husband. "It appears to me that I am probably not destined for a long life," she told Calvin Stowe. She dreamed of death; she was half in love with death. She constantly dipped into a gloomy self-betrayal and saw herself fading away enveloped in an interesting pathos.

Perhaps she was echoing her heroine Corinne, but she had also caught the wider echo of a theme which was prevailing in the West. In the early forties the thought of death was breaking into verse and hymns and common talk, not as mystery or as terror, never as that rushing pale horse of Revelation with Hell following after, with the sword and famine and the wild beasts of the earth, which had been all but figured forth in the revivals of the wilderness of a few decades before; death now was drifting ease or release or escape. The new generation was floating in fancy into eternity on flowery beds of ease, or seeking distant shining shores, as if their first visions of far horizons in the West had carried them boundlessly forward. In large as well as in personal terms Mrs. Stowe poured forth these soft anticipations; in insistent cataracts of language she poured out her new mild faith to Calvin Stowe, whose beliefs were of so different an order. Presently with a more practical resolution she began flying away for visits, as fast as one could fly in those days, back to New England; or she retreated to one cure or another because of her illness or her fatigue, the money therefor being raised by miraculous dispensations. Still she drooped and pined and wrote of the faint, sad, pensive theme. Slowly, a little heavily, Professor Stowe also took it up in their many exchanges of letters; he too tried to languish. But this, naturally, was a different thing; his wife dismissed his gesture with a curt and pointed raillery. "My dear Soul," she wrote on one occasion, answering a dark letter, "I received your most melancholy effusion, and I am sorry to find that it is just so. I entirely agree and sympathize. Why didn't you engage two tombstones—one for you and one for me? ... To see things through a glass darkly is your infirmity, you know. . . ." And she appended a little drawing of the tombstones. But Calvin Stowe had pertinacity. During his wife's longer sojourns in

Cincinnati he began to make long trips eastward for the sake of *his* health, when he was not departing for church conventions or fulfilling distant educational missions.

Once in the midst of a long separation ten years after their marriage Mrs. Stowe wrote of their "past failures," and declared that they had "now come to a kind of crisis." The crisis never broke; but it spent itself cursively in letters, in language, in the small oblique interchanges of a tedious daily life. Professor Stowe went his own way, seeing his visions; less and less often his wife was able to find avenues of escape. Her excursions to New England grew infrequent; she struggled with poverty as before, tended her children and taught them in a little school, cooked and sewed and wrote stories—and remained singularly isolated. Walnut Hills was still something of a wilderness; she had few contacts even of a casual sort, for Lyman Beecher's many battles had left his family in partial detachment. Below, in the chaotic town, the question of slavery was becoming acute; with much of its trade coming from across the Ohio, with a population which was preponderantly southern in tradition, Cincinnati had repudiated abolitionist sentiment with violence; its streets were often full of a terrible drama as slave-catchers raided the quarters of the free negroes, as houses were burnt, and women and children abducted, as a hunted people sought escape. For Mrs. Stowe these events passed like a distant phantasmagoria. Actually she knew little of them, because of her own absorbing occupations; as result of her father's close and eager surveillance she had accepted his neutral position; he still was importuned to declare himself an abolitionist, and he still declined to do so. Later Mrs. Stowe remarked of herself, using the lofty third person which became habitual in her public writings, that "in many years of her life the author avoided all reading upon or allusion to the subject of slavery, considering it too painful to be inquired into, and one which advancing light and civilization would live down. . . . It was a sort of general impression upon her mind, as upon that of many humane people in those days, that the subject was so dark and painful a one, so involved in difficulty and obscurity, so utterly beyond human hope or help, that it was of no use to read, or think, or distress oneself about it." Once her husband and her brother helped an escaping slave along the underground railway; once she visited a plantation in Kentucky for a few hours; but except for stories told by negro women who sometimes helped her with the heavier work of the household this was the extent of her contact with the institution of slavery. At the time of the Birney riots in Cincinnati she was concerned not with the issue of slavery but with that of free speech, or what she bitterly called "*any* violation of personal rights." If a single overmastering question impinged upon her it was the old religious question, in the persons of Calvin Stowe and Lyman Beecher.

Her burdens and her sense of them increased, with an unremitting double pressure; she was tired, no doubt, dismayed, and often overwhelmed. She rebelled—but to what end? Where was an escape or an outlet? Further and further she slipped into a haze of fatigue. Then, during a long absence of her husband's at a water-cure all the weight of her life in the West closed down heavily upon her. Pestilence stalked through Cincinnati in its most malignant form. The streets were crowded with funeral trains; charcoal burned at every crossroad; the women of the city, Mrs. Stowe among them, sewed endlessly, making shrouds. Death came with terror at last into her own family, after so many anticipations. When all danger seemed over, her sixth child, a little boy, was stricken and died. She was alone, and confusion followed; again she lacked funds. She tried to write, but could not; she was obliged to take in boarders; she maintained a little school for her own children and a few others. There followed, in 1850, the hard episode of removal with her entire family to Brunswick, Maine, where Calvin Stowe, at last resisting Lyman Beecher's persuasion, accepted a professorship at Bowdoin after seventeen lean years in Cincinnati. As it turned out, because of a delay in appointing his successor at Lane, he was obliged to remain at the Seminary after the arrangements for the departure of his family had been made.

So Mrs. Stowe set forth on her long travels with her five children— the seventh and last was to come within a few months—piloting her boxes and barrels along the slow route by canal boat and wagon and rail, a drab figure, as one sees her, her costume the billowing affair of the time, her anxious, slightly querulous face framed by her bonnet and side-curls. Beneath the effect of glamor which her countenance still kept might perhaps faintly be seen the bold, harsh outlines of the Beecher mask; and she had need of the Beecher resolution. More than ever she was cramped for money; she was obliged to make difficult, economical purchases in Boston; when at last she arrived by steamer it was in the midst of a heavy northeast storm, and she found the house which she was to occupy cold and dark and damp and moldering. She had welcomed the change to a more established civilization in the East, but Brunswick belonged to a comparatively late order; only a generation before the town had been cut into the rim of the forest; it was still fairly primitive. Mrs. Stowe was obliged to begin the work of the pioneer all over again. She papered the walls of her house, and painted and varnished the floors and the woodwork, and laid carpets and made barrel chairs and recovered sofas and decorated them with gimp, and rehabilitated pillows and bolsters and bedspreads; many of the plain cheap articles of her first housekeeping were worn out, and she was obliged to contrive substitutes. In the midst of her labors came a low-spirited letter from Professor Stowe, announcing that he was sick in bed, inquiring what his wife would do in case she was left a widow, as she almost certainly would be, warning her that she would have a mere pittance to live on, and so must not be extravagant. She read this communication in a mood of short, ironic humor, and thrust it into the stove. Professor Stowe finally came; her last child was born; she rested for two weeks. Then began once more the old round of taxing, wearisome duties. The winter was so bitterly cold that the children could scarcely sit through their meals even though the table was set in the room with a large stove; the house rocked with storms. More than ever she lacked privacy; her own room on the ground floor was freezing; a piano had been moved into the dining-room, and the twins, Eliza and Harriet, practiced there, each two hours a day; over-head was the noisy schoolroom. If she tried to rest, within a few moments one of the children was in trouble and rattling at the latch.

The following spring a clergyman from Harpswell happened to be loitering near the wharf late one afternoon, and saw the entire Stowe family seated on casks, apparently in silence. Tired and worn, unkempt and even dilapidated, with holes as large as silver dollars showing at the heels of her low shoes, Mrs. Stowe made an oblivious center of the group. Once more she had slipped away into the remote world of fantasy; and this time she was pondering with a vengeance.

THREE • *The year was 1851. Suddenly, amazingly, Mrs.* Stowe had begun *Uncle Tom's Cabin,* stirred by the letters from Mrs. Edward Beecher in Boston, describing the operation of the Fugitive Slave Law and urging her to write something in protest. "I will," she had said, clenching her hands—"if I live," she added, with her perennial sense of existing on the brink of eternity. Tranced, surrounded by her family, she had begun without premonition or plan, breaking into ecstasies of tears and sobbing as she wrote. In utter distress she produced her great book, writing installment after hasty installment for publication in the *National Era.* It was finished at last, with its strange scope and power.

Remote and unpracticed, Mrs. Stowe had created a protest which was to shake and shatter a national apathy and to spread with reverberations around the world. Slight as had been the little sketches of her Cincinnati days, she now at the desperate stroke commanded structure—for carelessly combined as it seems, the book has structure, with a free flow of narrative, and a wealth of invention. Slender as had been her observation of slavery, she used every touch of it, acquiring the basic gift of the creative artist, that of deriving the essential from the fragmentary, of judging the whole piece by the small bit of pattern. It has become the custom to belittle *Uncle Tom's Cabin* as a work which was always over-colored, which never had a place outside the turbid sphere of propaganda, and is now outdated. But propaganda sole and simple it is not; it declares no platform, and is unconcerned with measures; what it offers is a sweeping picture and an outcry. Battered though it has become through the overplus of excitement which has attended its career, defective though it is in certain essentials, it still has qualities which lift it above its contemporary position as a tract, qualities which should dismiss the easy, usual charge of exaggeration. Obviously the book lacks a genuine realism; but perhaps it should not be judged as realism at all. Obviously it lacks the hardiness and purity of view which belong to great writing; its emotion is never free, but intensive, indrawn, morbid, sentimental if one chooses, running an unchecked course which seemed created by hysteria. But the unbroken force of that emotion produced breadth; in its expansions and uncalculating balances, its flowing absorption in large sequences of action and its loose combinations of interwoven fates, the story at least brings to mind what is meant by the epical scale; it has above all that affecting movement toward unknown goals over long distances which becomes the irresistible theme of the greater narrative, rendered here with pathos because the adventure is never free, but always curtailed or fatefully driven. Diminish it as one may by stressing its sentimentalities or juxtaposing against it gentler glimpses of slavery, there is no denying that *Uncle Tom's Cabin* presents an elementary human condition with all its stark humiliations and compulsions, the straits of mind and body and feeling to which man can reduce man. Viewed at a distance, apart from its inevitable association with a cause, its worth becomes that of the typical or prototypical; subtract it from literary history, and a certain evaluation of human experience would be gone. Slavery is, unhappily, a point of reference for many human judgments.

The book was something of a miracle, a greater miracle than was realized by an enormous public. Out of a narrow and sheltered experience it had come—how? why? Mrs. Stowe herself wondered, for years; she could scarcely guess; her mind fluttered and wavered. In retrospect everything she had known of slavery took on a bewildering magnitude. When she remembered her visit in Kentucky it somehow seemed an extended sojourn; perhaps there had been many visits. Other episodes grew large. Building upon the circumstance of the escaping slave whom her husband and brother had assisted, she declared that the underground railway virtually ran through her house at Walnut Hills. On she rushed —into print. "It will contain all the original facts, anecdotes, and documents upon which the story is founded," she said rashly, announcing her *Key to Uncle Tom's Cabin*, "with some very interesting and affecting stories parallel to those of *Uncle Tom*." But the *Key* was packed with instances collected after the writing of her novel; and even these were largely hearsay. From these doubtful considerations she circled back repeatedly to the circumstances under which she had written her book; and again she grew confused. Most often she declared that she had written it wholly without foreknowledge of succeeding chapters or a glimmering as to the end. Then, carelessly, she explained that a sketch about a dying slave, written years before in Cincinnati, had formed the basis of her story. At another time she said that she had begun by writing the death of Uncle Tom; and she described a vision. "The scene presented itself to her mind while she was seated at the communion table in the little church at Brunswick. She was perfectly overcome by it, and could scarcely restrain the convulsion of tears and sobbing which shook her frame," she said, using the now familiar third person. At another time she wrote in detail of a visit which she had paid at Andover with Professor Stowe, and pictured herself as writing the death of Uncle Tom late at night when tired beyond endurance, suddenly, as if directed, while her husband slept. But this visit was paid months after the publication of her book.

Some of her discrepancies were pointed out to her, by Calvin Stowe for one; yet she allowed them to remain in print, and promulgated others. Out of her many mazy divergences at last began to appear certain consistent themes; she spoke repeatedly of exhaustion; and she considered herself to have been moved by something uncontrollable—by an unknown power. "The feeling that pursued her increased in intensity to the last, till with the death of Uncle Tom, it seemed as if the whole vital force had left her. . . . Mrs. Stowe felt herself so possessed that she became the conscious agent of a Power other than her own. . . . The story can less be said to have been composed by her than imposed upon her. . . ." "*Uncle Tom's Cabin* is a work of religion," she said. At last she solemnly declared, "God wrote it." And this pronouncement passed into widespread, breathless acceptance, though readers were not lacking who found in the propulsive strength of the book the work of quite another agent.

Mrs. Stowe was making a fable; but she may have been seeking the truth. Perhaps the writer always uses an allegory of experience or a concentrated metaphor. The figure may be obscure, the symbolism hardly apparent even to himself—often least of all to himself; but within those shadowy, troubled depths where the process of creation takes place the forms of deeply impressed experience will assert their strength. These patterns may not be the single conditioning force; in Mrs. Stowe's case they probably were not; no doubt she was moved in the writing of her novel by an instinctive compassion; but she seems to have been pushed by another, more personal motive, one which she touched upon again and again in her fumbling efforts at explanation. She had been caught in the toils of a formula as harsh and unyielding as any physical institution of bondage, in which torture was made the eternal destiny of a race whose earthly position at best was servile; the problem involved was one of the first magnitude, one of the great type problems of human experience; she had confronted it without remission for more than thirty years; it had been personalized by the unflinching presence of Lyman Beecher; since her marriage she had found it forever at her side in the solid dogmatism of Calvin Stowe; she had never truly resolved it. Then through her marriage had come an immense pressure of hard circumstance, with no remission; then tragedy; bondage of many sorts had claimed her. By her trials at Brunswick her sense of the restrictions of her lot had been profoundly stirred; and for the first time in her life she had moved decisively outside her father's dominion, and for a brief period, beyond that of Calvin Stowe. In the midst of a bitter climax of revolt she had caught the dark image of the endless restraints imposed by the Fugitive Slave Law; that baffling snare was the final image of restriction. Ardent and tired and overwrought, in that sensitive state where the imagination grows fluid, where inner and outer motives coalesce, she had taken bondage as her theme, had become obsessed with its conditions, morbidly obsessed by the concomitant of punishment, the terrible infliction of pain; freedom at any cost, at the last cost, became her immense preoccupation. In her story, down the great flood of the Mississippi, up and down the broad reaches of the South, journey numbers of human beings under a basic compulsion; to and fro they pass within a great, far-flung net, those hapless creatures; small, driven, forlorn, they take on stature as they confront the vast, impossible hope of escape. In the double story, that of George and Eliza, and that of Uncle Tom, the first two finally flee to Canada; but the escape among all the others which commanded

Mrs. Stowe's deepest feeling, that toward which the whole narrative constantly moves, is the release of Uncle Tom through death into soft unending rest and blissful freedom, the assuaging death which had so often floated before her in fancy. Little Eva likewise drifts away in a dim, dissolving mist; but it was Uncle Tom, the martyred Uncle Tom, with whom Mrs. Stowe most identified herself, covering him with a pity akin to self-pity, endowing him with a mild faith which she had struggled so long to attain.

These deep-laid patterns of escape, bondage, and rebellion were cloudy but familiar patterns for a public whose heritage in the main was identical with that of Mrs. Stowe, which had been bred largely in the same faith, and was breaking away from this with a prodigious sense of fortitude. The binding, passionate, highly personalized emotion of the book seemed to envelop something elementary in the temper of the time. It was an era of sentiment, of tears, of a billowing luxuriance in feeling; an intensive pleasure in emotion had welled up during the late forties and early fifties as if after an interminable age of suppression, cresting in the appearance of a hundred weeping heroines in the novel and on the still precarious stage. With its half-hidden insurgence and its sensational picturings of slavery the career of *Uncle Tom's Cabin* became torrential; it ran through numberless editions in the United States and in Canada and England, and was quickly translated into languages which ranged from French and German to Finnish and Wallachian and the Hindoo dialects. It swept the stage in versions that began to contain all the casual changes incidental to the production of a folk-play; indeed, on the stage the story was in all ways taken completely out of Mrs. Stowe's hands; through a hiatus in the copyright law she reaped none of the benefits of dramatic production. Licensed or not, its influence continued to spread in great widening circles. As result of its dynamic power more than through any other cause, for a time at least the enforcement of the Fugitive Slave Law became impossible; an enormous momentum was given to the gathering volume of anti-slavery sentiment. At a swift turn Mrs. Stowe was hailed as the leader, even the creator of the contemporary movement against slavery. At a stroke she reaped the reward of the long and arduous labors accomplished through more than twenty years by that small group of iconoclasts whose leader was Garrison Unwittingly she had written an abolitionist manifesto.

Mrs. Stowe seemed oblivious of the many implications of her book. At its close as a serial she had remarked mildly that she hoped "the foolish and unchristian prejudice against people merely on account of their complexions" would soon be done away with; and her casual advocacy of colonization was the despair of the rank and file of convinced anti-slavery workers. "Whether she knows anything of the real obstacles and difficulties of such a cause as ours, I cannot tell," remarked Wendell Phillips after an interview. Lifted high upon the tide of popular acclaim, controversy, and denial, she grew rapturously exalted, bent upon seizing all the happier emoluments of fame; she reveled in the joy of conferring favors. It is to be feared that she patronized Garrison, questioning him thoughtfully as to his religious faith, writing him letters on this theme. Sending a copy of her book to Queen Victoria and Prince Albert, she breathed a note of benediction. "May the blessing of God rest upon the noble country from which America draws her lineage, and on *her,* the Queen of it," she said solemnly, addressing the Prince Consort. "Though all the thrones be shaken, may *hers,* founded deep in the heart of her subjects, be established to her and *to her children,* through generations!" The giving of grace became habitual with Mrs. Stowe; she was soon applying to herself phrases usually reserved for another personage. "Dear one," she wrote to Calvin Stowe during a long visit which she paid in Brooklyn, "If this effort impedes my journey home and wastes some of my strength, you will not murmur. . . . I feel a sacred call to be the helper of the helpless. . . ." Speaking of the slave, Milly Edmondson, she declared with energy, *"I must redeem her."* "I am His chosen one," she wrote, "and I shall reign with Him when all the stars have done blos-soming. . . ." She began to describe the persecutions which were directed against her; she frequently mentioned her health; of her delicate health she was likely to write to quite unknown correspondents. "A frail little body," was her repeated image, a "feeble," a very feminine "instrument," and always, always, an instrument of special powers.

Suddenly from these precarious indulgences she slipped into bright pages of crowded, personal description, answering the sheaves of letters which reached her from all parts of the world. "So you want to know what sort of a woman I am!" she wrote to Mrs. Follen in London in reply to a brief note. "To begin, then, I am a little bit of a woman—somewhat more than forty, about as thin and dry as a pinch of snuff, never much to look at in my best days, and looking like a used up article now. I was married when I was twenty-five years old to a man rich in Greek and Hebrew, Latin and Arabic, and alas! in nothing else. When I went to housekeeping, my entire stock of china for parlor and kitchen was bought for eleven dollars. That lasted very well for two years, till my brother was married and brought his bride to visit me. I then found, on review, that I had neither plates nor teacups to set a table for my father's family; wherefore I thought it best to reënforce my establishment by getting a teaset that cost ten dollars more, and this, I believe, formed my whole stock in trade for some years. . . . The nursery and the kitchen were my principal fields of labor. Some of my friends, pitying my trials, copied and sent a number of little sketches to certain liberally paying 'Annuals' with my name. With the first money that I earned in this way I bought a feather-bed! for as I had married into poverty and without a dowry, and as my husband had only a large library of books and a great deal of learning, the bed and pillows were thought the most profitable investment. After this I thought that I had discovered the philosopher's stone. . . . When a new carpet or mattress was going to be needed, or when my accounts, like poor Dora's, wouldn't add up, then I used to say . . . I'll write a piece, and then we'll be out of the scrape. So I became an author. . . . I lived two miles from the city of Cincinnati, in the country, and domestic service, not always, you know, to be found in the city, is next to an impossibility in the country, even by those who are willing to give the highest wages; so what was to be expected for poor me, who had very little of this world's goods to offer? . . ."

Most of her glamorous excitement was spent in writing; among people that vagueness of mind which had proved vexing to Calvin Stowe seemed to increase. Once before a dinner in her honor in Boston she remained upstairs for an interminable period while the guests waited; her hostess found her standing before a bookcase, still in her bonnet and shawl, deep in *Sir Charles Grandison,* the entertainment forgotten. Around her, indeed, surged a clamant public; but she seemed to hear its roar like the faint echo in a sea-shell. Yet animation—or restlessness—burned beneath her hazy preoccupation; she persistently left Brunswick; she traveled; she visited her friends and her relatives; she spent weeks with her now famous brother, Henry Ward Beecher, in Brooklyn; and though she told Calvin Stowe not to murmur, he seems to have murmured a great deal. He disliked this translation of his wife into inaccessible spheres; he resented being thrust into a position of relative obscurity; he was proud of her achievement, but uncomfortably proud. Decidedly, the balance of domestic power was now established. Through *Uncle Tom's Cabin* Mrs. Stowe had obtained not only fame but financial independence—even domination; it was she who determined expenditures and made the larger choices. She began to speak of her "old rabbi," with a semi-affectionate but still quite positive stress upon her husband's impractical absorption in linguistic studies, or upon the long flowing beard that he now wore, and which somehow failed to make him impressive. "My poor rabbi," she called him with a note of deprecation, or even "my poor old rab." Presently in 1853 she carried him off to Scotland, hastening thither upon the invitation of the Anti-Slavery Society of Glasgow; and since Victorian custom denied her the privilege of public address, he delivered the responses on her behalf, and occasionally ventured a few words of his own. The rôle was inglorious, and he relinquished it within a few weeks, returning to his academic duties; but Mrs. Stowe went on, accompanied by her brother Charles, and her tour became a pageant. Crowds reverently watched for her at railway stations; hymns were composed in her honor, she was showered with gifts which ranged from enormous inkstands—because she was an author— to gold bracelets, which by an inverted symbolism represented the breaking of shackles; she received a penny offering amounting to thousands of pounds for the anti-slavery cause, and accepted a monster petition in twenty-six folio volumes, signed by hundreds of thousands of the women of England, urging the abolition of slavery. She met Dickens, Macaulay, Milman, Lord Palmerston, Lord John Russell, Kingsley, the Duke and Duchess of Argyll, the Duke and Duchess of Sutherland. Crowned at last, she entered the solid official world of English reform of the mid-nineteenth century.

Mrs. Stowe seemed oblivious of these heavier honors. She mentioned them; but her letters and her conversation were almost vacant of comment on notable personalities or on ideas. What she enjoyed most was great aggregations of people, or the shining accessories of romance. Whisked off to castles in coaches and four with liveried postilions and outriders, she happily caught every bright detail. Small and enraptured, quiet and gray and still a little shabby, she sat demurely in the great gilded hall at Stafford House while the Duchess of Sutherland hovered over her in splendid tall magnificence. "The Duchess of Argyll is of slight and fairylike figure, answering well to the description of Annot Lyle," she wrote; "Lord Blantyre is of the Stuart blood, a tall and slender young man with very graceful manners. . . . After the concert the duchess asked Lady Hatherton and me to come round to Stafford House and take tea, which was a thing not to be despised, either on account of the tea or the Duchess. A lovelier time we never had—present, the Duchess of Argyll, Lady Caroline Campbell, Lady Hatherton, and myself. We had the nicest cup of tea, with such cream, and grapes and apricots with Italian bread, etc. . . ." Though she herself wore the plain high-necked cloth dresses which were considered suitable for occasions in Cincinnati and Brunswick, though she maintained in these a quaint and confident sense of her Americanism, she descanted with enormous pleasure upon the velvets and satins and muslins and bright ribbons of her new friends —of the flounced white silk worn by Lady Mary LaBouchère, with a pattern of roses woven round the bottom of each flounce, and the sparkling diamond buckles adorning Mr. LaBouchère at knee and instep when these two were bidden to dine with the Queen at Windsor, actually—such was the happy fortuitous circumstance—while Mrs. Stowe was their guest, though she herself was not favored by the royal command. Presently, moving on to Paris and the Continent, she began to sprinkle little French phrases through all her writings, scattering them in fact with what she loved to call *abandon.* Her whole vocabulary grew lush and flowery; she marshaled adjectives in troops—or was it *troupes?*—she was often "fain" to do things, though she could still "presume" and "guess" and speak of her "folks." After a visit to the *Jardin Mabille* she remarked with an air of worldliness, "Aside from the impropriety inherent in the very nature of waltzing, there is not a word, look, or gesture of immorality or impropriety." Soon she was dipping into discussions of literature and painting—particularly painting. Raphael she thought pallid; Correggio she intensely admired; but her high favorite after a first shudder of revulsion because of his subjects was Rubens; and after all, in this new taste for a riotous paganism she had an august ally—had not Victoria, all domestic as she was, a yacht sportively named *Bacchante?*

Basking in wanton moods even in the Alps, she perched happily on the edge of a glacier, "feeding on the green moonshine of an emerald ice-cave." On she floated into Italy. . . ah, Corinne. . . . Perhaps something of her first vision of genius abroad came back; it seemed a final fulfillment. With pertinacity she clutched it, and wrote with shivering, sophisticated delight, "Rome is a world! Rome is an astonishment! Papal Rome is an enchantress! Old as she is, she is like Ninon d'Enclos—the young fall in love with her!" Here was *abandon,* indeed. Happily she hurried home and gathered up all these new emotions in a volume called *Sunny Memories,* which was described by a candid critic as a record of "spiritual inebriety," and was compared unfavorably in the matter of forthright pronouncements with Barnum's first autobiography, then recently published. But the carping note was small; *Sunny Memories* had a large success, as authentic impressions of Europe by an American, as a personal account by Mrs. Stowe.

On her return she was promptly summoned to the responsibilities of her position as a leader in the anti-slavery movement; she entered into the thick of the Kansas-Nebraska agitation, collected funds, and issued appeals. Grave and authoritative, she composed a shower of little pamphlets. With an abrupt gesture she also took the dark plunge into *Dred,* her second anti-slavery novel, in which the deep-laid, interwoven patterns of *Uncle Tom's Cabin* were again revealed. Out of the stilted pathos of the main story arises a bold and terrible fantasy—pure fantasy—which outstrips the obvious theme. Fear runs through the narrative, never quite like a passion, always a little suppressed; demonism haunts it. An impenetrable thick growth of cypress and wild vine and blasted trees in a deep swamp makes a wilderness where hunted negroes find sanctuary, from which emerges the figure of Dred, who cries in eerie places at dawn and sweeps down upon the huddled revivalism of a negro camp-meeting with something of the terror of the Hebraic God. Those signs and wonders and predicted overturnings which had filled Lyman Beecher's mind in the West as he considered the coming Millennium were turned to account—as if Mrs. Stowe were still under their spell, as if she had gained from them a touch of prophecy; for out of Dred's wailing utterances, his shouts of the fallen star called wormwood, of sharp sickles and ripe grapes, came an unmistakable foreboding of the black chaos of war. At the same time Mrs. Stowe fought her inheritance; like a sharp and acrid theme through the book runs an attack on Calvinistic doctrine and the Calvinistic ministry—an attack so bitter as to draw comments from its adherents on all sides, though few of Mrs. Stowe's contemporaries, it seems, were in a position to recognize its implications or the sources of her rancor.

Lyman Beecher was already slipping into that long clouded silence in which he was to spend his last years; his days of positive warfare were over; but Mrs. Stowe's indictment was by no means finished. "Snared" was the word and the image which he had used with gusto in speaking of his pursuit of souls; his daughter now ruthlessly described a minister who "sat quietly behind his face, as a spider does in a web, waiting until the unsuspecting seeker had tangled himself in incautious, impulsive, and of course contradictory meshes of statement, which were, in some future hour, in the most gentle and Christian spirit, to be tightened around the incautious captive." Her father had been immensely proud of his adaptability; and Mrs. Stowe ironically noted the trait. "He knew precisely all the gradations of smile which were useful for accomplishing different purposes," she declared of one of the ministerial prototypes who invade the story with conspicuous irrelevance. She described "the solemn smile, the smile of inquiry, the smile affirmative, the smile suggestive, the smile of incredulity, which encouraged the simple-hearted narrator to go on unfolding himself. . . ." She was indefatigable. Dealing shaft after shaft, she struck at Lyman Beecher's well-known suppleness in ecclesiastical debate; in a broad allusion she fairly mocked his heresy trial. And with a bulk of detail which all but ruined the story, she railed against that faction which had set the issue of slavery aside in order to advance the cause of the Millennium—as her father had done at Lane Seminary.

When she had finished *Dred* she wrote in triumph to her friend Georgeanna May that she now "walked in liberty" and "had done with languishing." The statement may have been reckless; languishing was an interesting habit, not to be lightly abandoned. As for liberty—had she attained it? At least she had her more obvious triumphs. "One hundred thousand copies of *Dred* sold in four weeks!" she wrote blithely. "After that who cares what the critics say?" Within a few months she was back in England again, placing her children in foreign schools—it is not clear what became of the younger ones—bringing Professor Stowe with her for a brief space, but soon drifting on without him through visit after happy visit. She stayed with the Kingsleys, perhaps enjoying a sense of daring radicalism in religion. Actually, by a careful prearrangement, she met the Queen and the Prince Consort and the blue-eyed royal children at a railway station for a brief moment, and presented the Queen with a copy of her novel. And ah, this was crucial, during this second sojourn she learned to know Lady Byron.

Elderly and frail, in lavender weeds, Lady Byron received her; from the beginning their friendship flourished. Soon Lady Byron was writing of "communion" with Mrs. Stowe; and Mrs. Stowe bubbled and purled in reply. "How glad I was to see your handwriting once more! How glad I should have been to see you! I do long to see *you*. I have so much to ask you, and need to be refreshed with the sense of a congenial and sympathetic soul." Each of them had encountered Calvinism; each had swung to a belief in the efficacy of love; but as to this, Lady Byron had gone much further than Mrs. Stowe, who still was doubtful as to the question of eternal punishment. Lady Byron calmly explained that there was *no one*—not even Lord Byron—of whose future she despaired, and adumbrated her theory that it was Calvinism which had driven her husband to extremes of irreligion and vice. A little occultly she portrayed herself as Lord Byron's redeemer, thus becoming—privately and tragically—a figure not unlike that of Mrs. Stowe herself. They talked together endlessly of death, of the "beautiful and terrible mission." "I often think how strange it is that I should really *know* you," said Mrs. Stowe mystically, "you who were a sort of legend of my early days." When at last Lady Byron imparted her secret Mrs. Stowe solemnly wrote to her new friend, "Considering the peculiar circumstances of the case, I could wish that the sacred veil of silence, so bravely thrown over the past, should never be withdrawn during the time that you remain with us. I would say, then," she added a little ominously, "leave all with some discreet friends, who after both have passed from earth, shall say what is due to justice." Did she suspect that she herself might issue the dramatic statement, that with a crusading onslaught she might offer to the world a dark and imperative theory as to Byron's private life? Certainly she was immensely stirred, immensely flattered; all this amazing story, this friendship—aureoled by nobility, a great name, and historic connections —was tendered to *her*. At something more than forty, with Lady Byron at sixty-one, she developed an adolescent idealization and flow of emotion. "I left you with a strange sort of yearning, throbbing feeling," she wrote Lady Byron after a last visit—"you make me feel quite as I did years ago, a sort of girlishness quite odd for me. I have a strange longing to send you something. Don't smile when you see what it turns out to be. . . . I send you a cup made of primroses, a funny little pitcher, quite large enough for cream, and a little vase for violets and primroses —which will be lovely together"—such things, she explained, as she had for her "own quiet meals, when, as often happens, I am too unwell to join the family."

FOUR • *Alas! these coruscations of romantic feeling and careless joys of fame came to an abrupt end.* Mrs. Stowe had just returned from her second visit abroad when she received the sad intelligence that her son Henry had been drowned in the Connecticut River at Hanover. The old misgivings rolled back over her; she was plunged into a torment of questionings. Henry had not experienced conversion. What—ah, what might not be his fate in the eternal life? Would she ever see him again? After all what *was* the eternal plan? She was overwhelmed. With all her strange, strong outcries it seemed she never would be free.

Spiritualism was in the air; the new assuaging cult had been precipitated scarcely ten years before in middle New York by the odd exhibitions of the Davenport brothers and the Fox sisters. With her husband, who was inured to the phantasmal, Mrs. Stowe sought out mediums and dipped into spirit writings; guitars twanged for both of them. Restlessly she went abroad again—this time for many months, leaving Professor Stowe at Andover and her children scattered. "I cannot, however, think that Henry strikes the guitar," she insisted in a letter to her husband written from Florence, speaking of a recent experience of his by which he had been greatly impressed. "That must be Eliza. Her spirit has ever seemed to cling to that mode of manifestation, and if you would keep it in your sleeping room no doubt you would hear from it oftener."

While Professor Stowe cummuned with Eliza, she wandered on; among the English residents in Italy the new devotion had become absorbing. By a happy chance she met Mrs. Browning, who was a convinced spiritualist; these two "sister souls," as Mrs. Browning truly called them, were wafted together on a faint and lovely sea of emotion; they exchanged letters on the nebulous theme for many years. "I don't know how people can keep up their prejudices against spiritualism with tears in their eyes," wrote Mrs. Browning; "how they are not at least thrown on the wish that it might be true, and the investigation of the phenomena, by that abrupt shutting in their faces of the door of death, which shuts them out from the sight of their beloved. My tendency is to beat up against it like a crying child." They both were like crying children, Mrs. Browning afterward enveloped by the chaos that came to her with her father's death, Mrs. Stowe still peering into the void, seeking a resolution of her doubts. Even to George Eliot, patient and admiring but skeptical, Mrs. Stowe poured out her evidences and arguments in letters, gravely mentioning certain communications which had recently been received from Charlotte Brontë.

But with all this literary authority Mrs. Stowe failed to find in spiritualism a permanent release. Within her own spirit she housed a ghost, an ancient ghost, which would not be laid; she was bound to a treadmill, and whatever her excursions, she paced it, with insistence, with obstinacy, with a kind of a rage. Through the extravagant years she still was arguing with herself, with Lyman Beecher. In *The Minister's Wooing,* written soon after Henry's death, she had chosen for a theme the tragedy which had overshadowed her sister Catherine's youth, and which was now being strangely repeated in her own experience: the death of Catherine's betrothed by drowning, without hope of regeneration, stirring a terrible fear as to his eternal fate. Her father had been remorseless as to the outcome; Mrs. Stowe was now remorseless in turn. Her minister was a genteel prototype of Lyman Beecher; and slowly, with penetrating thoroughness, she defeated him in both love and religion. By a harsh but positive minor gesture she made the black-hearted villain of the piece stem from the family of the great Beecher and Stowe spiritual leader, Jonathan Edwards; and her book was a long assault on the Puritan faith.

When its opening chapters appeared serially in the *Atlantic Monthly,* Lowell, then the editor, wrote an anonymous puff of them for a New

York newspaper, speaking of Mrs. Stowe's "wonderful eye," mentioning her in the same breath as Cervantes and Fielding, Smollett and Dickens. Later he implored her, as did others, not to load her narrative with what he called "doctrinal casuistry." But she had her purposes, and she maintained them in her next novel, *The Pearl of Orr's Island.* Its opening chapters are idyllic, fluent, yet hardly soft; within them humor rises easily, humor of a native tang, as in the romancings of Captain Kittredge; this prelude is a little gold and silvery perhaps, but its unexalted perceptions might have gone far toward establishing the tradition of a simple realism if they had been carried steadily onward. Mrs. Stowe had written these passages as a sudden venture after the turmoil of producing *Uncle Tom's Cabin,* as if in their freshness and clarity she had found a natural harbor. Here, perhaps, was something of the sweet and tranquil mood into which she had drifted as a child among the green hills of Litchfield, a serene emotion which had naturally belonged to her. But now she destroyed this mood; as she continued her story she transformed it into a buttress for the new faith which she had struggled so often to maintain; her tale became a dull and exaggerated glorification of a death glimpsed without terror; indeed the heroine, Mara, is made to endure the most lingering preparation for demise through which an innocent heroine was ever dragged. And once more the old enemy Calvinism was demolished; the novel became an argument.

The day was late; already a new drama of the spirit had been quietly precipitated across the sea by a book entitled *On the Origin of Species.* But a vast number of people—a New England public, of the settled regions, of the broad, second New England in the West—were being tormented by the same interrogations which harassed Mrs. Stowe, were seeking the answers she labored to assert, were concerned not at all with origins, but with the eternal future. Once more, in 1857, a great revival had swept over the country, no longer with the terrible violence which had characterized the recurrent waves of religious excitement a generation or two before, but with a mild alleviating fervor; death was again an omnipresent theme. In her small person, within her restless, troubled mind, Mrs. Stowe was summing up anxieties and pertinent questions of an era. Besides, her public found in these later novels another, happier fascination; her subject actually was themselves—was New England. At times, indeed, she argued against the stringencies of a native taste and character as if she belonged to another race and blood. "With all New England's earnestness and practical efficiency, there is a withering of the soul's more ethereal portion—a crushing out of the beautiful—which is horrible," she declared. "Children are born there with a sense of beauty equally delicate with any in the world, in whom it dies a lingering death of smothered desire and pining, weary starvation. I know, because I have felt it." She inveighed against the New England habit of introspection, and against the mode of logic. "Between you and me, if there is a golden calf worshiped in our sanctified New England, its name is logic," she said brusquely. But at the same time—inconsequently—her final commentary was gratifying; she never relinquished her belief in New England leadership; she might have been asserting her faith in herself, in her own destiny. She declared that the people of New England were "especially called and chosen by God for some great work on earth." This region was "the seed-bed of this great American republic and all that is likely to come of it. . . ." She portrayed "a country which is now exerting such an influence on the entire civilized world that to know it truly becomes an object." And she cast an unmistakable glamor over the New England scene. Her hand was often wavering and profuse, it is true; her most local characters, Miss Roxy and Miss Ruey in *The Pearl,* are made so volubly to deliver themselves of little native idioms, maxims, proverbs, and mere quaintnesses as to seem engaged in a brisk competitive match; but here as in her other New England novels the sheer character of people and place often breaks forth from the superabundant detail and the mass of dialectic; these books have their measure of salt and savor.

If Mrs. Stowe had chosen humbly to consider the work of a contemporary who never gained a tithe of her immediate fame she might have found a criterion for the uses of localism, for the true place in the novel of those doctrinal questions which so obsessed her. Some of Hawthorne's tales rested upon the great questions which had shaken New England, questions as to the nature and results of sin, and the final human destiny; but Hawthorne had penetrated far beneath the incidence of doctrine to those typical strata of mental and moral compulsion, to those tenser bases of personality, which may generate the springs of controversy but which underlie such matters, belonging to the elementary in the human character. Hawthorne too used the externals of place, but always with a spare and beautiful economy, never choosing material because it was quaint or odd or even lovely, but because it was revelatory of certain shy aspects of the human spirit. The consequence was one which Mrs. Stowe in her lavishness seems not to have suspected: that these portrayals have through their fullness of implication the closest texture, the richest color—local color, if one will have it so, for Hawthorne never lost a devotion to the New England scene. But Mrs. Stowe disregarded Hawthorne quite as positively as she disregarded Lowell.

She was never a reader; she was indeed profoundly uninterested in literature. But she knew her own wish; and slaying her private enemy, pursuing her private quest, she was able to prove in some measure that both Lowell and Hawthorne were wrong.

In that long effort toward self-recognition which peoples as well as individuals can undertake, her highly stressed New England coloring seemed to afford knowledge and perspective as well as pleasure; to numbers of people her long doctrinal discussions became perennially important. Her books were read and re-read; in spite of its laggard story *The Minister's Wooing* ran through more than fifty editions; and *The Pearl of Orr's Island* was scarcely less popular. Once more she was uplifted and transformed by an immense approval. Drifting on that great swelling tide, she forgot her ancient warfare for a time and remembered only her leadership; in fact, she grew a little arrogant, as perhaps was inevitable for a Cervantes or a Fielding. For an *Atlantic* dinner she wound a wreath of laurel about her brow—which Longfellow thought becoming—snubbed young Harriet Prescott, and flatly demanded that no wine be served. In the course of the meal it happened that a faint pink flush appeared in certain goblets of water; Longfellow, at least, was fond of Bordeaux. But Mrs. Stowe had made her point; and soon she was to make another and far greater one, with wide and terrible implications. As the decade drew to a close, in the West, in the North, were sounding the rolling echoes of *John Brown's Body*. The country drew shudderingly near to the abyss; at last the Civil War broke.

Out—out she swung into that terrible black emotion, into the orgy of death which was making an overwhelming climax in the rising life of the nation. It was Mrs. Stowe's war; every one told her so. With an augmented sense of divine appointment she tried to shout above the noise of battle, reproaching all but the most extreme of northern abolitionists, reproaching the women of England in a long open letter, quickly assuming the habit of the little messiahs who invariably create wild opposing myths. "Why do the horrible barbarities of *Southern* soldiers cause no comment?" she indignantly asked in a letter to an English friend. "Why is the sympathy of the British Parliament reserved for the poor women of New Orleans, deprived of their elegant amusement of throwing vitriol into soldiers' faces, and practicing indecencies inconceivable in any other state of society? Why is *all* expression of sympathy on the *Southern* side? . . . You see I am bitter. . . . I have long known *what* and who we had to deal with in this, for when I wrote *Uncle Tom's Cabin* I had letters addressed to me showing a state of society perfectly *inconceivable*. If I had written what I knew of the obscenity, brutality, and cruelty of that society down there, society would have cast out the books. . . ." Indeed, in this letter her hysteria ran to lengths which will scarcely bear repetition. "Remember it is the moment when every nerve is vital," she went on roundly in semi-public communication to the Duchess of Argyll. "It is our agony; we tread the winepress alone, and they whose cheap rhetoric"—the British abolitionists—"has been for years pushing us into it, now desert *en masse*. I thank my God I always loved and trusted most those who now *do* stand true—your family, your duke, yourself, your noble mother. I have lost Lady Byron. Her great heart, her eloquent letters, would have been a joy to me! And Mrs. Browning, oh, such a heroic woman! None of her poems can express what *she* was!" Prince Albert, too, had died—"the ideal knight, the *Prince Arthur* of our times, the good, wise, steady head and heart we—that is, our world, we Anglo-Saxons—need so much."

Alone—so she felt herself—in an empty and hostile world, she kept up her noisy vociferations. Shattered and tired and emotionalized, she became a little harp through which dire winds were blowing. Presently she decided that Lincoln was "too slow" and hastened to Washington to offer him advice. He seems to have received her gravely; after all he had been harassed by many evangels. "So you're the little woman who made this great war," she reported him as saying as he looked down upon her from his great height. "I do love an open fire," he went on inconsequently, and turned to the hearth. "We always had one to home." Mrs. Stowe stressed the locution in her account of this interview, but singularly enough she left no record of the subsequent conversation.

On she rushed, regardless of Lincolns, constantly under foot, it would seem, demanding special privileges for her son Frederick, who had enlisted, insisting that she be kept in touch with the opinions and decisions and movements of cabinet officers and major officials. Yet, as she swung to strange lengths in those dark years, she became engaged by a preoccupation of a very different sort. In 1863, while the war still endlessly continued, she began building a house—a mansion or a castle. As a child at her sister Catherine's school in Hartford she had walked by the river-side and had dreamed of grandeur; now on the same spacious area her house arose, with gables and turrets and towers and chimneys and a conservatory and a fountain that played. Presently the interior began to be crowded with drapes, easels, bronzes, with trophies enough to fill a museum out of the years of her first celebrity—memorials and books and portraits and handsome little remembrances.

The Stowes moved in while the house was still unfinished, and lived for many months with boxes lying about, a staircase without a railing, with carpenters coming and going, and plumbers and masons, and a bell-hanger who seems to have haunted the place. The state of chaos was prolonged; but a new aspiring social life began there in spite of the confusion. A year later, still in the midst of the war, when one of her daughters was to be married, Mrs. Stowe wrote to Fields of the *Atlantic* of "an immediate necessity of bringing everything out of doors and into a state of completeness for the wedding exhibition in June. The garden must be planted, the lawn graded, harrowed, rolled, seeded, and the grass up and growing, stumps out and shrubs and trees got in, conservatory made over, belts planted, holes filled. . . . I have back doorsteps to be made, screens, and what not; papering, painting, and varnishing, hitherto neglected, to be completed; also spring-housecleaning; also dressmaking for one bride and three ordinary females. . . . I send you today a *Chimney Corner* on *Our Martyrs* which I have written out of the fullness of my heart. . . ." She now began to speak for herself and her family as "simple gentlefolk," and assumed in Hartford a position as the leader of a *salon,* as a hostess and a great lady. Distinguished foreign visitors sometimes came; her Boston acquaintances dropped in. Presently, too, she began rushing away for more and more frequent sojourns in Boston, ascending the great literary pinnacle. It seemed a final area for conquest—that society of Boston which had rejected the Beechers in the ancient days of her father's bold revivalism, and which still regarded her as something of an outsider for all her triumphs.

Throwing aside her commanding air and becoming what she rarely was, a charming conversationalist—gay and responsive and witty—she slipped into a lasting friendship with Oliver Wendell Holmes, the most truly Augustan of them all. By an odd circumstance their ancestries were loosely interknit within the later history of Puritanism; for Dr. Holmes could all but claim relationship with brisk little Dr. Ezra Stiles—Dr. Magpie—who had turned Yale College upside down by his insistence upon freedom of thought and speech, and had left it to be rehabilitated in the Puritan manner by Timothy Dwight, the great exemplar of Lyman Beecher. Both Mrs. Stowe and Dr. Holmes had known the stringencies of Calvinism, Holmes likewise through his father; they compared experiences and discussed religious questions by the hour. Yet after all, perhaps what Mrs. Stowe most admired in Dr. Holmes was a certain easy worldliness; he could indulge in public repartee and toss off toasts with an adaptation to the mind and temper of his auditors which must have seemed to her sheer genius; he was full of delightful gallantries. "A health to dear woman!" he had cried long before at a temperance dinner to which ladies were invited—

"She bids us entwine
From the cup it encircles, the fast-clinging vine;
But her cheek in its crystal with pleasure will glow,
And mirror its bloom in the bright wave below.

A health to sweet woman! The days are no more
When she watched for her lord till the revel was o'er,
And smoothed the white pillow, and blushed when he came,
As he pressed her cold lips on his forehead of flame.

Alas for the loved one! too spotless and fair
The joys of his banquet to chasten and share;
Her eye lost its light that his goblet might shine,
And the rose of her cheek was dissolved in his wine.

Joy smiles in the fountain, health flows in the rills,
As the ribands of silver unwind from the hills;
They breathe not the mist of the bacchanal's dream,
But the lilies of innocence float on their stream.

Then a health and a welcome to woman once more!
She brings us a passport that laughs at our door;
It is written on crimson—its letters are pearls—
It is countersigned *Nature.*—So, room for the Girls!"

If the ending was a shade too exhuberant, certainly the sentiment
was faultless; and Dr. Holmes manifested the rippling idealization in
a dozen agreeable ways. Besides, he could express the most enchanting
contemporary prejudices. He had invented that famous cognomen, "the
Hub." With aggressive certitude he disposed of rash literary groups
manifest elsewhere. "Those whipper-snappers of New York will do well
to take care," he declared in stiff warning. "The noble race of men now
so famous here is passing down the valley—then who will take their
places! I am ashamed to know the names of the blackguards," he added,
mentioning a pamphlet which had sneered at the "Boston Mutual Admiration Society."

But for Mrs. Stowe suddenly neither the high enclosure of Boston nor
her own storied dwelling in Hartford was enough. In 1867 she swept
down to Florida, proposing to build a town on the St. Johns River,
which would provide labor and instruction for the neighboring blacks,
and a winter refuge for her son Frederick, who had come home an in-
valid at the end of the war, and for her poor old Rab, who had given up
teaching and was restless. "I am being *châtelaine* of a Florida farm," she
wrote when she was fairly established. "I am founding a place which,

thirty or forty years hence, will be called the old Stowe place. . . ." But her orange groves were ruined by frost and had to be sold for almost nothing; and Frederick sailed for San Francisco, disappeared mysteriously at that port, and was never heard of again. The loss was more terrible than death, for Frederick's injury was thought to have caused a mental derangement. Restless and desolate, Mrs. Stowe again found herself overwhelmed by heavy burdens; and again she was cramped for funds. With its enormous returns and the impetus which it had given to the sale of her other books, *Uncle Tom's Cabin* must have seemed to her a purse of Fortunatus; but even that productive source—and the others—had been drained. She had been open-handed, she was generous; she had flung away money during her visits abroad; it was always slipping through her fingers. "I have invested $34,000 in various ways, none of which can give me any immediate income," she remarked casually. She was always investing money without adequate advice; the house in Hartford had devoured money, without promise of return. Factories had sprung up in the neighborhood; and its cost—with ornament upon ornament appearing under her lavish touch—still mounted fabulously; yet it was badly built; it was never really finished.

She kept it; she had kept the house at Mandarin in Florida; and to meet her still increasing expenses she wrote endlessly—a multitude of little sketches, poems, essays, stories, novels. Still on the current of her great fame, she found herself with plenty to do; editors and publishers were forever at her heels; but the whole affair of writing had become an immense and dragging effort. Using some of Calvin Stowe's most vivid New England tales, she undertook another long novel, *Oldtown Folks,* which she made include many of his experiences in the realm of fantasy. She would write for an hour, and then call to Professor Stowe, "Do come—come and hear, and tell me how you like it." Briefly aroused, her husband would water her efforts copiously with tears if they contained pathos, or lapse into nervous boredom; with increasing fervor he disliked both fiction and poetry. Again she would push herself to the labor of writing, and summon hearers from another quarter; she was unable to continue without an audience. "To see the first part of my book in type will greatly assist me in the last," she declared to Fields, seeking another stimulus. "I am so constituted that it is absolutely fatal to me to agree to have *any* literary work done at certain dates," she explained later. Once the presses had to be stopped when one of her books was being printed, because she failed to supply the necessary manuscript. "I *mean* to have this story done by the first of September," she wrote to Fields, "but I am bound by the laws of art. . . . I am sorry to trouble you or derange your affairs, but one can't always tell in driving such horses as we drive where they are going to bring up." She could never tell; she was always making promises and forgetting them. "I have been hard pressed of late," she announced, "owing to a promise inadvertently given to a publishing house here in Hartford that I would get out a book called *Men of Our Times* for them this fall."

"I see that all the leading magazines have articles on Planchette," she wrote to Fields, who was awaiting a promised essay on quite a different subject. "There is a lady of my acquaintance who has developed more remarkable facts in this way than any I have seen; I have kept a record of these communications for some time past, and everybody is much struck with them. I have material for a very curious article. . . . Shall you want it? And when? . . ." Without waiting for a reply she dashed off another proposal. "I am beginning a series of articles called *Learning to Write,* designed to be helpful to a great many beginners. . . . My materials for the Planchette article are really very extraordinary . . . but I don't want to write it now when I am driving so hard on my book. . . ." Her proofs were never ready; her disregard of spelling, punctuation, and grammar became notorious; often whole sections of her work, written in haste, would have to be revised by impatient editors at the last moment. She was weary, she was ill; she wept; she was overcome by unaccountable gusts of feeling—"unregulated and unrestrained feeling," her son said. In the midst of a deepening chaos she decided to make Calvin Stowe produce an article on the Talmud, and accomplished this feat, at the cost of copying his Chaldean characters herself; she spent hours at the task.

Calvin Stowe had scarcely receded into the background with the passage of years. "Big, burly, sledge-hammery, with a loud voice," was the description of Samuel Bowles, who met him early in the seventies. "He looks like one class of German professors—poor clothes, red nose, opinionated, and wise; or an old-fashioned New England tavern-keeper, the oracle of the village." As his wife worked he would wander about the Hartford house, muttering that they were always "plagued and poor." Once he tried to mend a pane of glass with a sheet of tin and a tack hammer and two shingle-nails; and after breaking all the other panes in the window he went to his room in an agony of despair—probably to bury himself in French memoirs of the eighteenth century, in which he was now absorbed, or to consider his phantoms, which had increased in numbers. Indeed more than ever his strange visitants now assumed reality—or persons about him faded into ghosts. On one occasion when Mrs. Stowe was supposed to have left town for a visit but had missed a train, she returned to the room in which her husband was reading, moved about, and took a place at the window. When at last she spoke, Calvin Stowe replied absently, "Oh, I thought you were one of my visions." She had in truth the look of a trance-walker; her air of vague absorption had become an incorrigible habit. Off she went on hazy errands more and more frequently, chiefly to Boston, seeking companionship or scouting for copy, lunching with young Mrs. Thomas Bailey Aldrich on one such visit, partaking too well of claret cup by mistake, and tired no doubt, with confusion heaped on confusion, sleeping it off on Mrs. Aldrich's sofa with hoop-skirts indecorously disarranged.

FIVE • *She seemed to be repeating an endless pattern.* After her romantic flights, once again, as in the earlier years of her marriage, she was caught within the net of weary personal responsibilities; her old burdens were heavy upon her, magnified now with her increasing age. Once more, in the midst of a shadowy fatigue she was pondering. Something was wrong. Was it in our national life? With a touch of the grandiose, a little heavily, she offered her commentary. "Numbers is the king of our era," she declared, anticipating Matthew Arnold by a decade. "The power is passing out of the hands of the cultivated few into those of the strong, laborious many." "In America there is no class which will confess itself the lower class. . . . There has been a slow and gradual reaction against household labor." Yes, perhaps the servant problem would prove the nub of an enormous difficulty. Then there was the scale and glitter of the later American existence, borrowed from foreign lands. With a restless glance Mrs. Stowe considered Europe; like many of her countrymen after the Civil War she abandoned the romantic view of Europe. "The women of America can, if they choose, hold back their country from following in the wake of an old, corrupt, worn-out, effeminate European society, and make America the leader of the world in all that is good. . . . The genius of American life is for simplicity and absence of ostentation. . . . We have too many rooms, too many carpets, too many vases and knick-knacks, too much china and silver. . . . What earthly need is there of a grand regale of oysters, chicken salad, ice-creams, coffee, and champagne, between eleven and twelve o'clock at night? . . . If all of us were in the habit of having a regular repast at that hour, it might be well enough to enjoy one with our neighbors; but party fare is generally just so much in addition to the honest three meals which we have eaten during the day. . . . Large parties are not, as a general thing, given with any wish or intention of really improving our acquaintance with our neighbors. . . . I ask Mrs. Brown where she buys her lace, and she tells me how she washes it, and somebody else tells me about her baby, and procures me a new sack-pattern. . . ."

From the theme of social sophistication Mrs. Stowe drifted to that of a dubious personal embellishment. "Powder, paint, gold-dust, and silver-dust, pomatums, cosmetics, are all perfectly appropriate where the ideal of life is to keep up a false show of beauty, after the true bloom is wasted by dissipation," she announced severely. Considering elaboration in dress, she held up to scorn the light-minded little woman who in a single season bought a waterfall hat, an oriole, and a jockey. Women must learn to make their own hats and their own plain frocks, she trenchantly declared; if their homes needed decoration, this too could be contrived by adroit and willing hands. With her sister Catherine she compiled a thick household manual packed with precise instructions. Expensive prints, for example, were unnecessary; varnished chromos were within the reach of all, and could, moreover, be framed by crossed strips of native wood whose bark must be left intact, with the corners "garnished" by clusters of acorns or small pine cones or bits of moss or ocean shells. Barrel chairs could be contrived, and lambrequins—improperly called "lamberkins."

At last it came out, the whole familiar picture: the American domestic interior of the sixties and seventies in its homelier forms, with lambrequins indeed, with whatnots and stands, fresh matting on the floor, flowering plants in the bow-window, a round table in the center of the room with a fringed cover and a lamp, about which the family group was comfortably disposed. Mrs. Stowe sketched the scene again and again; at her best she gave it warmth and color and even a quaint enchantment. Was this the outer semblance of a life which she now coveted, the home which was a quiet haven, sheltered and tranquil and wholly safe from the incursions of public responsibilities? Perhaps the Mrs. Stowe who had ventured into the great world, who had longed for castles, who had dreamed long ago of the dominant figure of Corinne—perhaps this Mrs. Stowe was a transitory character who had vanished at last.

Undoubtedly within these homely pictures was contained the form of a wish; according to her invincible habit Mrs. Stowe was setting down her desires. Yet after all, in these many little essays, her *Chimney Corner Papers,* her *House and Home Papers,* and the collection which she called *Little Foxes,* she was not merely descriptive. Again she began to show the thread of an insistent argument; beneath her scattered musings ran something plain and relentless and familiar—a purpose. Her domestic scenes were not only peopled—they were dominated—by a small, resourceful, patient little woman who ruled the household, who indeed by one means or another had called it into being. Brightly and lightly, but none the less with inexorable firmness, this small feminine monitor invariably contrived to resolve every domestic problem, through tact, or ingenuity, or a determined forgetfulness of masculine shortcomings, or by the hard reality of labor. Mrs. Stowe was captivated by this little leader of the household; indeed, she could seldom rebuke any of her heroines; even her reproof of the frivolous woman was never really harsh; in the domestic essays she was prettily called "Hummingbird." In *Pink and White Tyranny,* a novel written in these years presumably as an invective against feminine extravagance, her wrath from the first was obviously factitious, and gradually dwindled before the charm of her slight and willowy heroine. When Mrs. Stowe discussed the wicked folly of expensive hats her style grew animated; she had always liked pretty hats; even in her second polemic against slavery, *Dred,* in the opening scene she had made Nina display a sweet little bonnet trimmed with cascading silver wheat.

Yes, Mrs. Stowe was enchanted by feminine vagaries. "She's a woman," sighed Mr. Sewell in *The Pearl,* marveling at the preternatural mental and emotional powers of little Mara. "And they are all alike. We can't do much for them, but let them come up as they will, and make the best of it." And they *were* all alike—in Mrs. Stowe's novels as in her domestic essays. The triumphant little woman who held the difficult reins in the *House and Home Papers* was only a little less gay than Hummingbird, who had no responsibilities; Nina was Hummingbird; and Nina was likewise Tina of *Oldtown Folks,* tripping up and down the halls of the old house, and oh, how heroically battling against the heaviest odds; and Mary of *The Minister's Wooing* and Mara of *The Pearl of Orr's Island*—they too were the same character, grown calm and secure, bearing heavy spiritual burdens, melting at times into pure ether, but essentially the same creature—the woman-child. And clearly they were all Dolly of the later *Poganuc People,* the liveliest, the gayest, the wisest of them all; and Dolly—the secret came out—was finally avowed as Mrs. Stowe herself.

There she stood or lightly twinkled through the novels, and now again in these tired and troubled years through the essays—small and vivacious, never quite reasonable, wholly mysterious—and powerful! Not only was this small embellished counterpart of Mrs. Stowe the center of every scene, not only had she dominated book after book, but she was mighty by contrast. "There is a temperament called the Hypochondriac," declared her author; and that temperament proved in the main to be masculine. Satirically and often Mrs. Stowe referred to "the lords of creation." "Marrying for a living is the very hardest way a woman can take to get it," she announced shortly. A masculine character named Enthusius appeared in the essays, who "never considered it a part of a husband's duty to bear personal grievances in silence," and the impractical hot-headed old Enthusius bore an unmistakable resemblance to Calvin Stowe. Frankly, in *Oldtown Folks,* the one solid novel of these years, Horace Holyoke *was* Calvin Stowe, visions and all—flattened and dim and more than ever ineffectual, but the very character; in the end Tina casually accepts him as second choice, after marrying the horrid Ellery Davenport, who dies. Indeed, this novel summed up the many-sided warfare of a lifetime. Its pages were crowded with ministerial characters, whose harshness of essential temperament were limned, whose marrying habits were freely discoursed upon; among other circumstances Mrs. Stowe pointed out the trials of their wives, who more frequently than not died under the strain; one of these stern apostles was married three times, like Lyman Beecher. Again she made the villain of the piece, Ellery Davenport—a black villain and a seducer—stem from the Beecher and Stowe spiritual ancestry, from the family of Jonathan Edwards. Filled to the brim with lively notations of people and places, this book remains the richest and raciest of Mrs. Stowe's novels; and ironically enough, its background was drawn in the main from the homely reminiscences of Calvin Stowe.

But for Mrs. Stowe this familiar rebellion could hardly prove sufficient. If she was the perfect Victorian, as she liked to picture herself, she sprang from a hardy native stem; it was not for nothing that Lyman Beecher had possessed a sense of drama. Out of her accumulated grievances arose a concentrated revolt. Her attention fell upon a review of the Guiccioli memoirs in *Blackwood's* for July, 1869, which praised Byron's mistress and denounced Lady Byron as a "moral Clytemnestra" or a "Brinvilliers" who had in effect destroyed a great life and a great talent. Mrs. Stowe blazed with indignation, and rushed to the defense, determined— well, determined upon many things. She dashed off *The True Story of Lady Byron's Life.* Members of her family tried to dissuade her from publishing this narrative, but she "set her face like flint." Submitting it to her friend Dr. Holmes, she declared that what she wanted was *"not* your advice as to whether the main facts shall be told, for on this point I am so resolved that I frankly say advice would do me no good. But you might help me, with your delicacy and insight, to make the *manner of telling* more perfect. . . ." Fields, then the editor of the *Atlantic,* was in Europe when she sent her article; and young William Dean Howells, who had been left in charge, dared not risk the displeasure of a valued contributor by its rejection. The magazine was nearly wrecked in consequence; cancellations of subscriptions were sent in by the hundreds. Publicly and privately, in the newspapers, in conversation, a vast furor of controversy raged as to the whole Byron legend, which was still immense, as to questions of fact and taste and interpretation; interchanges were made across the Atlantic; the debate spread up and down Great Britain, and to the Continent. Lord Lovelace, Byron's grandson, sent Mrs. Stowe a vigorous remonstrance at once through his solicitors; but she was only moved to wilder flights. She expanded her article into a book, *Lady Byron Vindicated,* preparing a special edition for English readers. As for Lord Lovelace, she roundly declared that she had had no reason to believe that any member of Lady Byron's family was living when she wrote the *Atlantic* article. Yet in her book she rambled on at length about Lord Lovelace, then Lord Ockham, as she had seen him during her visits with Lady Byron ten years before; and from her descriptions he would seem to have been a young man of uncommonly sound health. "His bodily frame," she said, "was of the order of the Farnese Hercules —a wonderful development of physical and muscular strength. His hands were those of a blacksmith. He was broadly and squarely made, with a finely shaped head, and dark eyes of surpassing brilliancy." Indeed, Lady Byron had told her that Lord Ockham "had a body that required a more vigorous animal life than his station gave scope for, and this had often led him to seek it in what the world calls low society; that he had been to sea as a sailor, and was now working as a mechanic on the ironwork of the *Great Eastern.* He had laid aside his title, and went in daily with the other workmen, requesting them to call him simply Ockham. . . . I said that there was to my mind something very fine about this, though it might show some want of proper balance."

As for the friends of Lady Byron who might have answered the *Blackwood's* article, Mrs. Stowe announced that they were "limited in view as aristocratic circles generally are." "When time passed on, and no voice was raised, I spoke," she said. Alas! the *Blackwood's* article had appeared in July, and Mrs. Stowe's answering article in September; she had rushed pell-mell into print. With a shrillness which cut through every page she continued her contradictory reproach, even threatening Lord Lovelace and the English friends of Lady Byron with divine wrath for their failure to assume the responsibility of telling the story. "I do not judge them," she said with a touch of menacing grandeur, "but I remind them that a day is coming when they and I must stand side by side at the great Judgment Seat—I to give account for my speaking, they for their silence." Finally she took the inflated position of a nationalist in the matter. "I have one word more, as an American, to say about the contempt shown our great people in thus suffering the materials of history to be falsified to subserve the temporary interests of family feeling in England. . . . We Americans have been made accessories after the fact to every insult and injury that Lord Byron and the literary men of his day have heaped upon Lady Byron. We have been betrayed into injustice and complicity with villainy. . . . I claim for my countrymen and women our right to *true* history. . . ."

For her narrative Mrs. Stowe had no materials, no documents; she had returned to Lady Byron within a few days the scanty memorandum of events with which she had been entrusted during her second visit in England; and she had made no copy. Nor had Lady Byron's secret in any sense been bequeathed to Mrs. Stowe, unless her own exhortation, "Leave all to some discreet friends," in the little note written many years before had constituted a bequest. She had asked for no proof from her friend in the first instance. "Of course I did not listen to this story as one who was investigating its worth," she announced flatly. There was not a line of proof in all her passionate asseverations. For her strange enterprise she had only her memory, which was always faulty, her power of weighing evidence, which was inconsiderable, and whatever lay within her own mind of irresistible compulsion.

Her purposes seemed mixed. At times, in her *Lady Byron Vindicated,* she seemed launched upon a project of autobiographical reminiscence. With a large irrelevance she discoursed upon her own movements in England, mentioning her visit to the Kingsleys', noting the emptiness of London out of season, speaking of a lunch-party of notables at which she had been a guest. From the mode of autobiography she slipped into that of fiction—and what sort of fiction? She was discursive; her headings were sensational; they were cheap; they might have been taken from paper-backed romances; significant italics broke from every page. Still in the personal vein she offered *Lady Byron's Story as Told to Me,* with such portentous statements thrust forward as "I shall yet have occasion to explain these words," or "There was more in this mention of Electra than meets the ear." Yet—her story still untold—she seemed bent upon the violent business of literary—or was it social?—criticism. With a sweeping gesture she indicted the whole society to which Lord Byron belonged, accusing both Moore and Murray of bad faith—particularly the "artless Thomas Moore," as she satirically called him; she went far out of her way to denounce Moore, whose vice, she said, was "cautious, soft, seductive, slippery, and covered with a thin veil of religious sentimentalism." Abundantly she quoted from his poetry; she quoted Maginn, lashed out at Christopher North and the *Noctes,* stormed over the "pretended negotiations through Mme. de Staël," and was haughty toward Lady Blessington. At times she seemed mainly bent upon portraying Lord Byron; and she made him the composite of all the wickedness which the masculine mind and heart can enclose; she fairly gave him the cloven hoof. At the same moment she irresistibly endowed Byron with enchantment; in the high notes of her lifted voice with its underlying hysteria sounded a repulsion so strong as to suggest the alluring, a hatred which indicated a corresponding appeal. "I told her"—Mrs. Stowe was speaking of a conversation with Lady Byron—"that I had been from childhood powerfully interested in him, and began to tell her how much as a child I had been affected by the news of his death." Yet after all, her true subject was not the fabulously wicked poet but his saintly wife; and at last, out of the long mazes of argument and discourse her contention came out; Lady Byron had been made the victim of a vicious, intricate conspiracy from the time of her separation from Lord Byron—no, from the time of her marriage; as to the precise beginnings of the plot Mrs. Stowe was never quite clear; she mixed her dates, and followed strange clues. But her main assertion was uncompromising: Lord Byron had driven away his wife in order to conceal an infamous relationship, and then had made her character the subject of an artfully planned attack which had been continued after his death by his friends, and now had lately been revived by *Blackwood's Magazine.*

Lady Byron was a tragic martyr; and Mrs. Stowe identified herself with her friend. "Lady Byron was slight and almost infantine in bodily presence . . . giving the impression of fragility. . . . She was gentle, artless, with a naïve and gentle playfulness. . . . Her motions were both graceful and decided. . . . Calm, self-poised, and thoughtful, she seemed to me rather to resemble an interested spectator in the world's affairs, than an actor involved in its trials. . . . I found I was in company with a commanding mind." Here, indeed, was the heroine whom Mrs. Stowe had for long been portraying; here again was the quaint familiar portrait of herself. And Lady Byron—or was it Mrs. Stowe?—was a terrible, typical instance. "Alas!" she wrote, "the history of Lady Byron is the history of too many women in every rank of life." Yet surely she did not mean that incest was common; she was announcing that domestic martyrdom was common; she was proclaiming a cause—the cause of woman. Again and again in the tortuous convolutions of her story she urged it, as though raising a special banner; she spoke bitterly of the "slavery of woman," picturing the conspiracy by which this condition was maintained, insisting upon the "feeling which seems to underlie all English literature—that it is no matter what becomes of the woman, when the man's story is to be told." Yes—it was the cause of woman which she was pleading—woman, who was constantly betrayed or defeated by a brutal masculine conspiracy; the cause of woman was a vague but high and ennobling cause. In a noisy crescendo Mrs. Stowe named essential feminine qualities: "womanly delicacy and sacredness," "a woman's uncalculating generosity." She mentioned "a woman's weapons." What these were she did not disclose, but clearly they were noble in use and design. "Much of the beautiful patience and forgiveness of woman," she incoherently cried, "is made possible by that utter *deadness* to the sense of justice which the laws, literature, and misunderstood religion of England have sought to induce in woman as a special grace and virtue. . . ."

"I see no generosity in Mrs. Stowe—I only see great defects of judgment and a great desire for a place in public estimate as the proclaimer of a secret—and the power to boast of the confidence placed in her by such a woman as Lady B," wrote Mrs. Barwell to Sophia de Morgan at this time. Clearly enough Mrs. Stowe was pretentious; she was garrulous and morbid; it was as if all the failings of her temperament had suddenly come to the surface in grotesque and exaggerated forms. But nothing so simple as snobbery can account for this amazing outburst, nor yet that troublous desire for authority by which she had often been moved. As when she wrote *Uncle Tom's Cabin,* she seemed entranced; obloquy was being heaped upon her; but on the whole she enjoyed obloquy; it was an inevitable consequence of her rôle. Solemnly she proclaimed her defense of Lady Byron to be "the severest self-sacrifice that one friend can perform for another . . . the most solemn and difficult tribute to justice that a human being can be called upon to render." Her obscure sense of rapture was noted by her friends. Mrs. Fields said that she spoke and acted as though she "recognized herself to be an instrument breathed upon by the Divine Spirit." Willful and baffled and confused, in her own view she had again exemplified the messianic purpose.

"After the slave, then the woman," Wendell Phillips had cried in the fifties, as the new feminist movement began to take bold and aggressive forms. Something of the accusatory stress had long underlain the feminist platform, first articulated publicly at the famous Seneca Falls convention in 1848. "The history of mankind is the history of repeated injuries and usurpations on the part of man toward woman, having in direct object the establishment of an absolute tyranny over her," declared a manifesto framed on that occasion. In the late sixties, taking fire perhaps from the turmoil of blazing emotion which had broken forth with the war, this new effort toward liberation had abated nothing of its element of antagonism, but was assuming forms which were sharply controversial, often gay, sometimes bizarre, and always picturesque. The left wing of the feminist movement, of which Mrs. Stanton and Miss Anthony were leaders, was not concerned with the ballot alone, but with an entire reconstruction of the social and domestic position of woman; candor on the problems of marriage and divorce was reaching astonishing lengths. Scanned for its feeling rather than its story, undoubtedly *Lady Byron Vindicated* was a feminist document, the wild offshoot of a sturdy movement; Mrs. Stowe's strained syllables were part of the feminist vocabulary of the day. With her extraordinary talent for slipping blindly into a public drama without knowledge or perception of its outcome, once more she found herself abreast of a momentous agitation.

Naturally she was importuned to avow herself as an advocate. The implications of her latest manifesto were promptly recognized; Dr. Holmes mentioned them. Mrs. Stowe was moreover the most famous American woman of her day and generation. "After the slave, then the woman!" she might have echoed, for her own two loudest utterances had followed the sequence. But with a positive gesture she repudiated the public issue. "No," she declared in a hundred small allusive statements. "No," she insisted in the many domestic essays which she still continued to write. When the furor of the Byron controversy had partly subsided she became an editor of *Hearth and Home,* a journal whose opposition to the feminist movement was special and pronounced, whose single interest was heralded by a woodcut beneath the title showing a rustic cottage with children playing round the door. This was the symbol to which Mrs. Stowe continued to adhere, suggesting an antithesis with all the light inconsequence of her many heroines. Whatever her private warfare, whatever the personal rebellion which pushed her to so broad and devastating an utterance, she kept herself within the picture which she long had fancied. As she looks out of an old photograph of this period, her high cheek bones show prominently, her face is worn; she shows the scars of battle; but her curls still cluster, she wears quillings and flutings, trinkets and laces and velvet bands; a little shabby, not so animated or so bright as Nina or Tina, she might have turned in another moment to an ornate little mirror to survey herself in a waterfall hat or an oriole.

Truly, as Mrs. Stowe was fond of suggesting, the ways of women were mysterious. In her small confused personal frenzy she had thundered and hammered and created a shattering furor; she had rebelled against the entire race of men; her rage against Byron had contained a personal fury. Perhaps a familiar figure lurked beneath that fabulous embodiment of romanticism. Surely it was not that of clumsy, stumbling Calvin Stowe. With another character there may have been emotional identities, in a great gusto, something whirling and insistent and persuasive. Long before when Lyman Beecher's harsh and restless judgment had fallen upon her in the midst of her reading of the *Corsair* the two characters might have been fused in fancy; her father's long domination had begun sharply at this point. Yet strangely enough, her pronouncements of Byron's character, his poetry, and the literary circle to which he had belonged were identical with those which her father had uttered in her childhood. Her thunder was louder than Lyman Beecher's had ever been, even at the height of his power; this, perhaps, was a circumstance which he might not have relished. But the final outcome would have received his most fervent sanction. Mrs. Stowe had fixed popular attention upon Byron's private life; and in her standards lay a lasting criterion. By her extravagant power she succeeded in building another arch in the already well-grounded temple through which the arts must enter to find an American audience—the temple of morality. One of the most rebellious of his children had given new life to the Puritan tradition fifty years after Lyman Beecher had furiously ridden up and down Connecticut, seeking to establish an antique censorship.

SIX • *She was tired, after her fierce polemics, battered now, and* elderly; she would gladly have floated into a quiet backwater. "I feel like a poor old woman I once read about," she wrote to one of her daughters,

" 'Who always was tired
'Cause she lived in a house
Where help wasn't hired,'

and of whom it is related that in her dying moments

" 'She folded her hands
With the latest endeavor,
Saying nothing, dear nothing,
Sweet nothing forever.'

I luxuriate in laziness. I don't want to do anything or go anywhere." But quiescence escaped her, and she was to be far from silent. Almost at once she embarked upon the adventure which beguiled nearly all the famous persons of her time—public lecturing under the auspices of the so-called lyceum, that early hope of a spare democratic culture, which had now grown to an affair of prodigious circuits. All the oratory of an abundant period was being poured out to audiences waiting to hear the best that was known and thought in the world; the fever was at its second great height, after a flare in the fifties. The feminists were on the road; P. T. Barnum was offering an inexhaustibly popular address on temperance and money-making; Ingersoll with vast arabesques of rhetoric was commanding an immense, far-flung public. In part because of her first famous novel but rather more as result of the notoriety created by her book on Byron, Mrs. Stowe was drawn into the great, steadily moving, noisy procession; the terms offered her were irresistible; and she still needed money. Some of her children, it seems, were still dependent upon her, as was Calvin Stowe; and she had her two houses to maintain.

Thus she began another of those long pilgrimages which had somehow woven themselves into her life since the days of her first hard journey across the Alleghanies into the West. She had never known her public; absent and remote, bent upon her own errands, she had remained consistently aloof from the immense numbers which she had commanded. Now at sixty-one she set forth to show herself before them, to lift her voice before people whom she scarcely saw, and would never see again, reading passages from *Uncle Tom* or from her latest book, *Oldtown Fireside Stories,* a collection of New England tales which, even more precisely than her *Oldtown Folks,* she had derived from the reminiscences of Calvin Stowe. Her first reading was a failure. Before her next engagement, at Tremont Temple in Boston, she galvanized herself into action, rumpled up her hair till it stood on end, told Annie Fields that she looked like Lyman Beecher, and swept her audience with her. She was always arousing herself; on she went over the widening distances with an immense determination, reading in great gas-lit wooden halls or dim church parlors, sometimes up at dawn to catch trains, often waiting for hours in bare little wayside stations. Travel was still slow and irregular; by day there was only the wretched accommodation of overcrowded, overheated, badly ventilated common cars, by night the even more dubious comfort of the so-called drawing-room. Often she had no chance for rest between her train and her engagement; at hotels bad coffee, worse tea, and ill-cooked food were the rule; she often suffered from cold. In a mild fatigued way she enjoyed seeing the shy young women or little girls named Harriet or Eva who mounted her platforms after the lectures; a deaf old woman came miles merely to gaze upon her, saying, "Bless you.

I come jist to see you. I'd rather see you than the Queen." But in the main she drove forward in a haze. From time to time Calvin Stowe would write to her querulously and beseechingly; as in the old days he thought himself on the point of death; and she replied as then with a faint asperity, yet with a belated tenderness. "Please do *want,* and *try,* to remain with us yet a while longer. . . . It grieves me to think you are dull and I not with you. . . . I check off place after place as the captive does his days of imprisonment. . . . On the whole it is as easy a way of making money as I have ever tried," she added wearily, "though no way is perfectly easy." When she had completed a moderately successful circuit she joined Professor Stowe in Florida, and found him still attempting to lift an obstinate head above the tide of her fame. "I would have you understand," he announced to a seeker after celebrities, and he pompously drew his stout figure to its full height, "that *I* am the proprietor and protector of Mrs. Stowe and of this place." And she too, at least in public, could have her arrogant turns: in Florida, to a southern audience, she chose to read passages from *Uncle Tom's Cabin,* and continued stridently even after many of her hearers had left the hall.

A second time she went out on a long tour, but either she found the labor too arduous, or the demand to behold a famous figure of the past had been satisfied; she abandoned the lecture field. Her work, however, was far from being finished. She wrote—she was obliged to write—incessantly: simple, fluent little tales, light and glossy novels, poems, sketches, small essays; she made compilations; the bulk of her hack work was enormous. At last she had to sell the great Hartford house and take a smaller one; when Professor Stowe grew feeble she sold the house at Mandarin in Florida, and lacked thereafter the warmth and comfort of that retreat. Her husband's demands were unceasing during his long last invalidism; she would write for a few minutes, and then turn to answer his plaintive questions, or run a little errand to find some object which he required. She grew more and more abstracted; all mental efforts taxed her; but still she wrote—*Palmetto Leaves, Betty's Bright Idea, A Dog's Mission;* these were the fruits of her struggling years. Her face changed, and grew still; it was now a mask, greatly simplified, with that obliteration of subtle chiseling which often comes to those who have appeared much in public—a face which could hardly be identified with the bright and willful countenance of her girlhood. Severity was there, yet with all the effect of stillness, no composure. Beneath the incidence of her deadening toil appeared again the burden of her old theme, the trouble of the old vexing question. *Poganuc People* was her final novel; faintly and charmingly it portrayed an idealized childhood in Litchfield, yet with the repeated hint of deprivation; with a touch of the old bitterness it drew Lyman Beecher, and traveled over the eternal issues. Then, at last, roused to an aggressive sense of her many triumphs, Mrs. Stowe prepared her papers for a biography to be written by her son Charles, and gave it a sturdy dedication borrowed from another pilgrim. "I am going to my father's, and though with great difficulty I am got hither, yet I do not repent me of all the troubles I have been at to arrive where I am. My sword I give to him that shall succeed me in my pilgrimage," she repeated with a touch of the old grandeur, "and my courage and skill to him that can get it." In 1887 Calvin Stowe died, and the band of her heaviest obligation was snapped.

Her long struggles were ended. She might have died, but she did not. For all her fragility she lived on to a hardy old age; and with something of her old pertinacity she realized a wish. Lyman Beecher had found in revery the path to damnation; her domestic cares had seldom permitted the indulgence; she had snatched only half hours. Now she fell into a prolonged daydream, as if she proposed to enjoy in freedom the mood which she had so often been denied. The vexing responsibilities of the household, of the publishing world, of the platform were gone; carelessly she let them go. Vanished too were the troublous questions which had long perturbed her; it was as if Professor Stowe had been the stubborn symbol of a heavy past. Now on the brink of an eternity which she had so often found terrifying, she drifted into a faintly colored, unstressed world, the realm of her earliest fancy. A tiny withered figure in a garden hat, like the faded replica of a romantic heroine, she slipped out to pick flowers, with a vagueness in her eyes; bird-notes and old melodies pleased her; in a thin treble she sang of that expectant faith she had labored to maintain, sang *The Shining Shore,* which had first become known in the years before her marriage, and had been sung over and again during the Civil War. Whitman had heard it as he walked the wards of the great soldiers' hospital in Washington—

> "My days are gliding swiftly by
>   And I, a pilgrim stranger,
> Would not detain them as they fly,
>   Those hours of toil and danger—"

Lyman Beecher would have kept them to the end—those hours of toil and danger; gladly enough his daughter let them go. She was hardly peaceful; in her dim habitation she was constantly moving, as though the habit of movement still lay upon her. She took many walks, made wide encirclements around the river and the town, restlessly, with unflagging vigor, a tall, raw-boned Irishwoman following in attendance. "Ma, where *have* you been," a sharp voice would cry when she came in, wet and bedraggled after her long wanderings. But in her unquiet ecstasy she could no longer be reached; the isolation which she had often sought was now complete. Occasionally, it is true, an insistent question would arouse her to something like remembrance; once a stranger spoke to her of *Uncle Tom's Cabin,* and after a pause she answered in a loud, harsh voice, "God wrote it." Now and then her discordant laugh would shatter the air. But for the most part time moved by for her in simple cycles, day by day, year by year. Amazingly, swiftly, her whole life slid into the past. As she lived on into the middle nineties, her books, the monuments of her many struggles, began to crumble away like her memories. *Uncle Tom's Cabin* was still read as the relic of an era; but the single novel, *Oldtown Folks,* which should have a claim to permanence, was already being disregarded because she wrote so much that was ephemeral. Throughout that long tumultuous effort, in the great mass of her writing, she had been herself only briefly, it would seem, in a few passages of untroubled grace that had floated up as by chance. Perhaps the natural country of her mind lay within the quiet unmarked distances of these last years, or in those forbidden regions of revery which she had known briefly as a child on Litchfield Hill. Yet these, too, had been a refuge. Haunted even in a final solitude, she fled. To the end the unfolding patterns of escape opened momentously before her.

Henry Ward Beecher

ONE • *Southern Indiana was a rich and ample Arcadia in the*
opening decades of the nineteenth century. Water-willows
fringed the streams; groves of beeches spread in calm perfection over
slope after gentle slope. Grassy intervales, deep bottom-lands, and scattered black-swamps gave the green heights an opulent root. Near the
Ohio River, tangles of blackberries and wild grapes were laced among
the hardier growth of trees; and yellow papaws grew thick.

At the river's changing edge the idyllic mood was shattered, or at least
transformed. Here and there were flung low clusters of flimsy huts and
cabins on muddy flats where trees had been ruthlessly cut, where even
the few pretentious houses had been set down at the side of rough roads
without yards or gardens. One of these, the village of Lawrenceburg, precariously caught within the bend where the Miami joins the Ohio, was
all but swept away each year by freshets and floods when the larger river
overflowed its banks and the rushing White Water poured down upon
the tableland above the town. Washed up by chance and preserved by
good fortune, Lawrenceburg kept its hapless character; for twenty years
or more after its settlement in 1802 the place remained a lazy hamlet.
In the warm, moist air even the scream of the bluejays was muted; across
the river were the Kentucky hills, green and rich and hazy; the river
flowed by; Hoosier fiddlers, always idlers, played expertly on single
strings, joined by a chorus.

> Old Dan Tucker, he got drunk,
> He fell in the fire, and he kicked up a chunk. . . .
>
> O—clear the way for old Dan Tucker. . . .
> Come too late for to get his supper!
>
> Old Dan Tucker was a fine old man,
> He washed his face in a frying pan,
> He combed his hair with a wagon wheel. . . .

Hoe-downs, barbecues, and shivarees rose to a wild and dubious hilarity; bold and fancy steps were invented; and corn-whiskey became plentiful.

At last, after a careless generation, new features appeared in this easy existence. Little river-boats began churning up and down with greater speed and frequency. Corduroy roads were ribbed fanwise into the north and west over wider stretches. Wagonloads of country produce were driven to the waterside; a small sudden business would break at the landing. Disapproval of the gay, the shiftless, the slack-twisted became manifest among certain of the more prosperous inhabitants, who had adopted Methodism.

Wedged in between the topmost stratum and the casual band below was a small group of Presbyterians, who seemed in doubt whether to be rigid with the thrifty or joyous with the stragglers. Obviously the Puritan tradition, elsewhere aristocratic in the West, had failed to gain a solid foothold in Lawrenceburg. The situation, indeed, was anomalous; and the Presbyterian Home Mission Board finally bent upon it a severe and anxious scrutiny. As result, in 1837, immediately after his graduation from Lane Seminary at Cincinnati, young Henry Ward Beecher was sent to augment the numbers and to guide the wavering purposes of the indifferent little assemblage.

Young Beecher was a handsome young man of twenty-four with a thick mop of dark hair, wide blue eyes, and full pressed lips. In a tall stock and a quilted coat with flaring lapels he looked the bold and dashing cavalier. Plainly he was being impeded on his way to an agreeable destiny; he all but glares out of an old picture of this period. "The fact is, I never had any choice about it," he once flung out, speaking of his entrance into the ministry. Born in Litchfield in 1813, one of the middle members of Lyman Beecher's large flock, as a child he had been stolid and shy, thick of speech and uncertain of memory; he had often seemed stupid. Riding with his solemn stepmother when he was still so small that his feet failed to reach the floor of the family chaise, he had heard a bell tolling a death, and Mrs. Beecher had inquired what his thoughts were on such occasions. Poor little Henry had no suitable thoughts. "*I* think, was that soul *prepared*," said his stepmother. Against such onslaughts Henry had not been altogether defenseless. Between himself and the noisy, purposeful mob of elders, ministers, parishioners, and striving other children by whom he had been surrounded—between himself and Lyman Beecher—he had interposed a barrier of indifference. When he grew older and his father had swooped down upon him with high insistence urging him to struggle for that desperately difficult state of exaltation and abasement which augured grace, Henry slipped out of reach. His feelings, as Lyman Beecher bitterly remarked, were like "the wind on the willow." His father had prayed and besought and questioned without avail; Henry remained irrepressibly light-hearted. "I was feeling quite jolly again," he said wryly of an interval between the elder Beecher's invasions.

Pushed into Amherst as a step toward the ministry, Henry had soon been carried away by the new science of phrenology, which provided a simple chart and compass for the knowledge of character, but not one which the Calvinistic mind was likely to approve. Phrenology bestowed upon the human creature large and pleasing virtues like Firmness, Benevolence, Philoprogenitiveness, and Moral Courage, when it was clear that man had no native virtues at all. Dipping into this dubious science —in which he believed all his life—young Henry began to speak in public, on any subject, on any occasion, as if now that he was out of the Beecher household some hidden inner gift had been set free. But for the most part he loafed: always a mediocre student, he nearly failed in his studies.

After his graduation in 1834 he had been dragged in his father's wake to Cincinnati, and entered Lane Seminary. Events then had fallen upon him thick and fast. He was one of the tiny remnant ignominiously left behind when the Lane students quitted the Seminary in a body as a result of the elder Beecher's equivocal attitude toward free speech. Henry's conviction do not appear in the record, nor do those of Lyman Beecher in relation to a bit of insurgency which promptly followed on the part of his son. At the time of the Birney riots, when a mob raged in the streets of Cincinnati threatening the destruction of Birney's press, Henry hurried to the defense and had even molded bullets. The issues at stake were those of a free press and free speech. But this was a brief excursion. When the elder Beecher's heresy trial was being noised through the Great Valley and throughout the land, with councils held and conflicts begun along many subsidiary lines and with the embittered foregathering of many ministers, Henry was kept at his father's heels, was singled out indeed as a special companion, and traveled with him to Pittsburgh and elsewhere.

"I know you're plagued good at twisting," Henry had drawled to his father before a tableful of elders and ministers at one stage of the contest. "But if you can twist your creed onto the Westminster Confession you can twist better than I think you can." Dashed for a moment, Lyman

Beecher had answered tartly, "All my boys are smart, and one of them is impudent," and had plunged into a further argument. Acquitted at last, he had turned to the case of Henry.

In the course of the long and perplexing debate his son had quietly lapsed into skepticism. He had, moreover, taken a leaf out of his father's own book. "You will have your troubles, young gentlemen," Lyman Beecher had cried to his small remaining class of students at Lane, "go where you will; but when they come, don't dam them up!" Naturally he was not referring to desperate troubles of the spirit, but to such minor problems as the lack of money in an unendowed seminary, or those cabals among ministers which induced heresy trials. But Henry had seized upon this counsel as the most salient his father had to offer. He was now letting all his troubles slide, eternal questions with the rest. "Here I mean to be at my ease," he wrote in an early diary, "and not molest myself with any obligations to write so much, or so often, or so anything; but in mental *dishabille* I shall stroll through my mind and do as I choose. . . ."

"I am not reflective enough to make a record of reflections and feelings very definite," he added lazily. Literary subjects engrossed him; he was reading the novels of Scott, and the poetry of Byron and Burns. Presently he began writing for one of the Cincinnati papers. Apparently he had turned his back on the ministry.

Lyman Beecher always kept an agreeable sense of any possible convert as a quarry; the language of the chase was still appropriately his own. Adroit, lovable, stringent, this rugged hound of heaven tirelessly pursued his son amid the thickly crowding evidences that the Millennium was at hand. With all his easy doubling and rebellion, Henry was no match for an old and subtle hunter. At last, after an abysmal depression and a perfervid inner questioning, he found himself striding through the woods at Walnut Hills wrapt in peace. Before he knew it he was ordained, though not without a lively steeplechase at the end. In the heresy trials his father was generally considered to have taken Old School ground; naturally when Henry was ordained he professed Old School doctrines. But in the few weeks that elapsed between his son's examination and ordination Lyman Beecher had suddenly committed himself to the liberal contingent. At a rapid gallop Henry had swung about and followed him. Perhaps his father failed to notice that Henry had carelessly ridden on—on—where, indeed?

Securing an advance on his first year's meager salary at Lawrenceburg, he went back to New England to marry Eunice Bullard, the daughter of a country doctor living near Worcester, to whom he had become engaged after a brief courtship as a lad of seventeen at Amherst. "Who would want to marry a girl who couldn't sing?" he had asked scornfully during a visit at the Bullard house with her younger brother; they were discussing the marriage of a classmate. Suddenly he had realized that Eunice lacked a singing voice, and that she had heard him; she was discomposed. In a rush of remorse he had fallen in love with her. A little older than young Beecher, she was mature, and she was scarcely joyful. She too had endured a Puritan upbringing, but without that relief of lively humor which Lyman Beecher could offer when he chose. Once when she and her sister had appeared at the table with new silk dresses of their own making, cut low in the neck, their father had flung hot soup over them, remarking with violence that they must be cold; and he had opposed Eunice's engagement because young Beecher had no money. She was persistent; she at last wrung from him an unwilling consent, and she asserted her taste in the matter of costume. A daguerreotype taken about this time shows her in a flowered delaine cut low enough to reveal her small sloping shoulders and fitting closely about her thin little waist. But the day the likeness was taken she must have smothered tears behind the direct and obstinate glance of her narrowly set eyes; her small mouth is closely curled. Clearly she harbored sensibilities; and these were to be sorely tried in the new life upon which she had been so eager to embark. Once Henry forgot her altogether in the confusion of changing cars at a junction; she was lost in the crowd, and found him at last, careless and comfortable, gazing out the window of the train. As the two pushed through the latter stages of their journey by canal-boat and wagon she grew immensely frightened. The sprawling hamlet at the end proved an unhappy climax. Two rooms over a stable fronting the river on one side and a dirty courtyard on the other made the only habitation which her young husband could afford; a deal table, an old bedstead, a husk mattress and pillows, some strips of calico, a pair of plated candlesticks, comprised their household equipment. Henry's money had been expended on the journey; so she sold her cloak to provide a small bit of capital; and since further installments on his salary were paid irregularly or not at all, like many ministers' wives before her she eked out the scanty sums by work as a seamstress, and took in boarders.

Except on the Sabbath young Beecher apparently found life in Lawrenceburg agreeable enough. In a happy-go-lucky, negligent fashion he helped bake, cook, and clean the house, and often did the washing. Likewise he swept the floors of his little church, built the fires, and lit the lard-oil lamps; but there was no doubt about it, he was hardly successful as a minister. "I mean to write down little plans and devices as they occur; else I may forget them," he had declared in an early diary; but he forgot them continually. Each week, depressed by the ordeal of preaching, he would resolve to leave the ministry and take a farm; but in a day or two he was buoyant again. With a happy crew he hunted and fished and spent hours on the river picking up driftwood— a beguiling occupation in that lazy climate. His people liked him in spite of his inability to rouse them. A year slid by, and another; two children came. Eunice Beecher spoke of "misjudged or unguarded friendships," and of "the true western dislike of labor." She was sure that her casual visitors came to "spy out the land." Beecher remained oblivious, with small thought for the morrow, and less ambition. In 1839 he received a call from a larger church in Indianapolis, but he let the question pass, and accepted the charge only at the command of the Synod.

Perhaps in his carelessness lay an instinct for self-preservation. The new town presented an arduous existence. Lying in the midst of flat and heavy country, Indianapolis was laid out like a sun, with streets for rays; but the brilliancy of hope seemed realized mainly in the pervasive hue of yellow. The clay was a thick yellow clinging plaster, often so deep that trips from house to house had to be made on horseback; the same color was repeated in the countenances of the inhabitants as result of perennial onslaughts of chills and fever; jeans and linsey-woolsey were dyed with copperas and butternut; and saleratus biscuit with fried corn-meal were staples of diet. Here and there were green lawns with white palings, and the hint of comfort; but these were the exception. The Beechers' first house, a one story cabin on an alley, proved so leaky and damp that they were obliged to leave it; from the first they both suffered from ague; and one of their children died. Little sympathy was offered them on this occasion; illness was a common matter; every one had been sick, every one had lost children. Later Beecher harshly described his people as the "refuse" of the stream of immigration—the "detritus"— and said that they didn't know how to feel. In truth they were a mixed lot, strays from New England and homesteaders who had moved on from Ohio or central New York; but they possessed certain qualities in common. Beneath their impassive languor lay a hard core of persistence; tired and somber and malaria-ridden, they gazed upon the young incumbent, demanded the shock of a revival, and meant to have it. Once, laboring desperately, he brought them to tears, and was told by an elder that they wanted tartar, not sugar. Vexed and isolated, he found himself overwhelmed by doubts both as to his calling and his faith. He tried shouting axioms of belief aloud to his congregation, and fell into a deeper slough of doubt and questioning. Presently he rode forth to the wilderness camp-meetings which were beginning to spring up at a dozen points in Indiana and Ohio, caught some of their excitement, hastened back and tried to break the apathy of his people; bit by bit he aroused them, but not to the pitch which they expected. Overstrained by excitement, he fell to farming on a small scale, and wrote essays for an agricultural gazette. Once when heavy rains had filled a ravine behind his house he sallied forth to rescue a cat perched on a rail half out of the water, and unable to float over the miniature bayou in a tub, he fastened together two tubs, contrived some oars, was upset, and spent a long morning lazily drifting about in the hot sun. The excuse for idling pleased him, but peremptory members of his flock noted the heedless waste of time.

At last with shrill hysteria, as if he were bodying forth some difficult inner stress, he burst into his famous *Lectures to Young Men,* shouting forth variations and progressions on the theme of indolence. Those ruminant do-nothings, those odd chips of character who never fall into any scheme and never wish to, those misfits who haunt river-fronts or the comfortable corners of the village store—he condemned them with violence; he censured every type of idler; employing to the full that language of the senses which moralists often make their own, he traced the terrible downward path which each inevitably must follow. Revery of all sorts was dangerous, he bitterly insisted. "The daydreams of indolent youth glow each hour with warmer colors and bolder adventures. . . . Mere pleasure, sought outside usefulness, existing by itself, is fraught with poison." Pleasure—all pleasure—the pleasures of the senses and even of the mind: he denounced them all. Rising to an angry inflation, he pointed out the "artful insinuations and mischievous polish which too often lurk in literature"; he condemned Chaucer, Byron, Moore, and Bulwer-Lytton, excused Shakespeare, and declared the French nation to be the fountain-head of licentiousness and the burial ground of religion. With a fierce eagerness he railed against the theater—"an expiring evil" —the circus, card-playing, dancing horses, boxing men, and Fanny Elssler.

On he went at a headlong pace to describe many a quaint and subtle snare for the senses—"luxurious couches, plushy carpets from Oriental looms, pillows of eiderdown, carriages contrived with cushions and springs to make motion imperceptible.

"Laborious occupations are avoided. Money is to be earned by genteel leisure, with the help of fine clothes, and by the soft seductions of smooth hair and luxuriant whiskers.

"All your companions have jewelry; you will want a ring, a seal, or a golden watch, or an ebony cane, a silver toothpick, or a quizzing-glass. Thus item presses on item, and you lose all sense of *the value of property!*"

Whatever his impetus, at a stroke Beecher had knit together the strands of a long tradition. The *Lectures* followed precisely that hard pattern laid down at the end of the eighteenth century by Timothy Dwight, president of Yale College, prime leader in the Puritan renascence, and the perceptor of Lyman Beecher, who had repeated the attack in the so-called "morals campaign" in New England when Henry was a child. Here was the same diatribe against idleness, against pleasure, against the arts, the same insistence upon the value of property. With the picturesque modern embellishments added by young Beecher these admonitions were to go rolling down the years. First published in 1844, the *Lectures* ran through many editions, were read up and down the land, continued in popularity for decades, and were printed without change as late as 1890.

His people were shaken at last. Perhaps a homely audience in a raw little town was flattered by the assumption that their vices were romantic and worldly. Bacchanalian feasts in Indianapolis were rare; the wraith-like Fanny Elssler was a legendary figure. At times a circus wagon straggled through with a blackface comedian, a juggler, and a sluggish animal in a rickety cage as the sum of its attractions; but fashionable actors—did they exist even in the vicious purlieus of New York? Then, after the grinding confusion of the first pioneering, any social cult must have seemed solid ground; stability spelled respite; order was a symbol of the good life; and the Puritan tradition promised both respectability and righteousness through denial. Men were soon expelled from Beecher's church for gambling and drinking; the taboo against dancing grew rigorous; the theater became the sum of evil. Of all the doubtful characters now coming under a strict surveillance perhaps the fiddler alone maintained a placid dignity—at least in Indiana—the single artist of the place and period, charming away objections, enchanting hungry listeners.

With young Beecher's assistance a solid social censorship was being established. Yet strangely enough, he had hardly delivered the *Lectures* when he wheeled about and passionately denounced social tyranny in any form. Roughly argumentative, he assailed the very type of social regimen which he had just been upbuilding, that austere supervision of private thoughts, morals, and casual pleasures which the community was ready to assume. His *Dissuasive against Moral Intolerance* was a bold word for personal freedom, spoken early, and remaining fresh, as if the oblivion into which it speedily fell had sealed it away, preserving its force. The narrow despotism exercised by religious sects, by clubs, societies, lodges, and even political parties, Beecher specified roundly. "Their authority, usually deemed moral, may be and full often is of the most enslaving kind." He pushed to the extreme instance of such control—over opinion. "Perfect emancipation is effected only when the mind is permitted to form, to express, and to employ its own convictions of truth, on all subjects, as it chooses," he cried. Hurrying onward, he cast a long look about the country. "The United States is, I believe, the only land in which offensive opinions are MOBBED. . . . America, with her Bill of Rights, her Declaration of Independence, her free Constitution, this land of liberty, which no man tires of praising, has had the sole honor of such mobs!"

In the end Beecher transformed the *Dissuasive* into an invective against mob domination. Perhaps he was moved in part by some occasion now lost to view; ironically he mentioned mobs against abolitionists as no mobs at all. But the anti-slavery cause can hardly have provided the goad for this outburst; his two or three anti-slavery sermons had been preached as matters of routine at the request of the Synod; he was not yet deeply committed to the cause. His antipathy rose to the sharp accents of a personal cry; his handling of the theme grew thick and labored with excitement; the mob—he hated it, hated its fury, its force, its possessiveness, the violent inflictions of its will. Liberty—the claims of the individuals within and against the implacable crowd—his insistence upon these ran through his speech as though he were pledging himself to revolt.

The singular circumstance was that during these years Beecher was yielding to the most powerful of mob emotions, overflowing all bounds, in the forest revivals. Here indeed was no willful infliction of harsh commands, but something more subtle and profound. That great primitive outbreak in the Cumberland region of Kentucky and Tennessee at the beginning of the nineteenth century had apparently created a deeply cellared consciousness from which later revivals were continually flowing in strange seasonal ritual. A bright and fervid certainty was again abroad, with its highest peak in the majestic West. In the forest camp-meetings the tempestuous joyful expectancy was reaching a confused exaltation, as though all the hopes of the great fertile region had been gathered there. In the light of camp-fires and blowing torches, by broad rivers at night or in the depths of forest groves, the watchwords of hope were being shrilly chanted, horns blown, hymns sung in blissful delirium, with crowds coming forward to improvised altars, where the rites of baptism were given in breathless silence, amid rushing waters and rustling leaves.

Into this huge rhythmic drama of regeneration young Beecher dipped and dipped again, as into an inexhaustible fount, a bottomless pool, as from an irresistible attraction. The expectant, plastic crowd seemed to offer him a haven; its lack of insistence might have been a blessing; by that vast surging overflow of feeling he was assuaged at last, swept into a consciousness outside himself; complexities were resolved, fatigue fell away. The liberty which he had been seeking might have been that of untrammeled emotion. At ease in that dark exultant tempest he began to appear as a leader among the many roving revivalists, preached at the camp-meetings with enormous freedom, swayed them, raised that extraordinary blissful hope to a higher pitch, and from the scale of those great assemblages seemed to gain a stature of his own. Riding back to Indianapolis he found his tasks there dull; his flock was small; he still felt the tension of their disapproval; he had never quite won them; even with his augmented power he was unable to win them now. But into the great forest meetings he could swing again and again, often at the cost of prodigious exertions as he rode all day or all night, slept for a few hours at dirty questionable little inns, and rode forth once more. Floated and buoyed, he preached daily for weeks, for months, without respite, exercising a power which was thrilling to his closely gathered hearers. His labors were a miracle of unbroken endurance. Nor were they without their tangible reward. Certain gentlemen from Brooklyn heard Beecher's triumphant revivalism during a visit in the West. In 1847 he received a call from Plymouth Church in Brooklyn, an organization recently formed on the Congregational principle. He was eligible for this pulpit; ministers still moved from the Presbyterian church government to the Congregational, and back again. Aglow with excitement he paid a visit to Brooklyn, and returned bent upon making the change; he had let a plummet into the life of the West—sounding what depths?—and was ready to go. Difficulties arose; to most clerical minds preaching in the West was a sacred undertaking; to leave it was a dereliction. Lyman Beecher feared the wickedness of New York for this incorrigibly careless son of his. There were debates; and Beecher's congregation accumulated resistance.

Eunice Beecher turned the scale. A defeated pioneer, she had steadily failed in health; and malaria still raged in Indiana. So with their four children the Beechers traveled away late in the summer of 1847, uncomfortably established in a wooden box-car with crosswise boards for seats; this was the first train to leave Indianapolis. Mrs. Beecher looked years older than her ruddy young husband; she was not only ill, she was disillusioned; and hers was a literal mind, working with an austere and relentless purpose. For twenty years she kept the outlines of her experiences in the West intact, and set them down at last in an anonymous novel called *From Dawn to Daylight*. This early novel of protest, one of the few personal indictments of American pioneer existence, began with her marriage, encircled her life in Lawrenceburg, and was completed by the lagging years in Indianapolis; and the inference was clear that in the midst of rough hardships and a relentless poverty Eunice had borne the heavier burdens. Small sharp observations on her husband's character broke through. In her portrayal of western villages, dirt, laziness, and a callous unconcern were exemplified almost without relief. Familiar persons thronged in her story; Mrs. Beecher had a knack for brief and salient characterization. In her preface she declared that her narrative was "literally true," and added that if "the still, small voice" revealed certain of the originals of her characters to themselves, this was a contingency which she could not avoid. Naturally the veil of anonymity was quickly pierced; Mrs. Beecher's novel was not relished in Indiana. But she was impartial; faithfully enough in this relentless tale, she drew a small portrait of herself: she was prim and hard-working and desperately thrifty; it was clear that her unspoken longings ran deep. What these were perhaps was never said, but at least for her the West—"that great enigmatical land," in the words of a traveler—had proved a harsh and endless battleground.

TWO • *Brooklyn spelled civilization. The fair-sized town was* spaciously spread upon its heights, fringing prettily into small farms and suburban cottages; its broad, trim streets, lined with ailanthus, had a look both decorous and exotic. "Cool, fragrantly airy, and no mobs!" exclaimed one of its inhabitants with rapture. Each morning gentlemen of Brooklyn stepped into their barouches and drove by way of the ferry to New York, where they conducted prosperous affairs; at evening they returned to an exemplary elegance and quiet. Plymouth Church was composed of such persons; the plain small wooden building without a spire housed their comfortable number. They were startled by their new young preacher who looked like a western farmer in his loose coat and low collar, who flung a broad hat on a table when he ascended the platform, who had shouted defiantly at the outset that he would wear no fetters and be bound by no precedent. It was quickly rumored that he lacked reverence. "There is something of the power of growth peculiar to the great western wilds about this young man, but somewhat of its rudeness also," said Fredrika Bremer a few years later. But his sedate congregation was soon captivated by the swift jolts and turns of his speech, his quick humor, his free conversation about himself in the pulpit. Over them he poured the flood of an accumulated and primitive excitement.

Beecher promptly had the pulpit cut away so that he could range the platform. When the old building burned and a new church was built, the broad galleries and the rows of seats on the main floor were placed in a close curve under his direction, with the platform brought well forward so that he stood in the midst of his audience. "It is perfect," he cried, "because it is built on a principle—the principle of social and personal magnetism, which emanates reciprocally from a speaker and from a close throng of hearers. . . . I want them to surround me, so that they will come up on every side, and behind me, so that I shall be in the center of the crowd, and have the people surge all about me!" They surged, they thronged; even in these earlier years it was necessary only to follow the crowd from the ferry in order to find Plymouth Church; the new, large building began to overflow. "Heretofore I have had to labor uphill; to carry everything, and do everything," Beecher wrote. "Now I seem to have gone to the opposite extreme. . . . Now it is a question how I shall come out of prosperity." Long afterwards he remarked, "I came East with a silken noose about my neck and did not know it." But the noose—if it existed—remained smooth and silken, indeed, and sufficiently long. "Henry's people are more than ever in love with him," wrote his sister Mrs. Stowe after a brief visit in Brooklyn, adding that they had raised his salary to thirty-three hundred dollars —a princely sum for a minister in those days—and had presented him with a beautiful horse and carriage, no doubt contrived with cushions and springs to make motion imperceptible, so that he too could drive to New York in elegance. When it became clear that he had overtaxed his energies by labors in the new church his people sent him abroad for a holiday.

Still fresh from the western wilds, one of the early innocents abroad, young Henry Ward Beecher, traveling alone, made the grand tour in 1850. At his first glimpse of a ruined castle he burst into tears and was "entirely possessed and almost demented. . . . I walked in a dream along the line of the westward wall. . . . I seemed to spread myself over all that was around or before me . . . or rather to draw everything within me. . . . I had never before looked upon an *old* building! . . . The cornices were not wood painted *like* stone, but stone curled, and carved.

. . . With us stairs are such matters of mere convenience that I had no conception of the architectural effects to which they are susceptible. . . . The fact is, *we* have no ceilings to paint, ours being low, circumscribed, and without grandeur. . . . The number of pictures—the great number of pictures—not stuff to fill up—but noble, enchanting pieces, some of vast size, of wonderful brilliancy, of novel subjects! . . ." Suddenly he was overwhelmed by an unaccustomed solitude, drifted into a faint melancholy, his bold excitement gone, and in a peculiarly feminine figure described himself as thistledown floating on the wind, or "a broken-stemmed flower that the river has cast upon the bank. . . . What if I should die abroad!" he wrote in a swift revulsion of terror. "A shock it would be to many—but in a month's time only a few would feel it!" As he turned once more to the galleries he was swept again by a confused exhilaration, wept, laughed, resolved to control this amazing cascade of feeling, but could not. "I am here," he cried, "I am yours; do what you will with me; I am here to be intoxicated."

"Vivacious even beyond the temperature of Paris, and mirthful even to wildness, seeming not to know that there is such a thing as a care in the world"—so he was described by an English acquaintance of the time. In a transport of enthusiasm he hastened home and began to form his own collections of paintings, engravings, bronzes, books. Books—he was nothing of a student; many of his volumes remained uncut to the end of his life. According to popular legend he had no study in his Brooklyn house. "A library is the soul's burial ground," he had declared at Oxford; the Bodleian was a "Dead Sea of books." Yet irresistibly attracted by some bright salience of idea or of title, by something color-ful or fabulous in character or tradition, he purchased books in quantities, Boccaccio and Rabelais, Baron Munchausen and Fielding, the tales of Aesop, the *Anatomy of Melancholy*, the Bhâgavâd-Ghita, and the vol-umes of a hundred contemporary writers. His walls were now thickly hung with paintings and engravings. Color affected him like an appetite; he became increasingly interested in small decorative pieces—perhaps because they could be touched or handled and slipped into a pocket—sweetmeat boxes, enamels, little trays, little jars and vases, small porce-lains, examples of Bohemian and Venetian glass; the tops of bookcases, mantels, and stands in the Brooklyn house were crowded by objects of decoration. He was entranced by rich surroundings; he seemed bent upon acquiring each last object of that dangerous luxury which only a few years before he had denounced. Friends who knew his tastes aug-mented his accumulations by gifts of bright silken scarves, embroidered cushions, velvet drapes, and plushy carpets and rugs. Absorbed in pleasurable fantasies of his own, Beecher made a collection of stuffed humming birds, and another of birds of paradise; jewels intrigued him; he assembled ornaments which were never worn, and entered upon a lifelong quest for fine unset gems—opals, amethysts, sapphires, topazes; his yellow diamond, acquired in later years, was said to have a European reputation. These stones he carried loosely in his pockets; he called them "color-opiates," and used them to induce rest or sleep at times of undue excitement; gazing at their small intense blaze he grew relaxed.

A resistant, somewhat grim and gliding figure in the background, Mrs. Beecher offered her protests. If she had resented a narrow penury in the West, equally she disapproved the new refulgence by which she was now surrounded; neither condition fitted her view of an appropriate life. From most of her husband's activities she held aloof; his friends seldom spoke of her; many of them found her ungracious. Beecher slipped his new acquisitions into the house in spite of her censure and if possible without her knowledge, joked in public and in private about his strategy, spoke in this connection of "cosy little bills for books and engravings" which it was his task to conceal. Indeed, it is in large part through his portrayal that the figure of Mrs. Beecher emerges during these years; in the familiar essays which he was now beginning to write for the newly founded *Independent* he was always finding grist for his exuberant mill from his own experiences; naturally enough these included domestic episodes. He declared that he disliked "an insanity of neatness," and repeatedly illustrated the point by circumstances which had to do with his study table, his bureau drawers, his letters, his pockets—in a mood of oveflowing good humor. Equally he joked about his own shortcomings. "There is no pleasure so great as that of buying a book you cannot afford to pay for," he declared, and continued his hunt for new embellishments.

"Art was the craze" in the fifties. Plunged into a bright new prosperity, men were spending money upon ornamentation of all kinds with lavish abundance. If the forties had roared, with a more specific intention the fifties clamored—clamored for things, novel, glittering, and costly. The art of painting had burst into efflorescence; private dealers were showing bold views of the spectacular West and quaint metropolitan street-scenes which cast a glamor even over poverty. Journeyman portrait painters did a thriving business; sculptors of similar rank hardly lagged behind; the owners of pink brick dwellings were beginning to crowd their rooms with furniture adorned by tricksy little turns and flourishes which were considered French. Largely enjoying their new leisure, the same persons were building ornate cottages in the Hudson valley or among the Berkshires. "Gentleman's places are springing up in every direction!" cried Beecher with high enthusiasm, and himself purchased a farm at Lenox—"Blossom Farm"—which was succeeded in later years by "Boscobel" at Peekskill.

With the attention of an epicure he turned to the natural world, and broadly mapped the new Zion which lay within New England and New York, a soft countryside, a semi-civilized panorama, a tribute to the human creature. In the fifties to an amazing extent the whole land still lay fallow to the eye; those tiny hymns to local and legendary beauty, so slow to arise but at last revealing the character of a landscape, were for the most part unsung. Thoreau, indeed, an unexampled pioneer, was chanting his cool and lovely praises, but his scrutiny seems to have been too delicate for the untutored perception; it was Beecher, writing and speaking in the baroque style, who became the popular naturalist of the age. Distances enchanted him—distances and profusion; if he seldom evoked exact images he suggested sensations, and by the frangible medium of mere words, familiar words, created those flowery beds of ease which had long been an object of contemplation in this country. Long past was the day when he had argued that idleness was dangerous: idleness became a duty, dream-culture a noble pursuit; indolent revery in the midst of a bosky countryside brought its own reward. Urging the still hardly respectable idea, he wrote of "delicious sensations of pleasure at life in general," of subtle experiences when "we seem to hang like a harp in the air, and all things reach forth to touch the strings for joy. . . . Flowers play their incantations upon the sense, and lead off the thoughts on many a curious wandering, in gay analogies or curious melodies of fantastic dreaming. . . . Today is goblet day. The whole heavens have been mingled with exquisite skill to a delicious flavor, and the crystal cup held out to every lip. . . . It is a luxury simply to exist." Carelessly he dipped into a warm pantheism, which had perhaps less to do with the presence of God in nature than with man basking in mellifluence. Boldly he accepted the life of the senses—that long smothered, dubious life—and celebrated good things to eat, wrote pages on apple-pie with country cream, lingered over sweet odors. The rose was "a floral nightingale," dandelions were "golden kisses." "When apple trees blossom," he cried in gaudy metaphor, "there is not a single breastpin but a whole bosom-full of gems!"

Swimming on the tide of a new opulence, Beecher became not only a poet, a naturalist—indeed the Shakespeare of the pulpit, as he was soon freely called—but the great apologist of art, defending with fervor what he called "the luxuries and embellishments of beauty." The influence of all splendid possessions must inevitably spread downward through all classes. "Be generous with beauty," he cried. In this country, out of the "great movement of humanity," was to arise such an art "as the world never saw, and would never see again in any other condition of society!"

"Why, these are the children of the antique to justify it. . . .
A new race dominating previous ones and grander far, with new
    contests,
New politics, new literatures and religions, new inventions and
    arts
These, my voice announcing. . . ."

All about lay the evidences of triumph; poverty he never saw except in the quaint, softened form in which it was appearing in contemporary paintings and chromos. Beauty was benevolence, and benevolence was everywhere; every scene was glorious and golden. A shimmering light overspread the present, the future. "Humor is the golden bounty of atmosphere in us," he declared not quite intelligibly. He spoke of the "golden light of conscience. . . . When we come to that golden gate which men have made black. . . ." Death indeed had receded to the rim of a widening golden circle; life—affirmative, immediate, in a highly ornamented Mayday world—he acknowledged and commemorated life!

In the midst of all this pride and pleasure admonishing voices were being sharply lifted. "Simplify—I say, simplify!" came a warning from the lovely wood about Walden Pond. As a new society swirled in a round of gayety, Saratoga became the symbol of a wicked silken idleness; Mrs. Potiphar appeared on the scene—gross, vulgar, and extravagant. Bitter attacks upon the new preoccupations were made by the older orthodoxy; hard-headed criticism was offered by the ranks of the reformers. Mrs. Stanton and the feminists found the "art fad" frivolous to the extreme. "The fine arts do not interest me so much as the coarse arts, which feed, clothe, house, and comfort a people," said Theodore Parker. "I would rather be a great man like Franklin than a Michael Angelo— nay, if I had a son, I should rather see him a mechanic like the late George Stephenson in England than a painter like Rubens, who only copied beauty."

"It's all moonshine," Lyman Beecher had once remarked in hard scorn of the quest for beauty—"with no doctrine, nor edification, nor sanctity in it, and I *despise it.*" Like a dark and broken emblem of the past he now crept into Plymouth Church, mute, uncertain of mind, stiffly taking a place on the pulpit steps as though to sit as close as possible to his old position of authority. He had come to Brooklyn for his long final years, as if a durable instinct had driven him to keep watch over this one of his children who was traveling farthest from his keeping. Over his oblivious head reverberated sentiments whose every sound and syllable he would have abhorred. Not only did young Beecher join the issue as to art, but he swiftly built up the resurgent, ample philosophy—so it was called—for which he became abundantly known. Transcending his earlier cry of liberty arose his new cry of love—warm and immediate, "a perpetual tropical luxuriance of blessed love. . . . I never knew how to worship until I knew how to love; and to love I must have something . . . that, touching my heart, shall not leave the chill of ice but the warmth of summer. . . ." Instinct, impulse, "secret chords of feeling"—he urged these as a motive and a guide, "the heart's instincts, whose channels you may appoint but whose flowing is beyond your control." Without a qualm he cast aside every trace of the old intellectual discipline; the absolute melted away. "My nature needs to fashion the thought of God, though I know Him to be a spirit, into something that shall nearly or remotely represent that which I know. . . . This idea of a central, inflexible, passionless God, unmoved and unmoving, that sometimes thunders, and then under certain conditions loves in a proper manner—this conception of the divine nature is freezing; it sets me upon the Poles, and all the revolutions of the year leave me but ice and icebergs. . . ." As God grew mild, man loomed in splendor. Beecher saw a vast human ascendency in the midst of a rich and luxuriant scene. "Ye are gods!" he cried; and the bold text was made to deny that sardonic perception of human weakness which had underlain his father's faith. "You are crystalline, your faces are radiant!" he shouted to the thronging numbers in Plymouth Church.

Eagerly he ranged through the high expectations which had been tiding up in this country for three quarters of a century, and which now at last in the midst of a bountiful prosperity, seemed to be overflowing the land through wide and easy channels. "We are standing on the eve of a great day—a day multitudinous with truths and struggles. . . . The life of the common people is the best part of the world's life. . . . The life of the common people is the life of God. . . ." Love, liberty, human brotherhood, the American idea, all ran together under his hand in a bright impatient stream; already proof existed that these were to spread over the entire world; every one saw it. In 1852 the arrival of Kossuth in this country, almost by national invitation, had produced an overwhelming outburst of confident excitement; the Hungarian liberator was seen as a fulfillment of the American prophecy. New York grew clamant "with millions of feet walking upon the pavements," said Whitman, "with all that indescribable roar and magnetism, unlike any other sound in the universe—the glad exulting thunder-shouts of countless unloos'd throats of men." Kossuth spoke at Plymouth Church; and Beecher was in the thick of the excitement.

"I strike up for a New World," he might have cried with that other, obscurer prophet who was mingling with the same noisy crowds, who was formulating many of the same themes in ways amazingly like and unlike no great distance away in Brooklyn. Whitman, too, was proclaiming the "great Idea, the idea of perfect and free individuals." Easily at home in a natural world of prodigious brightness and scale, he too saw "the most splendid race the sun ever shone upon," and was urging the life of instinct and impulse. Love was the key—Love, Democracy, Religion—a new religion.

"I am the credulous man of qualities, ages, races,
I advance from the people in their own spirit. . . .
I too, following many, and follow'd by many, inaugurate a religion . . .

Each is not for its own sake,
I say the whole earth and all the stars in the sky are for religion's sake.
I say no man has ever yet been half devout enough,
None has ever yet adored or worship'd half enough,
None has begun to think how divine he himself is, and how certain the future is.

My comrade!
For you to share with me two greatnesses, and a third one rising inclusive and more resplendent,
The greatness of Love and Democracy, and the greatness of Religion . . .
I say that the real and permanent grandeur of these States must be their religion. . . ."

In the lavish disarray of their period the major and the minor prophet met and passed in a casual, oblique fashion. After the publication of *Leaves of Grass* in 1855 Beecher called upon Whitman; and both were visitors at Fowler and Wells' Phrenological Depôt or Cabinet on lower Broadway where Whitman's book was on sale. Like Whitman, Beecher roamed through galleries, museums, shops, along the waterside, visited factories and wharves and mills and foundries, made friends with the drivers who were also Whitman's friends in "the flush days of the old

Broadway stages, the Yellow-birds, the Red-birds, the original Broadway, the Fourth Avenue, the Knickerbocker." Slowly and carelessly scooping up themes from many casual, half-known sources, Whitman may have gained a stress of subject and emotion from Beecher in the years when his book was taking shape, from 1848 onward. As a reporter on Brooklyn papers he must have seen accounts of Beecher's discourses; indeed, he must have heard Beecher, for he was a tireless frequenter at public gatherings. A moralist in his own mode, he too meant to spread his ideas by means of public speech; his lectures with *Leaves of Grass* were to form "two co-expressions"; and for a time speech was his greater intention. Yet Whitman failed to speak; and—the anomaly had often been noted—from Whitman, who belonged so completely to his time, crude, muscular, abundantly adolescent, his writings a mirror of popular enthusiasms and current reactions—from Whitman public favor was withheld. With all his passion for the crowd he failed to gain the public which he sought, either through writing or through speech. "Solitary, singing in the West . . . solitary . . . solitary. . . ." The word echoed through *Leaves of Grass* even before his larger solitude was assured.

Mixed multitude and solitude—who yet fathoms that strange juncture in Whitman? Certainly the public of the fifties could not plumb it; less than ever in this period was the popular mind prepared to accept a canon of detachment. The isolation of the pioneer might have been a chimera which haunted an entire generation; for a decade or more, crowds of insistent people had been surging together as if to escape solitude, as if to establish or enjoy emotions in common, at the revivals flaring up like watch-fires throughout the country, at the lectures of the lyceum system, rising through the forties toward their first great climax. As if in response to a powerful wish, a broad sonority was rolling all around; the country was filled with an oratory which seemed to catch and hold a multitudinous feeling. Here and there an irritable critic might be heard declaring that eloquence was the curse of the country; but the demand for a broad and moving overflow of speech only crested higher. Beecher, Theodore Parker, Wendell Phillips, Emerson, Greeley, John B. Gough, and a score of others were storming through the land, speaking on morals, religion, politics, reform, with a choral response to the hungry demand for articulation.

With an idiom which often closely approached that of Whitman, with an approach to rhapsody—often incoherent—which seemed more fluently or more crudely molded from the same stuff that Whitman used, Beecher kept the channels of public intercourse free; and—there was no doubt of it—among all the thronging number of public speakers he received the adulatory crown, the rosy native laurel. Sweeping out into lectures in New York, New England, and the West, he captured audience after audience by his wide encirclements, taking, as Theodore Parker said, the Rocky Mountains as his sounding-board: the tribute suggested both the volume of his speech and the ease with which it was flung from him. "I had great liberty." Beecher repeated the phrase in speaking of his most telling public efforts. Liberty—his was the liberty of great public laughter, of ready public tears, of ample movement, of uncurbed emotion; that wave of impulse toward sheer feeling, which ran back so far and had had so aborted an existence in this country, fairly arose under his hand; emotion was the medium in which he lived, the thrilling medium which richly floated between himself and his audience, something palpable which ran far beyond what he said. Did he create it—did they? Extraordinarily sensitive to the moods of his hearers, he seemed to shape his vast appeals to the changing responses of the sea of people before him; his coarseness seemed of their larger fiber, his drugged and drenched romanticism the stuff of their sentiment, his boundless candor born of their dangerous unreserve; from his large public interchanges he apparently gained in strength, as in the days when he had plunged into the primitive revivals of the wilderness; he could pass from one address to another within the space of a few hours without fatigue, without stress: the two would be wholly different in theme, mood, manner, and he would emerge as fresh as ever. "He is eternally young," said Parker, "and positively wears me out with his redundant, superabundant, ever-recovering, and ever-renewing energy." His speech was likened to great natural forces—with the Falls of Niagara; he was compared with Webster, Calhoun, Clay, the dead or dying leaders of the older oratory, and was considered their superior in "affluence of mental movement." In terms which were then at the early bginnings of a long, hard-working career, his "magnetism" was discussed and his "physic influence." "Mr. Beecher has great strength of instinct, of spontaneous human feeling," said Parker, still trying to plumb the secret of Beecher's power. "He has a genius to be loved. . . . He captivates men without an effort."

There he stood, or rather moved, scarcely more than forty, the strained look of earlier years smoothed away, his long loose locks brushed back in the leonine fashion common to many public speakers; he carried his weight so well as to seem taller than he was. Yet except for the mobility of his countenance and the translucence of his eyes there was nothing remarkable about his appearance; nor was his voice unusual in timbre, never golden or silver; so his most ardent admirers agreed, though its range seemed unlimited. He was likely to begin on a conversational level, so low as barely to be audible; he seemed to be talking to himself; then with a sudden quick turn his tones would suggest explosions, grow gay, fresh, sad, arise in full diapason, fall with a warm enveloping quality.

"The voice," said Beecher, "is the bell of the soul, or the iron and crashing of the anvil. It is a magician's wand, full of incantation and witchery; or it is a scepter in a king's hand, and sways men with imperial authority." Such unmistakable allusions to his own powers abounded in his speeches. "At times," he declared, "there are no gestures comparable to the simple stature of the man himself." He seemed intent upon giving himself, his many selves, the full range of his emotions, his thoughts, his purposes, and motives; his large themes uprose out of an amplitude of self-portrayal. "A living, outflowing heart carries away its sorrows down its own stream, and deposits them speedily far from the fount," he cried, echoing then and many times thereafter that counsel of Lyman Beecher's which had superseded all other counsels in his days at Cincinnati. With a rash candor he spoke of "everything that makes my soul a terrible house of imagery. . . . No man can go down into the dungeon of his own experience and not come up with a shudder and a chill." Freely he mentioned "dark chambers, and hidden cavities, and slimy recesses," as though to specify their existence in the realm of his own feeling gave him release. With equal frankness he discussed his gift for poetry, his sensitiveness to moral issues, his tender heartedness, his carelessness, impracticality, generosity, hatred of neatness, and love of disorder. He confided to his hearers that he disliked gutter-rats; he confessed that in Indianapolis he had been repelled when his parishioners were ill-smelling; he was pleased with people who praised him; in detail he described the tribute of a poor woman who once ran after him in the street with her little girl at her side, and said with tears in her eyes, "Mr. Beecher, I must take you by the hand. I want to tell you what you have done for me. I was nothing but a poor sewing-woman—" Then she had broken down. "I like to have persons come to me with tears in their eyes and attempt to tell me how much good I have done them, and fail with emotion because they cannot speak," he declared. An incomparable mimic, in relating such episodes, he could echo the very inflections of the other voice; he seemed easily to comprise or express other characters; he could imitate with exactness the gait and speech and usual movements of a drunkard, a blacksmith, a fisherman, a wood-cutter. Once in telling a story in which an old wretch of a sailor had figured he mimicked all the gestures, even to the slow action of removing a quid: at the end he furtively—a little regretfully—tossed the imaginary luxury behind him, and then with a sly, small movement which seemed unconscious, which only one person was in a position to see, wiped his fingers on the back of his coat—as if he were lost in the miserable old character.

Occasional critics complained that the mirth which he provoked was too loud, the transition to weeping too swift, that the stimulus which he offered was too exhilarating for many natures. He was called a mountebank; edification in his pulpit was said to give way to entertainment; Beecher himself admitted that people came to his church as they went to Barnum's Museum. "God is the only gentleman": such impulsive aphorisms were abundant in his discourses; he was still so careless of the usual reverential attitudes as to lead his friends among the phrenologists to proclaim defensively that his Mount of Veneration was increasing in size. Yet in the main, criticism was overborne; if he preached the great gospel of freedom, on a prodigious scale he seemed that extraordinary phenomenon, a liberated character. Insisting upon the doctrine of an abundant love, he bestowed upon his hearers the flowing warmth of his feeling—gave it without calculation or reserve, before a small audience as before a large one, before a group of friends as before a crowded lecture hall. Gone was the time when he was dependent upon the huge reservoir of emotion of a crowded gathering; he seemed now to contain that ample source as his own. Feeling—he played upon feeling as upon the suddenly released stops of a huge instrument; yet he seemed careless of his effects, he was never the wayward possessor of the crowd that Lyman Beecher had been. "I have never managed," he declared of his relation to Plymouth Church; "I have never sought to exert my authority," he insisted. He seemed to lack the proselytizing purpose; he was no more the shepherding pastor than he had been in Lawrenceburg; he seldom paid private calls; most of all he shrank from private troubles; he had few intimates, unless every one was his intimate. In all his speech—even in his private interchanges—there was scarcely a phrase which gives a sudden homely glimpse of inner character, of the sort, for example, that his sister Mrs. Stowe could offer so freely and unconsciously. In the large abstractions of the audience-hall he seemed to find a huge and happy replica. If he took the Rocky Mountains as a sounding board, streaming back across immense distances came his own wishes and purposes—ample and free.

"It was a spectacle," said Alcott after hearing Beecher, as though the effect had been that of a many-sided display. "I pronounced it good, very good—the best that I had witnessed for many a day." And Thoreau, who must have scoffed at Beecher's musings on nature, who may have ridiculed his easy exaltation of the people—"What *is* your people?" he demanded of Whitman—Thoreau nevertheless listened to Beecher with wonder and delight, and called him a magnificent pagan.

THREE • "*Men look upon him as a national institution, a* part of the public property," said Parker generously. Yet with all his fluent participation in the modes of the crowd, Beecher was nothing of a popular servant. He met occasional hecklers with a brutal and commanding humor, and faced the aggressive crowd, trenching upon personal liberty, with something of its own blind and basic rage. When the Rynders mob drove Wendell Phillips and other abolitionists from the Broadway Tabernacle in 1850, all of his old angry resistance flared up; he made a headlong offer of Plymouth Church to Phillips, defying the mob to do its worst; and though he was not an abolitionist—he was never an abolitionist—he swung momentarily to an ultimate challenging principle of the group—"to choose dismemberment and liberty, rather than union and slavery." Quickly retreating from this position he was soon at variance with the abolitionist leaders; but that outcry against mob compulsion which he had raised so consistently in his earlier youth he now lifted again and still again with a noisy belligerence—in behalf of free speech, a free press, and individual freedom in opinion, joining the clangor raised by Parker, Phillips, and a few others, and contributing with them toward that effort which made the fifties a climax, perhaps, in the articulate history of personal freedom in the country.

Freedom—freedom! the word became a shattering, threatening force as he uttered it. With all his drifting ease he fought for it. With all his bosky estheticism, with all his outcry of universal love, Beecher achieved his largest fame in the realm of violence, as he plunged into the tumultuous undertow of the anti-slavery agitation. Almost insensibly he had moved into a blind and gross opposition to slavery, lifted to drastic avowals by the intoxication of his own fervor, it seems, as he improvised a slave auction at a public meeting held to raise money for the freedom of two slaves whose case obtained a special sympathy. In Plymouth pulpit he continued the crude and terrible drama, selling women and children by public subscription. Once he led forward a woman who was apparently white, clad in a snowy garment; with a beautiful gesture she unbound her hair, and let it fall glistening to her feet. At some distance stood Beecher, silent, until his silence cast a hysteric spell;

then, shaken by sobs, he went through the ritual of the sale, sparing nothing of the possible horrors of bondage, stirring the depths of a tense and turgid emotion, until at the end in frenzy the audience as by a single concentrated gesture flung down gold, notes, pledges, tore off jewelry, and swayed toward the platform in a passion of protest. From these scenes he quickly passed to others, or conjured their semblance into being. At the passage of the Fugitive Slave Act—whose logic Lincoln thought to be unassailable—Beecher announced that Plymouth Church would become a shelter for fleeing slaves; and he himself towered as a refuge and a strength. His stormy and pictorial vehemence was continually heard in the pulpit, on the lecture platform, in the leaders which he was now writing for the widely popular *Independent*. Inevitably he moved toward the calamitous equation; in his so-called "Great Speech" of 1855 he pictured the differences between the northern and southern conceptions of society in terms of an irresistible clash. "The struggle between the North and the South is not one of sections, or of parties, but of *principles*—of principles that cannot coalesce, nor compromise, that must hate each other, and contend, until one shall drive out the other." *Peace by War*—he spread the desperate phrase. "Do not be afraid because the community teems with excitement," he urged. "Silence and death are dreadful!" Silence—he broke it on every hand; death—did he not induce it? At the outbreak of the struggle in Kansas he started a great fund for rifles with which to equip the northern settlers, insisting that for slaveholders rifles were a more effective moral agency than the Bible. "Beecher's Bibles" became a stirring emblem.

At this point he encountered the leveling criticism of the abolitionists, most of all that of Garrison who was a non-resistant, as if the white-hot fire of the radical mind held something temperate at its core. To Garrison's remonstrance against the sending of arms as unchristian, Beecher replied with lively scorn: "We know that there are those who scoff at the idea of holding a sword or a rifle in a Christian state of mind . . . but you might just as well read the Bible to buffaloes as to those fellows who follow Atchison and Stringfellow." Garrison answered coldly, "He will allow us to shrink without scoffing. We know not where to look for Christianity if not to its founder." A tacit battle broke out between Beecher and the Garrisonians, which continued even after the Civil War; the abolitionists never forgave his failure to declare himself unmistakably for the radical cause during his years in the West; years later Beecher declared that Garrison was a bitter man.

On his stormy middle ground Beecher abated nothing, but continued a rousing, confused fury of attack; a drastic and terrible tumult might have been his end. "With his hat jammed down over his eyes, red and dusty, I must confess that he doesn't look altogether clerical," said a contemporary. Deep in the counsels of the new Republican party, he swept Plymouth Church with him into the young movement, and became indeed the outstanding ministerial figure of the country in the arena of political affairs, continuing—if he had chosen to see it—that tradition of New England to which his father had belonged, by which the ministry was actively linked with government. He took the platform on behalf of Frémont, probably accumulating more votes for the first Republican candidate than any other single person; he repeated these labors during the campaign for Lincoln, when pro-slavery sentiment in New York grew dangerous, and Plymouth Church had to be guarded by police. For a space, on the brink of the sixties, Beecher was moved by an almost mystical sense of the unity of the country, that consciousness of the whole continent which in many minds had grown so great with the surge of the movement westward.

> "Thou transcendental Union! . . . Through thy reality, lo, the immortal idea! . . ."

For a moment he paused, as if aghast at the impending cataclysm. Then in a sudden outburst he cried, "Let come what will—secession, disunion, revolted states, and a ragamuffin empire. . . ."

Again he swung from one excess of principle to another. When John Brown assumed a messiahship at Harper's Ferry in the wake of a widespread revival, Beecher at first shrank from the brutal act and purpose. "I protest against any counsels that lead to insurrection, servile war, and bloodshed," he insisted. Yet in the same speech he shouted, "Let no man pray that Brown be spared! Let Virginia make him a martyr!" Brown, in prison, reading an account of the address, caustically pronounced it rhetoric; but for Beecher either the momentum of his own speech or some desperate lure of the public situation proved irresistible. He continued to find in Brown a wild and challenging symbol. At the fateful end of the fifties, when the strains of *John Brown's Body* were resounding through the land like a bugle-call, when a comet flared in the north to the terror of hundreds of beholders, when the country was shaken by every omen and grew breathless with suspense, Beecher built up before a vast audience in New York a swift resurgent concept of liberty and of bondage; in a climax of simple drama, he seized the chains which Brown was said to have worn, flung them with clangor to the floor and spurned them with his foot, creating "a jubilee of sublime emotion"—in the words of an adverse critic—a huge ecstatic, racking, sobbing impulse into which the feeling of the crowd seemed poured and fused and magnified far beyond its mere aggregation.

At last, when the war came, Beecher seemed to find his native element; stormy and violent, his power rose with the terrific impacts which followed. He was now the editor of the *Independent;* in Brooklyn thousands were turned away from the services at Plymouth Church; his every word was scattered over the land; he had the power of a dictator, and he used it. "Is thy servant a dog?" asked Lincoln with unaccustomed bitterness as he read Beecher's passionate and peremptory editorials during the early months of the war. "Slow—slow—slow! . . . Vacillating. . . . The President has no sense of the value of time." Fairly with the firing upon Sumter, Beecher had announced emancipation as an immediate goal, whether or not the President assented, insisting upon the measure as if a heated arrogance were the single great residuum of his character. In that black period abuse was heaped upon Lincoln from many quarters; Wendell Phillips was calling him a "slave-hound"; but the attacks of Beecher must have been hardest to bear because they were so amply mingled with contempt. When at last emancipation was proclaimed in its gradual stages, Beecher stepped easily into a position of enormous prestige. At one time or another many persons claimed to have provided the impetus which drove Lincoln to the momentous decision, Greeley with his *Prayer of the Twenty Millions* among them, and even a literary free lance like Charles Godfrey Leland; but at the moment, for the hundred thousands of persons who hung upon Beecher's utterances as a final word in public affairs, who viewed the *Independent* as a last oracle, an almost fanatical belief arose as to Beecher's influence with the President. A legend was created, persisting for decades and representing a popular sense of proportions, that Lincoln traveled by night to Brooklyn in the midst of the blackest months of despair to spend the night in counsel with Beecher.

With his English speeches of the late summer of 1863, Beecher's hold upon the public imagination reached a categorical climax. In the England of the *Trent* affair, with mills closed for the lack of cotton, with social as well as economic pressure steadily exerted in favor of the Confederacy, he confronted, or invaded, a hostile foreign nation, and broached a public argument at a time when failure might have spelled disaster through a deep revulsion in British feeling; intervention was still in the air. Ostensibly he went abroad for a brief holiday; he seems, however, to have had from the first the intention to speak if he could find a suitable opening. This was provided at last by a small and active anti-slavery minority; but his handicaps were still immense. He lacked any sort of personal foothold; he was scarcely a name in England; through *Uncle Tom's Cabin,* as result of her visits, Mrs. Stowe was far better known there; once he was introduced as the Reverend Henry Ward Beecher Stowe. Our reticent and troubled ambassador, Charles Francis Adams, seems to have remained aloof. When Beecher's purpose became known, resentment flared up all over England; he was rudely caricatured by *Punch,* assailed by the *Times,* confronted at every turn by bitterly denunciatory posters. With a blunt challenge he began his series of speeches in the heart of the manufacturing district; but as he passed from Manchester to Glasgow, and from Glasgow to Edinburgh he was barely able to hold his own against the rough and irascible crowds; and at Liverpool the concentrated animosity against him reached a terrific culmination. He was warned by the newspapers not to attempt to speak: on the night of his address everywhere men were armed; outside the audience-hall the streets were packed; inside, was crammed an angry boiling mass of humanity. Immensely fatigued, Beecher later confessed something of momentary terror at the prospect which lay before him, and declared that he obtained the requisite tranquillity by a method which he had often found effectual—through the hypnotic agency of a little handful of many-colored precious stones. Even with this assistance he had handicaps enough. As he tried to speak he found half a dozen riots in progress at the same time; lifting a voice already worn by his other difficult addresses, he consumed an hour and a half in making an opening. Afterward he said that he felt like a ship-master trying to shout "on board ship through a speaking trumpet with a tornado on the sea and a mutiny among the men. . . . I felt as though the whole Atlantic Ocean were under my feet."

The Liverpool speech constituted an almost unparalleled feat; yet it appears less as a prodigious triumph in eloquence than as a revelation of Beecher's relationship with that entity with which his life and character now seemed intertwined—the public; not his own public, indeed, but any public, the crowd. As he battled against that huge mass all his gifts were united in careless power. His anger—hitherto so quick to flame against the aggressive mob—had vanished; he seemed to cast aside that contemptuous rage which had informed his utterances in these later years. At last, in that seething cauldron, he was possessed of a simple equability. "There's luck in leisure," he roared, and awaited tiny lulls in the prodigious tumult; readily enough he fell in with the barbaric jokes of the crowd; his laughter seemed as huge and noisy as theirs. When in the midst of shouts, hisses, catcalls, groans, came a partial quiescence, he quickly filled it to the brim, flattered the colossal brute, began to build—a phrase here, a fragmentary sentence there—the beginnings of his argument. His violence now met that of the multitude, but without bitterness; the crowd hesitated between murderous wrath and reluctant admiration at some of his loud laconic retorts. "I knew that I could conquer them," he afterwards exclaimed; yet even then he echoed less a lust for triumph than a sense of equilibrium, enormous and secure. And though his sweeping intercourse with the crowd seemed on the level of instinct, gradually he established a solid link in a long argument; critics who have complained that Beecher lacked architectonic should read the English speeches. They constituted, in truth, as Holmes said, a single great speech. Punctuated as they all were throughout by interruptions, exhibiting a handling which was necessarily loose and large, their long appeal nevertheless marched relentlessly through the single theme of the rightful freedom of labor and its unity throughout the world. From a history of slavery within fifty years—in the Manchester address—he swung back to its history in many civilizations—at Glasgow—pictured its degrading effect upon standards of living for free labor—at Edinburg—and at Liverpool contrasted the demands for manufacturing products on the part of labor which is free in contrast to that which is enslaved, in each case gathering all his arguments into a single bold entreaty.

The speech at Liverpool, indeed, was never ended; after three hours of shouting above the whirlwind Beecher's voice failed him; he was obliged to stop; but he had established the large circle of his contention. The tone of the English newspapers changed; his courage was now admired; he was permitted to make the last of his addresses in London with comparative ease, and even with the accompaniment of some enthusiasm. No doubt the summer's victories of the Army of the Potomac were beginning to make an impression in England; the less spectacular resistance of Adams had maintained a groundwork for change; probably Beecher breasted a heightened wave of hostility just before it fell. A period of what Adams called "repose" began in England after his tour; and at home he was widely considered to have averted intervention. Returning to the still deeply riven country, he easily filled the ample outlines suggested by Holmes' phrase, "our minister plenipotentiary." Once more he swept his great public into something like a continuous revivalism, which spread and met those other blacker revivals springing up along the battlefront as though a wild fear with a wild hope had grown from the monstrous cataclysm of war. "Everything marches," he cried, and preached in the midst of the abysmal darkness of 1864 all that golden abundance which had informed his most glowing utterances of the fifties; again he lifted his old choral shouts of love, liberty, and universal benevolence, voicing the whole gamut of his simple philosophy, achieving—it seemed—the full breadth of his powers. Scale—an enormous equilibrium: the gathered triumph of years seemed his in the desperate long struggle; the war might have brought him a final conquest. What greater distinction could he gain? Who equaled him as a dominant public figure? Theodore Parker was dead; Wendell Phillips, always austere, commanded a less spacious, less responsive audience; the other popular orators strummed upon single emotions. Lincoln yielded the final tribute, which like many of his briefer notations, wears a slight air of the enigmatic. Asked toward the end of the war whom he considered the greatest of his countrymen, Lincoln answered after a moment's hesitation, "Beecher."

In the stormy epoch which followed Lincoln's death, out of the first floating wreckage of the reconstruction, naturally Beecher loomed as a public counselor. With his accustomed bravura he began to preach magnanimity, tolerance, brotherhood; his fluid happy sentiments welled up again. "Everything marches. . . . The style of thought is freer and more noble. The young men of our times are regenerated. The army has been a school. . . . The war has changed not alone institutions, but ideas. . . . Public sentiment is exalted far beyond what it has been at any other period. . . ." But—what had happened? These axioms fell upon the northern mind like a patter of light rain on hard clay. The temper of the country had grown cold and bitter and surly. In a rough scramble for enormous wealth men cut and clashed; swollen railway operations were under way; it was all but the heydey of the Erie gamble, of the many scarcely hidden governmental activities of Jim Fisk, of a loose public tolerance of Tweed and his gang. Gold flashed everywhere—in wallets, in enormous dinner-plates, in heavy ornaments; diamond fillings for teeth came into vogue; marble palaces were ascending to house the decked and riotous conquerors; yet the gold and the marble might have been lead or iron for all the effect of brightness or clarity they produced; a coarse, blunt mood was revealed on all sides. Even feminine costumes grew stiff and pompous; puffings and flouncings had a corrugated look. In household furniture the gloomiest style known to history was developing, a superabundantly high, jutting, overhanging black walnut which looked as if its designers had copied Gothic pieces from an uncertain memory but with a purpose to exhibit power at any cost. The aquatint touch had vanished. This was the age of the bolder sentiments or none.

In the midst of a brusque sensationalism revenge against the South was the prevailing outcry. In his familiar vein Beecher pled for reconcilement. His appeal fell upon deaf ears. With unmistakable courage and some vexation he shouted louder, and suddenly found himself on the southern side as to the harassing question of the civil and political status of the negro. At first, with one of his lavish encirclements he had cried for equal rights for every one, for the South as well as for the North, for blacks as well as whites. Then from a group of southern gentlemen he learned something of southern fears of negro domination, and drifted past a belief in immediate negro citizenship, vaguely declaring that this would be accomplished in time "by the operation of general laws." Indeed, he seemed bent upon enwrapping himself in all the myriad filaments of a complex situation. With a blind and careless gesture he endorsed the program of the Soldiers' and Sailors' Convention held at Cleveland in the autumn of 1866—writing his so-called "Cleveland letter"—and found himself in a strange gallery, that of Jackson, who faced impeachment, and of a rapacious political combination which was opposing political rights for the negro on the ground that the bestowal of these would eventually give to the southern states a disproportionate representation in Congress. Moreover, the Cleveland convention was widely considered to be in cabal against the Republican party, whose cradle Beecher had rocked, whose shield and buckler he had been during the trying days of its early infancy. And fairly as he dropped the cause of negro citizenship the Republicans as a party had picked it up. The official party ranks came down upon him in full thunder; Charles Sumner denounced him in the Senate. The abolitionists took up the cry with white-hot fervor. In a series of open letters in the *Tribune,* Greeley brushed aside Beecher's "soft-voiced lullabies," and assembling his usual battery of statistics, sketched a history of the anti-slavery cause in this country which effectually disposed of the possibility of obtaining any rights whatever by "the operation of general laws." Harshly enough, Greeley declared that Beecher had become "an enlightened patriot and statesman . . . in the conception of every blackleg, duelist, negro-killer, and rowdy, from the St. John to the Rio Grande. . . ." Beecher seemed to lose even his small and intimate public; from Plymouth Church came a sharp, semi-official letter addressed to him in unmistakable terms of reproach and remonstrance; and from the *Independent* came a blasting criticism. In 1863 he had relinquished his editorial responsibility to Theodore Tilton—a younger man and a disciple—because of the pressure of other affairs; but he still remained the leading contributor; the paper had long been regarded as his personal organ. Yet the *Independ-*

ent fairly outstripped Beecher's other assailants in the bitterness of its assault.

Beecher was both hurt and bewildered. "I have been from my youth a firm, unwavering, avowed and active friend of all that were oppressed," he insisted with his usual largeness of personal reference. Once more he proposed the routine of an easy confidence. "Better days are coming! Just now angry voices come to me as rude winds roaring through the trees. The winds will die; the trees will live!" But the winds continued to roar; and these misty assurances scarcely reëstablished his power. As if in the chaos of war he had spent some essential force, as if he had whirled too far with his vast authority, losing his bearings, his sensitive knowledge of popular reactions was gone; his great ascendancy was broken; and he seemed to possess no secure chart or compass of his own. He slipped into the lax and tepid mood which was to produce his sentimental novel *Norwood,* the single new expression of these years; and it was perhaps an ungracious circumstance that in this perplexing interval Mrs. Beecher should choose to indulge in her novel, with its acid and thorough-going survey of the Beechers' early life. Still striving to assume his old rôle of popular adviser, from time to time Beecher issued statements on public affairs: but he seemed unable to find a way out of the confusion of his earlier avowals; he floundered; and—there was no doubt of it—a censorious reaction had set in against him. His congregation was still cold; the *Tribune* still riddled his proposals; scarcely a statement which he made on the political situation was left unchallenged by the *Independent.* In this paper, side by side with his sketchy ephemeral essays or the reports of his sermons, ran Tilton's unmitigated attack. As cognate problems arose, or as Beecher issued new statements, his wide audience was relentlessly informed of the uncertainty of his course. At the culmination of these onslaughts, in 1867, Beecher resigned from the staff of the paper. A complex and dangerous rivalry had begun.

FOUR • *Theodore Tilton, something of a flutist by tempera-*ment, was assuming the trumpet, apparently bent upon becoming the great Beecher on a larger and more romantic scale. Six feet tall, dashingly called Apollo among the editors, at a little more than thirty he too had achieved something of the leonine style, with noticeable embellishments. The locks which he freely tossed back from his brow were richly golden; his benign look was frequently crossed by a subtle effect of tragedy, a kind of generic grief, as though he bore the sorrows of the world; he was far more royal than Beecher; he was said indeed, to pay tribute to great names with the air of one who confidently believes himself to be an object of homage. Undoubtedly Tilton was versatile. In a floral age he was master of a luxuriantly metaphorical prose; he indulged in rondels, triolets, ballads, was the author of *Baby Bye,* a highly popular lyric, and a sheaf of allegories; like Beecher he discussed art, nature, and the emotions. A witty companion, he had hosts of friends; he lectured, and wrote with a fluent pen and a boundless energy, contriving to edit the *Independent* and the Brooklyn *Union* at the same time, doing a day's work at one office in the morning and going to the other in the afternoon, apparently unfatigued. Tilton was attaining a recognized dominion in the turbulent era after the war; perhaps his clear and strident voice fell in with current moods; the Egglestons praised him, and other sober-minded journalists. He was liked by Garrison. Marching beyond Beecher, he had long since proclaimed himself an abolitionist; and his post-war utterances had the virtue of a consistent stress. His program of political equality for the negro was unequivocal.

Besides these troubled questions Tilton was attacking others, hardly less vexed. A radical in the now well-established field of feminism, on the lecture platform and in the columns of the *Independent* he was insisting upon a new freedom for woman at every conceivable point where freedom could be exercised. He was deep in the counsels of the more daring leaders of the cause, such as Mrs. Stanton, whom he called "a gay Greek come forth from Athens" and with whom he played chess, Anna Dickinson, "the peerless Girl of the Period," the gentle Lucretia Mott, Miss Anthony, Isabella Beecher Hooker, Beecher's younger half-sister, and Mrs. Horace Greeley. Indeed, throughout the mutations of the next few years this group remained outspokenly loyal to Tilton; in the midst of their waxing campaign they consulted him at every turn. Their purposes were sufficiently drastic; these ladies were bent—where, ah, where did their bounding fancy pause? They proposed to alter the entire condition of the servile creature, woman. As they proceeded on their ebullient way a whole movement was thrown into relief, that vague large movement for freedom in which Beecher had been so ardent a leader. In the late sixties and early seventies they created a lively fantasia on the theme of liberty; nor was the florid affair lightly sketched; it fell into terms of positive action.

Strangely—yet fittingly, since this was another climax in the appeal for liberty—Beecher became deeply enmeshed within these animated patterns. He was cast into a further antithesis to Tilton and driven into a great public drama. Other elements played their part in the final catastrophe, undoubtedly: traits of character, and the complex interaction of diverse temperaments; but it was the feminist movement which provided a groundwork for the clash. They were a potent group, those suffragists. During the stirring hurly-burly of two decades or more they had held their own, gathering momentum.

Even that coquetry of the demure downward glance, that heightened delicacy of figure, enhanced by hoops and wreaths and fans and laces, which reached so charming an excess in the late forties and early fifties, may be read as an aspect of a new feminine confidence. Coquetry, of course, is as old as the world; the picture was superlatively Victorian; but in this country, at least, its elements had novelty. The Puritan had not permitted wiles; the pioneer could not afford them. But with early inklings of the cry for freedom, with the spread of wealth, a quaint suspiring rush had occurred. Assuming an exquisite refinement, women hinted an impulse toward authority. The bold efforts of emancipated women showed a print of this subtle mode; the bloomer dress was advocated in a little journal called *The Lily;* the costume itself was patterned upon the garb of a race of women whose subjection was notorious; the long full trousers were cut in the Turkish style. At the same time this dress was richly assertive; fashioned of handsome black broadcloth, it showed more than a touch of the cavalier with its short overskirt, its Spanish cloak reaching to the knee, and broad beaver hat with feathers.

> "Heigh! Ho! in rain and snow
> The bloomer now is all the go.
> Twenty tailors take the stitches,
> Twenty women wear the breeches.
> Heigh! Ho! in rain or snow
> The bloomer now is all the go."

With a gay insistence the feminists had burst upon an astonished public, wearing the costume at fashionable gatherings in Washington, their men-folk at their sides, one of whom at least, according to Mrs. Stanton, "went through the ordeal with coolness and dogged insistence." In truth, if the lily was a feminist symbol, it was to prove a lily with a strong and elastic stem; the new movement had what was called "snap."

Dauntless and witty, with sharp tongues and an overflow of high spirits, from the first these ladies had been quite aware that they were leaders without example or precedent. Mary Wollstonecraft, indeed, had made a courageous venture in logic long before. Within their own memory another Englishwoman, Fanny Wright, had launched a manifesto in this country on behalf of women; in the early forties Margaret Fuller

had provided a many-sided feminist canon. But none of these person-
ages, not even Miss Fuller in her famous conversations and with her
worshipful auditors, had ventured upon feminism as an organized movement. Obviously the new band was the first of its kind in the world.

> "Sigh no more, ladies, sigh no more,
>   Men were deceivers ever;
> One foot in sea, and one on shore,
>   To one thing constant never—"

With hilarious laughter they sang these verses; but as a company they
seriously proposed to emancipate women once and for all from the deplorable habit of waiting for uncertain privileges carelessly bestowed by
the dominant male. Slavery! that undoubtedly was the virtual position
of women. "Nothing can exceed the whole-souled, all-absorbing, agon-
izing interest which I feel in the redemption of women." declared Mrs.
Stanton, perhaps the most articulate member of the group, falling into
the messianic phraseology common to many reformers of the day. "Our
religion, laws, customs, are all founded on the belief that woman was
made for man," she mused. Soon this determined group had reached the
nub of the question; the enslavement of woman came less from her lack
of the vote—though she must have the vote—or from her inequality
before the law—which must be rectified—or from her failure to receive
equal wages for equal work, than from the oppression which she endured in the marriage relation. "How this marriage question grows on
me!" exclaimed Mrs. Stanton. "It lies at the very foundation of all progress."

"I wish you would call a convention to discuss divorce, marriage, in-
fanticide, and their kindred subjects," wrote Lucy Stone to this ardent
leader in the early fifties. Suddenly feminist committees and conventions
and lectures abounded. Little by little the feminists gained a hearing in
the small towns of New England and New York. Freely they made hard
jaunts over the sparsely settled areas of Missouri, Kansas, Iowa, Nebraska, with Mrs. Stanton indefatigably showing mothers in trains, stations, hotels and omnibuses how to wash, dress, and feed their children
—herself the competent mother of seven—and sprinkling counsel at the
same time as to the needs and methods of feminine emancipation. With
an extraordinary degree of enterprise she and Miss Anthony even contrived to address the Mormon women in the Tabernacle at Salt Lake
City. Indeed, for a time they seemed highly fortunate in their daring
purposes; their outcries for freedom mingled with the exultant shouts

of the decade. The more conspicuous public leaders endorsed their cause, Beecher among them, though he added a questionable praise.

"Woman," he said, "is appointed for the refinement of the race." "Man," he went on, "is said to have been made little lower than the angels; woman needs no such comparison; she was made full as high"— a sentiment which was to echo down the years in the camp of the opposition with appropriate salvos of applause. He had also indicated something of pity for the weak in championing the feminist platform, and had plainly stated that he considered the home the single proper sphere for woman. Yet he supplemented his acceptance of the new movement in a dozen intangible ways which perhaps proved useful. The floral mode itself—was not this a form of delicate praise of woman? Amazingly enough it had spread; the so-called feminine touch was everywhere; even journalists indulged in feathery fine metaphors and a gracile style. Amazingly too, tributes to woman were being offered on every side, in sheaves of lyrics, in dozens of little familiar essays. A bevy of women writers had fluttered forward; female poets were suddenly a calculable element in American life—Elizabeth Oakes-Smith, Mrs. Whitman, Anne Lynch, the Cary sisters, and a dozen others. It fairly seemed that the long-neglected sex was stamping the times with its own print.

Alas! in spite of this flattering wave of sentiment, when the feminists came to the point of action they were not only thwarted but denounced. When they pressed for a change in the rigorous divorce law of New York, the opprobrious term free love promptly settled upon them; and they were plunged the deeper into controversy by the support of some of their high-minded advocates, among them the elder Henry James, who pushed the doctrine of freedom to a charming and lofty extreme. "Holding as I do," he declared, "that the human heart is the destined home of constancy and every courteous affection, I cannot but believe that it will abound in those fruits precisely as it becomes practically honored, or left to its own cultivated instincts." However delicately worded, this was little short of the hateful doctrine itself. The same cry was more noisily raised by the redoubtable Stephen Pearl Andrews with his claims for a perfect "sovereignty of the individual," and Andrews was an avowed exponent of free love. On the heels of this excitement Horace Greeley and Robert Dale Owen opened a debate on the subject of divorce in the columns of the *Tribune,* in which the issue again appeared; and Greeley marshaled his adroit and considerable energies to defeat the bill in the Assembly which the feminists were sponsoring. It was proof of their eloquence and skill, or of the liberality of public sentiment, that their proposal was nearly carried; the test measure was lost by only a few votes. Their disappointment was proportionate; New York was to have been the starting-point for a broad wave of reform. Then came the fiery curtain of the war, obliterating special causes.

Afterward, primed for a fresh campaign, the feminists witnessed what they regarded as a traitorous desertion from their ranks. "After the slave, then the woman," Wendell Phillips had handsomely promised in the fifties; almost as a body the anti-slavery leaders had been pledged to the feminist cause. Well, emancipation for the slave had come; now for the emancipation of woman! What the feminists desired in 1865 was a sweeping constitutional amendment granting the suffrage to all citizens of the United States regardless of sex or color. Political rights, thus easily attained, were to provide a basis for a further and wider freedom. But in cool response the anti-slavery group replied, "This is the negro's hour." The cause of woman was dismissed. Naturally Mrs. Stanton and her group were enraged at what they considered the plain evidence of broken faith. For a brief space, indeed, when he voiced his first ready counsel of unrestricted political rights for every one, Beecher had seemed to support their proposal; one of his statements was construed as favoring immediate suffrage for women. But as he had quickly altered his entire position in regard to the negro, his other pronouncement was robbed of its force. With the prize in sight the feminists were left to shift for themselves. They were comparatively few in number; but they were resourceful. Within the angry temper of the post-war period their determination took on startling proportions.

All the antagonism of years surged up. Freedom—they proposed to have it, and something more besides. Ascendancy! "Where will you poor men stand in another fifty years?" Mrs. Stanton asked Robert Dale Owen, and answered her own question: "You will be crowded off the horizon!" "The establishing of woman on her rightful throne is the greatest revolution the world has ever known or ever will know," the same intrepid leader declared in a more public utterance. "We are, as a sex, infinitely superior to men," she cursively stated somewhat later. Echoes of the aggressive comparison were heard among her embattled sympathizers. "While man is toiling up the rugged steep by slow and painful steps, with laboring breath and sweating brow, woman instantly flies to the summit, and wonders that man should be so obtuse and slow," wrote a fiery feminine correspondent in the New York *World,* who proceeded to discuss an occult faculty known as "psychometric power," possessed by woman alone.

Issuing manifestoes, calling conventions, the belligerent group hurried to the practical issue; and their new campaign was the more menacing because it contained the incalculable element of burlesque. For all their frustration and undoubted seriousness, this tried and seasoned band still had the air of engaging in an enormous lark. In the midst of the New York constitutional convention of 1867 they apparently became as much absorbed in playing a merry prank on Horace Greeley as in having the word "male" stricken from appropriate passages of the new instrument. With deliberate opportunism they made an alliance with George Francis Train, a slippery financial genius with a passion for rhetoric who later became involved in the *Crédit Mobilier* scandals, and who even then was being denounced by judicial observers as "a crack-brained harlequin and semi-lunatic, a ranting egotist and low blackguard." But Train was picturesque; he could always command an audience; he had money; and he was willing to finance a new feminist campaign in Kansas—surely already an ample battle-ground; with the bellicose leaders of the movement he traveled there in 1868 as a self-constituted candidate against Grant. Upon Mrs. Stanton and her group fell an avalanche of criticism in consequence of this coalition; the arrangement proved too much for the conservatives of the movement, who hailed in the main from Boston. After a pronounced clash as to purpose and policies, the feminist movement was split, in 1870, by a division which was to last for twenty years. At this point Beecher and Tilton again moved into opposition. Beecher became the president of the conservative society, which was avowedly concerned only with securing the franchise. Tilton led the unabashed radical ranks, which included Mrs. Stanton, Miss Anthony, Isabella Beecher Hooker, Lucretia Mott and Paulina Wright Davis. These ladies had not abated their primary demands by a jot; they still were concerned with a complete feminine freedom; and they still proposed to conduct their campaign with a certain sparkle. In opposition to the quiet *Woman's Journal* they promptly launched a paper appropriately called *Revolution,* which was financed in large part by Train. But the vituperation which they suffered—and rather enjoyed —because of this continued alliance was as nothing to that which speedily fell upon them through their brief association with another, far more startling character—Victoria Woodhull.

Undoubtedly Mrs. Woodhull impinged upon the popular imagination. With her sister, Tennessee Claflin, she appeared before the American public for perhaps a decade, and showed a large and zigzag scrawling handwriting upon the wall. Movements—she fairly enveloped them;

she seemed an epitome of a dozen large and elementary popular fantasies; she had a knack for touching popular absorptions. And for all her air of gentle clairvoyance, she possessed a drastic force.

A faint picture of the two sisters emerges, telling fortunes or lapsing into trances in a closely shuttered house at Cincinnati early in the fifties. A dim narrative of adventure can be unrolled, within which Victoria went on the stage, traveled to the coast, made an unfortunate marriage with a Dr. Woodhull, divorced him, and later married a Colonel Blood, a handsome figure of a man with a magnificent sweep of side-whiskers, who had been president of a spiritualistic society in St. Louis, and who subsequently manifested an extraordinary talent for silence; he traveled in the train of the two sisters but seemed content with sartorial effects. Indeed, Colonel Blood was soon superseded as a guide by another far more famous figure of the classic past. Years earlier than the Fox sisters or the Davenport brothers, it seems, Mrs. Woodhull had received intimations of the spirit world. A phantasm had appeared before her, "a majestic guardian," both solemn and graceful, clad in a Greek tunic, who kept his identity secret until she went to Pittsburgh, late in the sixties; there, as he offered a celestial mandate, he strode to a table and wrote his name in English letters which at first were indistinct but which gradually assumed such luster as to fill the room with brightness. The name proved to be DEMOSTHENES. The omen was obvious: like other great leaders of the day Mrs. Woodhull was to assume the popular mode; she was to become an orator. In the midst of the great resonance still flooding the land she was to lift her singularly pleasant and even thrilling voice. On the same occasion the illustrious spirit urged her to go to New York; she did so, and with her sister suddenly opened a broker's office at 44 Broad Street under the patronage of Commodore Vanderbilt, a bluff, elderly, credulous gentleman who tossed away small portions of his forty millions for many a garish enterprise, and who seems to have been inordinately proud of the exploits of the Lady Brokers. Indeed, they detected frauds which bewildered experienced frequenters of the street; they discoursed to reporters, offering novel views on projects like elevated railways and pneumatic tubes. Presently Mrs. Woodhull launched into a discussion of politics, persuading Bennett of the *Herald* to publish a long series of articles which she had composed on the *Origin, Tendencies, and History of Government.* "The world is rapidly becoming Americanized," she declared with a not unlikely touch of prophecy. Advancing into the field of science, borrowing a title from Professor Huxley's recent *Physical Basis of Life,* she contrasted the matter of life with the life of matter, and announced that the subsistence of the body upon elements contained in the atmosphere might be expected in the oncoming golden era. All about were flowing powerful magnetic currents; Mrs. Woodhull quoted a celebrated author as saying that the sea itself was as much magnetic as watery; and declaring that she was only laying the foundation for a complete philosophy which she would soon expound at appropriate length, she trenched upon spiritualism.

Within the round of two decades the spiritualistic movement had attained an extraordinary ascendancy over many minds. Whitman had chancily set down a belief in the manifestations of spirits—

"Living beings, identities now doubtless near us in the air that
    we know not of,
Contact daily and hourly that will not release me—"

Boston had become a fervent center of belief; the leading spiritualistic journal, the *Banner of Light,* was published at Boston. As usual, Mrs. Woodhull was floating with a current. In 1871 she was elected president of the National Association of Spiritualists. The brokerage business drifted from view. Under the guidance of Demosthenes she founded a paper called *Woodhull and Claflin's Weekly,* and with a firm grasp seized upon several other promising causes, including those of feminism and of the pantarchy, which when examined proved to be but another name for that universal government of the world which she had already predicted. In fact, the principles of the *Weekly* were shot through and through with universality; with hosannas Mrs. Woodhull prophesied the "Universal Religion of the Future . . . the Universal Home—Palaces for the People . . . the Universal Science, called Universology, based upon the discovery and demonstration of Universal Laws . . . and an accompanying Philosophy of Integralism." By a universal formula of universological science was to come the universal reconciliation of all differences and the reign of peace, love, and truth. For universal intercourse a universal language had been invented, whose name contained a high-minded cryptogram—Elevato-Ahl-Uah-To. With an easy confidence the *Weekly* was proclaimed to be the "organ of the most advanced Thought and Purpose in the World . . . the Organ of Cardinary News . . . News of the Aspiration and Progression of Mankind toward Millennial Perfection. . . ."

"Progress! Free Thought! Untrammeled Lives!" After a few issues out came these watchwords. "Untrammeled Lives!" Only the most untutored reader of the *Weekly* could fail to guess what that bold signal meant; indeed its implications were soon explained at sufficient length by Mrs. Woodhull at a long-famous meeting held at Steinway Hall. Her exposition was singularly free from gross implications; freedom meant merely the absence of legal constraint, the right to follow the dictates of feeling. She took occasion to mention Whitman's recent dismissal from office in Washington as evidence of the confining net now being flung over utterances of instinctive truth; she denounced the Puritan tradition as maintained by both church and state. Indeed, her statements seemed only with a small degree of rudeness patterned upon the exquisite axiom announced by the elder Henry James, that the human heart was the home of every courteous affection, and could safely be left to its own cultivated instincts. And Mrs. Woodhull, attaining the platform at last, impressed her auditors by her charming diffidence. Slender and modest, with a white tea-rose at her throat, she dismissed any presentiment of the adventuress; if her curly hair was short, so was that of far less conspicuous women after the war; it was a fashion; and the gaze of her remarkably fine eyes was candid. Then and afterward in beginning her addresses she betrayed a noticeable hesitation, and gained confidence only when she found herself in the full flood of her subject.

Beecher had been invited to preside at this meeting, but he declined to do so; and Tilton took the chair, fittingly enough, for his editorials on the question of marriage in the *Independent* had so increased in freedom and fervor as to earn him, late in 1870, a sudden dismissal from its editorship and also from that of the Brooklyn *Union.* Undismayed, he had promptly founded a new paper of his own, the *Golden Age,* whose name bespoke his glittering millenarian expectations, and whose utterances, at least on the question of marriage and divorce, ran no great distance from those of *Woodhull and Claflin's Weekly.* At the same time he had composed a rhapsodic biography of Mrs. Woodhull, in which he faithfully recorded the guardianship of Demosthenes, her powers as a healer, and her transcendent conquest over numberless picturesque obstacles. Upon the publication of this highly colored brochure Tilton received a deluge of criticism; Edward Eggleston wrote a mock-obituary in the columns of *Hearth and Home.* Rising to even more lilting periods and freer conclusions, Tilton announced that there was something in his temperament which made him averse to organization of any kind, and he compared Mrs. Woodhull with most of the notable women of the country, including Mrs. Stanton and Mrs. Stowe.

These were fair alliances, and presently some of them flowed together. Mingling all her hopeful pronouncements, Mrs. Woodhull proclaimed the birth of a new Cosmo-Political party, at whose head she placed herself, declaring that she would become a candidate for the presidency of the United States in 1872. At the same time she admitted that she was "the most prominent representative of the only unrepresented class in the Republic." Her next step had logic and perspicacity. She memorialized Congress, insisting that the right of suffrage for women had already been secured under the fourteenth and fifteenth amendments, and was denied only by election laws of the several states; her case rested upon the well-known pronouncement that "representatives shall be chosen by the people of the United States." In the subsequent history of the feminist agitation the argument was to be used many times; its simplicity was tantalizing; but it was seldom to appear with the triumphant effect achieved by Mrs. Woodhull. She obtained a personal hearing before the Judiciary Committee of the House and drew favorable comment even from the Washington journals most stiffly opposed to the measure which she was advocating; they were almost unanimous in their praise of her modest bearing and the quiet directness of her speech. Indeed, Mrs. Woodhull created a pleasant ripple in Washington; long afterward her reticent gayety was remembered. The majority of the Committee reported adversely upon the memorial, it was true, but a trenchant minority report was offered by three of its members; and finally, she was brought into a direct encounter with the leaders of the left wing of the feminist party, who were in Washington at the time, holding one convention and preparing for another. They were startled; here was an able free-lance who had obtained more official recognition by her sudden sally than they had been able to win through the prolonged struggles of years. But they had suffered from the charge of harboring free love doctrines; and Mrs. Woodhull, however abstractly, had avowed these. They pondered. "The result should be everything," declared Mrs. Stanton at last in a momentous decision. "Her face, manners, and conversation, all indicate the triumph of the moral, intellectual, and spiritual." If there were questions as to Mrs. Woodhull's earlier history, these should be silenced. "The individual experience" had "sacredness." In truth, these ladies were carried away by Mrs. Woodhull; and perhaps the most acclamatory of them all was Isabella Beecher Hooker, one of the youngest of Lyman Beecher's children, a large-hearted, impulsive woman who had inherited much of her father's resistless energy and some of his revivalistic talents. In her new admiration the bond of spiritualism provided a last enchantment; soon she was calling Victoria her "darling Queen." As for the hated phrase "free love" she debated its implications for tortured days, and at last boldly concluded that the words meant only a noble personal independence. Freedom was good, and so was love; popular misconceptions must be changed; and with Mrs. Davis, who had reached the same conclusions, Mrs. Hooker set about the enterprise.

Attended by that air of innocence which perennially seemed to belong to these ladies, they marched straight into the field of controversy, proposing to emblazon the dangerous phrase "free love" upon the very shield of the feminist party. A pamphlet launched their argument. But it was Mrs. Woodhull, not Mrs. Hooker or Mrs. Davis or even Mrs. Stanton, who made the principal speech at the second Washington convention; and a few months later at another gathering held in New York, with cataleptic rapture she proposed an entirely new feminist program in a speech which was commonly called *The Great Secession Speech*. In case the next Congress failed to grant to women all the rights of citizenship, Mrs. Woodhull threatened reprisals. "We mean treason," she proclaimed. "We mean secession, and on a thousand times grander scale than that of the South. We are plotting revolution. . . . We will call another convention expressly to frame a new constitution and to erect a new government, complete in all its parts, and to take measures to maintain it effectually, as men do theirs . . . ." Obviously this new scarcely visible feminine government would require a head. Rising on the crest of her philippic, Mrs. Woodhull again proclaimed herself a candidate for the presidency of the United States—of feminine America—and announced that she would promote any number of exemplary reforms, including a grand international tribunal which would settle the differences between all nations and be supported by an international army and navy.

Alas! she failed to pause with such abstractions; under the hasty momentum of her influence a series of resolutions was composed which threw the fat blazing into the fire. They were read at the convention at the request of the gentle Lucretia Mott, who seems to have been won to the enterprise inaugurated by Mrs. Hooker and Mrs. Davis. This new manifesto insisted that "the evils, sufferings, and disabilities of women, as well as of men, are social still more than they are political," and that "a statement of woman's rights which ignores the right of self-ownership as the first of all rights is insufficient to meet the demand, and is ceasing to enlist the enthusiasm, and even the common interest of the most intelligent portion of the community . . . . The basis of order is freedom from bondage . . . and . . . the principle of freedom is one principle, not a collection of many different and unrelated principles . . . and . . . freedom or bondage is the alternative and the issue, alike in every case . . . and if freedom is good in one case it is good in all; and we in America have built on freedom . . . and the woman's movement means no less than the complete social as well as political enfranchisement of mankind . . . or such order as reigns in Heaven, which grows out of that developed manhood and womanhood in which each becomes a law unto himself. . . ."

Innocent as this long concatenation of phrases sounded, every one knew what they involved; the newspapers came down in a loud derisive chorus with the shout of free love; quarrels developed in open session; Mrs. Woodhull grew arrogant and tried to dispossess Mrs. Stanton as chairman; and the ranks of the left split into two parts with Mrs. Woodhull at the head of one of them. Here was freedom! But Mrs. Woodhull's conquest was transitory; the rift was brief. Though Mrs. Hooker maintained her faith in Mrs. Woodhull through all the tempestuous events which followed, she soon joined the recalcitrant others and returned to the main ranks. The radical suffragists, companions of years, quickly drew together again and left Mrs. Woodhull outside, solitary with her proposal of a great feminine government by rebellion, alone on the road to the Presidency in the spring of 1872. At the same time she became aware that she had lost the support of Theodore Tilton. It was largely as result of Tilton's efforts that the divided left had coalesced—without the inclusion of Mrs. Woodhull. Quickly forgetting his prediction that she would soon reign over the Republic, a sovereign like the other Victoria, he now invented the notion of Horace Greeley in that rôle. In the bitter, ridiculous presidential campaign of 1872 Tilton spoke and wrote endlessly on behalf of Greeley. Mrs. Woodhull dropped from sight. But it was not for nothing that she had been exalted by one of the leading journalists of the day, or that she had triumphed in Washington and New York; nor was it in vain that she had been endowed with an infinite capacity for making public appearances. A few days before the election, on November 2, 1872, she emerged, bent upon destruction.

In a letter to the New York *World* some months earlier she had made an allusion which was generally considered to bear upon the private life of Henry Ward Beecher and that of Theodore and Elizabeth Tilton; she had referred to the adultery of a great public teacher with the wife of another public teacher. A few weeks before the election she had poured forth an amazing tale at the National Convention of Spiritualists, "seized," as she said, "by one of those overwhelming gusts of inspiration which sometimes come upon me." Now in her journal she repeated her narrative with names and with an ample stream of circumstance; so full of particularities, indeed, was her story, that the conclusion was promptly drawn that Tilton had at some time given her its materials, and possibly had suggested their ultimate publication. The story covered pages, and was floated on a cosmic purpose; Mrs. Woodhull proclaimed her intention of creating "a beacon-fire." "I am engaged in officering and in some sense conducting a social revolution on the marriage question," she announced. Hypocrisy, she insisted, was a consuming vice, secrecy the only wrong; Beecher's philosophy was identical with hers; with his power and position he could immensely advance the cause of freedom by an open avowal, and must be made to do so. Freedom was the watchword—freedom, love, and truth! In her utterances at this juncture Mrs. Woodhull reached something like frenzy. When some one told her that she spoke like a weird prophetess, "I *am* a prophetess," she cried with shrill ecstasy, "I *am* an evangel!"

The sale of this startling issue of her paper was enormous; but before new editions could be printed, her presses, types, paper, and office equipment were seized and destroyed, and she herself was imprisoned in Ludlow Street jail on a charge preferred by Anthony Comstock, a young clerk in a drygoods store who had assumed the rôle of voluntary detective, and who a few years earlier, almost single-handed, had obtained the passage of that federal act restricting the scope of printed matter which has since caused so considerable an agitation. Comstock now sought to prosecute Mrs. Woodhull under its provisions. His choice of a test case was unfortunate; her publication obviously did not come within the meaning of the act; though she was returned to jail on successive charges of the same kind within the next six months, he was unable to secure a conviction. In the end she succeeded in making him ridiculous, or at least she told an ingenious legend which contained a semblance of the truth. Out on bail, she engaged to speak at Cooper Institute; a crowd had assembled, but officers were posted at the doors with a new writ, secured by Comstock, to prevent her entrance. As the chairman of the evening was offering an explanation, an old Quaker woman sidled up to the front of the hall, sat down, listened for a few moments with an earnest air, then dashed to the stage, dodged behind a pillar, and quickly reappeared, triumphant but still modest, Victoria Woodhull, with a white rose at her throat. The police were said to be galvanized into admiration; her speech proceeded unhindered; and certainly, if the tale was embellished or even entirely fabulous, she succeeded even at this point in impressing many skeptical beholders by her charming diffidence, and still more with the conviction that she had been made the subject of an unworthy persecution. Conservative journals insisted that she had been unfairly treated; and Beecher, who was considered to have inspired the attack, was linked with the forces of suppression. Indeed, an arc of respectable support had been quickly described about Comstock by a group composed mainly of clergymen and wealthy merchants. A few months later the Society for the Suppression of Vice was founded, in close relationship with a well-known religious organization; Comstock was made its agent, as a reward for his many voluntary services. With this a sufficient war was on. Comstock's reports soon betrayed a system of espionage which covered the lives and pursuits of many persons. A literature sprang up which described the system in detail, and offered as well an unflattering analysis of the agent's character and his subtler motives as revealed by his heavy countenance. A bitter discussion of the relation of Puritanism to art was promoted by Comstock's attempt to suppress a public exhibition of Powers' *Greek Slave*. Insurgent critics noted a resemblance between the Society for the Suppression of Vice and the Moral Societies which had been established in New England fifty years before as a final thrust for authority on the part of the older Puritans.

In the midst of this vociferation might be heard the agreeable voice of Mrs. Woodhull. Freed at last from Comstock's charges, guided no doubt by the tireless Demosthenes, she mounted the lecture platform. With faultless personal reticence and unfailing audacity she delivered over and over two lectures entitled *The Garden of Eden* and *The Human Body the Temple of God*. In each of these she attacked the forces of suppression, again citing the dismissal of Whitman from a governmental office in Washington as an instance, dwelling upon her own experiences, and throwing in for good measure a generous amount of commentary on corruption in high places. But her main purpose was to develop a thesis. "If anything is sacred, the human body is sacred," Whitman had said. Perhaps Mrs. Woodhull derived her impetus from the writings of Whitman; in any case she proceeded to hymn the life of the body in terms which she might have derived from the 1860 edition of *Leaves of Grass;* but she drew her authority from the Bible. By ingenious parallels, geographical, spiritual, and biological, indeed with a wealth of detail in which she had not indulged hitherto, she proved that the Book of Genesis was an allegory woven about the central symbol of the Garden of Eden, which was the body. In the understanding of this truth lay the key to health, to happiness, even to the abolishment of death, which in turn was to accomplish the redemption of the universe. "The broad universe forever marching, marching, marching onward. . . ." Further upward and onward than even was lifted the millennial hope under her glancing touch, swimming now into the remotest parts of the sidereal heavens. The inhabitants of all the planets were watching the dwellers of the

HENRY WARD BEECHER [157]

great green earth with the intensest expectation, she declared, for the earth-dwellers, far more spiritual-minded than the inhabitants of the other spheres, were to solve the final mystery and fling it to the stars.

One after another, through decades, throughout the century, such prophets or evangels had been appearing, messiahs little and great, men and women: Ann Gilchrist, Jemima Wilkinson, Joseph Smith, Miller, John Humphrey Noyes, sometimes leading only small groups of followers, oftener arousing larger numbers, all of them resolutely announcing Zion with mixed or semi-mystical perceptions similar to those which Mrs. Woodhull had formulated. In these years the public prints were overflowing with discussions of Mormonism and of the complex marriages of the Oneida Community as these appeared against a background of the Millennium, impending or arrived. That long debate on free love, which had arisen so abstractly in the fifties and had followed so relentlessly in the wake of the feminists, was assuming gross proportions. For a brief interval the life of the senses was no longer a hidden theme. A strange latitude had developed, particularly in the second New England of the West; a movement was on—a half reputable, tramp movement, which included exploration and expression. With the sibylline touch which she had claimed Mrs. Woodhull had tapped a deep-running stream and had brought it to something of a head, or had clairvoyantly fallen in with its stronger currents. For three or four years she maintained an eminence on the lecture platform, particularly in the West, where little halls in quiet towns and villages were thronged to hear her complex doctrine, where she was accorded a respectful attention.

With something of the stubborn energy which had moved the other evangelists to lead unresisting bands into the wilderness, she had also precipitated a crisis which sent personalities and reputations toppling in a disastrous crash. To her first story, as published in her journal, Beecher had made no reply; his silence had been complete; to many persons it seemed singular. Tilton, on the other hand, had published in a Brooklyn paper a letter to a "complaining friend"—whom he afterward admitted to be mythical—and had crammed this to the last period with veiled hints and passionate asseverations whose meaning, he declared, would soon become apparent. In June, 1873, when at length she had escaped from Comstock's charges, Mrs. Woodhull republished her original narrative. At the same time two new papers were launched, the *Thunderbolt* and the *Rainbow,* whose editorship never became entirely clear, but which contained similar stories. At last, by the simple means of a "card," as it was called in the parlance of the time, Beecher briefly denied the accusations against him, and at the same time demanded an investigation by a committee of his church. Cards and letters now appeared in abundance, from Tilton, who constantly suggested imminent disclosures, from Francis Moulton, the so-called "mutual friend," from Beecher, who presently published a quaint agreement between himself and Tilton and Bowen—the owner of the *Independent* and the Brooklyn *Union*—in which the three had promised to bury all differences. It became clear that Beecher had had a hand in Tilton's dismissal from these papers. Further cards, notes, documents, and letters filtered into the newspapers; obviously the dramatic differences between Beecher and Tilton had run a subterranean course since 1870, and perhaps earlier.

After a considerable interval a prolonged church investigation of the charges against Beecher was held, which so excited the public imagination that a mere meeting of a Plymouth committee in a private house could induce a picturesque newspaper item describing lamplighters going about the streets in the warm dusk, and young ladies and gentlemen strolling, while strains of the *Beautiful Blue Danube* floated from a neighboring melodeon. The Plymouth investigating committee exonerated Beecher, but its proceedings remained secret. Still questions and disclosures and inquiries overflowed in the public prints. In the summer of 1874, a blue-eyed, solemn-faced young man with red whiskers who was described as having "a literary cast of countenance," and whose name was William J. Gaynor, procured the arrest of Theodore Tilton on the charge of libel against Beecher. Young Mr. Gaynor carefully disclaimed partisanship, but he insisted that the public had a right to know the facts. Obstinate and admonitory, he declined a private hearing. The case was several times adjourned, and finally discontinued; but the serious young man had assumed a representative attitude; the whole contentious matter was regarded as a public possession.

During strained and turgid months as the affair ran a blind course, reaching the stage of further church investigations and mounting toward a trial, everything which bore even remotely upon the situation came under public review—everything; not only personalities but principles and causes and modes of conduct and belief. All the feeling which Beecher had aroused through years seemed to seethe up in palpable multitudinous forms; he was made to compose within his own magnified person the larger emotional elements of his time. Scale was the most conspicuous attribute of the whole prolonged affair—scale and candor. With a lack of reticence which might seem incredible in this shyer age, questions of a difficult psychological import were discussed, questions which we are inclined to think we have invented, as to the nature of religious emotion, as to the motives of ecstatics, devotees, religious leaders, and mediums. With rigorous thoroughness the "new religion of sentiment" was surveyed, the "religion of love," or the "religion of gush," as it was more harshly called, of which Beecher was acknowledged to be the leading exponent. "Mrs. Woodhull only carries out Henry's philosophy, against which I recorded my protest twenty years ago," wrote Thomas K. Beecher of Elmira, one of the youngest of Lyman Beecher's children, and finally his father's favorite. Freedom—what was not the outcome of that loose and easy counsel, or of Beecher's exaltation of the life of feeling—of love? Indeed, the grotesque parallels which ran between Beecher's philosophy and Mrs. Woodhull's dubious doctrines were shouted on every side, in serious journals, in newspaper ephemera, in an immense volume of talk. On the other hand claims were entered for the intellect as a factor in human guidance; the loss of a structural theology was noted as a serious loss; the ghost of Lyman Beecher might have walked the scene; and a passion with which he was thoroughly familiar, the *odium theologicum,* burned like a prairie fire. The older orthodoxy, always doubtful of Beecher's sway, now at last obtained a drastic hearing. By a determined onslaught the whole affair was brought within the field of ministerial judgment. In Brooklyn two neighboring churches challenged the method of procedure of the Plymouth investigating committee; a national church council was called with Congregational representatives from the entire country. In the prolonged debate which followed a many-sided controversy took on an enormous momentum, with angry recriminations as to personalities, church polity, and belief.

The council endorsed the procedure of the Plymouth investigating committee, and thus tacitly sanctioned the exoneration of Beecher; but the question refused to die. Boiling up, the inquiry spread to the ranks of the feminist movement, already sufficiently agitated by its brief alliance with Mrs. Woodhull. Feminist motives were scrutinized with that minute consideration of psychological motive which seemed the brief fashion of the day. The same technique was applied to Beecher's writings, more particularly to his novel *Norwood,* with a finish and a thoroughness which later practitioners of the art of psychologico-literary analysis might well envy. Godkin, of the *Nation,* dubbed the language of Beecher, Tilton, and the others a "bewildering dialect," and declared that the letters and public statements in the case furnished "sociological revelations of the most singular and instructive kind." In a sharp enveloping phrase he summed up the result—"chromo-civilization." Indeed, the whole affair eventually ran to terms of social culture. In the West, where Tilton was popular, and where Mrs. Woodhull's modest presence told heavily against Beecher, a formula which had long been maturing now took positive shape; the West had long believed in the depravity of the East, and more particularly in the contaminated degeneration of New York; it now had proof. Even in England, as if by hastening fatality every region of Beecher's public life was to be raked and swept, the affair was not only canvassed but became a peg upon which to hang many an ironic survey of American tendencies, philosophies, and cults.

During this period statements from Beecher and from Tilton still appeared in the public prints. At last the inevitable occurred; the two clashed in civil suits; each sued the other. Beecher failed to prosecute his suit. In 1875 Tilton pushed his case to the issue; and once more, as the trial unrolled, there were recapitulations, rehearsals, and conclusions. Of all the many publications which then and earlier entered upon this turmoil of inquiry, few expressed an entire disbelief in the initial charge against Beecher. On every hand was sounded an almost pathological insistence that he be humbled. "Hands off until he is down!" cried a brother minister. "And then my pulpit, my home, my church, and my purse and heart are at his service." Down—down! The cry was echoed on all sides, on the public platform, in the public prints, in the interchanges of the street, in the cars; Beecher was publicly called upon to commit suicide; showers of lampoons, sketches, booklets, and skits appeared, heaping scorn and ridicule and anger; the minor literature of the case bulked enormously. Yet—was it sheer revulsion in the midst of an abysmal extreme? Or a resurgence of Beecher's old power, as if his hold upon the public after all were fundamentally rooted? Or had something of philosophy arisen out of the long fury of debate? At least for once the monster did not altogether turn against its favorite, but grew Janus-faced. Either face was distorted; in this turbid passage of emotion, belief in Beecher was scarcely less convulsive than hatred or blame. Faith rose to fanaticism. Plymouth Church rallied as in a revival, its devotion fanned to a white-hot blaze; it was noised through the country that the church would support Beecher, right or wrong. In the accumulated exultation Beecher was compared with David and Solomon and Paul—most often with Paul.

FIVE • *Every day for six months during the year 1875 Beecher* walked through the streets of Brooklyn from his home in Clinton Street to the City Court, ruddy and imperturbable, wearing the broad-brimmed hat that made him look like a prosperous farmer. His wife was on his arm. Mrs. Beecher, elderly in appearance, had a look of fragile immobility. Only by the sketchiest sort of inference was it possible to guess how she was affected by the Tilton affair, whether she was enraged or embittered or surprised, or unsurprised, whether her affection for Beecher survived it or whether it had long since died. She too had been brought within a large public consideration; her character had been analyzed, with an ungracious turn. Her severity of manner, her stringent housekeeping—of which Beecher had complained jocosely in his essays—her narrow tastes, her unyielding silences had not only been discussed; they had been used by his antagonists to build up the assumption that Beecher sought companionship outside his own household. What she thought of these accusations does not appear; she endured them like a predestined fate, a last hardship which she might always have expected, a final penalty of public life.

Beecher's serenity was apparently easy and natural; it was certainly abundant. In the courtroom he laughed heartily at the brisk sparring of the counsel or the unexpected sallies of the witnesses, watched each day's proceedings with fresh interest, grew solemn as the testimony became grave, and seemed untouched by anxiety. The ordeal was severe. Tilton's counsel spared nothing by way of satire; sordid byways were followed in the evidence; iteration and reiteration of the charges grew monstrous as the whole course of events passed through the endless processes of examination, as each step was again rehearsed by the newspapers. The amazing space given to the many aspects of the situation by journals throughout the land marked an epoch and broke a dike; some one remarked that the episode had produced nothing short of the abolition of privacy. Yet when the time came for his own testimony Beecher sat in the witnessbox with something of the boyishness which had often been part of his manner; he seemed at ease, with his fingers loosely thrust into his waistcoat; he had grown perceptibly older within a few years, but he scarcely looked his age, which was sixty-two. When questions pressed him close he flushed, trembled, and even wept; but with a candid memory he seemed to re-live scene after troubled scene, slipped into a vivid mimicry of the principal characters concerned—Tilton, Mrs. Tilton, and Moulton—and even appeared to derive pleasure from this exercise. In the cross-examination his answers were unfaltering. His counsel feared that with his invincible carelessless he might fail at essential points, but every episode came out fluent and clear.

Strangely chequered and anomalous, never quite lucid, this situation must have its place in the progress of Beecher's career like any other. Without it, the pattern of his later years loses color and identity. Without a view of this passage, indeed, certain of his triumphs must fail of adequate consideration, and something essential in the simple yet strange composite of his character must be lost.

Late in 1870 Tilton had charged Beecher with an unworthy attitude toward Mrs. Tilton, showing him a letter of accusation which she had written. The exact character of her statement was never proved; of all the many papers in the case this alone had been destroyed; Tilton had destroyed it. Later, in writing, Mrs. Tilton had withdrawn her charge, at Beecher's request. Then, at Tilton's she had withdrawn her retraction. All her statements were variable; she once wrote Moulton that it was a physical impossibility for her to tell the truth. She was small and pretty, pensive and appealing; she had tried to model her character upon that of Mrs. Browning; tears baptised her, she said; and she was afraid of Tilton. Undoubtedly Beecher found her charming; he had expressed his admiration both in and out of season, and the carelessness as well as the ornamentation of his avowals told heavily against him. Yet the whole tangled affair was plainly projected against Tilton's editorial downfall; Tilton's charges were made on the heels of his dismissal from the *Independent* and the Brooklyn *Union*. In the many-sided testimony he admitted that he had procured his wife's first statement to use as a weapon when he learned that Beecher had influenced Bowen at the time of his discharge from the two papers; and Beecher acknowledged in the trial that he had repeated to Bowen certain stories which he had heard as to Tilton's private affairs. Perhaps the relentless attacks of Tilton at the time of the Cleveland letters after the war had left a strain of bitterness in Beecher's mind which led him to retaliation; at least he declared that his immense and obvious contrition—expressed so freely yet so vaguely in his letters to Tilton and Moulton—sprang from the feeling that he had been guilty of slander "in its meanest form," and that he had contributed to, if he had not actually caused, the downfall of a young disciple and friend with consequent broken fortunes for him and for his family. Certainly Beecher's self-reproach had been extreme—too extreme for such a cause, said doubtful critics, accountable enough in view of his sensitive conscience, said his friends. Certainly, too, Beecher had become desperately panic-stricken. Starkly apparent in all the superabundant evidence in the case was the fact that for the two years or more before he made his public gesture of denial Beecher had labored under the emotion of fear—fear which was chaotic and disintegrating, fear of the public. This terror informed letter after letter in his voluminous correspondence with Moulton. Long before, some one had suggested that Beecher possessed courage as a prime trait; and Tilton had answered no, that Beecher was courageous before a multitude but a coward before an individual wrong-doer, that he could not utter a rebuke, that under any sort of personal accusation he crumpled. On this assumption Tilton had apparently proceeded, formulating his public and semi-public charges, arrogantly commanding Beecher to attend interviews, and pressing him into first one service and then another through Francis Moulton.

At the outset, in a breath, like a child, Beecher had turned to Moulton, a man much younger than himself, with whom his acquaintance had hitherto been casual, who had been Tilton's life-long friend, and who had brought Beecher and Tilton together for the first unhappy interview. It was Moulton whom Beecher had consulted at every fresh eventuality —and perils were constantly springing up. Almost habitually Beecher had poured out his depression or his dread in a note to Moulton early on Sunday mornings, and had received assuaging replies before he entered the pulpit. In innumerable letters—"effusions," as he afterwards drily called them—he had written to Moulton of having sold his birthright, of experiencing the tortures of the damned, of the agony of keeping up appearances, of his wish for death; before this enigmatic young counselor he had humbled himself unbelievably in apology, from him had accepted harsh and biting rebukes. To Moulton he had entrusted even the candid letters of his brothers and sisters about the situation as this became public, as well as a quantity of other similar papers. At last, at Moulton's suggestion, he had mortgaged his home in order to furnish Tilton with money to continue *The Golden Age.* Twice, following the guidance of Moulton, he had made large advances of money to Tilton. Naturally these transactions received an ugly name; yet they were compatible with the assumption that Beecher wished to repair the damage which he had done Tilton as a rival in the editorial field. The extraordinary circumstance was less this reckless propitiation than the continuance of Beecher's abasement before Moulton; and strangely enough, the relationship, which on Beecher's part was scarcely adult, which on Moulton's hinted an element of the mesmeric, looms as the single emphatic personal relationship of Beecher's long career. No other emerges with equal distinctness. He had remained, indeed, without close personal companions.

Moulton seems to have enjoyed his offices. Suave and courteous and formal, a little slow perhaps, he apparently had worn throughout a studious air. He had marked precisely the minute and the hour as well as the day when he first became part of the complex situation; he seemed to have all its innumerable details at his command; but his mind was as shuttered and barred as Beecher's was defenseless and open. Every item of his testimony was offered with an effect of quiet caution. "Did you dine on board the yacht?" inquired Beecher's counsel at the trial, requesting information as to a trip to a regatta which Moulton, Beecher, Tilton, and Horace Greeley had made together. "On board the yacht?" echoed Moulton softly. "No sir." "Will you tell us, Mr. Moulton, in what publication the name of that writing was changed from an 'apology' to a 'letter of contrition?'" queried the counsel. "In what published document —in what publication?" repeated Moulton with care. When he was asked on the witness-stand why he had tried to procure a letter of Tilton's to Bowen, he replied, "For the purpose of negotiating with Mr. Bowen, among others, and for the purpose of saving all the families interested. . . ." In secret, Moulton was always negotiating; by the unobtrusive method of absorption he had become the repository of nearly all the documents of every one concerned, excepting only Mrs. Tilton's first letter of accusation. In the end he had declined to return any of the papers which Beecher had entrusted to him. On the witness-stand he declared that his purpose in withholding these had been to prevent any one of the persons involved from injuring the others. Yet before the matter came to a trial every paper of importance had been given to the press; half a dozen journals carried facsimile copies of all the essential letters.

Though the chief actors in this long and puzzling drama lived but short distances apart from each other in Brooklyn they were forever engaged in the business of correspondence; even under the same roof Tilton and Mrs. Tilton were occupied by a considerable interchange of letters; and these communications of the entire group had certain qualities in common, except the letters of Moulton, which for the most part were aloof and self-contained. They were all highly literary, crowded with metaphorical fine language; they all overflowed with engulfing emotions; they all contained the extremes of hope and despair, with a persistent cry of anguished self-reproach, not only the letters of Beecher, but of Tilton and Mrs. Tilton. They were all enormously vague. At the trial and in the public mind many of Beecher's communications became evidence against him because they were so obviously charged with emotion. Snatched from their context, read apart from his other writings they seem, indeed, the vehicles of a deep-seated feeling. But even his letters to Mrs. Tilton were written in what Godkin called a "dialect." They were no different in kind from the empyrean of his oratory; he had used the same exalted metaphors over and over—thunderstorms with great trees bent to earth, misty landscapes, flowers crushed beneath the foot, the persistent shine of gold, the glint of sun and moon; if he spoke of the horror of a great darkness, he had often done so on the lecture platform with an intensity which bordered upon hysteria; the benedictions which he occasionally breathed followed the precise pattern which he had spoken again and again from the pulpit; they were scarcely personal; and his emotions had their characteristic tendency to accumulate momentum from expression. His letters were rather more dense and hurried and breathless than his platform utterances, but that was all. In a hushed and mingled frenzy all this group might have been voicing the extremes of idiom which Beecher had always used. They all seemed bent upon achieving the highest pitch and the deepest downward plunge. That accumulated life of sheer emotion upon which he had long since insisted might at last have become a whirlwind spinning within the tiny compass of their pages. They might all have been bewitched; they might have had their heads in bags; they seemed to be acting out a confused and colored drama to which they were unable to find a clew. Tilton was pursuing a course which meant destruction both for his home and for his career. Beecher was following a mazy path of whose outcome he seemed not to have the slightest notion. Whatever the confused situation in the background, a salty phrase, a downright declaration, most of all a touch of that knowledge of human character upon which—since the days when he first studied phrenology—Beecher had prided himself, might have cut through the ridiculous network by which he was surrounded.

Even during the most humiliating onslaughts of both Tilton and Moulton, he was insisting upon his own understanding of human nature in an extended series of lectures at Yale. His own great object in life, he declared, had been "to understand men." "Men are like open books, if looked at properly," he said. "I can do it with relative facility because I have in my eye the general outlines of a man's disposition and his general tendencies." Yet he took step after absurd step which showed not the slightest perception of the more obvious traits with which his antagonists were endowed. Why was it? From an overwhelming trust in the native human worth, based upon his own large and generous unworldliness—as his friends said? From an hysterical sense of guilt, arising from some small occasion, welling up now as if the whole Puritan sense of sin had broken forth like a submerged geyser? Long ago Lyman Beecher had warned his children against a "nervous conscience," and by his shattering onslaughts had perhaps induced it. All his son's buoyant self-confidence might have been counterbalanced by an equal self-depreciation.

The prodigious quantity of the evidence proved to be mainly in Beecher's favor. It was conclusively shown that Tilton's accusations had fluctuated with his fortunes and had increased point by point through the many months of subterranean intercourse; his charge of adultery was a climax. The heaviest batteries against Beecher lay in the desperate wish for concealment which had appeared not only in his multitudinous letters to Moulton but in every step of his course, in his failure to meet the accusations of Mrs. Woodhull's first story, and later in his reluctance to prosecute his suit against Tilton. In defense Beecher declared that he had considered the whole matter a private affair in which the public could rightly have no concern; he boldly insisted upon this argument; ten years before he had written a brief essay *On the Pleasures of being a Public Man,* in which he had declared bitterly that "public men are bees working in a glass hive, and curious spectators enjoy themselves in watching every secret movement as if it were a study in natural history." His contention in the larger instance had force; yet the silence which he had maintained had hardly been the silence of dignity. Looking out as through some single aperture, Beecher had seen with terror all the monstrous potential enmity of the crowd, had seen nothing else, had foreseen it, for in the end that murderous avalanche of criticism with a hardly less formidable mountain of faith had fallen upon him. Whatever the subtler factors, the whole matter had been fought out in terms of public recognition; and it was a stride into the public view which had brought him into relative clarity at last.

Some months after the first publication of Mrs. Woodhull's story Moulton had proposed the scheme of a new journal of which Beecher was to become the editor, resigning from the ministry. Tilton, who was to manage the foreign bureau, was to go abroad for a few years. Beecher was to raise money for the project. Actually, for a brief space, he had tried to promote the scheme. Whether he recognized finally that this involved robbing him of the essential basis for his career—the pulpit—whether by his consultation with a few friends he stepped outside the small purlieus by which he had been confined, the secret phases of the affair at last were over. Calmly enough he wrote to Moulton that he was willing to have it see the light of day, and added a trenchant note on Tilton's theatrical temperament. *"I will be free,"* he declared with his old belligerence. With his first public card of denial Beecher approached once more his accustomed mode of feeling; cramped and huddled and humiliated for many months, by that slender piece of print he finally entered the familiar areas of the public view. His demand for an investigation by his church seemed to complete his release. "What was most singular was that when the church came into the eclipse, I came out of it," he remarked. "I had had my time when I was dumb, and opened not my mouth . . . but when the trouble came upon the church . . . there came to me amancipation. . . . I had rolled off my burden." During the long-drawn battle of wits and evidence and oratory in the trial Beecher maintained the state of which he thus freely spoke—emancipation. It was as if, whatever the original circumstance, whatever the popular verdict as to his confusion or timidity, his sentimentality or his guilt, he had found his native medium. Beach, the opposing counsel, afterwards said that his bearing was "sublime," and declared that he had not been four days in the trial when he was convinced that Tilton's charges were unfounded; throughout the long aftermath of commentary it was freely argued that Beecher then and later could never have maintained his effect of splendid ease and scale except from a consciousness of innocence. Even when the case ended in a hung verdict—nine for acquittal, three for conviction—his tranquillity appeared secure. Even when he was summoned to a minute and taxing informal examination in Boston he carelessly or pliantly yielded to the indignity.

Still, after nearly five years of public or semi-public rumor, the many-sided question refused to die, either because of something complex and unfathomable about the whole affair, or because of the momentum which attached to Beecher's character and the forces with which it had become closely interwoven. When some of his antagonists declined to withdraw from the Plymouth congregation new problems of church procedure developed; once more neighboring churches entered into the controversy. At last another church council was called with representatives from the entire country, which reopened the whole matter.

Once more Beecher showed himself willing to submit to a drastic inquiry; but as the proceedings lengthened interminably he faced the council in anger and demanded to know how much more by way of questioning he was expected to endure. He shouted that he had been the victim of a persecution of the most unworthy kind. "I have not been hunted as the eagle is hunted," he cried with his old careless inflation. "I have not been pursued as a lion is pursued. I have not been pursued even as wolves and foxes. I have been pursued as if I were a maggot in a rotten corpse. . . . I have about come to the state of mind that I don't care for you or anybody else. Well, you know that is not so; I do care, and I don't, and I do again, and then I don't, just as I happen to feel. I am tired of you; I am tired of the world; I am tired of men that make newspapers, and men that read them; I am tired of a community that hasn't a particle of moral reaction"—forgetting perhaps his own long inertia. "I think people look upon my being tried as if it were a game of battledore and shuttlecock, and as if being tried was nothing but being tossed in the air by two clever fellows, and as if I ought to like it. . . . Is it possible for a man to live as long as I have, and as openly, and to have acted upon so large a theater, and been agitated by such world-shaking events, and be so utterly misconceived? . . . No man can take it from me that I have loved my kind without caste or distinction," he shouted, as though he were finding justification. "No man can take it from me! . . . I have lived in a minority all my days, contesting for the right and for liberty! . . .

"Tomorrow morning it will be said in the local journals, 'Well, Mr. Beecher—how rhetorically he managed the matter!' And it will be put in the religious papers, 'Oh, yes! That was a very plausible statement at the time—but—but—' . . . I am questioned and questioned and questioned, as I have been through months and years, on the supposition that the truth has not been got out. . . . I don't look with any great hope for the result of this council. I don't look for any hope from any council or tribunal. . . ." But the council vindicated Beecher and sustained the procedure of Plymouth Church at every point. Public references to the case grew less frequent. Beecher himself spoke an epilogue on his own course, which remains as one of his few pungent self-criticisms. Referring to the support of his friends and in particular to the assistance of his church—which had reached proportions truly colossal—he mentioned this as "the humane efforts of good men to drag an ass out of the pit."

The principal figures in the case resumed familiar attitudes, or struck new ones which held the old configurations. If Moulton had liked negotiations he was now submerged by these in the unpleasant form of civil suits; hurried by events, he had let fly incautious remarks about a number of persons who angrily determined to obtain redress. Mrs. Tilton vanished into an obscurity which was not without pathos. Tilton wrote a novel called *Tempest Tossed* which was full of biographical allusions, and soon went to Paris, where he lived for many years, gaunt, wasted, and flippant, continuing to write allegories on the hopes and illusions of mankind; appropriately enough, the volume of his collected verses was called *The Chameleon's Dish.* When the furor had lapsed, and the movement which she had sponsored sank once more below the level of repute, Mrs. Woodhull quietly went to England, and made an interesting marriage into middle-class wealth and respectability. Unwilling or unable to abandon a public career altogether, she founded a journal called *The Humanitarian,* a solid prosy organ which fitted snugly into the reform movements of the day, and was devoted to the science of eugenics. Its cover bore a tempered reference to the editor's career.

"How he lived and toiled and suffered
That the tribes of men might prosper,
That he might advance his people. . . ."

Obviously the source of this fragmentary motto lay on this side of the water; and in the end, an elderly woman, Mrs. Woodhull turned toward her native land with a broad gesture. She joined in a movement—the purest and mildest—for rehabilitating the ancestral home of George Washington. The gesture became, indeed, a handsome flourish; she was received into the counsels of an impeccable American organization composed of women, and achieved a highly respected and honored old age.

With these figures in the foreground of popular memory, with the whole long sequence of events graven upon the popular mind, Beecher confronted his multitudinous world. He at once appeared on the lecture platform. He lacked even the advantage which comes from abrupt contrasts; his larger public career had been interrupted long before in the years of dullness and confusion which had followed the Civil War; his positive triumphs lay more than ten years behind him. All his activities had suffered a severe check; the circulation of his books had fallen off; though he had become an editor of the *Christian Union,* this paper had never gained the widespread popularity which had belonged to the *Independent* under his sway in the fifties and early sixties. In the lecture field, instead of his old plenitude of engagements he was obliged to take what he could get. As he began his first tour he encountered something more definite than indifference—hostility. In many western towns he was received with hoots and jeers as he left the cars; he frequently passed to his hotel between crowds whose rough animosity was obvious; once the train in which he was traveling was invaded at a siding by a gang of roughs. He commanded hearers, but his audiences were cold and derisive. There they finally were, in a last line, the tangible public, with a multiple sea of faces, with figures solidly planted in repeated rows and circles and galleries, watching his every move, balancing his every sentence. If he had once seemed to draw his affluence of emotion from his public, he could scarcely do so now; and he lacked the easy elasticity of youth. Beecher was moving toward seventy.

He seemed oblivious of these popular attitudes; as he fronted the noisiest demonstrations he remained impassive. For himself, the whole episode which had cleaved his career might have dropped long since into a bottomless chasm. Without a tremor, without a sign, he took up the old threads of his discourse, the old sentiments, his accustomed manner, precisely where he had left them off in the more ardent years of his triumph. With his mild beginnings, with that deflation of egotistical effect which had always been part of his genius, he embarked upon the old careless business of self-portrayal. "Somehow I have always had a certain sympathy with human nature which had led me invariably, in my better moods, to see instinctively or to perceive by intuition how to touch the right chord in people, how to reach the living principle in them. . . . I have been blessed to an unusual degree as a comforter. There is nothing sweeter to me in this world than to meet one and another, as I do continually, who say, 'I never could have gone through my business troubles, Mr. Beecher, but for your preaching,' or 'When sorrow came into my household my heart was broken, and I owe it to you that I was lifted, as by the voice of angels, into the realm of peace.'" He declared that his nature was "designed" to interpret to men a "sense of justice as it is developed out of the divine love and sympathy. . . . That style of truth belongs to my own personality, and when I preach it, I preach a part of myself. . . . There are times when it is not I that is talking; when I am caught up and carried away so that I do not know whether I am in the body or out of the body. . . . I see things and hear sounds, and seem, if not in the seventh heaven, yet in a condition that leads me to apprehend what Paul said—that he heard things which it was not possible for a man to utter. . . . I am acting under such a temperament as that. I have got to use it, or not preach at all. . . . I know very well that I do not give crystalline or thoroughly guarded views; there is often an error on this side and an error on that, and I cannot stop to correct them. . . . I have my own peculiar temperament; I have my own method of preaching; and my method and temperament necessitate errors. I am not worthy to be related in the hundredth thousand degree to those more happy men who never make a mistake in the pulpit. . . . I make a great many . . . I am impetuous. . . . The average of a man's teaching will be more mighty than a single misconception, or misapprehension through misconception. . . ." Candid and unfaltering, he reviewed his purposes, his hopes, his triumphs, and struggles. Episode by large episode he discussed the course of his long career. He described his efforts in breaking away from that terror of the law which his father had striven to impress upon all his children; in these years he referred frequently to the influences of his youth. He recalled his participation in the struggle against slavery, with some carelessness as to dates, but a generous acknowledgment of the services of others. "I have had no ambitions," he declared. "I have sought no laurels. I have deliberately rejected many things that would have been consonant to my taste. It would have been for me a great delight to be a scholar," he said with apparent conviction. "I should have relished exceedingly to have perfected my thought in the study, and to have given it such qualities that it would stand as the classics stand. . . ."

Quietly, judicially, his audiences listened, as if they sought to penetrate beyond his words. Still he talked, as if he too were seeking something. At the height of his popularity a possession vast and generic had been his; he had attained on an enormous scale that equable relationship with the crowd which seems to lie in one or another form at the basis of so many human longings, whose absence is the secret of many a desperate struggle and defeat. He meant to have it again, on the old terms, without capitulation or sacrifice. There was nothing subservient in his apologia; he kept an abrupt and savage power over interlopers. Lecturing in Chicago against communism, he arose on the tide of an ample period to one of his old hopeful pronouncements, "The voice of the people is the voice of God!" "The voice of the people is the voice of a fool," shrilled a heckler in the gallery. "I said the voice of the people, not the voice of one man," roared Beecher. At times a gross stress upon his own powers broke forth. An obscure country minister told him that many persons had noted a resemblance between himself and Beecher, and that once he had actually spoken before an audience which had believed that he was Beecher. "Was it before or after the lecture?" queried the great man with a shout of laughter. Asked whether he had read all the books written by his brothers and sisters, he flatly announced, "I have made it a rule of my life to read none of the writings of my relatives; with two or three exceptions I have adhered to the rule," and with enormous gusto told the story of the man who death-sentence was commuted on condition that he read a long dull volume, and who declared at last that he preferred execution. Some of these narratives slipped into print; Beecher remained careless of such effects. In public and in private he showed the kind of sense of humor which might have belonged to his boyhood; he could be prodigiously entertained when a chair into which he dropped proved lower than he expected. Oblivious of criticism, he could fling forth dubious images, calling certain types of religious literature the "swill of the house of God." Considering for a moment a charge of sentimentality, he repelled it with a gross self-magnification. "I suppose I do *slop over* sometimes. . . . A man who has only a pint of feeling in an enormous bucket never slops over. . . . And as every flower or blade of grass rejoices when the rain falls upon it, so every recipient along the way in which a man with overflowing generous feeling walks, is grateful for his bounty."

A roar of sound and a tumult of feeling: these were his still to command; and a tempestuous sonority was again in vogue; there still were many voices. Gough was maintaining a loud ascendancy in the midst of the shrill clatter which Talmage and Moody were lifting; Ingersoll with his tempestuous sweep of oratory could outshout most of the newcomers. But even in the new era, among younger men Beecher regained his accustomed lead. In the many unspoken passages between himself and his hearers he triumphed; obviously he was giving them—the omnivorous public—himself, his many selves, without question or reserve; surely he had nothing to conceal. With renewed fervor his admirers spoke of the effect of "total character" which he seemed to offer on the platform; after years of turmoil, he was seen to possess a "primeval depth and freshness"—the quality which had impressed Thoreau long ago. Indeed, if he had suffered from strain this was not apparent, though a look of fierce determination showed upon his face when the excitement of speech had ebbed—a new look. Gradually his circuits widened; he pressed beyond the Mississippi toward the coast; triumph of all triumphs, he spoke successfully in the South. At first he encountered a bitter suspicion; he was faced by mobs; but he met them with a quick conciliatory strength; at Memphis he was greeted by a salute of twenty-one guns. He became easier, more companionable; bright images began to deck his discourses as in the old days. More and more frequently he drifted into exuberant picturings. When some one requested a copy of a prayer which he had offered, he replied that he would send it if his hearer would in turn reproduce "the notes of the oriole that whistled from the tops of my trees last June, or the iridescent globes that came in by the millions on the last waves that rolled in on the beach yesterday, or the segment of the rainbow last week, or the perfume of the first violet that blossomed last May. . . ." The diamond scepter appeared in his discourses; once when he was reported as saying "a diamond-studded scepter," he impatiently insisted that the scepter which he saw was made from a single blazing gem.

He wielded the gaudy instrument. Royal—the word echoed through his speech, was used to sum up his aphorisms; the effect was apparent in his manner. On an extravagant scale Beecher now apparently possessed all his old aptitudes and gifts, together with something else which was new and unwonted, the supple armor of a discipline. He who had always hated routine now forced himself to observe a careful regimen, exercised with careful regularity, ate sparingly, was immoderate only in sleep. With exquisite precision he would choose the diversion among many diversions which would create a mood harmonious with that which he meant to express. If he found himself over-stimulated by the thrilled animation of repeated successes, he knew how to block reflection, or to arouse himself to a new and sufficient emotional pitch. "A new excitement, *brought in from another quarter,*" he explained, "will meet the old one, and on the ashes of the past you will build up a new flame." With his accustomed carelessness he announced that most oratorical effects were the result of calculation. Candidly he declared that the majority of men were feeble in logical power, and that "every address should have dull passages to rest the audience." "If I can make men laugh I do not thank anybody for the next move; I will make them cry." At will he could move from bold distinctions and a popular vocabulary to something quite different; in these later years he refined his eloquence, and exhibited a taste and tact which were seldom present in the first noisy climax of his fame. His speech at the dinner given in New York in honor of Herbert Spencer was an admirable thing of its kind; nothing could have been more quietly fitting than his main allusions, nothing more slyly witty than his hints as to theological differences, though at the end he lapsed as in fatigue, and voiced the hope of meeting Spencer in heaven. Years before Matthew Arnold had called Beecher "a heated barbarian." Now he listened to a sermon in Plymouth Church and was immensely struck by the graciousness with which in a few words after the service Beecher acknowledged his "rebukes."

Once more he became the triumphant herald of new modes of feeling. With fluency he found a new and perfect passage to the Millennium in the theory of evolution. For a space, indeed, he had puzzled over *The Descent of Man,* and had grown deeply depressed; but quickly enough he had accepted its thesis, liking the stress upon a natural world, liking the fantasy of magnitude and change. By a broad and happy gesture he identified change with progress and science with religion; his series of lectures on these themes had an immense vogue, and shook theological bulwarks to their foundations. After his recent controversies he was expected to exhibit moderation or even a crouching acceptance of the usual formulas; but he continued, and enjoying the jolt and stir, severed his connection with the Congregational Association. In these flying years, indeed, he fairly linked himself with the skeptics and atheists by his tolerance; more than once in his public addresses he waved a friendly hand at Ingersoll.

In the same brief space of the early eighties Beecher again assumed a defiant political leadership. Once more he raised the old cries, as if he meant to encircle all the elements of his earlier triumphs. Again he sounded the rallying-call of liberty—for thought, speech, commerce, industry, liberty "around the whole conclave," from East to West, from North to South; liberty was the atmosphere which made men, and men made states, and states made the Millennium; our government was not intended to become a paternalistic government; the common people are competent to manage their own affairs. These counsels were highly popular with the hard-headed empiricists in *laissez faire* who had rushed to the fore since the Civil War. But fairly launched, Beecher swung into applications of the doctrine of liberty which were hardly acceptable to his allies. With an untrammeled gesture he urged international free trade at a time when a fast-bound tariff was a sacred wall for his more prosperous constituents. With noise and gusto he argued for unrestricted immigration, when for years the social prejudices against immigrants had been growing snug and secure. He even insisted that the Chinese would make desirable citizens. Looking about, he discovered corruption. Some years earlier he had seen dark rifts in the ever-golden horizon. "Money—money—money! Today the whole Atlantic seaboard is covered with smuggling—money! The whole land is a pandemonium of swindling—money! . . . The days are near at hand when money is to bear a relation to politics scarcely yet suspected, notwithstanding our recent experiences in corruption." In this address he grew incoherent and enraged, repeated himself, arose to rhetorical heights and crashed down again, as though he were struggling with some not altogether lucid conviction. But his main references were clear enough; he had dwelt upon the corruption revealed in the Tweed Ring; and he sounded a warning as to the place of money in politics. "Whichever party goes to Albany it is all the same. Men are about alike after being dissolved in that cauldron. . . ."

In 1884 there was no mistaking Beecher's indictment of the Republican party for its cynical disregard of the problem of corruption, shown through the nomination of Blaine. Flatly enough he declared the Republican leaders to be more concerned with political entrenchment than with the welfare of the nation. He stumped for Cleveland, became a chief of the Mugwumps, and once more faced a bitter and stormy anger within his congregation. Largely through his insistent energy Plymouth Church had become solidly Republican in the earlier and more perilous infancy of the party; now his people were as immovable and sure and solemn as though they contained the tables of stone on which were inscribed the final political commandments. Everywhere party faith had grown fanatical as result of the uproar over the dubious candidate; Mark Twain in Hartford considered it an act of conspicuous courage for a reputable citizen openly to cast a vote for Cleveland. Beecher was plunged into a political warfare not unlike that which had followed his incautious statements as to national policy at the end of the Civil War. Then he had been overwhelmed by the onrush of criticism; now he seemed inflexibly resolved not to yield a hair's breadth. His larger constituency outside the church turned against him; his friends grew cold or caustic; again the history of his recent years was dragged forth in relation to charges against Cleveland. To continue in the campaign was to court reminiscence of the whole episode.

"I will not be prudent," Beecher shouted in wrath. On the platform he referred in unmistakable terms to his own experience. To the end of the campaign he spoke repeatedly for Cleveland, and rode at last into calm water by the turn of the election. The roused antagonism of his special public died away. Less than two years later when he went to England many thousands of persons packed the wharves; he was escorted down the bay by a steamer crowded to the gunwales by his admirers, who had arranged an elaborate pageantry of farewell. At Liberty Island the liner slowed down, the crowded smaller boat came alongside, a band played *Hail to the Chief,* and a deafening salute of whistles went up from craft all over the bay. Among the many gifts with which Beecher was showered was a flock of homing pigeons which were to be released at intervals with messages during the voyage—flying emblems to span the lengthening space between himself and his people.

In England here and there he encountered coldness, criticism, or an air of speculation, but without apparent effort he swept questions away, and transformed indifference into enthusiasm. Throngs waited hours to hear him in London, listened with something akin to rapture, his addresses mounted to unbelievable numbers; he was acclaimed as the world's greatest orator, the greatest living American, one of the world's greatest citizens; the triumphs of his most thrilling years were repeated, those of 1863, now without a perceptible struggle. The world was again his own. Bringing home the spoils of many an opulent excursion—silks, velvets, plushes, pictures, sculpture, books—he received a welcome which like the farewell was appropriately royal, and resumed the life which he had so freshly known in the early fifties. Several years earlier he had begun to build his second summer dwelling, "Boscobel," a spreading edifice in the cottage style which had gradually assumed innumerable broad verandas and a wealth of carved and cut spindles and posts and ledges and cupolas. The grounds were those of a rich country place. Beecher's collection of rare shrubs was equaled in size and value only by a famous national collection; his flowers, endless in variety, were even more abundant and scarcely less notable. He bought fine breeds of cattle, horses, poultry; the whole place breathed an extravagant plenty. At the table he insisted that there must be such quantities of everything that any person could make a meal of a single dish if he chose. "Skimpy messes," he declared, were his abomination.

Again Mrs. Beecher moved into a scant antithesis; she still protested; her *Letters from Florida,* probably written for the returns the book would bring, indicate her constant preoccupation—thrift. In her book she wished to prove that people could live on almost nothing if they chose to reclaim the waste lands of Florida; but with a literal personal voice she seemed to be saying something else. "If you look for something sensational and romantic," she said by way of preface, "you are doomed to disappointment. That is not my vocation—more's the pity! . . . I can but look with longing on this promised land, this storehouse of poetry and romance; I may not unlock the gates and enter in. . . . Truth unvarnished is, however, full of elements possessing more abiding attractions than the most brilliant story; and to that I shall strictly adhere. . . ." Offering counsel, describing at length the conditions for fruit-growing and goat-raising and the means of combating malaria, snakes, and mosquitoes, she revealed her theme of a close economy; she spoke it even above the prosaic details of her extraordinary project. Perhaps she still was haunted by the narrow poverty of her life in the West. Indeed there was need for thrift in her household; after the huge drain of the trial Beecher had been in financial straits for several years, though his church had supplied him abundantly with funds. He seemed oblivious of stringencies; he became aggressively careless, lavish, open-handed. Once after a wedding ceremony he found that the envelope handed to him contained a thousand dollar bill; the large sum was offered because Beecher was known still to be laboring under financial difficulties. "We will consider that we found this money," he remarked to his agent, and proceeded to spent it for objects of household adornment which he had long coveted.

After his return from England, Beecher plunged into his usual activities—lecturing, preaching, writing. He agreed to write several articles a week for a newspaper syndicate, and forced himself to begin them; he promised an autobiography which was never undertaken; and he pledged himself to finish his long delayed *Life of Christ*. The first volume had been written in the two dark years of underground conflict in the Tilton affair; he once said that its interior history could never be revealed; and in truth the book was never ended. Long before, during his first visit abroad, he had seen a painting of the head of Jesus which he felt to be "approximately true," but afterward he was unable to find it; the name of the painter escaped him; even the portrayal itself grew faint and elusive; perhaps this was a revelation of the ascetic Christ. Whatever his conception, now in much the same way his great theme slipped away, the subject of a lifetime; its matter failed to take shape. He was spurred by the insistence of friends, by an explosive lawsuit, by a contract with a new publisher; he planned many times to begin work, but postponement followed postponement. It is a curious circumstance that the last chapter of his uncompleted book, picturing Jesus on the shore of Galilee, ended with a comment upon the fickle responses of the crowd; from that point Beecher never went on. Did he contemplate with anything like irony his own long battle? From the public, from the great antagonist and companion of a lifetime, he had gained what he sought—vindication and something more, the tangible right which he called liberty. Beecher seems to have known that his work was ended. He looked worn; his great figure had settled; the long locks which he had tossed back in earlier years with a leonine motion now hung spare and straggling; his florid countenance was heavily compressed, coarsened, and weatherbeaten; the fierce fire of determination was its single unmistakable expression, even in repose. He was stricken by paralysis early in March, 1887, overheard the statement that he could not recover, and lapsed into a profound lethargy. The end came quickly.

For a few months, for a few years, praise of Beecher was sounded on the old grand scale. "Our sense of vacancy is such as it might be if a great mountainous bulk which had always been the glory of our neighborhood had been withdrawn into some yawning chasm of earth," said one eulogist. The old comparisons were reiterated, with Paul, with Luther, with Bunyan. Certain critics declared that he must be considered not as a religious teacher at all, but as an esthetic force. He was linked with Ruskin and Carlyle. Again he was called the Shakespeare of the pulpit, because of his knowledge of human nature, the abundance of his poetry, and his dramatic gift; it was observed that his published works outbulked Shakespeare's ten times over, as indeed they did. Besides his many miscellaneous writings he had published more than seven hundred sermons; and these represented only a fraction of the expression of his fifty active years. Who, indeed, had raised so rich a voice in all the thunder of the century? Who remained to offer so ample a comfort, to arouse so thrilled an expectancy, to shake a huge public with his every emotion? Beecher quickly became a legend—is still a legend. His early moral lectures traveled on through the century, and beyond; his many discourses are still conned for their wealth of allusion to all the great subjects—life, love, the family, home, heaven, patriotism, religion—and for their floral wealth of figures. Even now he might recognize himself in many an obscure sermon in many a little pulpit, as his mountains and mists and dissolving views, his chaplets of flowers and glitter of gold emerge from expositions of the text; sometimes he is quoted. Here and there for a time after his death, evidences of a harsh and searching criticism appeared. A remorseless English critic called him the Barnum of religion. His style, his character, his influence were canvassed and condemned; some observers maintained that his influence had been disastrous, producing nervous excitement, hysteria, or something akin to intoxication in many of his hearers, with consequent exhaustion. Puzzled critics sought the inner springs of his character; captious ones announced that he had left no solid residuum of thought. But who shall say as to that? "What is Optimism? . . . What is Pessimism? . . . In looking at our own day and generation there is both light and shadow. . . . It makes a great deal of difference what you call things. . . ." These happy axioms and large abstractions, if scarcely the product of the mind, have served in lieu of thought, and have remained as a solace or an anchorage for large numbers of people. If the Rocky Mountains are taken as a sounding-board, subtleties can scarcely occupy a large place. Beecher kept the measurements which he had established. As for the inner springs of character, we must admit that these are often deeply buried.

Horace Greeley

POSED *on a slight eminence, governing a tiny triangle of* Manhattan, in the midst of clangor and confusion and change, sits an effigy in stone of Horace Greeley. Anxiety peers from the small and straining eyes; a long leg is thrust forward as in discomfort. An uneasy apparition, Greeley dwells within City Hall Park; and once more in far quieter spaces, as a final memorial, his image appears with a look of fretted, infantine grief.

Except for the singular emphasis, these commemorations are smooth and formal; the half-forgotten sculptors seem to have chiseled their contours in haste, boredom, or neglect. None of them has revealed the grotesque and shambling figure of the man, the friendliness of his odd countenance, or its complexity; and something of the same casual view has developed within the popular mind. In the fifty years that have passed since his death, the effacements of time have become fairly complete in the case of Horace Greeley. Newspaper men, it is true, still speak of him with amused companionship; he is sanctioned for a vague righteousness in upholding the cause of the negro; his counsel, "Go West, young men, and grow up with the country!" is remembered as the cry of an era. But even these remembrances have grown fragmentary and dim.

An obtuse contradiction exists between the insubstantial figure of today and the living presence of Greeley in the florid mid-century. He then seemed the liveliest pattern of the American ideal, a country boy who had risen by his own efforts within the almost classic mode of the printing office to a position of immense power. His every lineament and homeliest prejudice, his commonest phrases and shades of opinion, were known familiarly and affectionately up and down the land. *"Stop the Tribune"* was often roared in anger; but for three decades Greeley was able to outshout every cumulative noise, to outride every storm. Then he was hurled from public life, he plunged into death, as by a rapid propulsion of the public mind, to the accompaniment of loud and raucous public laughter, in a tragedy that lacked both dignity and scale. Oblivion closed over him without gradual ceremony.

The cataclysm which ended his career came with an unmistakable turn in public events. Was there then something transient rather than elementary in Greeley's character, so that he belonged to an era, and quickly passed with it? Or was the final calamity an outcome of something subtle and insecure in his own temperament? The answer may not be easy; certain aspects of those scambling times which Greeley knew were secret and remote. Whether we can discover the substantial Greeley as he pushes in and out of a crowded foreground must remain a question, not only because the human character is notoriously elusive, but because he seemed to possess many of its strange, clashing qualities. But Greeley draws us, perhaps, for this very reason, and by the warmth and ardor which he was able to inspire for years in his own era; he knew every one, he brushed against a multitude of events, large and small. Out of the panorama of his career—the scenic diorama, as it might have been called by the friend and contemporary, Barnum, who purveyed this entertainment at the American Museum—he may at least emerge as his contemporaries saw him, with part of the load of his times upon his capacious back.

ONE • *Hardy and long-lived, blacksmiths or farmers for the most part,* the Greeleys and the Woodburns were Scotch-Irish families which migrated to New England during the first half-century of the colonial settlements, the Greeleys in 1640, the Woodburns somewhat later. In the course of two or three generations members of each family had found their way into the neighborhood of the little town of Londonderry in New Hampshire, where other pioneers of their race were entrenched. The soil was unyielding, the country dark and still, whitened by the wind in summer and by the long snows of winter, and somber always; but the life of the settlers seems to have been anything but dour. They accepted a harsh faith yet failed to regard it closely; they grew boisterous, good-humored, given to ballad-making, drinking, dancing, and the celebration of funerals by gatherings which closely resembled wakes. By the end of the eighteenth century or the early years of the nineteenth, the people of this region, roaming well outside the Puritan tradition, had provoked a scathing comment by Timothy Dwight, president of Yale College, and tireless promoter of the Puritan renascence, who was exploring New England on his famous travels. Dwight declared that the moral tone of New Hampshire was low, and observed further that the moral declension had resulted in worldly failure.

The unexemplary course was illustrated by the fortunes of the Greeleys and the Woodburns; in these bleak uplands they barely held their own, and had little or nothing to hand down to succeeding generations. When the two families were united in 1808 or thereabouts by the marriage of Mary Woodburn and Zaccheus Greeley, the young pair slid into poverty. Tall and handsome, cold in manner but convivial of habit, Zaccheus grew gay at the smoky bars of taverns, or lifted his powerful tenor voice at apple-bees or husking-parties, often singing for hours when no fiddler was available for the dances. Mary Woodburn, a muscular, ruddy woman, smoked a pipe and could outstrip any man in the neighborhood at the heavy work of the harvest; she drank, sang, laughed, and told stories all day as she worked and all evening long when her work was done, and possessed a more contagious mirth than did her husband; but she was unable to marshal her energies for the purpose of getting on in the world. This young pair hardly solved the problem of farming in New Hampshire; their method of conquering a stubborn soil was to leave it. They moved frequently.

These were the parents of Horace Greeley, who was their third child, born February 3, 1811, on a stony little farm a few miles from the village of Amherst. The other two infants had died; and Horace was passionately cherished by his mother in consequence. He was sickly; and it was soon apparent that he was an oddity or a wonder. To watch the fall of rain made him violently ill; he could scarcely endure the sound of a gun. By the time he was two he had learned to read, so anxiously scanning the pages of his mother's books as she read that he soon could follow a text sidewise or upsidedown. The printed page entranced him; perhaps its shelter offered quiet. Before he was six he had read the Bible through consecutively, and was the marvel of the neighborhood as a speller. At about this time some one gave him a copy of the *Columbian Orator,* which contained a selection particularly appropriate for recitation by a prodigy. Again and again at school exhibitions and at other public gatherings Horace was thrust forward to declaim it, a tiny white-haired nervous little boy with a piping, pleading voice:

> "You'd scarce expect one of my age
> To speak in public on the stage;
> And if I chance to fall below
> Demosthenes or Cicero,

Don't view me with a critic's eye
But pass my imperfections by.
Large streams from little fountains flow;
Tall oaks from little acorns grow."

In the midst of these boastful homilies suddenly appeared a larger theme:

"But why may not Columbia's soil
Rear men as great as Britain's isle—"

Columbia could—Columbia would; in truth the pages of the *Orator*
were full of variations on the happy paraphrase "We are born in the
best of all possible countries at the best of all possible times." Grandeur
and glory, the ardors of patriotism and those of eloquence, were com-
mingled in this volume; Greece and Rome were resonantly mentioned
as the cradles of republican sentiment; indeed, a small and classical new
world emerged. In an inevitable and orderly progress the little speaker
himself was to prove a great example. Promptly and complacently the
couplets wheeled back to him:

"Or where's the boy but three feet high,
Who's made improvements more than I?
These thoughts inspire my youthful mind
To be the greatest of mankind—"

Classical echoes were to haunt the mind of Horace Greeley; and perhaps
in these exercises he received the print of a tempestuous purpose. A
timid child, he was thrust into vociferous speech; he was fascinated by
applause, though the sound must have smote his sensitive ear like
rifle-shots. He both liked and hated the hot confusion. In school he
craved approval, and cried when he failed to reach the top of his class
in spelling. Yet like many prodigies he remained solitary; among other
children he was shrinking and deprecating; he never learned to fight,
passively took whatever onslaught fell upon him, and went by the not
undescriptive name of Hod.

Before Horace was seven he was set to work picking hops, watching
charcoal pits at night, killing wire-worms in the corn, riding a horse
to plow; often he was late for school, and still more often did not go
at all. Other children were born to the Greeleys, another son, and two
daughters. Zaccheus still failed to prosper, and slipped further down the
social scale. Moving from one obdurate tract to another, the family at
last was forced into positive flight; with a lavish gesture Zaccheus had
given security for a boon companion who proved insolvent. Snatching

a few remnants of their possessions when the sheriff had all but invaded the house, Mary Woodburn drove with her children into Vermont, whither her husband had fled to escape imprisonment. Their remaining household goods were seized for the debt. For Horace the episode was full of haunting terror, ignominy, and confusion. The following winter the disconsolate family group was seen by a neighbor through the window of their wretched little hut on a rented farm at Westhaven near Lake Champlain, the two elders seated at a rough table, the children around a pan of porridge on the floor, all of them miserably clad. Again the family moved, farther north, where Zaccheus undertook to clear a pine swamp. In a rough wild country there began for Horace that dry and vibrant echo of woodchopping which he was to hear for many of his years. This enterprise failed, as did another of the same kind. The Greeleys seemed to pursue the fate of instability and change. In 1826, soon after the opening of the Erie Canal, Zaccheus was caught by the western fever, and decided to migrate with his family to the farther boundaries of Pennsylvania. Horace presented a blank front; he meant to become a printer. Walking many miles to East Poultney, he contrived to impress the owners of the village paper, who needed an apprentice; and Zaccheus bound him out.

Thus Horace entered upon another long period of drudgery, setting type, pulling sheets for long hours from the small hand press. Tall and uncouth, awkward and near-sighted, with a thatch of silvery-yellow hair and the face of a ten-year-old child, he stumbled along the streets or peered over his box in the office. His clothing was linsey-woolsey, rising high above his wrists and ankles. His fellow-workmen inked his hair and mocked his manner and his clothes; he became the subject of innumerable rough practical jokes. "Now, boys, don't," was the length of his rejoinder; with his odd head tip-tilted, he seemed oblivious of their gibes; he was wrapt, in truth, by a happy delusion, writing poetry in the manner of Campbell, Byron, and Mrs. Hemans—noisy, rhetorical verses, full of strong emotions and theatrical scenes. In spite of his appearance, in spite of a voice which was thin and beseeching, he plunged into the art of oratory on the rostrum of the village debating society. "Do we, as a nation, exert a good moral influence in the world?" This earnest query was being confronted in many parts of the country; the thrilling notion was afloat that Columbia was to become something of a Messiah among the nations; many heralds were proclaiming the national rôle. "Is marriage conducive to happiness?" This question boldly smacked of heresy. Happiness was scarcely viewed as a natural estate by the orthodox believers of this region. But the young people of the village were still more daring, and became favorably disposed toward Universalism, that rosy creed which denied the Calvinistic doom altogether, and proclaimed that the destiny of mankind was that of progress forever upward and onward with ultimate happiness for all. After running underground for a generation or more this dangerous theory had suddenly burst forth, and was spreading rapidly in New England. Like the others, Horace accepted the lavish argument; and at the same time, fairly treading the clouds, he entered another field of romance. His political opinions were given life and color by the dashing figure of Henry Clay.

As we look down the funnel of years Clay seems to have been forever facing the destiny of defeat; but in the late twenties glamor irradiated even distant portrayals of his character and of his person; he was eloquent at a time when eloquence was beginning to capture the fancy of an entire people; he had already promulgated his famous American system, with its barrier of a protective tariff—for the East—balanced against a network of internal improvements—for the West—and promising a country bound together in a passionate yet practical union. It was true that he had made startling reversals; Clay and John Quincy Adams were never anything but a strangely incongruous pair. But Clay, at least, had succeeded in riding the wave of amazement that arose at this last extraordinary juxtaposition. For our awkward young apprentice he became a legendary figure about which to wind a hundred impractical hopes. In his hero's early poverty, his rise from obscure beginnings, his lack of formal education, appeared a happy omen and promise. The singular circumstance was the depth and the tenacity of young Greeley's feeling. Upon Clay—a distant chimera—he lavished a romantic affection, as though he had never offered the tribute of affection before; Clay became the unmistakable idol of a life-time; and Greeley, once for all, turned against the Jacksonian Democracy. He became a Whig; his political alignments were to be conservative.

When the office in East Poultney was closed in 1830, Horace set out for his father's clearing in Pennsylvania with a collection of dazzled enthusiasms; and as he made the slow voyage down the Hudson, and thence westward along the Canal, he must have encountered others no less bright. By 1830 the flourish with which the Canal had been opened had arisen to the point of exaltation; the narrow dipping channel seemed to have flung the country wide for an irresistible conquest. At Troy surged and flowed a mixed population, joining the line-boats or leaving them: Connecticut tinkers and clock-makers, groups of gorgeously arrayed gentlemen who were not ashamed to show a metropolitan cognizance of affairs; traveling evangelists; occasional English visitors who grew vocal as to American manners and customs; and most numerous of all, Yankee farmers with their wives and children, seeking the West, and bearing with them, as a traveler observed, quaint and concentrated houses, churches, schools, and other boats to explore other swifter waterways beyond.

Walking along the tow-paths, joining the traveling company at tiny hamlets along the way, were citizens of the New Jerusalem in the rich Genesee country, who had begun to disperse since the death of the Universal Friend, and were seeking other colonies expectant of the Millennium elsewhere. The Shakers of New Lebanon were gathering thrifty, dancing members, and sending them forth to establish new communities in the fertile valleys of the West. At Palmyra on the Canal Joseph Smith had already entertained those visions which were to lead or drive increasing numbers on a long hegira; the Book of Mormon had just been published, the Mormon church established; mysterious tokens had appeared with a steady beckoning promise for the future. Men and women were on the march westward—in groups, in companies, in bands. Within a year or two the Beechers were to travel in the same direction over the Alleghanies in search of the Millennium.

Young Greeley, traveling for days on the slow line-boats, often walking to break the monotony of the journey, could hardly have failed to see and hear exponents of stirring enterprises or to catch the gusty emotions by which they were animated. Then, as he reached Buffalo and crossed Lake Erie to Dunkirk, came an abrupt change. He walked through the wilderness to his father's clearing. Here at last was the fabulous West. Winter and summer the ring of the ax was the steady accompaniment of existence; to pause was to yield the battle. The widely scattered settlers were cut off from each other, from markets, from the rough highways, by the endless wall of trees. Zaccheus Greeley had purchased a tract of forest of which four acres had been cleared, buying the whole for almost nothing because an early pioneer had given up the task as hopeless. Each year by the most exhausting efforts he and his younger son might add an acre to the small clearing; then the new ground, full of stumps and green roots, demanded a further extravagant outlay of labor. Poor as the Greeleys had been in Vermont and New Hampshire they had never lived in a log cabin. Mary Woodburn felt the stigma, and hated the isolation; like one of the minor fates she sat for hours spinning and weaving at a small window that looked toward the East, her high spirits gone.

Into a dejected household Horace came as a transient. During the winter he engaged in the huge labor of woodchopping, and sought work as a printer in the villages of the neighboring counties. The following summer he bade farewell to the West, though its impress was to remain, whether because of a filial affection which he never more than faintly intimated, or because upon the apparently impassive surface of his mind all experience was deeply, even harshly graven. Equipped like any hero with a few clothes in a bundle at the end of a stick, he set out to seek his fortune in what he called the Great Emporium, walking most of the way along the Canal, and at length reached the small city which lay thickly clustered at the lower end of Manhattan Island.

TWO • *In New York Greeley found himself as isolated as he had been in the wild country which he had left. He was now twenty;* but because of the babyish countenance which topped his tall figure he was taken for a runaway apprentice, and given only the most exacting odd jobs in consequence. In winter he still wore a shrunken linen coat and coarse shoes without stockings; his cuffs were tied with twine; he looked like a meek dilapidated young ghost. In the offices where he found brief employment his appearance became an irresistible subject for mirth, as in East Poultney. Stirred by these jests he at last purchased an antiquated black swallow-tail coat and a tall black hat for a small sum, and in this sepulchral costume tried to meet his fellow-workmen with a timid conviviality. A roar of derision went up; the suit was a cheap fraud, its black recently applied to thin and threadbare cloth. From such palpable absurdities Greeley passed to others, weathered a hideous epidemic of cholera, and saved but little out of his meager earnings. Yet at the end of three years, as though he had been following a rigid line, he found himself the editor and part owner of a new literary sheet called the *New Yorker.*

Within the plain pages of this journal was plucked a melancholy lyre. The grotesque and spectral lad still saw himself as a minstrel. With a loud rhetorical flourish, with a positive effect of noise, he celebrated the sentiments of renunciation and regret, sang the anguish of distant farewells, roamed through the past, haunted Nero's tomb, or considered the death of Pericles in verses dimly lit by stars or set with vague immemorial trees and pale crystalline streams. Melancholy waters, ruins, remote places only half terrestrial, and above all, the classic past—

"The grandeur of great Greece,
  The glory of old Rome,"

HORACE GREELEY [187]

as Poe first stiffly phrased the lines in these years: such themes were being poetized by numbers of obscure young writers; their verses, sad and illusory, had begun to adorn the many literary journals which sprang into existence in the thirties as by a concerted movement. Within the tumult of hope was heard the note of repining; that link with the classic past which had been so joyfully celebrated in such volumes as the *Columbian Orator* was appearing once more, with nostalgia. The classical reminiscence was everywhere, not only in verse, but in the urns filled with myrtle which appeared on many a lawn, and in the larger renascence of an architecture. Set in the midst of a deep thicket, even the small white chapel at Lane Seminary in Cincinnati, then recently completed, wore the faint guise of a Greek temple; taverns were said to take on the very semblance; country dwellings were repeating the ancient tradition: yet these new buildings were seldom equable and spacious as in the earlier classicism of Monticello; rather they became narrow and austere, as if adapted now to a native stringency. Were they only chance echoes? Or did they compose an effort to achieve dignity and peace in the midst of a thousand wild new intentions? The wilderness by which these buildings were often surrounded gave them an air both quaint and startling: there indeed it was on every hand, that archetypal unfathomable enemy and beckoning friend—the forest, glimmering faintly in the poetry of the day, densely present in the poems of its high tutelary saint, Mrs. Hemans, then known and admired far less for her calamitous portrait of the pilgrims than for her tangled picturings of life in the wilds of Louisiana or along the Mississippi, or in the scarcely known regions of the farther West.

Glancing over the many finely printed pages, letting the eye rest upon spare columns and porticoes, amid sassafras and pine, a questing mind might have caught the strange and contradictory fantasy. Perhaps Greeley caught it; he was lost in dim adventures; he continued to write poetry as if in pursuit of a final vocation. The *New Yorker* with its columns of literary news and exchanges was lifted on the wave of the frail new enthusiasm, and drew an increasing number of readers from the western states and territories. Alas! the pleasures of poetry were not those for which the pioneer was willing to pay; Greeley was soon in financial straits. Twice his office was gutted by those widespread fires which were epidemic in New York like cholera. Partners came and went as though they were taking brief outings in his shop. Overwhelmed by these trials, he found that his personal responsibilities had increased. In 1836 when his fortunes had seemed briefly in the ascendant, he had married a New England village teacher who had come to New York in search of cultivation.

Black-haired and animated, high-tempered and intense and somewhat Oriental in appearance, Mary Cheney glittered with a high and positive purpose; she never read, she passionately studied; and no doubt she hoped to find in the awkward young editor an ambulatory compendium of knowledge. Already his aptitude for statistics was amazing, like a gift for stiff and prosaic language. What Greeley had hoped to discover in this pedantic young woman remains a mystery; perhaps with a sensitive apprehension of popular tendencies he had become aware of the drift toward reform. Mary Cheney was a born reformer; if she meant to improve herself, she by no means intended to neglect others. This queerly joined pair had met at a boarding house dedicated to the principles of Sylvester Graham, who was preaching the attainment of health, placidity, economy, and a great old age by means of his regimen of boiled fruits of the earth and Graham bread. Greeley had accepted the novel program; his mother had been a poor cook; he had in fact that kind of a somber uneasiness in regard to questions of health which led Americans of this period to originate inquiries as to physical well-being as a mode of salutation. Greeley quickly tired of the tasteless and rugged Grahamite fare. Mary Cheney, on the other hand, never altered any of her tenets, once these were fixed; and throughout their lifetime the Greeley table was garnished by vegetables without condiments, by plain puddings, and Graham bread; no meat was served there, nor tea nor coffee, "and never a pickle," as Greeley plaintively observed.

At many points the opinions of these two diverged. Mary Cheney's inflexibility was met by her husband's unwinking stubbornness; if Greeley was a walking accumulation of knowledge, he often walked away; each seemed to inspire the other, along with a vague attraction, the instinct for contrariety; and they remained desperately poor. Soon after his marriage Greeley found himself in the midst of the widespread misery which followed upon the panic of 1837, when one person out of seven or eight in New York was receiving alms, and when an almost equal wretchedness flowed over the entire country. Harassed and uncertain, he still sustained the lyric note; but as if that supplicating voice of his could be made to achieve another register, he roughly attacked Democracy in his paper.

As he trembled on the brink of total failure, he attracted the attention of Thurlow Weed, the successful editor of the Albany *Journal,* the seasoned Whig leader in the State of New York. As early as 1824 Weed had possessed the outworks of political power; he had been credited with the reconciliation of the Clay and Adams factions. His work as political manager was by no means finished, nor were his precise ambitions apparent to the casual view. His tall and energetic figure, his shrewd glance under bushy brows, his humorous mouth, suggested the man of ready speech and action; but his voice was a whisper; Weed conserved his purposes behind the obvious scenes. His dramatic self was Seward, who was rougher, more irritable, more outspoken, more supple, more charming. Twenty years later in Washington, young Henry Adams saw the ultimate Seward—"a slouching, slender figure; a head like a wise macaw; a beaked nose; shaggy eyebrows; unorderly hair and clothes; hoarse voice; offhand manner; free talk, and perpetual cigar . . . a new type, of western New York . . . a type in one way simple because it was only double—political and personal." In the middle thirties the type was still newer, that of the political buccaneer, strangely encumbered by a load of principles. In Seward, at least, there was no doubt about the existence of the principles, even though at the moment they were taking the form of an intense hatred of Democracy, which had triumphed again in 1836 through Van Buren, and of burning hope, for the Whigs had come back into power in New York State in 1837 as result of the panic, though by a small margin. The following year Seward, who was a member of the Assembly, hoped to succeed to the governorship.

Late in 1837 Weed visited Greeley, proposing to found at Albany a small political weekly, to be called the *Jeffersonian,* of which Greeley could become the editor at a salary of a thousand dollars. The paper was to run for a year, and to enjoy something like free distribution. Promptly enough Greeley accepted the new post, though he still maintained the *New Yorker;* and a long run and fateful association was begun.

Driving the two days' journey by sleigh in winter, traveling in summer by the slow river-boats, Greeley contrived to attend the meetings of the Assembly, to write political news for the Albany *Journal,* and to edit the sober and decorous *Jeffersonian.* Seward's name was barely mentioned in its columns. Greeley printed for the most part solid matter on the sub-treasury bill, the hard pivot on which an indictment against Democracy was being swung. The reasoned attack seemed adequate; at the fall elections Seward was elected governor, though the Whig majority was small. In excitement Greeley snuffed the political air. "I say!" he wrote to Rufus Griswold, then a Whig editor at Vergennes. "I haven't any good reason for writing to you at present; but there is an unanswered letter from you in the bottom of my hat, and a few minutes to spare before I go to my dinner and the *Daily Whig,* so here goes. . . ." He spun out pages of lively political comment, referring to the *Daily Whig* as his "new pet," for which he was writing an editorial a day. To Weed he wrote in another vein, with authority, and in rebuke. "WEED: I will *croak*. If I am not a liar, that nomination of Glentworth has excited universal disgust and much deep indignation. I don't know the gentleman very intimately, but he is regarded as a blackleg. . . ." Deep in the new agitation, still without capital, late in 1839 Greeley launched a campaign organ of his own, the *Log Cabin,* which roared and bellowed with the fervor of the first great picturesque campaign in American political history.

"Give him a log-cabin and a barrel of cider, and he'll be happy," said an unwise opponent of Harrison.

Enraged and self-conscious, farmers throughout the country coalesced into a nation-wide mob. Small matter that the political issues were circular and confused; in truth, the Harrisonian Whigs had stolen the Jacksonian thunder. Old Hickory was merely supplanted by Tippecanoe, one rural western general by another; again was heard the noisy exaltation of the common people, of the farmer, of the West. The difference was one of scale. Popular self-consciousness had swollen to enormous proportions; the mass was creating a heroic self-image, that of the pioneer farmer. Cider-barrels and log cabins, with coonskins nailed to the door, were wheeled through the streets of hundreds of little villages in obstinate and tireless repetition. Enamored of their hero's emblems, they wore Tippecanoe medals, waved Tippecanoe flags, consulted Tippecanoe almanacs, washed their hands with Tippecanoe soap, blew their noses on Tippecanoe handkerchiefs—and initiated a ritual which was to prove perdurable. The political mass-meeting was born, where hundreds burst into song:

"Hurrah for Harrison and Tyler!
    Beat the Dutch or bust your bi'ler!"

In song they mimicked the lugubrious enemy:

"Oh, dear! What will become of me?
    Oh, dear! What shall I do?
I am certainly doomed to be beaten
    By the hero of Tippecanoe."

In belligerent assertion of a native creed, they scorned the silken snob.

"We know that Van Buren can ride in his coach,
    With servants, forbidding the Vulgar's approach—

We know that his fortune such things will allow,
And we know that our candidate follows the plow."

Greeley caught every echo of the mob. Gone was the quiet style of the
Jeffersonian; strident voices seemed to shout through his new paper. He
railed against the presidential palace as though he positively believed
that Van Buren dined from gold plate. He glorified the "hardy subduers
and cultivators of the soil" as though his dearest dream were to become
one of their number. Pioneer life in the West might have held him by a
close and invincible attraction. Catching the rage for emblems, he
showed woodcuts of Harrison's battlescenes, of pioneer accomplishments; nor was the cider barrel neglected, though cider in that campaign
was sturdy liquor, and Greeley had already announced his adherence
to temperance principles. Against the advice of Weed he spread the
many campaign ballads over the pages of the *Log Cabin.* The stroke was
fortunate. Subscriptions rolled up from all parts of the country. The
paper was a huge popular success.

When Harrison was elected, and Seward again achieved the governorship, Greeley was mentioned for the office of Postmaster General.
Griswold urged the appointment in a Philadelphia paper, with too broad
a touch. "I thank you for your kindness in respect to my Postmaster
Generalship!!!" wrote Greeley with an air of possession. "But, Gris, I
pray you to have a care as to your practice with the long bow!" he
added anxiously. "It is too adventurous, I assure you, and spoils the
marksmanship. The things you have said of me there are more incredible
than anything in Munchausen, and every intelligent man will know it.
I understand Thad. Stevens is to be Postmaster General. . . ."

Two weeks afterward he told Griswold, "Your letter opens up a
world of Greek to me. I have never said that Stevens would be P.M.G.
to my knowledge. . . ." Then he said that he had declined to become
an applicant for office. "That road is too muddy now; it is thoroughly
cut up with the throng of hungry travelers. . . . I will not have the
world say that I have given hours that were needed for rest and bread
to the Whig cause with the expectation or design of getting office. I
never thought of it. . . ." With agitation he labored the point throughout
a long letter; it was clear that he wanted the office.

The world seems to have said very little about Greeley at this juncture, the Whig leaders even less; perhaps they had never considered the
possibility of reward for this useful young printer, gawky, poor, and
out-at-elbows. And the question of bread, which Greeley mentioned,
remained a considerable question. His wife had fallen ill; their first child

had died; their staple of income was the twelve dollars a week which he received for his services on the *Daily Whig*. Again he was heavily in debt. In spite of the unprecedented popularity of the *Log Cabin* he had lost money through its publication, chiefly because he could not risk large editions without capital; the repeated printings had proved costly. With a rash enthusiasm he had continued the paper after the election, but the number of subscribers had quickly dropped. The *New Yorker* was involving him in heavy losses, for Griswold, who had been left in charge during the campaign, had abruptly quitted New York on errands of his own during one of Greeley's absences from town, leaving the paper, as Greeley said, "dead as a hatchet." A few months earlier the same enigmatic friend had joined in promoting two new journals, the *Brother Jonathan* and the *New World*, which were proving serious competitors in the literary field.

"The poor old *Yorker*," wrote Greeley mildly to a journeyman printer with whom he was to maintain a correspondence for years. "I am rather afraid the hand of death is upon it, though I am doing everything I can to keep breath in its body; and I do think some two or three of the last numbers have been a match for the abominable *Worlds* and *Jonathans;* but what's the use so long as that enormous ass, the public, won't think any such thing? What I shall do I'm blest if I know. . . ."

Surrounded by dead or dying papers, he wrote an endless number of letters, with an air of leisure, as if he had not another preoccupation in the world. Throughout his life, in the midst of a myriad active enterprises Greeley was to write thus, tossing off letters with or without excuse in his fabulous script, as though he were driven by an insatiable thirst for communication. Frequently he now wrote to Griswold.

"Gris, I'll bet you a York shilling you're sorry you left us. Cause why? Your paper don't look as though it had the bump of payology very strongly developed, and the only principle that I ever found you tenacious of is that of having your pay at least as fast as you earn it. . . . My new hands are terribly raw . . . Raym"—Henry J. Raymond—"is one of the best of his class, but that class is awful. He can write rather better than you can (though slovenly English and on uninteresting themes) but he knows (or did know) nothing of the details of Editorship . . . and has no judgment with regard to selections. There you are unrivaled. I was never afraid that you would down the paper unless by writing for it. . . . O I have had a weary time of it! for my other man, Darlington, is dull and heavy. . . .

"I wish that you would write me each Wednesday evening a junk of literary Intelligence," Greeley urged plaintively.

"Rufe Gris! . . . Get a right notice in the *Ledger* if you can. Swain would like to do me a kindness. But pay for it rather than not get a good one. . . . Remember some *Yorker* poets in your volume of Poetry if consistent with the quiet of good conscience. . . ." Griswold had turned critic, showing some of the animus which was to give him an unwelcome celebrity. "But *won't* you catch it for serving up Dr. Thomas Dunn English the way you have?" queried Greeley.

"Ah, Gris, Gris, shave your horrid claws! . . . *Don't* Raym quietly poke it into Bryant's volume in the last *Yorker?"*

Greeley seemed casual enough, yet in the midst of this eager gossip he was pondering a new project. During these weeks late in 1840 he had formed a high and abstract friendship with Albert Brisbane, a young man of varied talents who had returned to this country after making the grand tour. Speaking of what he called his psychical forces, Brisbane once declared that his complete keyboard was deficient in most of the lower notes; Thoreau, more harshly, said that he seemed a person who had lived in a cellar. But whatever his removal from the common levels of existence, there was no doubt of Brisbane's lofty absorptions; if he often seemed to be blowing enormous soap bubbles, upon those irides- cent spheres the human creature might be seen to glisten in magnificent attitudes, to move on splendid errands. Brisbane was a reformer, an inventor, an orator, a poet. Moreover, he seemed to have been born with the purpose of spurring the race toward an entire orientation with the universe; and in France he had encountered a philosophy which precisely suited the character of his own mind, that of Charles Fourier, who had arranged the material and spiritual activities of mankind, indeed of the universe itself, within a series of perfect patterns.

Naturally, since the Fourieristic system embraced so much, it offered a solution for the vexed problems of labor; what Fourier called "attractive industry" was a crucial element in his scheme. Accordingly Brisbane had addressed himself to Greeley, who had given vent in the *New Yorker* to certain sharp and uncompromising utterances on the human right to work, stirred by his own bitter experience during the panic of 1837. With all his abstractness Brisbane was a persuasive speaker; and Greeley was entranced by the whole intricate design, captured, as he had been at East Poultney, by something glittering and large and ecstatic. Fourierism promised—what did it not promise by way of a new and happy human existence? In February, 1841, the two launched a little paper called the *Future,* whose purpose it was to explain the Fourieristic philosophy.

This modest venture received an onslaught of criticism out of all proportion to its size. "Don't you think the *Future* a tremendous humbug? Greeley's got himself into a scrape by connecting himself with it, and the city—especially the Sunday papers came down upon him with a vengeance," wrote Raymond to Griswold. "He's rather sorry he enlisted, and is trying to take the curse off by advertising Brisbane's name as editor. It doesn't sell at all." Indeed, Bennett, Beach, Webb, and New York editors had attacked the paper with ridicule and abuse, crying communism. Griswold reviewed the paper in sharp disgust; and Greeley wrote to him tartly: "As to the *Future,* the great mistake on your part is that you don't begin to understand our system. You are ignorant as a hoehandle."

Weed printed in the Albany *Journal* a long and reasoned diatribe against the Fourieristic philosophy, as this was expounded in the new paper. "To have you join in the cry was more than I could relish, though I did not expect you to look with favor on the new notions of our little band of reformers," wrote Greeley with hurt indignation. He insisted that Weed took "the wrong view of the *political* bearing of this matter, though *I* act without reference to *that.*" In the same breath he continued the theme of politics, elaborating an argument as to the political affiliations of labor, insisting that "all the social discontent of the country has been regularly repelled from the Whig party, and attracted to its opposite."

Undoubtedly the political bearing of the new reform occupied a considerable place in Greeley's calculations at this moment—perhaps always. But the *Future* perished at the end of two months; and quietly enough, within a week or so, in April, 1841, Greeley launched the *Tribune,* a Whig penny daily which Weed had urged him to establish.

THREE • *Nothing could have been more precarious than the* new undertaking. Greeley was still carrying the dragging load of the *Yorker* and the *Log Cabin,* hoping to sell them for a flat sum, however small; he was still encumbered by debt. For the new enterprise Weed supplied only encouragement; Greeley was obliged to borrow his small bit of initial capital elsewhere; and he had entered a field thickly populated by competent enemies. Looming in the distance with a subscription rate of ten dollars a year was the *Evening Post,* Democratic and highly successful under the placid editorship of William Cullen Bryant. At the same rate appeared the *Courier and Enquirer,* a Whig paper edited by the redoubtable Colonel Webb, who was not without power in Albany, and who was bitterly antagonistic to Greeley. Nor was the low price of the *Tribune* a novelty, for the *Sun,* founded in 1833, sold for a penny; and the *Herald,* established by James Gordon Bennett in 1835, though selling for two cents, likewise commanded a public with slender purses. Both were sharp-toothed, unscrupulous, and highly entertaining, the *Sun* maintaining a Democratic bias, the *Herald* wholly untethered by political principles. "Many talk of principle—political principle, party principle—as a sort of steel trap to catch the public," Bennett had said, announcing his paper. "We ... disdain ... all principle as it is called, all party, all politics." And his multiplying small parcels of infamy, slander, obscenity, and blackmail, with a handsome dash of foreign news and free-handed pronouncements on governmental affairs, enlisted the satisfied attention of thousands of readers, who saw in his boldness candor, and were amused by his brutal narrations of circumstance.

Greeley seems to have been aware that in founding the *Tribune* he was taking a hazardous step; but the regrets which impinged upon him were not those which Weed, for example, might have expected.

"Perish the dream of shapes of beauty!"

he cried in a long poem which appeared in the *Southern Literary Messenger.* With that effect of loud speech which so frequently informed his verses he announced the purposes upon which he now had fixed:

"To war on Fraud entrenched with Power—
    On smooth Pretense and specious Wrong—
This task be mine, though Fortune lower;
    For this be banished sky and song!"

But, after all, fortune grew bright; the *Tribune* was an almost instant success, encountering only a few picturesque obstacles, like a cabal on the part of Beach or his minions on the *Sun* to prevent the circulation of the new paper, which resulted in so tumultuous a rise in his subscription list that Greeley was all but overwhelmed, and so persistent a demand for advertising space that he was obliged to implore his clients to wait for a day or two, when their insertions positively would appear. It was true that he was tried by difficulties; his presses were small and inadequate; he complained that he had "an awful sawney" to help him; he told Weed that he had been given almost no Whig advertising. But from the first the *Tribune* had a look of authority. Cheap as the paper was, it offered large folios of excellent typography, in contrast to the often hastily composed sheets of the *Herald* and the small and smudgy *Sun.* And punctually enough, when the paper was fairly under way, like a god out of the machine appeared the figure of Thomas McElrath, a methodical lawyer, a life-long friend of Seward's, who offered himself as a partner in the enterprise, and added a considerable amount of capital to Greeley's small initial sum. New equipment was purchased; within a few months the *New Yorker* and the *Log Cabin* were merged into the *Weekly Tribune;* at the end of a year the price was raised to two cents; and McElrath, with his quiet collection of practical qualities, achieved for both papers the solid ritual of adequate publication, something which Greeley's adventures in journalism had hitherto lacked. Both issues of the *Tribune* were advertised, they were circulated, promptly and well.

Yet undoubtedly it was Greeley who made the paper, *was* the paper; the legend which quickly sprang up around the old dingy office in Ann Street ran close to the truth. Bent over his high desk with his nose nearly touching it, he composed from three to four columns a day and often more, listened to reports which he could deliver almost *verbatim* afterwards though he had not ceased to write, supervised details throughout the whole sheet, and often did not stir out of his chair from eleven in the morning until after midnight. In moments of rage over mistakes he could let out a bellow which was plainly audible at the American Museum half a square down Ann Street at the corner of Broadway, though his voice in its ordinary ranges was still husky and thin. If he could bawl in anger he also bawled with jubilation; the *Tribune* office was a noisy, nervous, highly stimulating place; that voice with its rapid changes was everywhere; Greeley was an incessant talker. As a result of his shouting importunity riders—often relays of riders—were always posting from remote localities where events were clustering, bearing fresh news for the *Tribune*. His tireless, drudging insistence sent a corps of printers slowly shuttling back and forth on the river boat to Albany during sessions of the Assembly, prepared to set up the reporters' accounts on the return voyage. Though he was never so brilliant a newsgatherer as Bennett, Greeley made up for a final lack of organization by a perceptive touch which bordered upon fancy; his free-handed letters drew numberless bits of odd local narrative and a variety of political soundings from distant correspondents; he smelled out strange corners. As if the pleasure or the strain of daily utterance gave him an enormous impetus, his own mixed and changing interests flowed forth like an avalanche; no one who had known Greeley of the *New Yorker* could have predicted the superabundant variety of his themes or the range of his style. Spread on the front page, indeed, was literary news, an insistent discussion of current books, with poems, with *Barnaby Rudge* and other novels as serials, with extracts from essays: in any portrait of the American mind in this period, the backwoods mind, this bold stress must be taken into account: these gave the stamp of the *Tribune*—or *Trybune*. Along with the news of crops appeared a review of Hazlitt's *Table Talk*. In his editorial columns Greeley turned from a high-pitched grandiloquence which smacked of the *Columbian Orator* to a style which was jogging and companionable and mixed with salty humor; he was as likely to announce his habit of taking two cold baths a day and to urge their hygienic virtue as he was to argue the benefits which must accrue from a nationally established Whiggery. "We have now had two or three days of sour spitting North-East weather, but not half so much rain as we need," he observed in a casual note; yet in the same moment combat suddenly seemed his native element; principles—or causes—if Bennett scorned them Greeley nailed their bright and manifold insignia to his mast; Whig candidates were extolled with stentorian urgency, or bitterly scorned if they seemed unworthy of the high excellency of his party; Clay—Harry Clay, as Greely fondly called him—was "the eagle-eyed and genial hearted LIVING Master-Spirit of our time," and was mentioned in the same breath with Washington, Hamilton, Jefferson, Madison. Positively, every enemy was black; the *Sun* was "that slimy and venomous instrument of loco-focoism . . . jesuitical in politics and groveling in morals."

As result of such indulgences Greeley was peppered with lawsuits, his less flagrant commentary often drawing the larger fire; but at least in one instance, that of his legal tilt with Fenimore Cooper, he succeeded in wringing from the case laughter and acclaim. That touchy aristocrat had sued because of a letter of Weed's which appeared in the *Tribune*, with a few sentences of derogatory comment on the part of Greeley. Cooper won damages of two hundred dollars at a lively trial at Ballston Springs, at which each of the protagonists spoke in his own behalf. Rushing back to New York on one of his quick-driving trips, Greeley spread his account over twelve columns of the *Tribune;* he rollicked through the story, mimicking the pompous Cooper and his even more inflated nephew, who had acted as counsel. In his long and pointed raillery he sported with the picture of the "handsome Mr. Effingham, "who in Cooper's *Homeward Bound* had unquestionably been the figure of Cooper himself. Tirelessly Greeley repeated the allusion; in the trial he had much of his argument turn upon hypothetical questions of appearances, inquiring whether he would be entitled to sue for libel in case Cooper pronounced *him* not handsome. With a heavy-handed thrust in rebuttal Cooper had replied that in such a suit his course would be not to plead the general issue, but to justify. Greeley, missing nothing of the humor of this retort, set down the whole of it, weighty phrasing and all.

Nothing could have been more fortunately planted than Greeley's acceptance of this gibe at his appearance. Undeniably Greeley was absurd. Somewhere he had picked up an old light drab coat of Irish frieze and a battered hat of similar toneless hue; the garments were long since out-dated; wearing them he looked more than ever the ruined ghost. Tall and gangling, he still stumbled as he walked, as though he were pushing forward on a blind errand. He was always rumpled, his pale silver-yellow hair awry under his singular headgear, his collar riding up or retreating from sight; but the phantasmal was belied by his full front glance from behind narrow spectacles, by the pursed and sudden smile which could transform his countenance into that of a happy infant. Rival editors, seeking a vulnerable point, had begun to jeer at him, insisting that he was a boor or a clown; Webb, who led the racket, declared that the old white coat and the dismal hat were eccentricities assumed to attract attention. Greeley drily answered that his own appearance was hardly so eccentric as Webb's would have been, in striped garments, had not Seward pardoned him for dueling. Greeley had a dozen things to say on the question; his attachment to his strange costume was plaintive, bold, yet obscure. Over and over he disclaimed perversity; he grew pensive, even drooping, and declared that when he came to New York he was only a poor farmer's boy, and had made his way without assistance. By his pallid garments he might in truth have been trying to perpetuate the very figure he had cut when he had arrived in the Great Emporium.

Obstinately enough, in any case, he maintained the effect; when one rough white coat and hat wore out he contrived to find another; and ridicule, which had long been his portion, began to serve him well. His retort to Webb received a wide circulation; rough verbal sketches of his odd figure were scattered over the country. His make-up quickly became an asset, not only for a reason which Barnum down the street would have understood, but because—by luck or some other agency—his appearance was somehow a sculptured emblem of the moment. He looked the avowed rustic, the homely sage, the hardy young wiseacre, the budding pioneer who had abandoned the plow for the composing-room for sufficient purposes, but who had by no means left behind him his rural sympathies. He appeared guileless; but in the backwoods it was still the day of the blank countenance, a face useful in times of pioneer danger, never betraying the jolt of fear or surprise. Greeley was considered enormously shrewd behind his infantile mask. With pioneer self-consciousness still rolling up since the Harrison campaign there could be no doubt of the advantage of these impressions; around him sprang up a strong personal partisanship. Subscriptions for the *Weekly Tribune* poured in from the rural districts; farmers began to consider him a bold but prudent neighbor; if, a decade later, visitors from New England and the West made it a high point "to hear Beecher" in their trips to New York, in these earlier years they were determined to "see Greeley" and ask his advice. In numbers they began climbing the stairs of the old Ann Street building, to consult him about the condition of the world, of the country, about ensuing elections, about their crops; they took his abrupt counsel like that of the last oracle; they wrote him sheaves of letters, which he invariably answered. When he moved about in rural districts they nudged him and asked when their subscriptions expired. Here was the poor lad risen to eminence, one of themselves; the American legend was crystallizing, and Greeley with his rustic ostentation composed it.

He looked a crank; but cranks had come into their own in the early forties. Far from exhibiting the uniformity of which Cooper had so bitterly complained in his preface to *Home as Found,* the national temper seemed positively to assume those angularities and effervescences which must have been apparent to the boy Greeley along the Canal. There could be no doubt now as to the thronging urgency of strangely insistent characters throughout the country, or of the welcome with which their amazing proposals were being greeted. At last, after an age of nascence, it had come—the era of reform, loosed and violent, insecure but assertive, the old drama of regeneration assuming strange guises. "In the history of the world the doctrine of Reform has never had such scope as at the present hour," cried Emerson in 1841. New schemes—panaceas: men were thunderstruck by panaceas—the abolishment of money, of rent, of idleness, of meat as a food, of animal labor—the beasts, too, were to be free as glorious man—the abolishment of fermentation even in the making of bread. Abolishment was the favorite device, as if from a purpose to wipe the slate clean and to begin afresh; but new faiths were springing up in abundance, predicting an instant Millennium. Indeed, the thousand years of peace seemed to have begun. In 1840 a convention had been held in Boston by the Friends of Universal Progress, at which advocates of these many causes joined in hopeful, friendly congratulation, where Abolitionists saluted Agrarians; Grahamites joined with Millerites; Calvinists met on friendly terms with dubious Unitarians, and the two groups mixed with Vegetarians, Groaners, Come-Outers, Dunkers, and Muggletonians. It was a noisy gathering, and aggressively picturesque in its outward guises. Freaks of costume played a conspicuous part, as if a badge or a signal were needed for reform; these persons were characterized, according to a writer in the *Dial,* by "a certain plain sylvan strength and earnestness." The rustic note was everywhere.

In his old white hat and coat, with his entranced smile, Greeley could have mixed naturally enough with the members of this gathering; in the early forties he attended many other aggregations no less motley in appearance, and quite as hopeful in intention. In truth, he was deep in the most fantastic project of them all. There it was, in the very forefront of the *Tribune,* a rainbow vision of the universe rising above the mixed plenitude of the paper, mating oddly with the thickening politics of Whiggery. Deaf to the protests of Weed, oblivious of the ridicule of Raymond and of Griswold, equally unregardful of the mounting sneers of rival newspapers, Greeley had clung to the cosmic scheme which Brisbane had revealed to him, that of Fourier. The Fourieristic philosophy was written up and down the columns of the *Tribune;* Brisbane was unraveling its intricacies in a daily exposition; Greeley was thundering his personal allegiance. With this strange load upon his back he fought his way into a sudden personal popularity. Waving the banner of this new improbable cause, he had pushed his paper into a circulation which ranged from the seaboard to the Mississippi. The puzzling circumstance was that the official prophets were confounded, for the Fourieristic movement was coming with a rush.

FOUR • *Like a great* pavanne, *or a child's dream of a far country, or a perpetual circus,* the Fourieristic scheme spread its sweetly assembled elements.

Fourier, a quiet little descendant of the Encyclopedists, a pedant and a solitary, never moving from the small orbit of a commercial traveler in the provinces of France, had discovered that the twelve passions were the motivating power of existence. These prime agents were social in their effects, causing men to join together for pleasure, for many-sided action, for industry. Naturally in such pursuits they assembled in groups; in turn many groups might be combined to form what Fourier called a series; while many series would naturally merge into a phalanx, an organization of some two thousand persons who would occupy three square miles in an opulent valley, and be housed in a single palace or phalanstery. Around the spacious interior of this building was to wind a great gallery, the street of the phalanx, a fine and tasteful promenade where groups and series might meet and mingle regardless of the weather; at one end of the building was to arise the Temple of the Material Harmonies, consecrated to music, dancing, gymnastics, painting, and poetry;

at the opposite end was to stand the Temple of Unityism, where members of the phalanx would celebrate man's essential unity with the universe. Scattered over the rich domain at appropriate intervals were to be huge granaries and stables, dairies and mills, with plotted gardens on every hand, trim woodlands, and well-tilled fields; for the phalanstery was to become no simple bower of ease; the great climactic product of the passions was industry. Artisans, intellectual leaders, craftsmen, and pastoral laborers would freely and naturally join in harmonious production for the common good. With a charmed absorption in numbers, by his favored method of analogy, viewing the passions together with colors, curves, metals, and musical notes, Fourier proved that harmony is inherent in all human existence.

Harmony—in one form or another the word rang through Fourier's utterances and those of his American disciples like a cry or a prayer. In harmonious companies the entire race was to march—not forward perhaps, since progress was an illusion—but round about in universal unison; by its very name the phalanx suggested solid troops irresistibly moving. Swiftly many phalanxes were to spring up, until the entire planet was to be dotted with these joyous bands, each communicating with the others by means of signal towers placed on the roofs of the phalansteries. At Constantinople, which was to become the capital of the Globe, an Omniarch would unite myriads of phalanxes under a common rule, assisted by three Augusts, twelve Cæsarinas, forty-eight Empresses, one hundred and forty-four Kalifs, five hundred and seventy-six Sultans, with a suitable number of minor retainers. In this wheeling pageant of government women were to occupy a free and exalted position; a universal language was to be established; and the entire rigidly mathematical arrangement was to move with the prodigious cycles of the universe, whose separate elements of planetary youth, maturity, and decay Fourier had precisely discovered and subdivided. In the early nineteenth century the earth had reached the fifth era, or that of civilization; in the eighth universal harmony would be achieved; this happy condition would be accompanied by the appearance of the polar crown, which would alter the physical aspect of the globe, transforming it into a green and balmy Eden. Climates would become uniform; wild beasts would vanish; other creatures, wholly useful to man, would be created; and—as if Fourier had been starved of circuses—the sea would acquire the taste of lemonade. If the pensive note at last was sounded by a picture of the earth at last swinging down the ages to dissolution, the prophecy was balanced by the promised rise of happy new existences on new and more splendid planes, or on other planets.

This quaint cosmography was never widely accepted in France; only one or two phalanxes were formed during the lifetime of Fourier, and these were soon disbanded. But in America numbers of people might have desired and awaited these precise patterns of existence. Little Fourieristic papers were blown over the land as by an irresistible wind, the *Harbinger,* the *Phalanx,* the *Present,* another *Future,* the *Tocsin,* and many others; Fourieristic conventions were held by the dozen and in many states; in the City of New York even conservative organizations like the Society Library began to open their doors to speakers on association, as the new cult was promptly called. Emerson, while deploring a tendency toward rigidity in the system, declared that "it strode about nature with a giant's step. . . . One is admonished and cheered by a project of such friendly aims and such bold and generous proportions." From 1841 to 1846 Fourieristic colonies sprang up in haste, with urgency; farmers pooled their farms; a group undertook to found a community around the unpromising matrix of a stone quarry. The North American Phalanx at Red Bank in New Jersey began its flourishing career. Under the influence of Brisbane the community at Brook Farm, organized in 1841 as an experiment in transcendentalism, was changed to the Fourieristic plan. In Pennsylvania and New York fifteen or more phalanxes were formed, with a large cluster on the shores of Lake Ontario; at least six appeared in Ohio, four in Michigan, others in Indiana, Illinois, and Wisconsin. Certain of these announced special missions, like the Peace Union Settlement in Pennsylvania, where some forty or fifty persons were planted on ten thousand acres for the purpose of spreading universal peace throughout the world.

In these years Poe spoke of our "anti-romantic people," yet this incredible romanticism was everywhere, in a dozen similar guises. The wish to establish the small Eden or Arcadia—which inevitably must spread—was faintly sketched at Fruitlands, where life was "consociate, not associate," at the vigorous Universalist colony ruled by a patriarch at Hopedale, at Putney and later at Oneida, where the golden era of the Millennium was believed actually to have dawned, in the second group of Owenite communities, and among the Icarians now preparing in France for a long journey into this country and finally across the heart of it to establish still another economic paradise. The Mormons—now imperially marching on Utah—the Shakers, the old communities at Zoar and Economy and Harmony were flourishing with new vigor and abundance, drawing added members, sending forth offshoots into neighboring territories.

Gazing backward, a speculative observer might have concluded that this ample burgeoning was the culmination of an impulse not only deep but stubborn, appearing even in the Puritan settlements. All these groups had glinted with some form of the millenarian dream; all had accepted the most radiant and difficult of all hopes, that men could unite in simple concourse without fear, or jealousy, or restless ambition; all were driven by the belief that in a closely banded association lay happiness; peace was to be contained within tiny boundaries. Now, in the early forties, an effort to find stability surged up as never before. With the rolling impact and heavy backwash of a world expanding with gigantic strides, with perennial shifts and oscillations, with the push forever westward, life in this country must often have seemed intolerably loose and unstructured. The effort to compose and maintain a society in the midst of enormous change seemed to underlie many wishes in the middle years of our history, a struggle pushing through many struggles, often dumb and affronted, indeed, its character swiftly buried beneath more tangible memorials of the age, but surely potent. If the Fourieristic movement was a form of escape, it also contained the pattern of a far-reaching purpose. Order was Fourier's great cry—"Not Justice, but Order." With Fourier a happy and fluent companionship was not only a method of life but a religion. Unity was the goal of his quaintly diagrammed faith, the union of men with their kind, of men with the pleasant earth—a multiple harmony.

Undoubtedly in this sweet and vain fantastic movement Brisbane was the original force; but he could hardly have found a foothold without Greeley; he would have looked far and long for an organ which could provide as a background the force and authority of the *Tribune*. With a headlong energy, with color and breadth, Greeley sketched the system in *Tribune* editorials, spread accounts of the new communities over his news columns, and lectured tirelessly. Association—union—unity— UNITY OF EFFORT, for so he constantly magnified his theme: these words and phrases were constantly on his lips, settled in the heart of his growing argument. Isolation rang in sharp antithesis, as if the solitude which he had for years seemed to ignore had weighed heavily upon him. He protested against the many forms of isolated effort, against the isolated household—"We maintain that the isolated family is *not* the most perfect form of the household"—against the insulation of the individual from a consciousness of the life of others, pleading for a society— a SOCIETY—"a more intimate and trustful Society . . . an intimate Social Relation . . . a more intimate and trustful Social Relation." He preached a longing for peace until his insistence bordered upon discord; and the cry which he raised was not so much for a resolution of material hardships as for a less drastic pressure upon the human spirit. As from desperate experience he spoke of "the Soul's indignant protest against its own perpetual involvement in a system of heartlessness and war, of chaffering and struggling for daily bread . . . the surrender of itself to a perpetual round of ignoble anxieties and petty yet exacting collisions . . . the exposure to rude rebuffs and wounding suspicions. . . . It is *this* that gnaws and kills." "There is a small number," he declared—"very small, it may be, but I think it increases—to whom the old ways, the old purposes of life have become impossible of pursuit—who must breathe freely or be stifled—who cannot live longer to merely personal ends—who will readily dig ditches, if that be the most useful employment which solicits them, but who must do even this heroically, not sordidly, or not at all. They are ready to welcome drudgery, privation, obscurity, but not willing that the covering and cherishing of their own bodies shall be the purpose of their life-long struggle." All this was to be changed by Fourierism—"the Reform which shall embosom almost every other . . . the vast Reform . . . which is destined to render our age memorable in the History of Man."

"Let none accuse me of the enthusiast's common error," Greeley insisted—"the presumption that the world is to be transformed in a day." Charges of this sort rained upon him once more in a large and scornful commentary, from the Whig leaders, most of all from Weed, who again admonished Greeley as though he were a callow if talented schoolboy. "Coming from another, I would think it insufferable impudence," wrote Greeley in blunt rejoinder. Even so Weed seems to have pressed him close; and Greeley finally addressed a long and formal pompous letter to this monitor, full of pensive dignity because of Weed's contemptuous tone, but clear enough in its conclusion that he differed from Weed "on the general policy and objects of political controversy."

Perhaps because of these criticisms Greeley tried to check or measure his enthusiasm: but he could not. In the midst of cascades of statistics, his cynical exchanges with Bennett, his denunciatory rhetoric, his humor, uprose his conviction that a miraculous change was at hand. Like an ardent revivalist he was swept from height to height, and chanted the "unmeasured reign of Truth, Purity, and Bliss . . . the glories of the second Eden. . . . The idle, thriftless, improvident tribes and classes will disappear, leaving the earth to those who . . . by tilling, irrigating, fertilizing, and beautifying the earth, prove themselves children worthy of her bounty and blessing. . . . Wiser in our very follies, less cruel and wanton even in its crimes, our Race visibly progresses toward a nobler and happier realization of its capacities and powers. . . ."

Intoxicated by his great subjects Greeley slipped into one of the largest of them all. *Human Life* was the subject of a lecture which he delivered again and again, a showy piece packed with a flowery rhetoric, a noisy drama of words, which he warmly fancied: he wrote to Griswold that it was "fearless and dashing throughout." "Horace Greeley will lecture before the New York Lyceum at the Tabernacle, this evening. Subject, *Human Life*. The lecture will commence at half-past seven precisely. If those who care to hear it will sit near the desk, they will favor the lecturer's weak and husky voice."

His voice had remained a high trembling falsetto, weak and querulous, without persuasion or appeal, never achieving on the platform the bellowing force which he could so easily loose in the *Tribune* office; he used no gestures except an occasional awkward sidewise movement of one hand. "I suppose it to be a fact universally admitted that I am the worst public speaker in America," he drawled in a shrill sing-song to a western audience. He seemed driven to lecture, drawn out of his odd personal configuration into speech; the effort can never have been pleasing to himself, but still he spoke, as if from a restless passion for communication or for response; and strangely enough, in the midst of all the rising accomplished thunder he was a success, surpassing as an attraction not only Emerson and Channing but the bold Theodore Parker; Henry Ward Beecher was still an obscure minister in the West. Part of Greeley's triumph sprang from the growing power of the *Tribune,* part perhaps from the enigma which he presented of a startling, many-sided personality. But undoubtedly much of his early popularity as a speaker was derived from his proud and glittering themes.

Amazingly, for a brief moment in the middle forties the hope of association seemed at the point of happy achievement. Life in the urgently composed phalanxes assumed a serene and lovely glamor. "We worship only reality, we are striving to establish a mode of life which shall combine the enchantments of poetry with the facts of daily experience," ran a manifesto from Brook Farm. In truth, poetry was tangible there. Like the strange gay pageant of Hawthorne's romance, the rhythmic groups and the Fourieristic series were looped over the earth amid the whir of partridges and the springing maize; life was a picturesque game, with music and dancing at the Eyrie, with Christopher Cranch imitating the notes and cries of birds and beasts, with the symbol of Unityism offering a religious sanction to pleasure on appropriate occasions. "The freedom from care, the spontaneousness of labor, the absence of all toil and anxiety, the sense of equality in condition, and the abolition of all class distinctions . . . made work a delight," said George Ripley. "There was exhilaration, joy, and gayety." At the North American Phalanx in New Jersey where the early work of organization had proceeded more slowly than in the other communities, the pastoral figment assumed even broader, brighter colors. In the pale yellow house, which had been a large mansion, the pattern of the phalanstery was maintained with the spreading wings which the master had dictated. The dining-hall, airy and well lighted, spare and fresh with an abundance of snowy linen, showed a painting of the ideal phalanx of the future, with the words "The Great Joy" formed in evergreen leaves above; and actually joy, little or great, perhaps somewhat overstressed and intentional, seemed at hand. Labor—the cultivation of melons, peaches, tomatoes, or the making of hominy at the great mill—had a classic air; about the workers hung something simple, merry, and secure; they seemed like those happy improbable Huskers, Drovers, Lumbermen, and Shoe-makers whom Whittier was evoking in his *Songs of Labor* in these years. All the members wore coarse clothing; many of the young women appeared in short dresses and pantaloons with jaunty caps and blouses; in the evening at the little dances some of them wore the bloomer costume, which Fredrika Bremer found far more modest than most ball-gowns. In the part at the end of the day's work, young people—and some of the older ones—wandered or played, crowned by leafy garlands. The wreath was a favorite adornment, as if the days were a long celebration; when Marcus Spring met Miss Bremer at the little wooded gorge which formed a portal for the phalanstery he wore a chaplet of wild clematis; and his staid horse and buggy were equally adorned with flowering strands.

Like glimpses of an idyll these experiments floated before the public fancy, portrayed in part by zealous lecturers, suggested by news items in the *Tribune*. If Greeley himself never wore a garland, certainly he was crowned in spirit; he moved about among these communities with an air of happy participation. To finance the American Phalanx he dipped with a lavish hand into his earnings; he was often there helping with the harvest, sewing hominy bags at night with Channing. Considered enormously shrewd and practical, he was made treasurer of the Sylvania Association of Pennsylvania, where some seventy persons had founded a phalanx with hurried enthusiasm, captivated by an abundance of wood and water on a tract of two thousand acres, careless of an altitude which brought summer frosts, disregarding a stony soil. Greeley often visited the Universalist colony at Hopedale; he spent hasty days and nights at Brook Farm, where one of the more prosaic spectators remarked that he looked like a wandering Moses at a fair, ready to be duped by any fakir. Unsettled and restive he certainly was, talking, forever talking in his high falsetto or sudden shout, moving in and out of these communities as though he could neither stay nor keep away, always on the wing, seldom at home, staying at hotels to be near his work when he was in the city, always hastening with a quick, drudging step, pushing through crowds like a draft horse with a heavy load, and arriving once more in Arcadia.

FIVE • The load which Greeley had thrown together in these early years was in truth huge and preposterous. Shouldering the vast superstructure of Fourierism, he still balanced the ponderous bulk of Whiggery. Was it because he loved any scheme or program? Was it another wish—how ironical, and inverted!—for companionship, sought in the unlikely region of the political machine? Fourier had insisted that the problems which afflicted humanity were social, not political; yet Greeley was not only entangled by the political struggles of the day; plainly he regarded himself as a political leader. Late in 1841, when he was still a shabby young printer engaged in a precarious enterprise, he had traveled to Washington to offer himself as a mediator between Tyler, who had turned his back upon Whig principles, and the angry Whigs in the country. The Whigs mentioned in the possible bond had grown still more infuriated; Weed, however, had maintained his gift for silence. The prompt and startling rise in the circulation of the *Tribune* had given Greeley a power which could scarcely be overlooked. Greeley quickly had become the most brilliant exponent of protection in the country; with his extraordinary control of statistical materials he was issuing the *Whig Almanac,* a political handbook which no competent Whig could do without. In 1842, when the Whigs were hopelessly out of the saddle, Weed had quietly offered Greeley a nomination to the State Assembly; and Greeley, apparently unaware of a satirical intention, had accepted the favor. Now in 1844, the high year of the Fourieristic enthusiasm, he had plunged headlong into Whig plots and counterplots as a partisan supporter of Henry Clay, who again was seeking the great national honor in the face of a considerable opposition.

Surely—to bring incongruities to a climax—Clay was a strange taskmaster for one who was basking in a theory of transcendent harmony, unless harmony was to be read as an equivalent of compromise. To the end, it seemed, Greeley loved a rogue, though with what acute knowledge, what bold inner laughter, what entire innocence, no one can securely tell. A humorous dash or a supple charm drew him to one character after another, had probably drawn him to Weed and Seward, for example; but none of these attachments equaled in warmth or persistence his feeling for Henry Clay. A member of Congress once declined to be presented to Clay on the ground that he did not care to submit to a dangerous fascination; but Greeley yielded completely to the spell, as though he were perennially drawn by something immoderate in that great equivocal character. Stories of Clay's gallantries must have reached him at every turn; to begin to unravel Clay's political history even within recent years was to uncover a hundred tattered edges; and Clay could be imperious with his admirers. But Greeley haunted Clay's rooms whenever his captivating leader was in New York, watched his suave and studied movements, listened to that grave melodious voice, hearkened to his counsel, and joined with huzzas—which sounded through the *Tribune*—in the riotous popular acclaim which invariably greeted him upon his arrival in the city. New York was one of Clay's firmest strongholds.

After a long series of balked endeavors, in 1844 Clay at last secured the Whig nomination for the presidency. Greeley's labors on his behalf were tireless and uncalculating. He enlarged the daily *Tribune* one third in size and packed it with political argument; he published a *Clay Tribune* similar in popular appeal to the *Log Cabin*. Writing many columns a day, dashing off an endless stream of letters, speaking at political meetings five or six times a week, he continued his services long after he had reached a state of almost unbearable physical exhaustion. Fevered and unable to sleep, he was covered with boils; still he worked; he seemed to have an enormous stake in the election. But the campaign lacked spontaneity; with all his swift persuasion Clay was unable to arouse a lasting popular ardor; and at last in his famous Alabama letters he took the step which elected Polk, announcing that he was opposed to the annexation of Texas, though not because he feared the extension of slavery. Clay was a slaveholder; and northern anti-slavery sentiment was deeply antagonized. An abolitionist ticket was put into the field which commanded enough votes in New York and Michigan to split the Whig majority in those states, and thus to turn the election for Polk within the nation.

Greeley's disappointment was angry, noisy, and extreme. Greeley instead of Clay might have been running for the presidency. He afterward declared himself "the worst-beaten man on the continent." And, as if the central episode had only riveted his loyalty, his views on slavery now precisely followed the mild contours prescribed by his leader. "Be quiet! I know it!" he wrote to De Frees in 1845. "We are to be flogged in Indiana. I feel it in my bones. That beastly abolition nomination in the Switzerland district cuts us down to three congressmen." Greeley declined to accept the more radical Whig sentiment on slavery, represented by Seward, who was out of office, it is true, and absorbed in private practice, but who still was a large recognized factor in Whig politics. In a letter to the Anti-Slavery convention held at Cincinnati in 1845, Greeley refused to pledge himself "to any special or isolated Reform in such a manner as to interfere with and fetter my freedom and ability to act decisively and effectively upon more general and immediately practical considerations of National interest and Human well-being." This vague statement threw the convinced anti-slavery workers into a turmoil of rage: they too coveted the liberal power of the *Tribune*. But their anger was nothing to that of the Whig leaders when confronted by Greeley's further avowals.

Blazoned with capitals and aglow with rhetoric, set off in subdivisions so that no one could miss his point, Greeley's letter pictured the harsh conditions imposed upon white industrial labor as those of virtual slavery. Labor—as a new rallying cry—began to run through the editorials of the *Tribune* like harmony, an equal abstraction. "The toiling millions" frequently appeared there, with broad statements as to "the great Social Revolution which our age is destined to commence, in rendering all Labor at once attractive and honorable, and banishing Want and all consequent degradation from the earth." Following the Fourieristic canon, Greeley insisted that the difficulties which beset the industrial classes were "social not political, and are to be reached and corrected by social remedies. . . ." Changes were to come through peaceful agreement. "Legislation to correct such abuses can seldom do much good, and will often do much harm." In 1845 exponents of association and land reform, of abolition, temperance, peace, of the ten-hour day, were invited to meet in New York at a single grand convention with the hope that by pooling all these movements a monumental wave of reform would arise throughout the country, the power of each adding momentum to the others. Greeley was foremost in the extravagant preparations, and expected an immense and sweeping result: that the gathering would draw an equal attendance of wage-earners and capitalists, that the employers in amiable converse would promise to divide with their workmen the benefits obviously accruing from the tariff, and that by prompt voluntary stipulation they would establish a ten-hour day throughout the country. Unfortunately the employers failed to attend the convention.

Within a few months Greeley had accepted the program advanced by the new formed Workingmen's Party, or the National Reformers, or the Young Americans, as they were intermittently called, a small group which had been active since the late twenties, under the leadership of George Henry Evans, and which possessed a hard and acrid humor. The new movement was distinctly a class movement. Reversing his attitude toward legal compulsion, Greeley followed in their wake. "To talk of the Freedom of Labor," he wrote, "the policy of leaving it to make its own bargains . . . when the fact is that a man who has a family to support and a house hired by the year is told, 'If you can work thirteen hours a day, or as many days as we see fit, you can stay; if not you can have your walking papers; and well you know that no one else hereabout will hire you'—is it not the most egregious flummery?"

From this novel and daring agitation Greeley quickly passed to another. An agrarian bias had been marked in the labor movement at the outset. "All men are equal, and have an inalienable right to life, liberty, and *property.*" Thus had run a declaration in a labor manifesto in 1829. Now in the middle forties the small new party urged land reform as a further great remedial measure, fastening upon the vision of the free homestead. Pamphlets entitled *Vote Yourself a Farm* were achieving an immense circulation. At first Greeley argued that the opening of the public lands free to actual settlers would result in a disastrous exodus from the older states. Then, suddenly, he wrote of "the creation of a universally land-holding people such as has not been since the earlier and purer days of the Israelite commonwealth."

Land—free land—the picture of the individual homesteader entrenched upon his own clearing in the wilderness, relieved from undue care, now obsessed Greeley like some personal desire. Fear—struggles—hardships: he portrayed these accompaniments of the life of the pioneer with imagination and exactitude, as though they still weighed heavily upon him. One by one he described the handicaps of the settler, who had not only to purchase his land, which usually absorbed his savings, but to mortgage his tract at the outset for tools, fertilizer and other necessities, thereby incurring an almost inescapable load of debt. Day in and day out Greeley dealt with the evils of land speculation. "Wherever, upon a natural harbor, a bay, a head of navigation, or a waterfall, a village begins or promises to spring up, there the speculator or his agent is early on hand, and pounces on all the unoccupied land within a circuit of a mile or two." In detail he pictured the circumscribed choice, the economic limitations, which followed, and the resultant high prices. His arguments were bold, and his proposals still bolder. By the mid-forties Greeley had not only given wide currency to the agitation for free homesteads, but was urging legislative measures which would limit individual holdings and restrict the inheritance of land. His confidence in this startling program was unbounded. "It needs but to be discussed and understood to secure it an overwhelming approval and support."

A howl went up from New York newspapers which was echoed along the seaboard, as Greeley advanced these doctrines. The *Sun* appealed to "men of all parties to PUT DOWN doctrines which strike at the very root of the social system." The *Express,* a Whig paper, charged Greeley with "attempting incessantly . . . to excite the prejudices of the poor against the rich, and in general to array one class of society against the other . . . all of which is used by our opponents to prejudice the poor against the Whigs as a party." Anti-Whig—anti-Whig: the cry of apostasy rose against Greeley on all sides. "There can be no peace in the Whig ranks while the New York *Tribune* is continued to be called Whig," said the *Courier and Enquirer,* whose staff young Henry J. Raymond had joined, leaving the *Tribune.* In phrases which all but quoted Greeley, Raymond remarked that the Whig party was one of order and stability, eschewing radicalism in every form. "The better way for the *Tribune* would be at once to admit that it is Whig only on the subject of the tariff," he declared, "and then devote itself to the advocacy of anti-Rent, Fourierite, and Vote-Yourself-a-Farm doctrines."

Weed was silent, perhaps because young Raymond, whom he favored, had become vociferous. Greeley calmly assumed that his alliance with Weed was bedded in rock. In midsummer of 1845 he was eagerly urging Weed with his family to join the Greeleys in a charming diversion. "I write this line only to ask when you and your folks will probably come down and pass a Saturday. . . . I ask, first, because we count on the visit, and secondly, because we shall probably spend one Saturday this month at Rockaway, for sake of the sea-bathing, and want to be sure of not missing you. . . . I went down to Coney Island on Saturday afternoon— a savage place, but cool, capital bathing. . . . Please send me three lines at once, saying whether you can come down next Saturday or the next, or at any other time, and whether you wouldn't like to go down with us to Rockaway. If you never bathed in the sea by moonlight or at sunrise in July, it is a pleasure you ought not to miss much longer. Rockaway is magnificent—I mean the ocean, there is nothing else there; for one night I know not its equal. . . . I should like to go down with you and your folks any Saturday that you would."

As for his outspoken critics in the field of politics, after a few blasting retorts Greeley seemed unaware of their existence.

After all, during these years, his overmastering interest might have been in literature. The old delicate American instrument was still tinkled in the *Tribune,* more like a melodeon now than a spinet; there were candid reviews, which Greeley himself often wrote; he kept a bracing tone in this department, for all the soft thin melody of much of the verse, and often excluded contributions as "too essayish." "No descriptive letters!" he told young Bayard Taylor, who was going to Germany. "I am sick of them." His criticism was by no means always impartial: he wrote what he called "a tall puff" of Griswold's *Poets and Poetry of America,* when at last this volume appeared; but plainly he regarded himself as a literary guide, able to set the critic in his place.

"O Gris, you have not taken sufficient time with that work!" he wrote after Griswold's anthology of translations had appeared. "Your choice of translations is often dreadful. . . . *The Garret* kills me. . . . Gris, you *must* not get books up so jobbingly. You will never get above the journeyman's wages unless you amend. O if you only caught me reviewing in right earnest, you would imagine your hide was off and you in a hogshead of brine. . . . What about Praed? As he is English you haven't a chance to show your bad taste or carelessness by choosing wrong translations. But you may omit something. . . ."

Surely it was after a glance at *The American Scholar* that Greeley wrote, "The world is a seminary; Man is our classbook; and the chief business of life is education." He frequently quoted Emerson and would gladly have given the essays a place in the *Tribune* if Emerson had been willing to have these appear in a newspaper. With an eye upon that trenchant luminosity he fairly scrambled for aphorisms with which to adorn his own flowing observations. When his supply ran low, he appealed to Griswold—"Gris, make up for me a brief collection of the best epigrams in the Language, say three folio sheets of mss. A page may be given to epitaphs, though I don't care." He printed excerpts from the essays of Carlyle, and two early poems of Whitman's. He despised Poe, believing Griswold's elaborate tales; yet he lent Poe money for the purchase of the *Broadway Journal;* he was always lending money to impecunious young writers, forever helping them to find publishers; they came to him in numbers. "O so many!" he cried. He railed at them; his editorials and his letters began to be filled with the theme that most people took to writing because they were too lazy to do anything else; theoretically his advice to the pleading author was "Work or starve! Root, hog, or die!" But he seemed unable to refuse them. Thoreau came to him. "Now be neighborly!" Greeley counseled him, disapproving of Thoreau's drift toward solitude, as well as his "defiant pantheism." Thoreau, on the other hand, remarked that Greeley was "as hearty a New Hampshire boy as one would wish to meet." In spite of misapprehensions on both sides, Greeley took infinite pains to assist Thoreau, urging his essay on Carlyle upon the editor of *Graham's,* who accepted it, hastening the publication of the piece, advancing money to Thoreau meantime, and procuring from *Graham's* the final payment. He drew young writers about him as by a hungry wish for companionship. When the *Harbinger* was discontinued at Brook Farm he established the paper on the top floor of the *Tribune* building. With excellent musical criticism, witty notices of books, translations of continental novels—as well as the principles of association—in train above his head, with the loyal instigators, Ripley, Channing, Dana, Snow, passing up and down his stair, Greeley found a happy element; here perhaps was association once more, unplotted but tangible.

Was it a wish for brilliant contacts, or sheer knack for drawing talent within his orbit that led Greeley to add Margaret Fuller to the staff of the *Tribune?* Once, with a deprecating air, he remarked that he had offered the post to Miss Fuller because Mrs. Greeley had wished her "monitor and friend" near at hand. Restlessly wandering, Mrs. Greeley had gone to Boston for Miss Fuller's famous conversations, in which certain opening guns of the new feminism had sounded. "It is the fault of MARRIAGE, and of the present relations between the sexes that woman *belongs* to man, instead of forming a whole with him," Miss Fuller had boldly declared, afterward developing the theme in her *Woman in the Nineteenth Century.* An avowed feminist, Mrs. Greeley had been enraptured. Greeley likewise had been impressed by these pronouncements; they accorded with the philosophy of Fourier, who had given women an equal place in his scheme; Miss Fuller frequently quoted Fourier; and though she had not participated in the experiment at Brook Farm, she regarded association as the great contribution of the age to the technique of living. The boldness of her literary judgments had pleased Greeley most of all. "This is the thinnest of all Mr. Longfellow's thin volumes," she had written; and she found a tradition for candor already established on the *Tribune.* Greeley persisted in calling her a maiden, it is true; and he always assumed that she was very young: she was thirty-four and he a year younger, when she came to New York. But these were cursory disparagements; soon he was sending a cordial notice of her *Woman in the Nineteenth Century* to Griswold. "I want this as much better as you can make it, in *Graham's* for March, and no mistake. Don't disappoint me. . . . P.S. Margaret's book is going to *sell.* I tell you it has the real stuff in it." A month later he prodded Griswold: "I tell you it will make its mark. It is not elegantly written, but every line talks." Before the publication of her *Papers on Literature and Art* he wrote again to Griswold, with a proviso against that editor's habits as a reviewer. "Miss Fuller's book will be out soon, I understand; try and see it before you write about her." He was urgent with other editors; he was immensely proud of Miss Fuller.

Together they visited the new literary *salons* which were forming in the middle forties at the Lawsons', at Dr. Dewey's, at the home of Miss Charlotte Lynch, who had been secretary to Henry Clay, and who was now writing guileless verses. Indeed, a regiment of women appeared at these gatherings, "a swarming sisterhood," as they have been often and joyfully called: Mrs. Ellet, Mrs. Osgood—"doing the infantile act," said an irreverent observer—Mrs. Hewitt, the redoubtable and picturesque Mrs. Elizabeth Oakes-Smith, Mrs. Whitman, Mrs. Mary Gove, "a mesmerist, a Swedenborgian, a phrenologist, a homœopathist, and a disciple of Preissnitz, and what more I am not prepared to say," as Poe remarked. His scornful, shadowy presence often adorned these companies. Nor had Poe alone fluttered the dovecotes; Griswold had omitted the effusions of some of these ladies from his first anthology; and their movements had hardly been those of shy woodland creatures. Now with his long proposed *Female Poets* in preparation intrigue was in the air. Wisely perhaps, Griswold was seldom present at these gatherings; but the elegant N. P. Willis, another editor, was usually at hand, posturing against a mantelpiece and uttering rippling fluencies. Some of the twittering artifice flowed and surged about Greeley, who was inclined to print some of these feminine verses, or about Miss Fuller, who was less responsive. The air must have been at times electric, when Miss Fuller was in good vein, and when Poe with his antipathy to the transcendentalists was besought to speak, and did speak, with eloquence.

Naturally Miss Fuller held a preëminent place in these youthful and somewhat self-conscious *conversazioni*. She was the American Corinne. Like hundreds of young women of her generation she had read the book; the difference was that while the graceful, immensely energized portrait had only stirred an ambition in other minds, to Miss Fuller it had presented contours which she could fulfill. Her swan-like movements suggested something of the floating charm of the original heroine; her rhetoric swept as easily and as far; she could create the effect of a *salon* in any unlikely place, in a tram or a stage or up the dingy stairs of the *Tribune* office, or in its plain and crowded rooms. But there were differences between Miss Fuller and her great prototype. She betrayed a hint of the pythoness which seems to have been absent from Corinne; her voice had a harsh and nasal note, though its excited roughness was pleasing to many hearers; she strangely opened her eyes very wide, and closed them with a fluttering movement. She possessed, indeed, according to Hawthorne's portait of her as Zenobia, "an uncomfortable surplus of vitality." "We seldom meet with women nowadays, and in this country, who impress us as being women at all: their sex fades away, and goes for nothing, in ordinary intercourse. Not so with Zenobia. . . . Not that I would convey the idea of special gentleness, grace, modesty, and shyness, but of a certain warm and rich characteristic, which seems for the most part to have been refined away out of the feminine system." Emerson declared that Miss Fuller made him laugh too loud and too long. Amid the lisping, fading delicacy of the forties she was a phenomenon indeed; and the warfare which she helped to open was as blazingly full of sudden fire as was her own temperament. As a result of her now famous Boston conversations she was known as a leader toward a new feminine freedom, and was drawing about her some of the young exponents of the new feminist movement, like Mrs. Stanton and Miss Anthony. Around her, indeed, transiently appeared a considerable number of admirers, most of them women, flocking to see her at the Greeley's, with whom she lived.

If Greeley were seeking a society, something of the sort tided about him within his own home, in the purlieus of a faint deciduous elegance. The Greeleys now lived in a spacious old mansion, showing signs of decay, built long before as the summer home of a rich merchant, at Turtle Bay, on the East River. The situation was charming; the house was surrounded by old fruit trees, shrubbery, and a garden, with a pond and a brook, with dim gravel paths leading to the river, and a box hedge all around; a wild and leafy lane led to the Boston Post Road at Forty-ninth Street, where hourly stages might be taken to the city. It was true that over this romantic habitation was thrown a mask of rigorous principle; Mrs. Greeley disbelieved in curtains, carpets, and rugs; and she still maintained the simple exactions of the Grahamite diet. But the spell was partially broken by the small figure of Pickie, the Greeleys' third child—the two others had died—who was hardly a year old when Miss Fuller joined the household, but who swiftly grew to look like one of the more sprightly seraphim, graceful and sparkling, moving through the spare, forbidding rooms as with the wind, a small free angelic Horace Greeley of higher spirits and warmer coloring, with red-gold hair. His father adored him, crowning him with what seemed his highest praise; he called Pickie "a poet." And his mother, in words even then becoming popular allowed him to illustrate as completely as might be the possibilities of his own selfhood. At an early moment he was painted at full length, naked and exquisite, with a cluster of lilies in his hand; in this posture he was thought to resemble the infant St. John; but he seems rather to have been a perverse and delightful imp—delightful at least to the mature company by which he was invariably surrounded: he never saw other children. At an amazingly tender age he became a fluent conversationalist, and would trip or pace with Miss Fuller by the hour in the unkempt garden, deep in talk. They all talked, with Miss Fuller in the brilliant lead.

SIX • *That exigent drawing-room by the river came into being* only for a few months, like some swift penciling by an eager artist, soon to be effaced by the clash and rub of dissident characters. No precise record remains of the circumstances under which Miss Fuller left the staff of the *Tribune.* Ostensibly she departed—in 1846—to go abroad with the Springs: but surely a change was inevitable.

During a visit to the *Tribune* office Pickie once seized Greeley's watch, and whizzing it around by the chain let it fly against a wall. Bewitchingly —so Greeley thought—the child explained that he was nervous; and his father attributed his excitability to the continued presence at Turtle Bay of the argumentative phalanx of ladies—"ladies," said Greeley, "whose nerves were a source of general as well as of personal discomfort." Greeley himself was nervous; and his growing exacerbation became manifest in relation to Miss Fuller. He complained that her feminine disciples regarded her "with a strangely Oriental adoration." On the other hand he argued that she was accustomed to rather more comfortable surroundings than she found in the Greeley household, that she liked tea and coffee, which were not served there, and perhaps other luxuries. Certainly Miss Fuller expected from Greeley courtesies which he was unaccustomed to bestow, such as the offer of his arm in crossing the street, and even in crossing a room. He marked her requirements, and took up the question in debate; his rejoinder was that if she were truly emancipated she would not demand such attentions. Miss Fuller's response seems to have been a growing air of condescension. Though she acknowledged that Greeley was generous—he was, she said, with the exception of her mother the most disinterestedly generous person she had ever known—her other commentary was almost wittily neutral. She repeated the careful observation that he was "in modes of life and manner ... a man of the people."

Indeed, at one of the *salons* of the day he had been known to take off his boots and dry his feet on the fender. "Madam, do you call that a poem!" he exclaimed loudly to a young and pretty poetess who had asked him what he thought of her latest effusion. Yet with his ranging, high-pitched conversation he could obliterate the effect of such episodes, for a time at least; he could even talk down Miss Fuller, though this climax occurred rather more frequently outside of his own household than in it. His annoyance grew; whether or not he was aware of her aloof amazement, he expressed his own vexation. He insisted that Miss Fuller's style lacked elegance. Fastening again upon her wish for feminine equality he complained that she could write neither so fast nor so fluently as he could; loudly and often he reiterated the personal comparison, even after the passage of years. "If quantity only were considered, I could easily write ten columns to her one: indeed, she would only write at all when in the vein; and her headaches and other infirmities often precluded all labor for days. . . . A sufferer myself, and at times scarcely able to ride to and from the office, I yet did a day's work each day, regardless of nerves or moods. . . ." Later he made—and printed—his remark about the "three or four bouncing babies" who might have provided Miss Fuller with equilibrium.

Greeley himself seems to have managed the literary department alone for a time. Uneasily he still frequented the gatherings at Miss Lynch's, Dr. Dewey's, and the Lawsons'; and his was a strange fate. For all the power of his position, for all his easy volubility, he seemed unable to command a place in these mixed and restless gatherings. No one was moved to set down the substance of his talk; what he said failed of lasting impression. A few persons in letters or memoirs wrote of his rude habits; most of these minor notabilities did not mention him at all. In this tiny bubbling literary microcosm he was not considered a significant figure. When Griswold was composing his *Prose and Prose Writers of America,* Greeley all but begged him, in one letter after another, to include his own essay on *Human Life;* he had the air of a small boy reaching expectantly over the counter for sweets. But Griswold failed to include the piece, or any essay of Greeley's; and the sting must have been sharper because Miss Fuller's essay on Niagara appeared in the bulky volume, and Greeley himself had tried his hand at a lyrical outburst on the same theme. A strained eagerness informed his attitude toward this now powerful wayfarer in American letters; undoubtedly he was still fascinated by this small, smooth, slippery critic, whom Greeley himself called "the most expert and judicious thief that ever handled scissors," and who was widely regarded by newspapermen as a magnificent liar; they declared him able to talk longer with a small capital of truth than any man in existence. Undoubtedly his talk was charming; and undoubtedly too Griswold knew how to play an admiring friend as a skilled sportsman plays a lively fish on a hook. He never saw too much of Greeley, who was forever writing him, forever begging Griswold to write, begging him to spend an hour in the *Tribune* office when he was in New York. A single frequent reproach appeared in Greeley's letters, "O Gris, how could you run off without saying Go'd b'y'e?"

Large as he loomed to his great newspaper constituency, Greeley lacked a circle of his own; the brief interlude in which an easy or brilliant conversation had seemed to come into gracious bloom within his own household was over. Members of the fledgling feminist movement still came to the house by the river; and for a time Greeley gave their public efforts a sufficient support in his paper; but in the end he was bored or annoyed by their presence.

Then, in 1846, the Fourieristic movement crashed downward, overset in part by the determined efforts of young Henry J. Raymond, still of the *Courier and Enquirer,* who after a series of maneuvers engaged Greeley in a disastrous public debate on the philosophy of the movement, their arguments appearing jointly in his paper and in the *Tribune.*

With an adroit intelligence Raymond fastened upon an element in the Fourieristic scheme which had scarcely received a sufficient scrutiny —the passions, which were indeed basic in the whole mechanism. The passions had, it was true, been mentioned in the new discussions. "How could the passions lead to crime," Parke Godwin had cried in hasty rhetoric, "when everything should be arranged to satisfy them in the most agreeable manner, and when their exercise would determine the lot of each one as to wealth, enjoyment, and pleasure? By what strange caprice, when every honorable way would be left open for the action of the passions, would a man set to work out base methods, which could only conduct him to the contempt and ruin of all his affections!" Fourier had, indeed, imposed certain severe conditions; he had declared that the passion of love must undergo what he called an organization by the series, a discipline which was bound to eventuate in purity. He had insisted upon what he called the Vestalic Corporation and the Corporation of Constancy. But he had also declared that there were many persons who would never fit into either the Vestalic or the Constant order. With his amiable habit of taking human nature as it was, Fourier had planned to have such characters form an order of their own. Parke Godwin had made the astonishing interpretation.

"Such characters as Aspasia, Ninon d'Enclos, etc., Fourier regards as essential parts of the variety of the human race, who will always exist, who must be allowed for in every scheme of philosophy, and whom society, instead of rudely thrusting from its charities, must turn to some good account. The most irregular natures must be made to coöperate in the production of Harmonic results." Fourier did not expect that these persons would be altered even by organization within the series; their order, scarcely strict in its requirements, was to be designated by such titles as the Bayardères, the Bacchantes, and so on. Further, he had plainly declared that the system of marriage was imperfect, and that in the future it would become impossible for man to maintain a monogamic proprietorship over woman.

Such were the alarming principles to be found at the basis of the Fourieristic argument, and launched by a group of heedless enthusiasts upon an innocent people! By some enchantment these implications had escaped the earlier critics; but they did not escape Raymond. His cool logic revealed them one by one; with all the fury of an orderly and orthodox mind he made them plain. Greeley, the rustic sage, the good, the homely friend of the farmer, was revealed as clasping the hand of a distant Ninon, a vague but vicious Bayardère, as accepting all the moral horrors which for two generations had been freely designated as French. Not that his personal character was questioned; it merely became clear in the course of the debate that he had seized upon the entire scheme without suitable examination. In vain did Greeley try to draw the argument toward the theme of industry. Raymond replied that under the name of association lurked the dread monster communism with all its moral horrors; or else it was but a new and cheap disguise for the familiar capitalistic system.

Back came Raymond to the passions. Presently Miss Fuller was reported to have made a Fourieristic marriage; and the hideous contingency was laid at the door of the *Tribune*. With a rush came the onset of many anti-Fourieristic pamphlets, published in New York, published here, there, and everywhere; all of them raised the shout of immorality; most of them mentioned Greeley; and for some reason a feature of the Fourieristic scheme which had strongly appealed to Greeley, which he had been mentioning with increasing frequency, that of music as an accompaniment for industry, became the subject of special derision. Raymond had coldly tossed aside the idea as one more evidence of a wild impracticality. The others found in it inexhaustible material for humor. They wrote with variations of "the favorite hard-beaten dancing-ground . . . where the Fourier warriors, with an occasional whoop against civilization, much to their own satisfaction, after the old Indian style, dance the war-dance in a kind of stationary trot, with many a vigorous antic, to a humdrum kind of music."

Themselves uttering whoops, they rode rough-shod over the promise of the good time coming. With something of the ancient Calvinistic fervor they insisted that the evils which the new system proposed to remedy were conditioned by the human character, and could not be changed. In truth, here and there skepticism might be heard as to ultimate human hopes. Said Brisbane's father when a Millerite shouted to him that the end of the world was at hand, "Damned glad of it, sir! Damned glad of it! The experiment of the human race has proved to be a total failure!"

By the end of 1846 the scheme of association had broken down. In a land overflowing with fertility the founders of the new communities had almost invariably chosen stony uplands, tracts of untouched forest, sandy or exhausted soil; most of the members were unused to agriculture; few of them had trades. In their haste to achieve Arcadia they had made their beginnings with insufficient capital; the whole movement might have been founded upon a private rapture, a puff of longing or desire. That faint ephemeral picture of the good life, painted briefly upon the American ether, was gone. Within little more than a year after its foundation the Sylvania Association, of which Greeley was treasurer, had disbanded; the members of the Brook Farm community dispersed; by 1847 nearly every remaining phalanx had reached or was approaching dissolution, with the exception of the Ceresco community in Wisconsin, and the North American Phalanx at Red Bank, two groups which had been slowly and carefully organized, and which were destined to last another decade. Worst of all, critics less conventional than Raymond began to philosophize the movement. Thoreau said bluntly: "My objection to Channing and all that fraternity is, that they need and deserve sympathy themselves rather than are able to render it to others. They want faith, and mistake their private ail for an infected atmosphere. . . ." There were other voices, and hints that beneath the poetical aggregation of the communities there had been something sickly, that the glamor which lay over them was the faint shine of decadence; the movement seemed one of despair rather than of hope. It was a curious circumstance, scarcely noted at the time, that the prime movers in the plan were nearly all in some sense solitaries—scarcely rooted in any society— Channing, Brisbane, Greeley, even the Springs, besides many more who surged up—who knew whence?—and back again into a dim background as the movement rose and expired. Then from Emerson with increasing force came an indictment against the whole effort toward reform—"the demon of reform"—against any sweeping temporal measure; if they had chosen to heed it, Greeley and his fellow associationists might have heard that grave voice lifted against them at the beginning of the forties.

"How frivolous is your war against circumstances! . . . The impulse is good, and the theory; the practice less beautiful. The reformers affirm the inward life, but they do not trust it, but use outward and vulgar means. . . ."

Ridiculous among the ruins, Greeley dropped the theme of association from the columns of the *Tribune*. But conventions were still held with unabated fervor and scarcely diminishing frequency; and he remained a constant attendant; in 1849 he became president of the still existent American Union of Associationists. With Pickie on his arm, as if to school the child from infancy in the idyllic, he continued to visit the North American Phalanx, where he remained a director. And as if the pattern of association were cellared in his very being, he turned to the project of engrafting it in a new form upon the growing labor program.

Coöperation—here was the new guise. After all, Greeley had never abandoned the notion of a benevolent union of labor and capital; he now proposed a profit-sharing plan. Alas! the employers did not consider the scheme benevolent; even the small aggressive labor party regarded it with an unfriendly eye. At the middle point of controversy Greeley was challenged by some of his Whig newspaper antagonists to place the ownership of the *Tribune* on a coöperative basis, if he believed in coöperation. He promptly did so, creating a joint stock company in which shares were owned by the principal editorial assistants and the foremen in the composing rooms. In spite of this demonstration labor still held aloof. Failing to enchant the group with one scheme, Greeley tried another, cast in a similar mold, proposing a system of coöperative labor leagues which were to combine the functions of capitalist and wage-earner. Wages were to be abolished, coöperative stores set up; the problems of fluctuating hours, rents, and the congestion of cities were rapidly to be solved. With hurried enthusiasm he persuaded workers in several trades in New York to embark upon the enterprise, poured money into the project, acted as treasurer for one of the leagues, and urged their cause in the *Tribune.* The scheme failed, leaving an aftermath of loss and disappointment. Moreover, Evans and his fellow-spokesman of the labor party regarded with growing resentment Greeley's assumption of the post of chief counselor. A clash came toward the end of the forties. The labor group endorsed unionism; and Greeley bitterly opposed the growing policy. He became an unwavering enemy of the strike.

Greeley insisted that the only unions which he could endorse were those designed for peaceful and productive industry. In truth, he wheeled back to the phrases of Fourier and of Whittier's songs, or those of a popular ballad of the time, whose vague but happy promises were frequently on his lips.

"There's a good time coming, boys, wait a little longer,
   We may not live to see the day,
   But earth shall glisten in the ray,
   Of the good time coming!"

With a careless gesture he flung together the miscellaneous and contradictory papers of a decade, including the florid essay on *Human Life,* called the volume *Hints toward Reforms,* and stated his expectation that the book would prove a golden mean between radicalism and conservatism.

The small realistic labor group was disgusted. "If ever there was a nondescript, it is Horace Greeley," said the *Workingman's Advocate* tartly.

To this description Weed might have assented, for Greeley seemed bent upon disrupting the proper plans of the Whig party. In 1848 Weed had invented the notion of General Taylor as the Whig candidate for the presidency. Greeley wanted Clay. The rounds were fought in the convention; and Clay was defeated for the fifth time in his great aspiration. Greeley sulked, with logic and reason. Taylor was not a Whig, he belonged to no party, he had never voted, and was a slaveholder; the circumstance which had captivated Weed, that he was a hero of the Mexican War, antagonized Greeley, who had been from the beginning inalterably opposed to the war. For many weeks after Taylor's nomination he declined to print the Whig ticket at the head of his columns. Called upon by a crowd for a speech at a Whig mass-meeting in New York, he announced that he would support Taylor only as a means of defeating Cass, adding flatly that he considered the nomination "unwise and unjust." A little later he wrote Schuyler Colfax, "If I could make Van Buren president tomorrow, I would. . . . I do like the principles he now embodies—Free Soil and Land Reform. . . . The Free Soil party is the only live party around us."

Here was the substance of his own deep-rooted contention. But Greeley did not join the small new group of irregulars. By an adroit move of Weed's, he himself was now appearing on the Whig ticket as a candidate for Congress from New York, to fill the unexpired term of a member who had died. He could hardly have won his election as a bolting Whig, particularly as popular enthusiasm for Taylor developed much as Weed had predicted. In the end Greeley supported Taylor, went to Congress, and swung into the prime purposes of the Free Soil party, or of the early labor group—as one likes. Land, free land—land free to the actual settlers; this cry he raised above all others, and remained first and last the most conspicuous advocate of a dynamic measure. For twenty years his agitation was to continue; an adequate homestead law was not passed until after the Civil War. But in that tepid session his warfare was rather more than vain; and alas! he assisted in the passage of a measure which once more rendered him absurd, as if absurdity were to follow him like a familiar shadow. A proposal reached the Public Lands Committee, of which he was chairman, that all bogs, swamps, and marshes in the unsettled regions should be removed from federal ownership and ceded to the new states; the argument was that these watery tracts were a menace to health, producing ague and malaria, and that the proceeds from the sales could properly be used by the states for drainage. Easily enough, Greeley accepted the scheme; here was another means of lightening the burden of the pioneer, of opening a fair and spacious country. Apparently he never saw the subtle hand of the speculator. The entire measure was a gigantic hoax, a fraud and a swindle, promoted by a skillful and rapacious lobby. Greeley had become an easy tool.

"Never was a cat rolled whiter in meal," he said with wry candor. "Millions on millions of choice public lands, whole sections of which had not enough muck to accommodate a fair-sized frog . . . went . . . with a good deal more besides"—went to speculators—"while never a shake of ague has any pioneer been spared by reason of all the drainage done under this specious act."

Nothing daunted, Greeley maintained his many-sided insistence. With increasing frequency he traveled westward, went twice to northern Michigan, circled the Great Lakes, visited Chicago, then "a smart and struggling village," and became one of the prime leaders in a series of Grand Rivers and Harbors Conventions whose purpose it was to improve transportation facilities by water in the newer regions. "Go West!" The way was to be made swift and easy. Greeley joined in the activities of railroad conventions—likewise "grand"—which resulted in the spiking down of the first ties west of Chicago, in 1848. Two decades before the Union Pacific was built he was urging the construction of a transcontinental railroad. "Go West, young man!" His classic counsel began to reverberate in the columns of the *Tribune,* in his lectures, in his brief interchanges with the country lads who still trooped up his stairs or accosted him in the street or in the lecture hall. "Go West, young man, and grow up with the country!" The broad advice roared with the palpable loud confusion of similar sounds throughout the country. From the backwoods, from a half-tilled acreage, from tracts exhausted by casual or untutored farming, the movement westward was now streaming far into the Valley of the Mississippi and past it, over the plains, with breaking fringes in California or within what Greeley had once doubtfully called "the barren solitudes of Oregon." At the end of the forties a sweeping and tempestuous march seemed the very pattern of existence. The swing toward empire in its loudest, noisiest phases had begun, in the conquests of the Mexican War, in the climax of the Gold Rush. Talk of a "manifest destiny" was rife—the inevitable occupation of the entire continent by the English race, the American possession of Canada. Behind this huge intoxication lay indeed that exhausted land which Greeley more than most men understood and deprecated: with every wave of the westward movement, in New England, in New York, in Pennsylvania, even in the more fertile regions of the Ohio Valley, the country had been harried by reckless farming until whole sections looked as though they had been devastated by fire, blight, or war; over the next ridge, certainly a few days' journeying by wagon, lay abundant new ground. Greeley might never have dreamed of the small, still pastoral within quiet enclosures. In truth, the whole urgent centrifugal movement toward the West, into wild land, seemed a denial and a contradiction of his personal choices, most of all those which he had made as a boy in the deep oppressive solitude of western Pennsylvania.

None the less his absorption in the hastening stampede remained ecstatic; more and more frequently he was out of the *Tribune* office, traveling westward. He wrote with freshness and excitement of the Ohio Valley, of the broader range of the Mississippi, and pushed further into the West through the services of other writers. In the *Tribune* appeared stories of Kit Carson, of Lieutenant Beale's journey, and accounts of the Mormon settlement. "Try to see the upper waters of the San Sacramento in October, and give us a screamer on the cañons through which the river passes Mount Shasta," wrote Greeley to Bayard Taylor, who had been commissioned to write of Eldorado for the paper. "I reckon there is grandeur there if not gold." Gross as was the contradiction between his earlier picture of a good companionship and this restless wide insurgence, often as he had turned from one proposal to another, fickle as were his changes, none the less the scattered alphabet of all his main proposals now spelled something like an American legend. Greeley had built up a large fantasy which might become substantial. Through all his expectations ran that passion for the land which had been part of his response to the Fourieristic scheme. His vision of the country was still predominantly rural, Arcadian on a homely but enormous scale; even in his commentaries on the Gold Rush what he saw was not treasure-trove, but an intoxicated human movement, and an effect of magnitude in a superabundantly rich, uncharted country. At every point he consistently opposed anything like imperialism, most of all during the Mexican War. "We do not believe it possible that our country *can* be prospered by such a war as this. . . . These victories, these acquisitions, will prove immense calamities, by sapping the morals of our people, by inflating them with pride and the lust of conquest and of gold, and leading to look to the commerce of the Indies and the dominion of the seas for those substantial blessings which follow in the wake of peaceful, contented labor. . . ." Peace was a solid benediction: Greeley urged it without remission, in the face of apathy or a concerted sentiment for war within his own party or in the country at large. "Peaceful, contented labor"—he saw this still as a great salient abstraction, the vision of a country blessed as all men worked usefully on plotted homesteads of their own. Around the happy half-continent was to be kept the high steep wall of protection: in season and out, Greeley urged this doctrine until at last it seemed less an economic safeguard than a positive means for producing an ultimate Millennium in which new inventions, new products, new ameliorations of the human lot were to arise in a large new Eden set away from the history of an older world. For a moment at least, in his broad sketchings, the wild new excitement seemed the pastoral dream on an immense scale, another movement toward a splendid society, a new movement toward association.

"This people associate as easily as they breathe," said Fredrika Bremer in these years of the late forties. "This free association is evidently an organizing and conservative principle of life, called forth to give law and centralization to the floating atoms, the disintegrated elements. . . . It is not at all difficult to predict that the Valley of the Mississippi in consequence of the variety of nations by which it will be populated, and from the variety of its scenery and climate, will at a future time produce a popular life of a totally new kind, with infinite varieties of life and temperament, a wholly new aspect of human society on earth. . . . I imagine to myself a Millennium in the Valley of the Mississippi, a resting-place in the history of the earth, where . . . love, beauty, joy, and the fullness of love, becomes the portion of all . . . with mighty rivers bearing from these flowery prairies with their ocean-like views, and from these golden fields of maize all the treasures of earth to mankind, and mild fresh winds to blow over them. . . ."

For Greeley that accelerated movement became a sign and a token; he gave to his brief and scattered journalism a glamor which stirred his wide constituency to the core. Doubtful as his economics might be at certain stages, or unpopular—for the country was going through revival of belief in free trade—and imitative too, for the framework of his vision rested upon Clay's American System—still by his quick large sense of common motives and inarticulate purposes, Greeley captivated the American fancy. His public often and violently disagreed with him. The marvel was that an enraged "Stop the *Tribune!*" was not a more frequent command, when the clashes between Greeley and his readers were so many and so deep. He struck constantly at habits, attitudes, and beliefs which they ardently cherished. The backwoods of the West in this era were far from being temperance communities; his rural readers were often habitually hard drinkers; and Greeley hammered his conviction against the use of alcohol. Tobacco was a special solace in country places, for women as well as men; Greeley's mother had not been singular in smoking a pipe. His crusade against tobacco, if anything, outmatched his temperance crusade. He declared tobacco to be "if not the most pernicious, certainly the vilest, most detestable abuse of his corrupt sensual appetites of which depraved man is capable." He discoursed upon the natural affinities of tobacco with blackguardism. At a time when violent death was a common episode in the West, when summary punishment for simple crimes was as casual a matter as a sunrise, Greeley unflaggingly wrote and spoke against legal punishment by death, indeed against physical punishment of any kind for crime. When the Irish immigration was growing unpopular, he spread the native Irish cause across the pages of the *Tribune;* before an insular public he expounded the case of Hungary. At a hundred points, it seemed, he was crusading against the sentiments or the interests of his public.

In the words of a contemporary, remembering a psalmist, a man was popular in those years as he laid his ax against the thick trees. The violence of the pioneer struggle seemed to demand violence in return; the prime trait of energy in any form perhaps appeared good. Undoubtedly his public enjoyed seeing Greeley fly in the face of the Whig leaders, of any established authority; certainly they relished his harsh epithets as though these were flavorsome morsels. "Uncle Sam! You bedazzled old hedgehog!" Greeley's schemes might dissolve in a huge flood of schemes, but they were aggressive, they continued the positive stir and throb of novelty. Likewise, for a brief moment, in the midst of all that cataclysmic change, something like tolerance flourished, with a liking for the rough-edged, divergent type—the pioneer; to most of his readers Greeley seemed one of themselves. They thumbed the pages of the *Tribune* and wore it to tatters, then passed it on to the nearest neighbor, or to others less lucky who could not afford to subscribe. With all his contradictions and assaults Greeley cried their momentary needs, their dangerous, persistent hopes, for less pressing hardships, for a recognition of the toil which was their lot, for a more bountiful possession of the rich extravagance of the country. Vague indeed his vision of the land might be, a swift and broken sketch: yet who in a time of huge and restless change could be wholly clear? In the midst of dissolving parties and a world on foot or on wheels, Greeley perhaps seemed more lucid, certainly more positive than any other single leader. The Whigs might howl: the labor party might cavil or complain: but Greeley commanded his public despite his changes and inconsistencies, and caught the wraith of a broad public companionship. His first sudden popularity seemed rooted in the continent.

SEVEN • *When Greeley sailed for Europe in 1851 to act as* a juror at the Crystal Palace Exhibition, he went as a magnified rustic with a vision of the country in his pocket, and a parcel of rural prejudices to keep his grandeur company.

He stalked through Prince Albert's marvel, that great translucent shell, and considered the triumph of the exhibition to be the McCormick reaper, which had been flouted in the London papers as a "cross between an Astley's chariot, a treadmill, and a flying machine." He was immensely proud of American locksmiths. He regretted that more Yankee notions had not been sent over, nails, pins, wood screws, brassware, clocks, as well as light Jersey wagons, Yankee ox-carts, and farming implements. With some condescension he tossed the Prince Consort a word of praise—"the solid and practical Prince Albert." By an apt touch he contrived to make Victoria monumental "on her slow and measured progress from side to side and end to end of the mighty convocation," but he declared the procession to be only middling. "Our New York Fire Department could beat it. So could the Odd Fellows." Nor did he find the applause of the crowd equal to that which invariably saluted American leaders on similar occasions. "One who has seen General Jackson or Harry Clay publicly enter New York or any other city, finds it hard to realize that the acclamations accorded on like occasions to Queen Victoria can really be deemed enthusiastic." Noblemen were "lucky descendants of Norman robbers," lords-in-waiting "uncouth fossils." Westminster Abbey was inferior for practical purposes to a dozen New York churches. Of the French opera Greeley said with pedantry, "It is not only a National Institution but a National Trait, and as such I visited it." Nor was he pleased with what he found there. "Its entire, palpable, urgent tendency is earthly, sensual, devilish. . . . I am, though no practitioner, a lover of the Dance. Restricted to proper hours and fit associates, I wish it were far more general than it is. Health, grace, muscular energy, even beauty, might be promoted by it. Why the dancing of the theater should be rendered disgusting, I cannot comprehend." In Venice, indeed, he broke into an exalted rhetoric. "Venice! Queen of the Adriatic! How can I ever forget thee? . . . My first day in Venice must ever hold its place among the most cherished recollections of my life." But he remarked that spacious Venetian palaces might be bought "for less than the cost of an average brick house in the upper part of New York. . . . Cheap as they are, they are a poorer speculation than even corner lots in a lithographic city of Nebraska or Oregon. . . ."

In Rome Greeley liked St. Peter's chiefly because its semi-circle reminded him of Niagara Falls. "I saw nothing in Rome with greater pleasure or profit than I derived from the hours I spent in the studio of our countryman POWERS," he declared. And lest some of his larger constrictions be missed, in the preface of his *Glances at Europe* Greeley took a rough shot at those other Americans even then trooping abroad with more pliant backs, who wished to learn "how my Lord Shuffleton waltzes, what wine Baron Hob-and-Nob patronizes, which tints predominate in Lady Highflyer's dress, and what is the probable color of the Duchess of Doublehose's garters." Such readers, he declared, would only waste their time looking through *his* book. Whether or not Greeley wore in his foreign travels the old white coat and hat, a conscious rusticity clothed him like a garment; he had shed that sweeping largeness and gusty energy which in his own country had given him an extraordinary stature, and became one of a long, little processional—noses in the the air—winding down the years through Europe.

Still a rustic, Greeley returned to his native country, and discovered a new era. The sea might have divided one decade from another. Instead of peaceful agriculturists tilling the western soil, building a happy empire, the farther rim of the continent now held a mad and noisy multitude of gold-diggers, with rustlers, renegades, rakehells, courtesans among them—splendid adventurers no doubt, and magnificent adversaries of fate—but none the less torrential scramblers for yellow dust. Back over the continent the glittering powder which they unearthed seemed to sift, lightly touching every palpable object on the horizon; a spreading opulence was everywhere; the decade grew richly gilded and floridly scrolled. That lust of empire which Greeley had feared as result of the conquest of Mexico seemed to have come in a thousand minute forms—in costumes, in household decorations, in social habitudes, an ironical climax to the broad movement which he had helped to accelerate. The virtues for which he had fought were being ignored—industry and a homely simplicity. Idleness was actually being celebrated by ministers like Henry Ward Beecher; the rustic note was shown as a pretty affectation in country villas, in paintings, in colored prints. Even on his own paper sentiments were now freely aired to which he could not subscribe. With that power for attracting talent which he had exhibited from the beginning of his journalistic efforts, Greeley had continued to swing new voices into his expanding chorus. Most of the Brook Farm writers were now solidly entrenched on the paper. Dana was the managing editor: that "wit in ethics," that enigmatic traveler from the exquisite idealism of the *Harbinger* toward the snug, worldly humor which he was later to exhibit as editor of the *Sun*. Ripley, Fry, and Curtis were regular contributors. But Curtis was writing his florid, descriptive *Lotus-Eating* papers; and Greeley detested a semi-worldly idleness. Fry, the composer of *Eleonora,* was discussing the feasibility of grand opera in New York. Greeley had not moved an inch from the views which he had expressed in Paris; he wrote of "the putrefying opera," and said to Dana, "I don't believe three hundred people who take the *Tribune* care one chew of tobacco for the matter." He was no more hospitable to the theater; and the department of criticism, in spite of Ripley's thoroughness, was leagues away from the fresh belligerence which Greeley had inaugurated in the forties, and to which Margaret Fuller had given her own positive print. Ripley's heart, as Godkin said, was "too much for his head." With the paper again increased in size, with mounting subscriptions, the *Tribune* in some measure raced beyond Greeley. Though his voice was still unmistakable in its columns, though historians then and since have said—till the phrase has worn thin—that Greeley *was* the paper, by the early or middle fifties he was no longer the single powerful agency.

The turn of the decade seemed to have altered the whole drift of Greeley's career. Pickie had died, smitten by cholera in the midst of terrible midsummer heat; and Greeley declared with despairing reticence that henceforth his course must be "downhill." It may be that Pickie's death was a final blow; this was almost the only personal emotion of which Greeley ever spoke. Another child, Ida, had been born before Pickie's death, and another son, Raphael, soon after, but he was not a "poet" like Pickie, "only a very good, bright, noble boy," Greeley said. The family moved from the spacious mansion at Turtle Bay to a house in Nineteeth Street, where Mrs. Greeley kept goats in the backyard; a tale survives that she insisted one Sunday morning upon going up Broadway during the hour when people were assembling for church, in a procession to consist of Greeley, the children, herself, and the goats, and was only dissuaded by a long and stubborn argument on the part of her husband. Mrs. Greeley was abrupt; her words had "a kind of crack like the report of a rifle," said a visitor; she always appeared to be washing something, and was usually disheveled. In the late forties and early fifties she became absorbed in spiritualism, and invited the Fox sisters for a week's stay at her house; Jenny Lind had come to watch the exhibits, and had imperiously ordered Greeley to take his hands from under the table. Greeley himself was transiently absorbed in the new cult. "What have you seen or heard about Spirit Rappings?" he wrote to an old correspondent. "There's something in 'em! What it is, I am not yet sure; but it isn't kneejoints nor toe-snaps notwithstanding the wise pill-peddlers of Buffalo." But this diversion was brief; the Greeleys soon gave up spiritualism; nor was their household a stable one. With a sudden movement, Mrs. Greeley went abroad with Ida and Raphael in 1853, deciding one autumn morning at breakfast to take a steamer the same day and remaining in Europe for nearly two years. Greeley joined them for a few weeks in the summer, but soon was back again, sleeping in hotels, wandering in and out of town, visiting the North American Phalanx, where the members still sported on the green and where he could help with the haying.

Then with a sudden blast of fire in 1854 the great mill of the Phalanx was destroyed. Greeley offered to lend the sum necessary to replace it; but when the directors gathered to discuss a new location, a casual suggestion was made that it might be better to disband; and with a sudden resolution the thing was done.

En Masse! On a huge scale Whitman was to repeat the intrinsic passion:

> "Come, I will make the continent indissoluble,
> I will make the most splendid race the sun ever shone
>   upon . . .
>   With the love of comrades. . . .

> "I will plant companionship thick as trees along all the rivers
> of America, and along the shores of the great lakes, and
> all over the prairies. . . .
> I will make inseparable cities with their arms about each other's
> necks,
>> By the love of comrades. . . ."

But Greeley not only scorned Whitman in a public address on poetry;
he retreated as in terror from the magnified area, bitterly regretting the
passing of the small community, the moment of intimacy, the close
bonds, the quaint and tiny lyricism. With singular unanimity most of
the members at Red Bank stressed in remembrance the sense of enclosure, "within walls which beat back the storms of life." Even in the later
sixties Greeley wrote of the disorder and harsh struggles existent in
"isolated society." Stubbornly he again urged the ennobling influence of
grand and harmonious common dwelling places, or labor pursued with
a common purpose, and gravely asserted the desirability of uniforms in
such communal efforts, and the pleasure of working to the strains of
music.

Perhaps it was in quest of an idyll that he haunted the Sunday evening
salons of the Cary sisters, now superseding the earlier, crowded gatherings at Miss Lynch's or Dr. Dewey's which had been at their height in
the forties. Within the limits imposed by architecture and furnishings,
the two sisters had striven to create the effect of a leafy bower. The carpet of the hall showed a pattern of oak leaves with scarlet tints; ascending to the drawing-room, the visitor discovered a long apartment which
was thought to glow like woods of maple and beech touched by frost—
or like a jewel—with its many vases of ruby glass, long mirrors, carpets of crimson and green, many brilliant paintings, quantities of handsomely bound books, and rosewood *étagères*. All was exquisite order
within this bright shining frame; Greeley said that it was "the sunniest
drawingroom (even by gaslight) to be found between King's Bridge
and the Battery." Alice was his favorite, a calm and stately figure in
shawls, clad in gray satin, with an inevitable touch of crimson. Her eyes
were wide and fine; she was thought to have a sealed and tragical past,
which seems to have borne some relation to the restless character of
Rufus Griswold. Phœbe, who was dark, vivacious, quick-witted, and always dressed in a bright bewilderment of color, pleased Greeley less; it
is doubtful whether he liked animation in women. But he enjoyed the
company; the Cary sisters drew about them all the notabilities of the
day: Bayard Taylor, Robert Owen, Fanny Fern, James Parton, Beecher,

Curtis, Samuel Bowles, Whittier, Mrs. Stanton, Miss Anthony. In any gathering Greeley was still likely to talk incessantly, to elbow, to become authoritative, to administer rebukes; yet at the Carys' he found perhaps the nearest approach to tranquillity that he ever found. Here was poetry —nearly every one who came there dipped into poetry. "Come, girls," he cried one stormy, snowy night, "let's read Tennyson," and himself declaimed the verses in his high voice, rolling out the words of Bedivere, "For now I see the true old times are dead," and repeating more than once a passage from *The Passing of Arthur.*

> "I am going a long way
> With these thou seest—if indeed I go—
> For all my mind is clouded with a doubt—
> To the island-valley of Avilion;
> Where falls not hail, or rain, or any snow,
> Nor ever wind blows loudly; but it lies
> Deep-meadow'd, happy, fair with orchard-lawns
> And bowery hollows crowned with summer sea,
> Where I will heal me of my grievous wound."

In an elegiac mood he purchased a farm at Chappaqua near White Plains, mentioning his "great namesake," the owner of a Sabine farm. "Long tossed on the stormiest waves of doubtful conflict and arduous endeavor, I have begun to feel, since the shades of forty fell upon me, the weary, tempest-driven voyager's longing for land, the wanderer's yearning for the hamlet where in childhood he nestled by his mother's knee, and was soothed to sleep at her breast," he mused before an agricultural society in the West. "And so I, in the sober afternoon of life, when its sun, if not high, is still warm, have resolved to steal from the City's labors and anxieties at least one day in each week wherein to revive as a farmer the memories of my childhood's humble home."

Chappaqua seemed filled with ghosts, and was dense with trees. Perhaps with a wishful reminiscence of her own, Mrs. Greeley had demanded that the new place should contain a spring, a brawling brook, and a grove of evergreens. In order to include these natural features, and remain within an easy distance from New York, Greeley purchased a wooded hillside, which sloped north by west with a bog at its foot, and with a further tract of rocky and exhausted soil. As if by instinct he had chosen a farm that was almost a precise replica of those hard, unpromising areas over which he had toiled with Zaccheus Greeley in his childhood. He poured money into the place, with small results; Chappaqua had a slip-shod look. His harvesters left grain in quantities on the ground. Stumbling across his fields to show them to a friend, dragging his feet, Greeley could collect enough rye, wheat, or oats to make a bundle before he had walked a hundred yards. "I should have been a farmer," he now frequently said. Yet he could never make or mend the smallest tool; he was struck with surprise when a visitor fashioned a cup for spring water from a thick leaf; he lacked the ingenuity to tie a sailor's knot. When some one told him that May was not the best season for cutting alders, Greeley replied, "*Now* is always my time for anything. Pretexts for putting off work are a lazy man's argument." Trees grew as thickly at Chappaqua as in the thickets of Vermont or the wilds of Pennsylvania; and Greeley became an inveterate woodchopper, hacking away at hickory, ironwood, oak—not for fuel, not for clearance, but as if he were obsessed to perform the mere labor, obsessed by the noise and movement, and perhaps by reminiscence. Presently, as if they both obscurely sought a common life together, the Greeleys began building. The original farm-house was rebuilt; in the course of a little more than ten years two other houses appeared on the place, each larger than the last, and Greeley had built two huge barns.

In and out of this rural medley Greeley ranged, seldom at Chappaqua for more than a day or two, talking and writing of the place constantly, as if its picture filled the foreground of his mind. In the midst of the myriad preoccupations on a great paper, in the thickening clash of the fifties, he stole time to read the country exchanges; agricultural interests and inventions still crowded forward in the *Tribune.* Outside these interests he was sharp, tired, and irritable, roaring in the office louder than before; many persons declared that he was immensely overwrought; in these years developed the fulminations for which he became famous; he was forever calling his opponents liars or villains. He had nothing now publicly to say of the good time coming; he wrote of "this stammering century," "the Age of Brass we live in." Instead of the rough and lively humor of earlier years he was beginning to develop that form of disillusioned fun which Mark Twain was to perfect, beginning with elegant apostrophes—"Saratoga! Bright city of the present! Thou ever enduring one-and-twenty of existence!—" and then suddenly giving the unwary reader a hard jolt by a bald prose. Greeley's diatribes against literature as a vocation became more pronounced; he thundered against colleges; and he quarreled. At Poe's death he had permitted Griswold an extraordinary liberty in the *Tribune,* which he had used in the initial blast of his posthumous attack on Poe in the famous "Ludwig" article: but Greeley now quarreled with Griswold over a minor matter, and pilloried a book of his; they never were reconciled. He grew distant toward the feminist group, and wrote Mrs. Stanton tersely, "You know already that I am thoroughly committed to the principle that *woman shall decide for herself,* whether she shall have a voice and a vote in legislation." Over minor newspaper attacks, over the pricks of inferior persons he could become exasperated to the point of desperate explosion; yet he passed over important commentaries on matters of the *Tribune* policy without a word, and in the office steadily became more exacting. "You crucify me, yes, you will crucify me with such management," he cried to Dana over some trivial omission. He railed at all writers, and lent them money more freely than ever, or endorsed their notes; he was forever lending money. Even in the earlier years of his first more moderate prosperity he had lent five thousand dollars, then four thousand on the same day, and soon afterward five hundred dollars, endorsing a note to keep an acquaintance out of jail "because his wife was sick and suffering here, while he was jugged at Rochester. Now I believe he has just got into State Prison for two years. . . . Such is the fun of living in cities, having friends, and knowing how to write your name. I go agin writing." But he continued to lend and endorse, giving to almost any man or any cause. He lent to wastrels, to the merest mendicants; he lent to any one who had the sketch of an agricultural invention on paper. He lent until his habit became a byword, flinging money away as though the impatient gesture satisfied him, as if he meant to obliterate the hard years when he had lacked money.

The extraordinary circumstance was that in the midst of his fumbling indifference and exasperation, during the first half of the fifties, Greeley's reputation had swiftly mounted; it was as though during the first ten years on the *Tribune* he had acquired an impetus toward popular recognition that nothing could stay. Young James Parton was already at work on his ardent biography, which was to run to a sale of thirty thousand copies within a few months—an unprecedented record for those days—and then rapidly to double and treble that number, passing through edition after edition. Critics, indeed, might be heard saying that Greeley could "hardly conceive an honest opposition to his own views," that he was "a sort of John the Baptist, one crying, literally, in the wilderness, 'Prepare the way!' but with no power to lead the way himself. . . ." "Owing to the want of consistency in his own mind, he is practically dishonest to an eminent degree," said one harsh observer. But a shrill and carping noise was all but overwhelmed by the praises of writers who were describing Greeley's looks and habits with a lavish touch, his farm at Chappaqua and his cluttered office in the new *Tribune* building. Perhaps few public men have been so frequently photographed and painted;

from the early fifties onward he sat again and again for one or another form of portraiture; he seemed to be reversing the fate of caricature. Some of these likenesses show him with skeptical eyes and a querulous curl of the lips, or with a rigidity which suggested porcupine quills; others showed him still baby-like, with his aureole of silver-yellow hair, his countenance revealing a celestial calm, his mouth, wide, sensitive, and finely cut, sometimes serenely smiling.

Clearly the public was intrigued by this vigorous yet enigmatic figure; and the *Tribune,* like Greeley's image in the popular mind—most of all the western mind—gained an increasing magnitude. In 1851 Henry J. Raymond, still Greeley's unremitting antagonist, had founded the New York *Times,* receiving the support of Weed. Within three years the new paper had gained a city subscription which trebled that of the *Tribune,* but in wider areas the *Tribune* held its own, and quickly reached far beyond the popularity which it had commanded in the forties. Between 1850 and 1854, subscriptions to its weekly and semi-weekly editions had nearly doubled; between 1854 and 1856 they doubled once more. In the country at large the *Tribune* had become, in truth, an oracle.

Oracles were needed; if the fifties were gilt, they were also changing, clashing; beneath the bright gayety of a new worldliness ran the mixed and troublous issues which were to disrupt the nation. The anomaly, with Greeley's reputation, was his uncertainty. Clay had died in 1851; Greeley had been profoundly moved; his leader and pattern for twenty-five years was gone. Ironically enough, much of Greeley's immediate confusion came from his effort to accept Clay's great Compromise Measure of 1850. He tried to defend it, but he was swept by the current horror of the Fugitive Slave Law, and at length was obliged to admit that the only clause of the Compromise which he could accept was that which provided for the admission of California as a free state. Yet the more vigorous aspects of the anti-slavery cause had never captured Greeley; he still followed the middle course of Clay; except as it involved violence the plight of the negro did not move him deeply. On a public platform in 1850 he had complained that the free negroes of the North were dependent, lazy, inefficient. In a time of doubt Greeley grew lax; nor was he able to find clarity in the movements of the Whig party. In 1852 Scott was nominated as the Whig candidate for the presidency, a candidate who was unwilling to define a platform. When the election was over, Greeley publicly renounced politics. "I have had enough of party politics," he declared. "I will speak for temperance, and law, and agriculture, and some other objects; but I am not going to stump the country any more in the interest of party or candidates."

New auguries appeared, as the radical Republican party came to birth. Free homesteads—free soil—free labor: these promises, it seems, mingling with the effort to prevent the extension of slavery, might have commanded Greeley's allegiance: but he held back. "Remember that editors can only follow where the people's heart is already prepared to go with them," he wrote to Bovay. "I faintly hope that the time has come which Daniel Webster predicted when he said, 'I think there will be a North. . . .' But I am a beaten, broken-down, used-up politician, and have the soreness of many defeats in my bones. However, I am ready to follow any lead that promises to hasten the day of northern emancipation. Your plan is all right if the people are ripe for it. I fear they, too," he added skeptically, "generally wish (with John Mitchell) that they had a good plantation and negroes in Alabama—or even Kansas."

Greeley hesitated: then the political scene claimed him once more. Within a few weeks he had decided that public opinion *was* ripe for the move. If he did not christen the Republican party—the honor frequently has been claimed for him—at least he gave the new name a wide publicity by a striking editorial, pledged his allegiance, and in the summer of 1854 attended the first Republican or anti-Nebraska convention at Saratoga Springs. In these moves he had passed beyond Seward, who had overpassed Greeley in radical anti-slavery sentiment during earlier years; it was as though the two could never march together. "The business of reconstructing parties and platforms is a difficult and delicate one," wrote Seward at this time. "Let those undertake it who will, and those perform it who can." The body of New York Whigs held the same view; there was no question in that year of submitting a Republican ticket in the state elections, as was done in Michigan. Greeley assented to this moderation in New York; indeed, absorbed as he was in the counsels of the new party, he proposed to lead the Whigs of New York at the same time. He wanted the Whig nomination for governor.

With Weed he was still in close communication, asking patronage for needy Whigs, discussing the exigencies of the new political situation, and flatly insisting upon his own hatred of Raymond. "Well: on Tuesday I was met by a letter from Raymond, which I shall send you as a literary curiosity," Greeley had written to Weed a few months earlier. "I had said or written nothing to him, made no request of him— yet just see the insolence with which the little viper talks to me of his 'benevolence,' 'favors,' etc., to those who prove worthy of them! . . . Well: this letter, you will see, repeats a falsehood coined by St. John"—as Greeley insisted on calling Raymond—". . . namely, that I am offended with St. John and 'abuse' him *because he did not give the advertising to the* Tribune!—and this after all that has passed between us! Ought I to bear this?"

The next step is shrouded by contradictions; but at least Greeley asked Weed for the nomination. The discussion apparently centered upon the feasibility of choosing a temperance candidate to head the Whig ticket. Temperance sentiment was strong in the state at the time; and undoubtedly Greely was the leading Whig advocate of the cause. But with cool security Weed told Greeley that while he had undoubtedly "shaken the temperance bush," another man "would catch the bird." Weed declared —after Greeley's death—that Greeley came to him again, and requested the nomination for the lieutenant-governorship. Weed's answer was that it would be impossible to place two advocates of temperance at the head of the ticket. In his later narrative Weed declared that he had entered the convention in entire ignorance as to the probable Whig candidate for the lieutenant-governorship. Greeley did not believe this; nor need any one else. Weed's power in the Whig organization was still strong; and since Seward was a candidate for reëlection to the Senate, he would have left no loophole in the plans of the party unguarded. The Whig nomination for the lieutenant-governorship went to Henry J. Raymond, Greeley's strongest rival in the newspaper field, and his avowed antagonist.

Greeley's bitterness overflowed. He at once wrote to Seward, declaring that after the election he must have "an earnest talk." "I have tried to talk with Weed, but with only partial success. Weed likes me, and always did—I don't think he ever had a dog about his house he liked better—but he thinks I know nothing about politics."

The conversation with Seward seems never to have been held: but after the election—when both Seward and Raymond were elevated to office—Greeley addressed to Seward a long and furious letter, full of half-revealed affection, hurt, and reproach. Apparently he had hoarded resentment against Seward for years for his lack of assistance after the election of 1838.

"You were governor, dispensing offices worth three thousand to twenty thousand dollars per year to your friends and compatriots, and I returned to my garret and my crust, and my desperate battle with pecuniary obligations heaped upon me by bad partners in business and the disastrous events of 1837. I believe it did not then occur to me that some one of these abundant places might have been offered to me without injustice; I now think it should have occurred to *you*." With increasing rancor he rehearsed the details of the Log Cabin campaign, resulting in "the great scramble of the swell mob of coon minstrels and cider suckers at Washington—I not being counted in. . . . I asked nothing, expected nothing; but you, Governor Seward, ought to have asked that I be postmaster of New York. . . ." He declared that he had been promised financial assistance from Seward's friends when he founded the *Tribune,* and had not received it—forgetting perhaps the timely advent of Seward's friend McElrath. He forgot, too, his many pronounced differences with Weed on questions of policy and principle, forgot that he had served notice on Weed as far back as 1845 that he would go his own way.

The astonishing circumstance was that after a hundred divergences he should have expected the support of Weed. Sharp, angry, full of recriminations, he now remembered the few sops which had been tendered him for his services, his merely formal nomination for the Assembly in 1842 when the Whig party was hopelessly out of power, and the ninety days in Congress which had been permitted him in order to hold down the seat for another Whig. He covered page after page, and came back to his bitter reproaches. "I suspect it is true that I could not have been elected Governor as a Whig. But had he"—Weed—"and you been favorable, there would have been a party in the State, ere this, which could and would have elected me to any post, without injuring myself or endangering your reëlection. . . . I should have hated to serve as Lieutenant-Governor, but I should have gloried in running for the post. I want to have my enemies all upon me at once—I am tired of fighting them piecemeal. And although I should have been beaten in the canvass," he added in mingled obscurity and clarity, "I know that my running would have helped the ticket and helped my paper. . . . No other name could have been put on the ticket so bitterly humbling to me as that which was selected. The nomination was given to Raymond—the fight left to me. And, Governor Seward, *I have made it,* though it be conceited for me to say so. What little fight there has been, I have stirred up. . . .

"I know that some of your most cherished friends think me a great obstacle to your advancement—that John Schoolcraft, for one, insists that you and Weed shall not be identified with me. I trust, after a time, you will not be. I trust I shall never be found in opposition to you. . . . All I ask is that we shall be counted even on the morning after the first Tuesday in February . . . and that I may thereafter take such course as seems best, without reference to the past."

With these words Greeley dissolved the "political firm of Seward, Weed, and Greeley, by the withdrawal of the junior member."

This angry and naked self-revelation was not taken seriously by Seward, who made a quiet reply. Greeley rejoined in further explanation, not without pathos, that what he had wanted was "some sort of public recognition that I was esteemed as a faithful and useful coadjutor. . . . Office as such is not within my line. I should make no reputation and many enemies in any responsible position." Seward had asked Weed about a possible vacancy on the Board of Regents, a position which might have interested Greeley; but nothing came of the suggestion; and Greeley's long letter dropped from sight in Seward's compendious files.

Weed and Seward also seem to have buried their remembrance of Greeley's services, which had in truth extended far beyond the scope which he had mentioned. Greeley had always given Seward a large place in the *Tribune;* his greater speeches in Congress and in the country had been reported in full in Greeley's paper—a tribute which even Raymond had not always offered; and because Greeley was supposed to be his spokesman, Seward was now enabled to cover his laggard step into the Republican ranks during the rush of Whig sentiment thither in 1855. Weed not only disregarded these services; that astute politician failed at this point in judgment of Greeley's character, and of the surrounding circumstances. For all that Seward was soon included in the new Republican party, he had moved there a hair's breadth too slowly. Greeley rather than Seward commanded the liberal sentiment of the country. With the changing temper of the North, with events hurrying toward conclusions on the western plains, with the Republican stress of a new homestead law—Greeley's favorite measure—in conjunction with the moving cry of Free Soil, his swift decision before the Saratoga convention was standing him in excellent stead; he had swung toward a position of decisive leadership. Moreover, if Weed had taken the trouble to gauge Greeley's temperament, or even to pass his career in quiet review, he might have perceived that while his erstwhile henchman had the broad back requisite for the rôle, Greeley had always done something more than carry loads for other men; and whatever he hoisted into that conspicuous position was likely to remain there in one form or another. With all his effect of veering change Greeley seldom abandoned any opinion or principle, enthusiasm, or hatred; he merely thrust these into new positions and let them mix with their opposites as best they might. He might subside or change his tune, but the likelihood was that he would keep any deep-seated feeling intact. Probably Greeley both loved—and hated—Weed and Seward to the last; and his affection gave impetus to his hatred.

Casually considering Greeley negligible, Weed made the single great mistake of a long, closely guarded career. Yet even if he had been disinclined to reminiscence, he might have found a warning in Greeley's subsequent tactics. During 1855 Seward was being freely mentioned as a desirable Republican candidate for the presidency the following year. Greeley urged Frémont, who received the nomination. And in the winter of 1855-6, with an unerring premonition of a growing climax, Greeley went to Washington to watch the struggle for the speakership, which promised a definition of new political alignments. The session was thick with contention; and Greeley, seated at a reporter's desk day in and day out, watched every move, reported every significant rumor in bulletins to the *Tribune;* but he was something more than a reporter. By his zealous analysis and criticism he was plainly attempting to jockey doubtful votes into line for Banks, the candidate of the still scarcely formed Republican group; he was deep in political manipulation. His purposes were generally recognized. As result, he was twice assaulted on the streets of Washington by a member from Arkansas. "I presume this is not the last outrage to which I am to be subjected," he wrote in his next letter to the *Tribune.* "I came here with a clear understanding that it was about an even chance whether I should or should not be allowed to go home alive . . ."

Of Greeley's hysterical excitement at this juncture Weed could hardly have learned; but the index of a wild unruly power was unmistakable. Greeley began to write to Dana of "perpetual treacheries on our own side." He complained that the *Tribune* was not supporting him. " I shall have to quit here or die, unless you stop attacking people here without consulting me. . . . Do send some one here and kill me if you cannot stop this, for I can bear it no longer. My life is a torture to me. . . . I will stand my chances or be horsewhipped or pistoled, if you will keep me clear of being knocked down by the *Tribune.* . . ." Sometimes his budgets of news failed to reach New York in time for fitting publication; he could make no allowances; his complaints grew higher pitched. "Dana! for God's sake speak the truth to me. The *Tribune* is cursed all over the house as having beaten us today by your untimely article on Bayard Clarke in yesterday's *Tribune.* . . . I must give up and go home. All the Border Ruffians from here to the lowest pit could not start me away, but you do it, and I must give up. You are getting everybody to curse me. I am too sick to be out of bed, too crazy to sleep, and am surrounded by horrors. I shall go to Pittsburgh on the 22nd, and I guess I shall not return. I can just bear the responsibilities that belong to me; but you heap a load on me that will kill me. . . ."

"You must not get cross with me," he wrote pleadingly a few days later. "You see it seems hard to stay in this dreary, infernal hole to write letters, which mere delay makes a good deal more stupid than they naturally are. . . . My letter would have been middling on Saturday, while it will be sour as whey and flat as dishwater on Monday. . . ." Four days later he was back in the old vein, with the difference that his despair now embraced the entire management of the paper. "The infernal pica-yune spirit in which it is published has broken my heart. . . . We ought to get back to our noble size soon, and print a supplement at least every Saturday. No Jew ever managed a pawnbroker's shop in a baser, narrower, more shortsighted spirit than the *Tribune* is managed, and I am heartsick. I would stay here forever, and work like a slave if I could get my letters printed as I send them, but the *Tribune* is doomed to be a second-rate paper, and I am tired," He wrote continually of his plans for the paper, wrote of it as dead or dying, though within the current years its subscription list was making another unprecedented upward surge, rising to half again the numbers enrolled in 1855. Greeley complained of a new magazine project undertaken by the paper—"because I regard the *Tribune* as a great idea just begun to be developed, and don't wish anything else to interfere with it. . . . To make the *Tribune* the first paper in America is fortune and fame enough for me, and that *we are not now doing. . . .*"

Soon he was offering a new vein of criticism, on an enduring theme. "If a man should invent a new locomotive that could readily and profit-ably be used in cornfields or on common roads, I should wish to see it announced in a leader on the very day after it was patented, whereas by your method it would probably appear the next month in a supplement, buried up under new raspberries and improved bee-hives. Is that the thing? . . . I want to have less and less to do with politics, and more and more with the Productive Inventions. I feel that the path of Empire —journalistic and all other—stretches in this direction. . . ."

With these pronouncements Greeley might have been headed toward Chappaqua or the Crystal Palace: but before the year was out he seemed to have left far behind the thought of peaceful production, and was in the thick of the Frémont campaign. As the struggle for Kansas mounted, like Beecher he plunged into its most belligerent phases. "Let the North furnish men and money, settlers, and Sharp's rifles," he cried. "Pour into Kansas, brave men and true, with your rifles in your hands."

Then in 1857 and 1858 Greeley espoused the cause of Douglas. Among the strange fortunes of these turbulent years was the rise of Douglas to popularity. The Republicans might never have considered Douglas the arch-trickster who had given them a battle-cry and pushed them toward the formation of a party. The furor and black bitterness which had followed the passage of the Kansas-Nebraska Act was forgotten. By his adroit and powerful sophistry, Douglas was now enabled to appear as the defender of Kansas; popular sovereignty was seen as a bold solution. Greeley took up the phrase; no man in public life seemed so wholly captivated by Douglas as Greeley. He frequented Douglas's house in Washington; the *Tribune* sounded his praises; it began to be whispered, largely through the agency of the *Tribune,* that Douglas was after all a Republican at heart, and that after the election of 1858 he would so declare himself. With his magnetic flow of oratory, with a kind of diabolism or artifice, Douglas was one of a procession of types that Greeley had found irresistible; and for Greeley a further attraction must have lain in Douglas's program of roadbuilding and expansion, and his dreams of prairie grandeur. As though he regarded himself as the authoritative national leader of the party, Greeley now issued a call to the Illinois Republicans to rally around Douglas in the forthcoming contest, and privately urged the party leaders of the state to put no candidate in the field. The prospective candidate, as every one knew, was Lincoln. "I saw Greeley," wrote Herndon to Lincoln in March, 1858. "He did not say so much in so many words, yet his *feelings* are with Douglas. I *know* it from the spirit and drift of his conversation."

"Let the future alone; it will come out all right," said Greeley on this occasion. "Douglas is a brave man. Forget the past and sustain the righteous."

"Good God, righteous, eh!" wrote Herndon.

Even after Lincoln had received the Republican nomination, and the great debates had opened, Greeley threw the weight of his influence toward Douglas, or was silent. In September Herndon wrote to Parker, "We were like innocent fools waiting out here to hear Greeley open in his great *Tribune;* we expected that he would open the ball, but no signal boom came out, and we grew restively cold, and our party slumbered as with a chill—a bivouac of death upon an iceberg. . . ." A month later Herndon queried bitterly, "Who could know by Greeley's paper that a great race for weal or woe was being fought all over the wide prairies of Illinois? Who would? It is strange indeed!" It was clear that Lincoln feared Greeley; his allusions to Greeley's support of Douglas were unmistakable in speech after speech. In truth, with the foremost Republican editor in the country turned against the Republican candidate in the great battle of the issues, the outcome might well have been precarious; and the *Tribune* was widely read by the farmers of Illinois. As Lincoln's classic argument proceeded, as the force of his dialectic rang out over the country with the unmistakable emptiness of Douglas's rejoinder,

Greeley wavered, it is true, was "sorter, sorter," as Herndon said; but his genuine support was never offered to Lincoln. At length in a letter to Theodore Parker, Herndon came out with the explanation:

"Greeley, Seward, Weed, and Douglas, by accident or otherwise, met in Chicago in the month of October, 1857, and soon afterward it was announced to me *officially,* but *privately,* that Senator Douglas was a Republican. I did not see these men in Chicago, though I believe they were so informed. This is the substance of the Chicago contract. Douglas said to Greeley, etc., *'You support me for the Senate, and I will support Seward for the Presidency, and take my chance for the office in time.'* 'Agreed,' said the crowd."

The bargain was sufficiently amazing; that it was made seems plain from the prompt endorsement of Douglas late in 1857 by the New York *Times,* Seward's official organ, by Seward's own extraordinary reversal toward Douglas, by a network of minor drama in Illinois, and most clearly of all, by Greeley's continued opposition to Lincoln. But a puzzling circumstance remains: what was Greeley doing in that gallery? Why had he agreed to such a transaction? Had he after all buried his animosity toward Weed and Seward? Or was he supporting Douglas in the hope that he might outstrip Seward in the race for the presidency in 1860? Obviously Douglas was aiming for that office: and at least a framework for this interpretation of Greeley's motives exists. When Lincoln lost the election in the state senate, it was largely through the opposition of Greeley, as Herndon and others thought; and Greeley at once began to urge Douglas as a candidate for the presidency, in conversations at Washington.

Outwardly his relations with Weed and Seward were serene. Seward's charming account of his trip to Labrador in 1857 had been printed jointly in Weed's paper and in the *Tribune.* Before Seward went abroad in 1859 he dined with Greeley; and both Weed and Seward gained the impression that on his forthcoming overland journey to California—he was making his farthest journey west—Greeley proposed to spread the enthusiasm for Seward as the Republican candidate in 1860. When Seward returned from Europe late in the year, and received public demonstrations on every hand, the *Tribune* was generous in its acknowledgments; and Greeley printed in full Seward's great conciliatory speech in Congress, of February, 1860, praised it, and had it reprinted as a pamphlet. Weed, quite as much as Seward, might have supposed himself reinstated in Greeley's favor. Late in 1859 Greeley wrote to Weed's friend, George E. Baker, "Weed is a giant. . . . Weed loves those who never seem to oppose his will, but he is after all the greatest man we have left, Seward *not* excepted."

Yet by the early spring of 1860 Greeley had begun openly to inquire in the *Tribune* whether Seward, if nominated, could be elected. He announced that Seward was unpopular in Pennsylvania, whose electoral vote was considered essential; and he gave an increasing prominence to certain recent, dubious transactions of Weed. During the winter of 1859-60 Weed, the undying politician, had promoted a scheme by which the New York legislature was to grant charters to certain New York city railways in return for a substantial enrichment of the Republican treasury. The smirch was black; and Greeley made the most of it, arguing that while Seward's character was above reproach, his election to the presidency would inevitably mean the entrenchment in Washington of a similar corruption. These charges received a doubly serious hearing before the country because of the long—and so far as public knowledge was concerned—unbroken alliance of Seward, Weed, and Greeley. At the same time it became clear that late in 1859, privately at least, Greeley had begun to agitate for quite another candidate for the Republican nomination, dropping Douglas at last, who after all could not be shaped into the Republican pattern. As if the Whig print were cut deeply into his mind, Greeley turned to Judge Bates of St. Louis, an old-time Whig, a Clay Whig, never a Republican, whom Greeley had seen as the presiding officer at a Rivers and Harbors convention in Chicago which he had attended with enthusiasm in 1847. His argument was one of expediency. He insisted that Bates could carry Missouri, a doubtful state, could command the old Whig vote of the South, yet arouse northern enthusiasm, since he had promoted the cause of gradual emancipation in Missouri.

At the Republican convention in Chicago in May, Greeley was early on the ground. Within a few hours flyers were scattered over the city, reading, "Greeley at the Tremont, Weed at the Richmond House." From the first Greeley was in the thick of affairs, constantly moving about, followed by crowds of people in the streets who recognized his legendary figure at sight, tirelessly warning delegation after delegation that Seward would fail to carry the doubtful states, but that Bates could do so.

"Massachusetts was right in Weed's hands, contrary to all reasonable expectations," said Greeley afterward. "It was all we could do to hold Vermont by the most desperate exertions. . . . Indiana was our right bower, and Missouri above praise." At the last moment, indeed, Seward seemed on the point of success; on the evening before the nomination,

Greeley telegraphed the *Tribune* that he believed Seward would be nominated. But in the huckstering of that night Greeley played a decisive part; convinced that Seward could be beaten only by Lincoln, he assisted in the transfer of the Indiana votes which gave Lincoln a rising ascendancy on the second ballot; some of the Bates votes from Missouri followed; and in a storm of popular applause which spread over the city, Lincoln received the nomination.

"Greeley slaughtered Seward and saved the party," wrote DeFrees to Schuyler Colfax. "He deserves the praises of all men, and gets them now. Wherever he goes he is greeted with cheers." With entire candor Greeley acknowledged his part in the final outcome, but complained that his "share in the load was unreasonably heavy, considering where I live, and the power of the soreheads to damage me. I don't think you wanted to come face to face with Weed in a case where his heart was so set on triumph," he wrote to Colfax. "I ought not to have been obliged to expose myself to the deadliest resentment of all the Seward crowd. . . ." But Greeley was at little pains to allay that resentment. The day after the nomination, with blatant triumph, he wrote in the *Tribune,* "The past is dead. Let the dead bury it, and let the mourners, if they will, go about the streets!"

Weed had burst into tears when the defeat of Seward was announced. Seward's magnanimous gesture was promptly made. Awaiting a tremendous ovation at Auburn, he turned at once, and in his own hand wrote a cordial endorsement of Lincoln. It was left for St. John, as Greeley still called Raymond, to take up the cudgels. In a letter dated from Auburn, he accused Greeley of having wreaked the "long-hoarded revenge of the disappointed office-seeker." In reply, Greeley demanded the letter which he had written to Seward in 1854, and printed it *verbatim* in the *Tribune.* Apparently he believed that its publication would clear him of Raymond's charges: but the effect was otherwise. Godkin said that public amazement at the terms of the letter was the highest tribute that Greeley ever received. The barb—"disappointed office-seeker"—remained; and Greeley himself seemed bent upon confirming its intention. Strident and secure, contemptuous of Weed, in 1861 he sought the Republican nomination in New York for the Senate; he meant to step into Seward's shoes. Weed's candidate was Evarts. At the outset, in a triangular contest, Greeley received a flattering plurality; Evarts lagged a considerable distance behind him, with the third candidate, Harris, far in the rear. The Harris delegation began to break in Greeley's favor; he all but had the nomination in his hand when Weed, marshaling his forces, swung the nomination to Harris by sacrificing Evarts. Nothing could have been clearer than that Greeley had been publicly beaten by Weed, unless it was that Greeley craved office.

Greeley's motives for months and even years seemed to have been conditioned by a disillusioned enmity; yet perhaps no act of his was ever truly simple. Beneath this obvious driving purpose ran other attitudes, which had at least the virtue of large terms. Herndon, to whom Greeley had early confided his confidence in Bates—and who thought Greeley honest—phrased one interpretation. "Greeley is getting quite conservative: he is a timid man; he is willing to agitate for an idea during its abstract state, but he shudders when it is about to concrete itself amidst living events. He is fine for theoretic principles—not heaven-high ones applied." An ardent abstract mind, naturally a quiet mind, lost in the tide of tremendous events, but with a blind and raging restlessness—how begotten? who shall say?—this seemed Greeley. Undoubtedly he feared and dreaded the climax of war, in spite of his own brief perverse violence. His opposition to Lincoln was plainly enwrapped by a fear of the extremities to which an articulate anti-slavery policy might lead. Long before, in the forties, Greeley had considered Seward "too radical" as an anti-slavery leader. His advocacy of Bates was consistent: as a compromise candidate he believed that Bates might stay the tide. Even after the nomination of Lincoln, Greeley flatly declared that he thought Bates, "to whom I never spoke nor wrote, would have been the wiser choice." At once, when the election was over, from the *Tribune* came the cry, "No war! No war!"

EIGHT • *Frantically Greeley all but thrust the measure of* secession before the gathering delegates of South Carolina, declaring that "the South had a good cause for leaving the Union as the Colonies had for leaving the British Empire. . . . The right to secede may be a revolutionary one, but it exists nevertheless. Whenever a considerable section of our union shall deliberately resolve to go out, we shall resist all coercive measures designed to keep it in. We hope never to live in a Republic whereof one section is pinned to the residue by bayonets. . . ." These sentiments were widely quoted in the South; hammering them for weeks, Greeley carried with him an immense bulk of northern sentiment. Asked in Boston on a public platform, "Will the South secede?" Henry Ward Beecher answered roundly, "I don't believe they will, and I don't care if they do." Loud as were the echoes which Beecher could always raise, the voice of Greeley carried farther and more remotely; he seemed bent upon shouting down Lincoln's unmistakable plea for the union in the first inaugural address. Yet by February, 1861, when secession was taking a tangible form, Greeley announced, "I deny to one State, or to a dozen States, the right to dissolve this Union. It can only be legally dissolved as it was formed—*by the free consent of all parties concerned.*" He went further, writing a contemptuous denunciation of the abolitionists, who had long entertained the view that secession was a logical possibility. "Our only doubt is whether it is even worth while to set them right. Perhaps it would be most merciful to leave a mill-horse to stagger in his circle to the end, for he will fall down if taken out of it. . . ."

"No war! No war!" Greeley had shouted. But as state after southern state seceded, from the columns of the *Tribune* was lifted the shrill cry, "On to Richmond! *On to Richmond!* ON TO RICHMOND!" followed by as vengeful pronouncements, in the spring of 1861, as ever proceeded from any public organ. "The rebels of that State [Virginia] and Maryland may not flatter themselves that they can enter upon a war against the government, and afterwards return to quiet and peaceful homes. . . . We mean to conquer them—not merely to defeat, but to conquer, to subjugate them—and we shall do this most mercifully the more speedily we do it. But when the rebellious traitors are overwhelmed in the field and scattered like leaves before an angry wind, it must not be to return to peaceful and contented homes. They must find poverty at their firesides, and see privation in the anxious eyes of mothers and the rags of children."

These fearful words may not have been written by Greeley, but they appeared in successive issues of his paper; either he had sanctioned them or he had lost control of his instrument. "Forward to Richmond!" Still that fateful and threatening cry uprose from the *Tribune* during the weeks that preceded the rout at Bull Run, creating the impression that the administration was hesitant, possibly precipitating the ill-prepared and hurried march. When disaster had come, when that first shattering cataclysm was over, in the midst of war at last, Greeley collapsed, and a week later wrote to Lincoln a long letter, filled with self-reproach, desperation, and confusion. "I think I shall not die, because I have no right to die. I must struggle to live, however bitterly. . . . You are not considered a great man, and I am a hopelessly broken one. . . . Can the rebels be beaten after all that has occurred? . . . If they can—and it is your business to ascertain and decide—write me that such is your judgment, so that I may know and do my duty. And if they *can not* be beaten —if our recent disaster is fatal—do not fear to sacrifice yourself to your country. . . . I pray you to decide quickly, and let me know my duty. . . .

I do not consider myself at present a judge of anything but the public sentiment. That seems to me everywhere gathering and deepening against a prosecution of the war. . . . On every brow sits sullen, scorching, black despair. . . . It would be easy to have Mr. Crittenden move any proposition that ought to be adopted. . . . This letter is written in the strictest confidence, and is for your eye alone. But you are at liberty to say to members of your Cabinet that you *know* I will second any movement you may see fit to make. . . . Send me word what to do. . . . I will live till I can hear it, at all events. . . ."

Greeley fell into a critical illness, a brain fever—whether before or after writing this letter is not clear—emerged to discharge Dana from the staff of the *Tribune* without explanation, but apparently because Dana's leaders had equaled or outstripped his own in violence, and became the huge stormy petrel of the war, darkening every disaster, circling continually in the public view. Since they sprang from similar homely origins, each of them preserving so unmistakable a rusticity, it might seem that Greeley would have been drawn to Lincoln; but wildly, blindly, throughout the war Greeley patronized, instructed, scolded, or exhorted Lincoln, as though chaos had left him stripped of everything except a clamor for authority and a desire for peace. "If after sixty days' more hard fighting the enemy is not beaten, it will become the duty of the government to make peace ON THE BEST POSSIBLE TERMS," he wrote in a double-leaded editorial in 1862. Repeatedly he proposed an armistice; in the midst of the blacker months of the same year he issued his *Prayer of the Twenty Millions,* insisting upon immediate emancipation, urging Lincoln to "write to the United States ministers in Europe, and ask them to tell you candidly whether the seeming subserviency of your policy to the slaveholding, slavery-upholding interest is not the perplexity, the despair of the statesmen . . . and be admonished by the general answer."

Lincoln's instant, grave reply was a measure of Greeley's power. With immense simplicity, as though striving to make clear an old lesson, Lincoln explained his object, "to save the union." In a bluff rejoinder Greeley hoped that Lincoln might realize that "slavery is to be vanquished only by liberty." When, four weeks later, the Emancipation Proclamation was announced, Greeley, like a few other leaders in public life, Beecher among them, received credit for the act from the anti-slavery forces.

Greeley also reaped quite a different reward. Violence began to roll up against him as though all the violence of his own mind had become tangible. In New York pro-slavery sentiment was strong; and Bennett, Greeley's enemy of years, harking back to Greeley's cry of "On to Richmond," played upon mob feeling to the utmost, insisting that Greeley was not only responsible for the war but for its continuance on behalf of the negro. Bennett's attacks upon Greeley were unremitting, unscrupulous, and foul, culminating in the contention that Greeley was a traitor who should be hanged to the nearest lamp-post. With the passage of the draft laws of 1863 that consummation was nearly realized; the draft riots surged and centered about the *Tribune* office in Printing-House Square. The first story was gutted, the building set on fire; and though the fire was extinguished, a siege was on, lasting for three days, with the police only intermittently in control. Greeley at last was calm; in the midst of a frantic madness which exceeded his own, he found tranquillity. "I want no arms brought into the building," he said with his old mild and deprecating air. "I am not quite through; I will go in a few minutes," he replied when urged to leave. But he had no doubt of the momentousness of the occasion. "It was a tidal wave that struck at Vicksburg, Gettysburg, Helena, and Port Hudson, and dealt its last and worst blow right here—in the *Tribune* office and this city of New York. . . . Had it not been resisted here, it would have swept the North and would have broken the union to pieces."

The ironic circumstance was that even as Greeley was being mobbed as a war-monger he was again agitating for peace. Read the cause as one likes—whether from remorse or hysteria, or an overweening and obstinate wish to direct affairs—Greeley offered his proposals so frequently and in so many forms as suggest the elements of a constant wish. Undoubtedly he was shattered by the war; it may be that the disaster at Bull Run, coming after months of excitement and strain, struck him an irremediable blow. War had always seemed to him an ultimate evil, violence, in spite of his own violence, intolerable; and he too had had his vision of the union. What all but exhausted the unending patience of Lincoln was his mode of procedure. Without counsel or advice, as if to trench upon the province of Seward as Secretary of State, Greeley began to advocate the intercession of a European power; he entered into prolonged correspondence with Mercier, the French minister, who went to Richmond. He wrote to Vallandigham; and at last in a long series of letters, full of the blackest despair, he urged upon Lincoln the necessity of a conference with Confederate officials who were reported to be in Canada. Lincoln seized the opportunity, and sent Greeley to Niagara as his agent, but stipulated that negotiations should not proceed unless the southern representatives could present written credentials from Jefferson Davis, and unless they would treat on a basis of restoration of the union and the abolishment of slavery. The southerners were not official representatives of Davis, nor were they willing to discuss a possible peace on the terms which Lincoln had laid down. But Greeley, with the chance of stopping the war still dangling before his view, could not halt; he invited the trio to travel to Washington; and they accepted. With the arrival of Hay, bearing a repetition of Lincoln's instructions, the whole fiasco was exposed. Greeley, ridiculous on a huge scale before the nation, declared that the President had originated the negotiations, adding that he had reluctantly become a party to them, and demanding that his correspondence with Lincoln be published. Lincoln declined unless Greeley would "erase some of the lamentations in his longest letter." This Greeley refused to do. Lincoln told Welles that he thought it better that Greeley should put him in a false position "than that the country should be distressed by such a howl," and that Greeley was "an old shoe—good for nothing now, whatever he has been."

In truth, Greeley seemed to have found a worn trackway which he could not avoid. His feeling toward Lincoln was perhaps the chilliest he had ever entertained. In his *American Conflict,* begun in 1863, an enormous task in the midst of his editorial labors, Greeley drew a continued portrait of Lincoln as "habitually cautious, dilatory, reticent . . . by nature slow, cautious, tentative, and far from sanguine." He spoke of Lincoln's "obstinate tameness during the earlier stages of the war." Even in later years he did not modify his judgment. On the day of Lincoln's assassination he had prepared a sharp, short attack on the President, which was withheld from publication by a sub-editor when word that Lincoln was dying reached the paper. The next day Greeley seemed more concerned by this overpassing of his authority than by the disastrous tidings. Later, in an estimate of Lincoln, he remarked, "I cannot say how many distinct, written notices that *my* life was forfeited, and that the forfeit would soon be exacted, I have been honored with certainly a dozen— possibly a hundred." During the final months of the war he kept up his old insistence upon peace or an armistice precisely as though these questions had never been discussed. "Lincoln is already beaten," said Greeley of the coming election of 1864, and harked back once more to the Niagara negotiations. He joined with Sumner, Bryant, and others in the formulation of an attack on Lincoln which led to the nomination of Frémont by the radical Republican convention. But after the summer's victories the horizon changed; Frémont withdrew; and Greeley urged the cause of Lincoln before the country. At last, when the war was ended, as if the old shoe had the length of at least one good firm stride in it, Greeley returned once more to the latitudes of peace, this time with measures which Lincoln, it is plain, would have furthered.

With his old stubborn, strident uproar Greeley urged the cause of conciliation and good will, of peace and amnesty. Up and down the land, in the face of a popular opinion that was either lax or vengeful, he cried the difficult cause of amnesty, not for a few weeks or a few months, but through the slow hard years of the middle and late sixties and even on into the seventies, when decisions were either postponed or fought down in Congress. In 1867, joining with Gerrit Smith, Commodore Vanderbilt, and a few others, he went to Richmond to provide bail for Jefferson Davis, who still was confined there on the baseless charge of participation in the plot to assassinate Lincoln. No one could have known better than Greeley what denunciation he would bring upon himself and upon the *Tribune* for this step, consistent though it was with his large contention. Popular antipathy in the North, seeking a scapegoat, had centered upon Davis. As a result of his act, subscriptions to the second volume of Greeley's *American Conflict,* then appearing, were canceled by the thousand; its sale was almost negligible, though that of the first volume had run well toward a quarter of a million. Greeley was personally ostracized in New York. A move was made in the Union League Club to expel him from its membership. He dared its members to do so; and in the end they took no action; perhaps they were quelled by the vituperative thunder of Greeley's letter.

"I do not recognize you as capable of judging, or fully apprehending me," he wrote. "You evidently regard me as a weak sentimentalist, misled by a maudlin philosophy. I arraign you as narrow-minded blockheads, who would like to be useful to a great and good cause, but don't know how. Your attempt to base a great, enduring party on the hate and wrath necessarily engendered by a bloody civil war, is as though you should plant a colony on an iceberg which had somehow drifted into a tropical ocean. I tell you here, that out of a life earnestly devoted to the good of human kind, your children will select my going to Richmond and signing that bail bond as the wisest act, and will feel that it did more for freedom and humanity than all of you were competent to do, though you had lived to the age of Methuselah. . . . Don't sidle off into a mild resolution of censure, but move the expulsion which you propose, and which I deserve, if I deserve any reproach whatever."

NINE • *The quiet level of feeling upon which Greeley seemed* to enter after the war was broken by only a few major episodes. He entered upon a brief and bitter engagement with the radical feminists in 1867, when this small determined group proposed to have the word "male" stricken from the proposed new state constitution. Greeley's indifference to the feminists had mounted to antipathy when these intransigeants had demanded a more liberal divorce law in New York in 1860. Through his untiring efforts the liberal bill had been defeated; and in his current debate with Owen he had given vent to certain singular statements. "Marriage is an obstacle, a restraint, a terror. . . . I distinctly remember that *my* marriage covenant was for better, for worse, and until death do us part. . . ." These avowals had caught the attention of the militant group; and Mrs. Greeley was still one of their number. She was, in fact, deep in the campaign which again was centering at Albany, at the time of the constitutional convention. Greeley, as chairman of the committee on the right to suffrage, opposed the measure of the feminists, declaring that "public sentiment does not demand and would not sustain an innovation so revolutionary and sweeping . . . involving transformations so radical in social and domestic life." When Greeley arose in the convention to present his report against the bestowal of the suffrage upon the women of the state, he was followed by G. W. Curtis, who offered a petition from women citizens of Westchester, praying for equal rights before the law, and headed by the name of Mrs. Horace Greeley. A battle was on. Slowly approaching Mrs. Stanton and Miss Anthony at the Carys' soon afterward, Greeley shook a long finger at them, and served notice that henceforward the *Tribune* would have no word of praise or encouragement for the suffrage movement. With a fling at "George Francis Susan Pillsbury Stanton Anthony," he kept his word, remarking in an editorial, "As to woman's voting, our judgment does not favor it because it would double the cost and trouble of elections to no purpose." Worst of all, he spoke of "the father's vote," as "representative, paternal, comprehensive." And presently, in *Hearth and Home,* he came out with a volley of arguments against the entire feminist position.

In 1867, to the proposal of the Alaskan treaty, Seward's darling project, Greeley offered a violent opposition, drawing upon himself the charge of a narrow personal antagonism. But at least his repugnance to this move was part and parcel of a long opposition to any form of national expansion.

Except for these few raids and forays Greeley seemed to be settling into peaceful pursuits. Like many men in later years he appeared to be reconnoitering, as if to stalk the character of his own existence. Haste seemed to be what he found there: haste and solitude. Dashing off his reminiscences in a rough pedestrian style, he called these *Recollections of a Busy Life.* "My life has been one of arduous, rarely intermitted labor— of efforts which have absorbed most of the time which others freely devote to social intercourse and fireside enjoyments." Once more he dwelt upon the project of association. "I deem it impossible that beings born in the huts and hovels of isolated society, feebly, ineffectively delving and grubbing through life on the few acres immediately surrounding each of them, shall there attain the stature of perfect manhood. They are dwarfed, stunted, shriveled, by their petty avocations and shabby surroundings. . . . Our dwellings, our fields, our industries, all tend to belittle us; the edifice which shall yet lodge commodiously and agreeably two thousand persons, giving each the requisite privacy and independence, though as yet unconstructed, is not a chimera; nor more is the prosecution of agricultural and other labor by large bands, rendered picturesque by uniforms, and inspired by music. . . ." Yes! after a span of twenty years, after dismal failure and derisive laughter, Greeley insisted upon the Fourieristic scheme from its palace to the last garland.

Scarcely a personal sentiment crept into the book, except as he mentioned Pickie, or, with less ardor, his second son, Raphael, who had died in 1856. Greeley spoke of himself as "caught in a monotonous round . . . as yet a horse in the barkmill"—an image which in one form or another he had used with increasing frequency in these years. "Fame is a vapor; popularity an accident; riches take wings; the only earthly certainty is oblivion; no man can say what a day may bring forth; while those who cheer today will often curse tomorrow. . . ." With a melancholy pleasure he returned to his old efforts at poetic aphorism. "Life is a bubble which any breath may dissolve; Wealth or Power a snow-flake, melting momentarily into the treacherous deep across whose waves we are floated to an unseen destiny. . . ." His commentaries on his vocation were ironical. He declared that the editor was to the author what the bellows-blower was to the organist. The image seemed to please him. "Another hand at the bellows would have ruined me."

As the sixties drew to a close Greeley sketched another, briefer, and more intimate memoir in a series of letters to a young woman whom he seems to have met at the Barnums', where he now frequently stayed during his wife's absence abroad. This lady friend, as she was called in the volume of letters published in the nineties, appears only under the initial M—; and she apparently regarded Greeley as rather a quaint old gentleman. "Dear old Horace . . . the old man," she dubbed him in a letter to her sister which was included in the collection. "I'll never say again Mr. Greeley isn't *queer*," she wrote, describing a picnic at Chappaqua, to which she had gone with the Tiltons and some others. "He drove slow, of course, and *such* driving you never saw. His old horses knew him, no doubt, and they paid not the slightest attention to his chirps and gentle shakes of the lines. He held one line in each hand, with elbows sticking out, and his hat on the back of his neck, while his horses went all ways but in the road, and sometimes took us over stumps. . . ." In her further account M— chirped and twittered: but Greeley seems to have enjoyed her light music. "I have a large acquaintance with those who are regarded as brilliant women," he wrote. "They appall and fatigue, while you charm and cheer me. I pray you not to be like unto them." In response to a further question he begged her to cease from self-depreciation. "My friend, I charge you not to disparage yourself, and especially not to regret that you do not, when I have the pleasure of seeing you, talk mainly philosophy or epigrams." He sought her out; he thanked her for "the happy day at J . . . the only day of many months that was one of enjoyment and not of work." At a Universalist convention—she too enjoyed that faith—he watched for her in vain through part of an afternoon among streams of people. He insisted that she must come to New York from her home in New Jersey for a considerable visit, apparently at the Barnums'. "Now I want you to be without care and unlikely to be called suddenly home when you visit our city. . . . Please let me hear what is in prospect, and when we may expect you to come over, resolved to remain not less than two Sundays. . . . I hoped that you would write, but did not request it, wishing it to be your own unprompted act."

Letters of sentiment these certainly were—sentiment relaxed, grave, and scrupulous. To the improbable character of M—, created in part by his own wishes, Greeley seems to have offered as full a revelation of his more intimate moods as he ever gave to any one. "I have not many friends. My life has been too hurried, and too much absorbed in pressing duties and anxious cares." Hurry—work: the double demon seemed upreared about him. "Work crowds me from every side . . . I have hardly known what home meant for years, and am too busy to enjoy anything." He wrote briefly of his wife's ill health, of his regret that his daughter Ida's youth should be absorbed by a difficult attendance upon her mother, of his younger daughter Gabrielle, born after Raphael's death. With a disarming candor he asked M— to read the opening passages of Froude's history of England, and then the first chapter of his own *American Conflict,* "so as to mark the difference between the work of a great historian and a little one." Most frequently he wrote of Chappaqua. He was often there in these years, still chopping down trees, watching the building of a new house.

"My life is all a fevered march, and I now seem unlikely ever to sit down and have a quiet talk with you. I have some dry cedar wood up at

Chappaqua, which I have long proposed to burn in an open fireplace on a succession of winter evenings, while I sit before it with a few dear friends, read poems, and talk over our past lives. But I guess that cedar will remain unburned until after my funeral." The picture of congenial company at Chappaqua continued to haunt him; he wrote increasingly of poetry; Swinburne had become a favorite poet; he could repeat numbers of the longer lyrics; he urged Browning upon M——, though a little dubious of her comprehension. "I send you two volumes of Browning, whereof I only expect you to read half. I know how subtle and obscure he is; but then he is mighty when he is in his happy mood. . . . You must like *My Last Duchess,* and *The Flight of the Duchess* is nearly as good. . . . I have been chopping wood at Chappaqua nearly every Saturday of late, and I have a lot of red cedar cut up into firewood and well seasoned. You know how pleasant is the odor of burning cedar. Well, I reserve this to warm and light my hearth when I can—at some future day with my family about me—go up and spend three or four consecutive evenings, long bright evenings, reading choice poems, and discussing higher themes than those which engross such dreary letters as this."

"The new village of Greeley, youngest cousin of Jonah's gourd": so he described to M—— an enterprise which he had hastened to sponsor, in the pattern of association—the Union Colony, founded on the coöperative plan in the Cache à Poudre region of Colorado by a large company who were mainly lifelong readers of the *Tribune* and his admirers. At the first opportunity Greeley visited the colony, in 1870; he was enormously hopeful: "We hope to incite the foundation of many such colonies on every side of us," he wrote to M——. He poured money into the enterprise, bought a tract there, in the end bought several tracts, though with scarcely better judgment than he had exercised at Chappaqua; eighty of his acres ran up the side of a long bluff. Returning, he wrote constantly to Meeker, one of his former sub-editors, who was the leader of the experiment, lending money—though he repeatedly insisted that he was burdened by debts—offering advice, and steadily insisting that his acreage be planted with trees. "I am in no hurry about the plowing of my lot, but want it seeded *thick* with trees—thin out and trim up hereafter. . . . Be good to my trees. . . . Now please, if my evergreens fail, ask Ralph to get a cask of acorns, hickory nuts, and chestnuts, to be planted in rows next November, and send me the bill, and don't let them go to ruin any more than they must. . . . Do push on my forest trees. . . . It may be I shall come out to live with you after my trees get a start. Please start all you can this spring. . . ."

Greeley spoke and wrote as though he hoped to spend increasingly long holidays in this new and rugged Eden, and eventually to live there. By a dozen allusions in his letters to M— he pictured himself as ready to leave active life. He looked old. M— was not the only observer who found him a kind of relic of another age. "He tends to be fat, is shambling, and bowed over in carrying himself," wrote Mrs. Stowe in one of her portraits of contemporary notabilities, adding that he wore "a habitually meek sort of smile, which must not be trusted as an index of the mind within." Greeley regarded himself as old, though he was hardly sixty. "I am overworked and growing old," he stated in a letter to a group of admirers in Illinois, declining to lecture there. Early in 1872 he was given a birthday celebration at the home of Alvin Johnson which had something of the effect of a final milestone. In a bower of orchids, in the midst of balladry and music, during a long and formal reception, Greeley received the tribute of representative men and women throughout the country; he was surrounded by Ripley, Bayard Taylor, Oliver Johnson, his "young men" who had grown up with the *Tribune,* with John Hay now added, Whitelaw Reid, William Winter, and a score of others. Bret Harte was present, Mark Twain, Samuel Bowles, Beecher; Barnum was "among the surging crowd," Greeley afterward wrote to M—; and those who could not be present framed their praises in appropriate letters or articles, among them Whittier, Holmes, and Edward Eggleston. "In Mr. Greeley the average American sees himself magnified," said Eggleston. Greeley's "constant pursuit of the ideal object" was frequently mentioned. He was declared to have impressed his character more deeply upon his generation than any other American of his time, saving Lincoln. "Philosopher Greeley": the designation which Herndon and Parker and others had used in the fifties was revived. In a gentle tribute to Alice Cary, who had recently died, Whittier had spoken of "that old friend, so sage and bland, our later Franklin."

Sidney Howard Gay, of the *Tribune* staff, in a private conversation offered a digression from this pleasant chorus. He declared that Horace Greeley was a myth, like Hercules, Diana, Hebe, and Mrs. Harris. "There never was such a man," he stated with emphasis. "When the truth is known it will be seen that the Horace Greeley of popular fancy never existed." What the truth was, Gay seems not to have said: but it soon became clear that Greeley entertained a somewhat different notion of himself from that which was being entertained by his friends. "Our later Franklin": undoubtedly the designation pleased him; his editorials contained frequent references to Franklin. But he seems to have missed the valedictory note in the praises raining in upon him, the note, indeed, which seemed clear now in so much of his own expression. Bit by bit he had been edging toward an old pursuit, one quite different from chopping cedars at Chappaqua, or reading poetry, or directing the affairs of a new Arcadia in the West, or writing to M—. In 1869 Greeley had sought an office for which few persons could have been more unfitted, with his notorious inability to manage financial affairs, that of State Comptroller. Weed had stepped in; Greeley had lost the election, running behind his ticket. The following year he had sought and gained the nomination for the senatorship. Weed, still a power, had set the whole Republican machine in adverse motion, preferring a Republican defeat to Greeley's election. Greeley was defeated. Seward, now failing in health, was outside the combat; but Weed, extraordinarily hearty at seventy-three, and quite as tenacious as Greeley in his ardors, was still in the midst of a lively strategy. The Republican forces in New York were dividing, with Weed on one side, Greeley on the other. Godkin declared that Greeley's affiliations were with "the worst set of politicians outside the Tammany Ring." But the battle array soon swept outside the state.

"You see I am drifting into a fight with Grant," wrote Greeley to M— in March, 1872. "I hate it; I know how many friends I shall alienate by it, and how it will injure the *Tribune,* of which so little is my property now that I dread to wreck it; yet I should despise myself if I pretended to acquiesce in his reëlection." To Meeker he wrote in even stronger terms. "You see I don't want four years more of Grant. I won't stand it, if there is any reasonable alternative, and that may drive me out of politics and newspapers. I feel that my trade is a *mean* one, because it compels me to think other men's thoughts. I prefer my own. I heartily wish I was out of politics, out of journalism, and able to work moderately for a humble livelihood. . . . I do not yet see my way out."

Greeley's quarrel with the administration began with the question of a complete and final amnesty for the South, which Grant had done nothing to further, which Greeley had urged without remission for seven years. And few acts could have stirred Greeley to such consistent anger as Grant's proposal to annex Santo Domingo; the anti-imperialistic policy of the *Tribune* had been unmistakably manifest from its foundation; Greeley had never wavered in this respect. By quiet and continuous efforts Grant had tried conciliation, mainly through Schuyler Colfax, an old friend and political associate of Greeley's in early Republican days, who was now Vice-President. Through Colfax an informal offer of the English mission was tendered to Greeley; remembering Franklin, indeed citing Franklin in the *Tribune* as an editor who had become ambassador, a year or two earlier Greeley had angled for such an appointment. He now declined exile. By the spring of 1872 the political horizon was gusty with change; an insurgent political movement was arising in the West under the magical caption of reform. At first governed by the purpose to secure a general amnesty, the Liberal Republicans—as they were called—soon included in their program far more than this conciliatory principle. They were as flatly anti-imperialistic as Greeley. Attacking corruption in the administration, they came out for civil service reform; and with prices soaring, they adopted a policy of a thorough revision downward of the tariff, with a move toward an entire removal of duties on raw materials.

By April, 1872, the new movement had gained a formidable strength, attracting not only the original group in Missouri under Schurz and such tireless enemies of Grant as Charles Sumner, but Charles Francis Adams, Samuel Bowles, an entire group of influential editors of smaller papers in the East and West, as well as a large popular following. Greeley's support was greatly desired. Naturally he belonged with the insurgents, except on the question of the tariff. He had been for years the most consistent exponent of protection which the country had known; and his enthusiasm for a country ringed about and self-sufficient had by no means abated. "We should live wholly within ourselves," he had told Garfield in 1870.

At the outset, even after much discussion, Greeley declined to identify himself with the new movement except on the condition that tariff revision be dropped from the platform. Then suddenly he signed the call of the eastern Republicans for a convention to be held in Cincinnati early in May. At about this time a strange herald began trumpeting the name of Horace Greeley for president. This was Theodore Tilton, not yet notorious through his suit against Beecher, lately the editor of the *Independent,* now the editor and owner of a new sheet, the *Golden Age,* and also the ecstatic biographer of Victoria Woodhull, whom within a year or two he had also announced as a candidate for the presidency in 1872, and as certain to win the prize. Tilton belonged to the long line—and was the last—of Greeley's romantic enthusiasms. Roguery, an imposing presence, facility, poetry, oratory, wit: in some measure Tilton possessed the gamut of qualities to which Greeley seemed so irresistibly drawn. Nothing could have been stranger that this last alliance, nothing plainer that on Greeley's part it rested upon affection, overriding his distaste, even his abhorrence, of Tilton's extreme feminism, which bordered perilously upon the current doctrine of free love, and his communism, which he announced that he wore in his buttonhole "like a rosette." Even within a year Greeley had engaged Tilton in the debate on marriage and divorce in the columns of the *Golden Age.* Now without a thought, without a regret, it seems, these two tossed away their differences, and flung together their fortunes. Tilton went to Cincinnati as one of Greeley's spokesmen.

It was a strange convention. "Full of fun and history," Bowles called it; but fun in an ironic sense was more apparent than history. Along with some of the truest and soberest minds in the country was a parcel of cranks. George Francis Train was there, who had long been gunning for the presidency, and who expected now to capture the nomination. Drawn by the promise of a new movement, single-minded exponents of many a cause were present, leaders in temperance, in feminism, in peace, in a hundred minor schemes. Office-seekers from many states had trooped in. The make-up of the convention was highly irregular; some states had sent incomplete delegations, some an excess number, who were used to fill the vacant places. In a coarser fashion the gathering seemed a replica of those mixed assemblages which Greeley had frequented in the forties, in which high-mindedness was mingled with quackery. Greeley was trebly and solidly present, represented by Tilton, who consorted with the radicals, by Whitelaw Reid, who could speak the language of the sober and substantial reformers, by Fenton of New York who spoke only a political dialect. Greeley's influence, the still magificent spread of the *Tribune,* was considered indispensable for the success of the new campaign; and at the outset, in the opening round of the many battles which seem inevitable in any convention, through his agents, he won a substantial victory. By the bargaining of Reid with Schurz, Bowles, and the other originators of the movement, an equivocal plank on the tariff was inserted into the platform, leaving the question for settlement in the congressional districts. Thus, in deference to Greeley's lifelong conviction, the only really broad and sweeping national issue was submerged. When the convention opened, Schurz and his group believed that Greeley's manipulation was at an end; the New York delegation was expected to give him a good complimentary vote, and that was all. On the opening ballots Charles Francis Adams led, in spite of the cool primness of his public letter—a typical Adams letter—declining the nomination in advance except upon express proof that he was desired. It was even believed that if a motion to nominate Adams by acclamation had been made just before the final vote the whole mixed gathering would have been swept into assent. But Gratz Brown, a leader in the original liberal movement in Missouri, angered by Schurz, who was attempting to swing the votes of the Missouri delegation from Brown to Adams, suddenly appeared on the scene. What followed is not entirely clear in detail. Whether through Brown's wrath, or—as Schurz charged—by "political huckstering" between Brown and Fenton, the votes of the Missouri delegation were swung to Greeley; a scattering few from other states went, then a larger number, enough to give Greeley a slight lead over Adams. A wild stampede to Greeley followed. An amazing circumstance had occurred; Greeley had seized the convention root and branch; he had molded the platform; Gratz Brown—his ally—was nominated for the vice-presidency; and the final, coveted honor was his own.

Schurz and the others were appalled. Schurz telegraphed to Greeley, begging him to decline the nomination. "I shall accept unconditionally," Greeley replied, and yielded the editorship of the *Tribune* to Reid. "I believe I shall receive 75,000 Republican votes in Illinois, and her electoral vote. . . . We shall carry New York, Connecticut, New Hampshire, New Jersey, and the South with hardly a break. I hope the Northwest will help us some; if she does not, we must endeavor to get on." In his despatch of acceptance Greeley said that he "would be glad to see the lies Sam Bowles has been circulating to the prejudice of Senator Fenton contradicted." Bowles made a courteous reply, and in the Springfield *Republican* supported Greeley in the campaign, though he remarked privately that Greeley's political affiliations in New York were certainly dubious, and that "his training had been in a school—the same school to which Seward and Weed belonged—which regarded office as the be-all and end-all of political discussion."

In the end Schurz likewise joined in support of Greeley, as did Dana, now of the *Sun.* Tilton was still well to the fore. "He drops easily into statesmanship," said a contemporary. But Tilton, speaking and writing on behalf of Greeley early and late, disdained the implication with a fanciful modesty. "Lest we be charged in advance with a vain-glorious daydream of some foreign mission or cabinet portfolio," he wrote in the *Golden Age,* "we hereby foreswear all future honors of the new administration—except perhaps an old friend's privilege once in a while, of taking a cup of tea at the White House, provided the Master of the frugal feast should not happen to be overcrowded with better company." Barnum joined in the campaign. With his mixed following of strange enthusiasts, disappointed reformers, politicians, and the nobler political constituency, the train of incongruities might have seemed complete. But another was added.

"May it be written on my grave that I never was its follower, and lived and died in nothing its debtor," Greeley had said a few months earlier of the Democratic party, in one of the less violent of the many diatribes which he had uttered in a long lifetime. Yet he received—and accepted—the Democratic nomination. Obviously the basis of its bestowal was his long policy of conciliation with the South, and southern antipathy to Grant. "I shall carry every southern state but South Carolina," said Greeley briskly, and plunged into the early hopeful pageantry of the campaign.

> "There is a chap at Chappaqua who lives upon his farm,
> And raises beets and cabbages to keep his soul from harm,
> He feeds on mush and milk and sich, and never takes a dram,
> But strange to say he keeps himself as happy as a clam.
>   Old White-Hat Greeley is his name!"

It became a song-singing campaign, a costume campaign, following the outlines of that first large political adventure in which Greeley had taken part. He was apparently being proffered a popular festival at last. Woodchopping clubs were formed; white hats became a badge; Greeley received hundreds of letters demanding hats of assorted sizes. Old Horace, Old Honesty, the Sage of Chappaqua, the Doctor, Our Later Franklin, Our Modern Cincinnatus: such designations abounded; the rural note was uppermost.

At the outset, for a few weeks, as if in kindly reminiscence, popular feeling surged up warmly about Greeley from the North and the South, from the West, from many an obscure backwoods community or small hamlet. There was no doubt that Grant was coldly regarded in the country. The outlook for Greeley seemed bright. Then the grim enemies got to work. The campaign became the bitterest known in American political history.

Weed came forward. With the talent and training of a journalist he had searched the files of the *Tribune* from 1860 onward, had pored over Greeley's speeches and his correspondence with Lincoln; with a laconic clarity he let Greeley's own words reveal violence and lassitude, acceptance of secession and insatiable thirst for war; his insistence upon peace now seemed a cry for surrender. Greeley emerged as little short of traitorous to the North, as a brute to the South. Weed's compendium, printed as a campaign document, aroused a last violent enmity, and gave rise as well to a similar small synopsis of Greeley's most urgent battle-cries, designed for southern readers. Nor were Weed's efforts purely literary; expending the wealth of his political technique, he set in motion against Greeley every force under his hand in New York and elsewhere; and his alliances within the nation were not inconsiderable. Raymond took up the cry, giving it an uproar of reverberation through the large medium of the *Times*. Raymond, always thorough, threw into relief every inconsistency in Greeley's present position. In 1868 Greeley had endorsed Grant without qualification. "It is a glorious ticket," he had cried. "Grant never has been defeated, and never will be." Even late in 1871 Greeley had said that Grant would be "far better qualified for the momentous trust in 1872 than he was in 1868." Raymond exposed Greeley's lifelong distrust of third parties; within a few years, even within months, his pronouncement against third parties had been shouted over the land. As for charges of corruption against Grant, what had been Greeley's attitude toward corruption in the matter of the Tweed Ring? Undoubtedly the *Tribune* had been apathetic; Tweed was the special quarry of the *Times*. In view of the magnitude of the scandal Greeley's brief and tepid arraignment seemed all but incredible; and the *Times* was able to prove that Greeley had never lost confidence in that handsome scalawag, Oakey Hall, who had been mayor of New York during the great thievery.

Men whose own integrity was unquestioned, whose intellectual power was enviable, added their invectives. Godkin, despising Greeley's recent political alliances in New York, wrote in the *Nation* of the "inevitable semi-contemptuous laughter which Mr. Greeley's name always excites," declaring that his nomination was calculated "to throw an air of folly and absurdity over the very name of reform," pointing out the futility of entrusting the cause of civil service reform to a man "whose whole life had been in a large measure devoted to a glorification of the Rule of Thumb."

Remorselessly the quest for inconsistencies went on, as if some monstrous hand were bent upon revealing Greeley's mind and his career as a long vast jumble. To the South he was pictured as a fanatical advocate of the negro—by his own words; to the North—also by his own words—as long having nourished contempt for the blacks. The abolitionists brought up their guns; Garrison had never forgiven Greeley the violence of his "On to Richmond" battle-cries; and to make matters worse, when Greeley went over to the war party, he had abused every one hoping for peace, Garrison and his party in particular. "As for his honesty," said Wendell Phillips, "for twenty years it has been a by-word with us that it would be safe to leave your open purse in the same room with him; but as for any other honesty, no one was ever witless enough to connect the idea with his name. . . . A trimmer by nature and purpose, he has abused even an American politician's privilege of trading principles for success."

Multitudes of pamphlets appeared, searching out Greeley's last foibles, turning to account every tale of absurdity, ridiculing his dress as an affectation, his farming as another, lifting to public derision his lack of natural skill in farming. Greeley's caption *What I know about Farming* was made the framework of innumerable pseudo-self-revelations. So deep was the allusion made to cut that more than ten years later, long after Greeley's death, Henry Ward Beecher was able to command a loud laugh at a country fair by a mere repetition of the phrase. Over and over Greeley's appearance was derided; even Godkin and Bryant entered into the race for epithets. Fans were popular, formed of a ridiculous image of Greeley's face with white whiskers waving about the edges and a phrenological analysis of character on the back, whose theme was the monstrous size of the bumps of Ambition and Calculation.

Harsh as these many squibs were, they were all but outstripped by the bitter, unflagging attacks in pencil by Thomas Nast. Fresh from his triumphs in depicting the Tweed Ring, Nast from the first poured into the caricatures in *Harper's Weekly* a venom for which there was scarcely an accounting. Curtis, now the editor of *Harper's,* once on the *Tribune,* tried to dissuade him; his ferocity scandalized even many of the anti-Greeley papers. The incompetent drawings for the opposition in *Leslie's Weekly,* attacking Grant, can hardly have aroused Nast's ire; his own work had reached too high a point of technical accomplishment. Nast was at the height of his fame; and the public honor which he had won seemed to multiply the malignant volume of his attack a hundredfold. He never displayed a keener, a more cunning, or more brutal invention than in his onslaught upon Greeley. By way of a mild beginning, after the May convention, Greeley's head was shown crowned by a fool's cap at the end of a stick with bells which was being presented to a horrified Miss Columbia. As Nast went on from week to week he not only made Greeley appear foolish, he caught the look of fatigue by which Greeley was increasingly enveloped, made him look strained, slow-witted, slow-footed, like some absurd puppet galvanized into painful action. Greeley was shown as fat, sagging at the knees, his mouth stupidly open, holding out an instrument called the New York *Trombone,* and maintaining that whoever called this instrument an organ was a "liar, a villain, and a scoundrel." "Horrors Greedey" was one of Nast's favorite designations, with a glancing allusion to the grossness of Greeley's table-manners. In one cartoon Greeley appears, fat and stupid, dancing with a hat in one hand, a bandanna in the other, shouting his own cause, ready to drop in bewilderment and exhaustion. In another he is seen painfully eating his own words about the South, about the Democratic party, red-hot out of a porridge bowl, again with the effect of extreme and violent effort. In still another, entitled *The Whited Sepulchre,* he is covering with the old white coat and hat a monument of infamy across whose base Ku Klux was sculptured. Once the coat, hat, and Greeley's spectacles appeared on a stick like the garb of a scarecrow, swept by the wind in a thunder-storm, entitled, "Something that will blow over." He was seen white-washing the Tammany tiger. He was shown gloating over the ruin of southern firesides, and again extending a friendly hand toward the South across the graveyards of Andersonville, and again, as Old Honesty, mar-shaling an army of jail-birds, thugs, and crooks. Finally Nast drew Gree-ley clasping hands with Wilkes Booth over the grave of Lincoln.

"Thank God for death, the one deliverer who never fails us!" Greeley had written to M— in March, 1872, when the possibility of the nomina-tion was glimmering before him. He complained now of sleeplessness, and wrote in June that he wanted "to last at least six months longer." His daughter Gabrielle had come home wasted by illness; and Mrs. Gree-ley with his older daughter Ida followed soon after. Mrs. Greeley was hopelessly ill. Chappaqua was constantly invaded, by newspaper men and daguerreotypists, by numbers of picnickers who seemed to consider the place common property; and the summer was a long blaze of heat. In the midst of a hideous fatigue, along with the endless labors of the campaign and the responsibilities of his wife's illness, Greeley had begun work on a chain of articles for an encyclopedia. He was in need of money. "My skies darken, and I must not agree to pay out more money unless it be very little," he wrote to Meeker in August. "But don't starve my trees. . . . My wife is going at last. I do not think she can last the month out. She may. I am urged to go out West . . . but I do not think I shall be able to leave her."

In the early summer Greeley had mounted the platform, the first pres-idential candidate to do so with the exception of Douglas, who had made a brief circuit in 1860. Then, as for some years afterward, such appeals were considered a breach of political decorum. "A national mendicant" —the rebuke was quickly hurled at Greeley. But he set out again toward the end of August in spite of his wife's precarious condition, beginning a long tour of six weeks or more, traveling through New England, into Pennsylvania, Ohio, Indiana, and the farther West, speaking at country fairs and from the end of railway trains, often delivering as many as twenty addresses a day. Still a notable figure, he drew enormous crowds; he spoke well; and his listeners fairly liked him. They listened with ap-proval to his tired oratorical efforts, grown dangerously smooth now with the piling up of fatigue. None the less he appeared as an innocent silly old sheep on the way to a terrible slaughter. He came before his audiences as a farmer, as one of themselves; but the small and insular as-semblage of farmers had been broken up; war had seen to that. A rest-less younger population was looking largely toward the cities, looking with a vexed and cynical temper; the popular mind was still raw, turbulent, and angry. Even the scandals of the Tweed Ring had failed to cut deeply into popular sensibilities; the Gold Conspiracy and the plunder of the Erie had sharpened the public mind but had scarcely shocked it; the shooting of Fisk, coupled with the story of Gould's offensive dealings afterward, had only added another fillip. As for Greeley, his public was perhaps less concerned with the revelation of his twists and turns than amused by cynicism of the attacks upon him; they roared with laughter at Nast's savagery.

Where was Greeley's old-time violence? That they might perhaps have relished, as it had jolted and pleased them for years in the columns of the *Tribune*. It had been spent, obviously, spent in some fashion on their behalf, with sensibilities which had played for years upon the turbulent convulsions of the public scene, rising at an instant command from day to day. With his old-time vigor gone, something of the hard and brittle shell of Greeley's natural mind must have become apparent in the footless exhibitions of the campaign, the rigid pattern of a quiet temperament pushed perennially into flux. There he stood, going through the old motions, speaking the old sentiments; yet even his platform had turned to thin air. His fine gesture of conciliation had only a reminiscent force; a universal amnesty bill had lately been passed by Congress; and the platform of the new party, in the main as result of Greeley's suasion, contained little else. One by one all of his old tenets and convictions had been riddled or left behind; nothing remained to him except his prejudices against liquor, tobacco, and gambling, the outline of a Puritan mode, with a faint abstract wish for peace. With little to say, in the devastating heat he spoke, an antique figure, a wraith out of the forties when for a time he had been at home, a strayed classicist, perhaps, out of place and out of season. Yet even in the forties the causes which he had espoused had been chimeras, dim resurgences of an earlier simple dream in the Republic—of happy excellence for all and equal participation in the bounty of the land.

Greeley was picturesque still; but the public had done with picturesqueness for many a long year, and with the homespun image perhaps forever. Most disastrous of all, as he stood before them, his old white hat was all but in his hand; his supplicating voice was reaching its most insistent pitch; he was begging the public after dictating, threatening, storming, for thirty years—asking a last companionship. Who had ever heard of begging from the monster? Flattered perhaps for an instant by his entreaty, they laughed at his jokes and shook his hand till he was exhausted by pain, watched the queer old whirligig disappear round a bend of railroad track, and voted against him. The young men who had grown up on farms, reading the *Tribune* from boyhood, voted against him. Gradually, even while he was speaking, the drift of the election became clear. The returns from North Carolina came in first, in August—against Greeley; then from Vermont and Maine in September—against Greeley; in October, from Pennsylvania and Ohio. Mrs. Greeley died a few days before the November election. At last came the deluge. Greeley carried only six states, Georgia, Kentucky, Maryland, Missouri, Tennessee, and Texas. The State of New York went against him by more than 50,000 votes, Massachusetts by 75,000, Pennsylvania by 137,000. Greeley was the worst beaten candidate who had ever sought the presidency. And Nast's efforts were not yet over. On the day following the election the cruelest of his cartoons appeared, showing Greeley distraught, abject, ragged and dirty, with stark horror looking out of his eyes, dancing on one foot, his hand clutching the air.

"I have been assailed so bitterly that I hardly knew whether I was running for President or the penitentiary," wrote Greeley on that day to a friend in New Hampshire.

To M— he sent a final letter. "I write this because I wish to relieve myself of some bitterness, but I do not expect—in fact, I scarcely desire —that you should write me again these many, many days. I am indeed most wretched. As to my wife's death, I do not lament it. Her sufferings since she returned to me were so terrible that I rather felt relieved when she peacefully slept the long sleep. I did not shed a tear. In fact, I am far beyond tears. Nor do I care for defeat, however crushing. I dread only the malignity with which I am hounded, and the possibility that it may ruin the *Tribune*. My enemies mean to kill that; if they would kill me instead I would thank them lovingly. And so many of my old friends hate me for what I have done that life seems too hard to bear. Enough of this. Speak of it to no one, not even Mrs. R—, but return to cheerfulness and life's daily duties, forgetting, as soon as may be, Yours, Horace Greeley."

On the same day there appeared in the *Tribune* a card—in the vernacular of the day—upon the editorial page, announcing Greeley's resumption of the editorship of the paper, which he had given up, as he said, "on embarking on another line of business." He also set forth a program which harked back to some of his earlier, more tranquil preoccupations, saying of himself as editor, "Since he will never again be a candidate for any office, and is not in full accord with either of the great parties which have hitherto divided the country, he will be able and will endeavor to give wider and steadier regard to the progress of Science, Industry, and the Useful Arts, than a partisan journal can do; and he will not be provoked to indulgence in those bitter personalities which are the recognized bane of journalism. Sustained by a generous public, he will do his best to make the *Tribune* a power in the broader field it now contemplates, as, when Human Freedom was imperiled, it was in the arena of political partisanship."

This statement, so temperate in the main, so honest and humble, was followed by an editorial entitled *Crumbs of Comfort,* which might have been written by Greeley in one of his old rough moods. In it the writer declared that for years the *Tribune* office had been considered a kind of federal employment agency where every red-nosed politician who ever voted the Republican ticket or cheated at a caucus or fought at the polls might seek his reward. "It is a source of profound satisfaction to us that office-seekers will keep aloof from a defeated candidate who has not influence enough at Washington or at Albany to get a sweeper appointed under the sergeant-at-arms, or a deputy sub-assistant clerk into the paste-pot section of the folding-room. . . . At last we shall keep our office clear of blatherskites and political beggars."

Greeley did not see this manifesto until it had appeared in print. Hastily he wrote a rejoinder declaring it to be "a monstrous fable, based on some other experience than that of any editor of this journal." But his repudiation was never published. A few weeks before the election many persons had heard that the Tribune Association would soon offer the editorship to Schuyler Colfax. Certainly early in November, Sinclair, one of the largest stockholders, had written to Colfax to learn whether he would consider the editorship, and whether he would also attempt to secure a controlling financial interest in the paper. According to rumor, receipts for the *Tribune* had fallen off at the rate of a thousand a day since the opening of the campaign; and the weekly edition, still a bulwark, had suffered even more heavily. Colfax postponed his decision for personal reasons; but negotiations were still in train throughout November for the purchase of a controlling interest.

Greeley was far from being able to assume financial control. Little by little since the early fifties, from need of money, because of heedless debts, he had sold blocks of his own shares of *Tribune* stock until he had only a handful left.

The story henceforward is a broken one. Oliver Johnson, a warm and loyal friend, testified that on the Sunday preceding Mrs. Greeley's death, Greeley had met him, grasped his hands, and had told him with a wild look that he was ruined; he had repeated the word many times, though Johnson had tried to efface the conviction. Alvin Johnson, also a close friend, declared that he had noted signs of insanity in Greeley after the death of his wife. Stanton, who had known Greeley for years, declared that after the returns came in he said, "I have ruined all my friends in the election, and now they are destroying me." And at a meeting of the *Tribune* stockholders, held about the middle of November, he arose suddenly and with a frantic gesture insisted that he had ruined the paper and every one connected with it, that he had tried to do right but that everything he did was wrong. The decisions made at this meeting have not come to light. Possibly then, or soon afterward, Greeley learned of the ironic circumstance that Jay Gould was ready to furnish the sum necessary for some would-be editor to purchase the controlling interest in the paper. Whether he was told that Colfax, for long his friend, might supersede him, whether he guessed that Reid, who had been his adjutant, might outstrip Colfax in the race for the prize, must remain a question. Within a few months Reid had gained control of the paper, and was its editor.

For a few days after the meeting of the stockholders Greeley seems to have been clear of mind. Then he began to lose weight with extraordinary rapidity, was wholly unable to sleep, and developed an inflammation of the brain similar to that which he had suffered after the defeat at Bull Run, but far more acute. He died on the 29th of November. His physical vitality was enormous to the last.

Nast alone was credited with the catastrophe; and there followed the obvious outcry that Greeley had been unable to endure defeat. The theory became popular, but who shall say as to its truth? His loss of the *Tribune,* his unavailing clash with a later age, even—long ago—the death of Pickie, may have robbed him of a final energy. Whatever the cause, Greeley's death precipitated a solemn deluge of respect. *Exit Greeley.* A Brooklyn paper had heralded the event in the cold strain of brutality which had become common during the campaign; but the jest was quickly felt to be unseemly. Greeley's body lay in state at the City Hall; Grant came from Washington for the funeral ceremonies, with Justices of the Supreme Court, and a hundred other notabilities. Perhaps it was scarcely fitting that Thurlow Weed should have been one of the great gathering, but he was there; every one was there; and the praises said by the galaxy of ministers were splendid and formal. When these were ended, and the vast company had dispersed, another wayward adventurer in the nation, Charles Sumner, spoke with a grave music. "Parties are always for the living; and now, standing at the open grave of Horace Greeley, we are admonished to forget the strife of party, and to remember only truth, country, and mankind, to which his honest life

HORACE GREELEY [269]

was devoted. In other days the horse and armor of the departed chieftain have been buried in the grave where he reposed. So, too, may we bury animosities, if not the badge of the past. Then, indeed, will there be a victory for the dead which all will share."

Animosities were forgotten: all was forgotten; a more rancorous mood might have been a greater tribute. His opponents—or his own clashing inconsistencies—had done their work well; nothing remained in the popular memory but the symbolic white hat and coat, with a faint recollection of the odd figure that had worn them. For a brief moment the public laughed again when the list of Greeley's assets was published, or found them pathetic: these included stock in the wildest of wildcat schemes, in gold-mines which existed only in the eloquent fancy of a prospector, in companies for the manufacture of inventions which were bizarre beyond belief. Years later the tracts settled by the community at Greeley, Colorado, became green and fertile, and thickly planted with trees; but at the time his investments there yielded little. His debts were large; but through the efforts of friends a substantial competence was contrived for Greeley's two daughters. And the farm at Chappaqua remained.

At Chappaqua, the summer after Greeley's death, there was unrolled a little pageant, a kind of postscript to his career, a light cadenza, or perhaps an ironic epitaph. Ida and Gabrielle Greeley were joined there by Greeley's sister, Mrs. Cleveland, and her two daughters, Cecilia and Marguerite. They took up their residence in the new house, which had not yet been occupied, and became vastly interested in the task of unpacking the treasures which Mrs. Greeley had brought from abroad, "the superb linen," "the heavy damask tablecloths with their beautiful designs, and the immense dinner-napkins, protecting one's dress so admirably against every possible accident," and the "exquisite silver and *Sèvres.*" "Everything is perfection, even to the little gold, lily-shaped handbell," cried Cecilia, who set down all these discoveries in her diary, and afterward made of this a book called *The Story of a Summer, or Leaves from Chappaqua.* They wandered over the house, gazing at the paintings which Mrs. Greeley—or Greeley—had brought from Europe on one occasion or another, of the Cenci, a St. Francis, a portrait of Galileo, a Carlo Dolce madonna, the head of Juno in relief, and the mother of the Gracchi. There were tables made of variegated marble, taken, it seems, from the palace of the Caesars; there were rich imported hangings, and handsome pieces of drawing-room furniture. The house, which had not been completed in Greeley's lifetime, was obviously intended to be a country mansion; it would seem that Mrs. Greeley had relaxed her rigorous principles as to household furnishings, and even as to nature. Around the house was now a charming little park, fringed with lilacs, sown with pansies, violets, heliotrope, mignonette, and planted with brilliantly flowering shrubs.

Here the little company played croquet or ring-toss, or arranged a sylvan picture with a blue boat, water-lilies, and a marquee on the shore of the little artificial pond. Here they strolled, wearing, as Cecilia said, "our broad-brimmed garden hats, with their graceful trimmings of *crêpe* and gauze." Or they drove to the village in "Ida's stylish new phaëton," behind Gabrielle's "irrepressible ponies." Or they were merely idle. "We girls have become habituated to the luxury of breakfasting in bed from residence abroad or in the tropics," said Cecilia, and drifted on to a description of lazy mornings at the "Villa Greeley." "We indulge in very simple morning toilettes here," she explained, "with our hair brushed plain from our faces and flowing loosely *à la belle sauvage*. . . . Even Marguerite, who is the most conventional of our quartette, has conformed to the reigning fashion here, and is no longer coifed in the stylish *Impératrice* mode; her sunny brown hair floats over her shoulders unconfined by hairpins, cushions, or rats. Truly we live in Arcadian simplicity, for under our roof there are neither curling nor crimping irons, nor even a *soupçon* of the most innocent *poudre de riz.*"

"Servants are proverbially the *bête noire* of American ladies, and the prospect of having to train some unskilled specimens of foreign peasantry weighed heavily, I fancy, upon our beautiful Ida in her new responsibility of a young *Dame Châtelaine*. However, we have been singularly successful in obtaining servants. . . . Lina, like all *cordons bleu,* is a great despot, and impatient of *surveillance;* but as she can be trusted to arrange an entire menu without any hints from Ida, *la Dame Châtelaine* gladly leaves the responsibility to her. . . . Minna is the perfection of neatness, and her plain stuff or print gowns are *sans reprôche* in their freshness. . . . It is quite refreshing to see a servant dressed as a servant. . . ."

Many a pleasant little party was planned, though always with the proper remembrance that the company was in mourning. For one of these gatherings a Signor Delmonte arrived, "a very agreeable gentleman, and quite a favorite in New York circles. In figure he rises far above ordinary humanity, six feet two inches being, I believe, his exact height—and his dark complexion and stately gravity render him quite conspicuous in a drawing-room. He is reported extremely wealthy." All the ladies who came were exquisite, all of them charmingly dressed, some of them in black, so that their friends at Chappaqua would not feel too much out of it in their black bombazines, but with occasional bursts of color which commanded the admiration of them all. "I love to describe stylish *toilettes* as well as any fashion-writer," said Cecilia, "so here is hers"—that of a charming Mrs. Acheson—"in all its details: steel-colored silk trimmed with turquoise blue, *demi-traine,* her hair beautifully dressed (or *coiffured,* to use the fashionable newspaper word) in puffs and rolls, and finished with a little blue feather; while an elegant fan attached to half a yard of gold chain depended from her belt."

For two birthdays which came close together a truly elegant *fête* was given. The young ladies wore their black bombazines with black velvet *ceintures,* from which depended fans, *vinaigrettes,* whistles, and tablets. Many friends came from New York, including Mr. Reid, Colonel Hay, and two friends from Paris; from the train "my dear friend Lela Paraf then tripped out, assisted by her elegant husband . . . a surprise party, indeed." Lela Paraf, it seems, was a "born Queen of Fashion." No other ladies were invited, for Ida Greeley feared "that if she sent out invitations to ladies for dinner, some enterprising reporter might announce that she had given at least a *fête champêtre,* if not a *bal masqué,* which in our deep mourning would be an agreeable report to be in circulation." But it was a gay party none the less. They played croquet, they played cards, and sang ballads; they sat three hours at table. "Lina had exercised all of her art in preparing the birthday dinner; and as Ida gave her *carte blanche* in her most extravagant demands—such as twenty pounds of beef for gravies, and an entire bottle of Madeira for the soup, the dinner was very elegant and satisfactory."

Through the record of idle and luxurious days ran an appropriate thread of reminiscence. "Ah," said Mrs. Cleveland with a sigh, "you children have never known my dear parents! . . . You remember, Cecilia, that all the foreign sketches you have ever read of brother, announce that his parents were 'common peasants,' while many American writers, although they do not use the word 'peasant,' convey a similar impression . . . I told you that father was a handsome man. He had large blue eyes, soft silky brown curls clustering around a magnificent brow, a set color in his cheeks, and a hand that the hardest field labor could not deprive of its beauty—long, tapering fingers, and pointed nails such as novelists love to describe but which in real life are rarely seen outside of the most aristocratic families. . . . He was slenderly built without being thin, and his carriage was almost military. To this fine presence was added an air of dignity and almost *hauteur,* that was very unusual in a poor farmer. But father was proud to an unparalleled degree. Indeed, it was his pride that caused him to plunge into the wild forests of Pennsylvania. His haughty nature could not bear the life of subordination that he led in Vermont, where he did not own an acre of land, and was obliged to work under the orders of others, often far inferior to him, and where he fancied the story of his flight from New Hampshire was known to every one. Smarting with mortification, he toiled until he could save a few hundred dollars to buy some acres in the wilderness, far from all his former associates. . . . He was always as particular about the etiquette of the table as though we were served by footmen in livery; and in our poorest days when cups and saucers were scant and spoons more so, we were obliged to observe the utmost decorum till we were helped. . . ."

In the same lucid vein Mary Woodburn was described. She was handsome; she was *not* tall and muscular. Though above medium height she had a graceful, slender figure; it was her pride that water could flow under the arch of her instep; and as for field labor, she may have assisted at harvesting time occasionally for a day or two, but for the most part she was occupied with the many duties of her home.

"Auntie, is it possible," said Gabrielle indignantly, running into Mrs. Cleveland's room one morning with an open volume in her hand, "that papa was as homely and awkward when a boy and a young man as this writer describes him? 'Tow-head,' 'gawky,' 'plain,' and 'clownish,' are some of the most uncomplimentary epithets applied to him. He is described as having 'white hair with a tinge of orange at the ends,' and as 'eating as if for a wager,' while grandpapa, the writer says, was so poor that papa had to walk barefooted over thistles, without a jacket, and in trousers cut with an utter disregard for elegance or fit; and it was remarked that they were *always* short in the legs, while one was invariably shorter than the other. Was it possible that grandpapa could not afford an inch more of cloth to make poor papa's trousers of equal length, and was it true that papa never had two shirts at a time until he came to New York, and that he never had any gloves?"

"I will do my best to refute this writer's unpleasant statements," replied Mrs. Cleveland. "First as to personal appearance. You say your papa was 'plain' as a boy. That is absurd, for his features, like mother's, were as perfect as a piece of Grecian sculpture. Brother's hair was never at any time tow-color, and the tinge of orange at the ends existed only in the author's imagination. Tow-color is a sort of dirty white or gray, whereas brother's hair, until he was thirty years old was like Raffie's, pure white. After that time it commenced to change to a pale gold-color, which never, however, deepened into orange."

"About papa's wardrobe," said Gabrielle, her cheeks still flushed with excitement; "were you indeed so miserably poor, auntie?"

"We were certainly very poor after father failed," said Mrs. Cleveland firmly, "but we were by no means reduced to abjectness." She explained that the elder Greeley always had a fine shirt, that Horace never had gloves in his youth, it was true, but was always well supplied with mittens, that a lameness might have accounted for the legend of the short trouser leg; and she pictured him as opening a ball in the little village of Westhaven with the prettiest girl in the neighborhood on his arm, himself a model of deportment. "His slender boyish figure," she said, "with the ponderous white head poised on his long slim neck, always reminded me of a lovely swaying lily." And Greeley's sister went on to describe the whirl of society in which Horace and his beautiful wife lived during the early years of their marriage, in the days of the *New Yorker*, at "124 Greenwich Street, a most beautiful situation close by the Battery, then the fashionable promenade of New York."

Once the rude stories of the journalists were contradicted, these young people seemed to have little to say of Horace Greeley; but the romance of their ancestry seemed to attract them invincibly, though they clearly surveyed it from an immense distance. "Were they veritable forests?" asked Ida as they considered early life in Pennsylvania. "Pray, auntie, in what way did you travel to advance at such a snail's pace," queried Gabrielle at some mention of the journey thither. "Bears!" exclaimed Gabrielle, her eyes sparkling with excitement, "how lovely! Darling auntie, do tell us more of them. It must have been like one of Captain Mayne Reid's stories, to live in that delightful Pennsylvania!" She took out her work-box, drawing forth a little roll of canvas on which she was delineating in yellow wool a stiff small canary with a surprising eye and an abrupt tail. "Oh, do tell us about it!"

In the end they prettily sketched the whole Greeley background, seeking perhaps to create an idyll of their own, proposing certainly to obliterate a spare and homely American legend. At Chappaqua, where Greeley had hacked away at his trees with a vexed reminiscence of a cruder past, they were absorbed in an occupation which had often engaged him; they too were considering the good time coming. It was coming with a vengeance, cascading down the years with the surge of wealth, an elbowing for position, for family, for prestige. "A cottage at Newport is my ideal for the summer," said Ida. "Newport air," Mrs. Cleveland replied, "would, I think, be too strong for me. The most agreeable sea air I ever experienced was upon the Isle of Wight." Yes, they looked continually toward Europe; and they had their standards; they were critics. A Miss Hempstead, they agreed, was "strikingly foreign looking for an American *pur sang.*" "A little English reserve is all that our bewitching American girls need to make them perfect, but I fear they will for several years yet bear the stigma of 'Charming but too wild.'" At last, in the late summer, their immense French trunks were brought from one of the unused houses on the place. "I am somewhat of a novice in packing," said Cecilia, a granddaughter of the defeated Mary Woodburn. "During the preparations for our eight ocean voyages, that duty never once fell to my lot." They were in the midst of a happy stir. Letters came from friends who were absorbed by similar tasks, or who had lately returned to the city, and were busy with upholsterers and *modistes.* With a swirl of excitement they were off at last, leaving Chappaqua in anticipation of the gayeties of the coming season.

P. T. Barnum

THE *great Barnum was tireless in the practice of autobiography.*
His first volume appeared in 1855, in the full flower of his
middle life; and the book was a flowing bowl of candor. In later years a
friendly apologist declared that the narrative should never have been
taken as the literal truth. "The soberer, matter-of-fact public did not see
the Pickwickian sense of humor and the Orientalism of statement that
pervaded it," protested this anxious gentleman. "The cold type could not
carry with it the twinkling of the author's eye." But it was part of Barnum's genius that he could convey the twinkling of his eye whenever he
chose; as for the soberer, matter-of-fact public, Barnum's friend had been
misinformed as to its attitude. In England, a notable church quarterly
was set quivering with decorous mirth by the volume, and found an excellent lesson of righteousness in the author's career; in this country
Barnum's rise from humble origins, his struggles with adversity, his
achievement of fortune were discovered as evidences of the American
genius; he was hailed as a national example. The few captious critics
were cried down.

Barnum soon outgrew this portrait. Fifteen years later he was moved
to tell another and longer story; and as the years passed and brought
fresh triumphs, he offered ample additions, sequels, and appendices, that
the public might be kept apprised of his later phases. The book went on,
a rising, swelling stream, under many titles and in many forms. The first
volume had been homely, racy, naïve; in the second, with all its accumulations, Barnum blew the summoning trumpet note. "Few men in civil
life have had a career more crowded with incident, enterprise, and various intercourse with the world than mine," he shouted. "With the alter-
nations of success and defeat, extensive travel in this and foreign lands;
a large acquaintance with the humble and honored; having held the pre-
eminent place among all who have sought to furnish healthful entertainment to the American people, and, therefore, having had opportunities

for garnering an ample storehouse of incident and anecdote. . . ." On rolled his rhetoric; episodes were piled on episodes as though to provide a mountainous view across a continent. As the public note salutes the ear for more than a thousand pages certain queries arise in the mind of the pigmy listener. Barnum had the public story-teller's habit; everything was his grist. In this semi-public performance of narration now and then he seized upon episodes which suited his taste or his purpose, and made himself the sublime hero, whether or not he was a leading figure in mortal fact. Here and there in his stories are obvious inflations, made with irresistible gusto. After describing the poverty and the miserable hardships which he had endured traveling in the South and West with a tiny circus during the thirties, he carelessly asserted that he purchased a steamboat for six thousand dollars and went down the Mississippi. After the great clock failure, when he had dismally pictured himself as at the lowest ebb of fortune and the dupe of shrewder men, he alertly explained to Thackeray that his wife possessed a neat fortune, which he may have sequestered; and he told the story, and the amount. In Barnum's long career remain innumerable small alleys or byways which it might be amusing or instructive for the humble student of character to follow. But such delights are forever barred; the regions which Barnum traversed were too obscure for easy penetration after the long lapse of years; his life was most often interwoven with mean or humble lives, which have left behind them no trace. And strangely enough, almost nothing substantial about him emerges from the ruck of contemporary evidence; scarcely another figure of equal proportions has left so little behind him by way of personal print. Necessarily he becomes a legend—an outcome he would have relished.

Perhaps, indeed, Barnum had no personal character. In a strict sense he had no private life. He lived in the midst of the crowd, in the peopled haunts of his great museum, on the road, on the lecture platform, on steamers, in caravans or circus trains, near the smell of sawdust or under the spreading lights of the city. He lived in public; at times it seemed he was the public. There was scarcely a murmur of popular taste or desire in his long era which he did not catch and use and fling back—magnified; his swelling cacophony became much of the noise of the nation, the smaller sounds mixing and mingling with the greater: he was carelessly orchestral. Yet, as we follow him over his widening course, we find that he was something more than a creator of emporiums to give the public what it wanted. He took his cues, he kept his ear to the ground; but he let play upon the faint stirrings of popular desires the energy of a sportive imagination, a fancy primitive but dramatic. There in the white glare of the public gaze, in his own proper figure of public middleman, he created an amused conglomerate. With numberless exhibits he traced patterns of his own, beginning with a familiar theme.

ONE • *"As well attempt to revolutionize the Kingdom of Heaven as the State of Connecticut,"* cried Pierrepont Edwards in despair in the first decade of the last century. Clash after clash could be heard in the struggle to entrench Calvinism as a state established religion and to restrict the franchise to authenticated professors of its harsh dogmas. Lyman Beecher had lately come to Litchfield, and was in the thick of the bitter contention. Yet the small hamlets and villages of Connecticut, so often pictured as held remorselessly in the Puritan grip, contained a stirring admixture of other elements. There were Jeffersonian Democrats of all creeds or no creed who raised the cry of Toleration; there were indigenous Tories who were resentful but inarticulate; and there was a rabble. This last included tipplers and tavern-keepers, storekeepers, peddlers, tinkers, and an occasional squire: the unregenerate, the unheeding, unthrifty, or merely jovial of many orders and occupations. Artfully they eluded the severe legal restrictions upon personal conduct contained in the blue laws, kept a watchful, realistic eye upon the shortcomings of their God-fearing neighbors, and established a supremacy of their own. "In New Haven," said Timothy Dwight, "a trick in trade is rarely heard of; and when mentioned awakens alike surprise and indignation." But whatever the cool virtue of New Haven, in other Connecticut villages like Danbury and Bethel, Middletown and Norwalk, tricks in trade were not only frequently accomplished but boisterously enjoyed, alternating with rough practical jokes as a means of releasing lively wits and surplus energies. To trick a peddler or a storekeeper in a trade—still better a minister or an elder—was to achieve something like public prestige. To lead any neighbor into a home-made trap where he became ridiculous was to acquire an equal dominion. With high spirits his ruff-scuff made puppets of others and pulled the strings. There in Connecticut, under the awful shadow of the Calvinistic doom, the members of a casual brotherhood lived by their wits and enjoyed their natural talents, and conducted their private anti-Puritan campaigns.

It was to such a loose community that young Taylor Barnum belonged by inheritance. He was born in the little village of Bethel near Danbury in the year 1810, of a numerous New England family which claimed Revolutionary connections, but upon whom dignity of any sort sat lightly. Barnum's grandfather and namesake, Phineas Taylor, was a Justice of the Peace, but he was also an incorrigible practical joker and trader who consorted by choice with the village wags and tricksters, and who relished a joke on a minister above all good jokes, and roared with laughter over adroit evasions of the blue laws. The Taylors and the Barnums were solidly on the defensive in Connecticut; their orthodoxy was questionable; and they had accepted the heated tenets of Democracy. Besides, in a frugal community, Barnum's father was thriftless. A farmer, a tailor, a tavern-keeper by turn, he improvidently died while his children were still young and left to his wife the rough and arduous business of keeping an inn. In this small hostelry our hero spent his earlier days—already in public life, a predestined anti-Puritan and a born adventurer. At fourteen he was a tall limber lad with dark restless eyes and a quick tongue who was considered "up to snuff." His favorite companion was an older boy who pilfered horns from his employer, a comb-maker, and sold them for fair sums to the same person.

Young Barnum soon was pivoted in that prime location for the display of equal talents—a general country store. All classes in the village came and went. Yankee peddlers—outlaws even among the clever community of village traders—bobbed up, tried their talents, and disappeared. Here came farmers who offered corn and buckwheat, ax-helves and hickory nuts for rum and tenpenny nails. Small manufacturers entered with their wares—clocks, razors, and whetstones. The hatting industry had already sprung up in Danbury; combs were made in Bethel; clocks were made everywhere. There was a constant babble and the crack of many exchanges; young Barnum himself drove many of the bargains, which were sharp and hard. "Some of the smaller fry shaved us prodigiously," he admitted in candid reminiscence. "The hatters mixed their inferior furs with a little of their best, and sold us the hats for otter. We in turn mixed our teas and liquors and gave them the most valuable names. . . . If we took our pay in clocks, the chances were that they were no better than a chest of drawers for the purpose—that they were like Pindar's razors, made to sell; and if half the number of wheels necessary to form a clock could be found within the case, it was as lucky as it was extraordinary." The changing miscellany of goods was endless: feathers, flax, beeswax, bright calico and gay ribbons, hickory nuts, oats and corn—novelties from the larger world, the spoils of the seasons, and the fruit of country labor. Freely enough at the store flowed Santa Cruz rum, Holland gin, and Jamaica spirits as well as many inferior brews; every one drank, even the clergy. "I suppose I have drawn and bottled more rum than would be necessary to float a ship," said Barnum afterward.

P. T. BARNUM [279]

Barnum shifted from store to store, from Bethel to Danbury and back again; he went to Brooklyn where he engaged in similar adventures on a larger scale, and to New York, where still a youth, he opened a porterhouse for Danbury and Bethel hatters and comb-makers. From this he was obliged to retreat; he had not yet reached the metropolitan pitch: he went back to Bethel and entered into partnership in a general store with an uncle, Alanson Taylor, painting a small frame building bright yellow, and laying in a large stock of hardware, crockery, and notions. At about this time he married a capable young tailoress named Charity Hallett. But he apparently felt that none of these matters required all of his time or his talents. He launched a lottery. Once as a boy he had acquired by a slip in trade a large consignment of worthless green glass bottles from a traveling peddler. He had promptly made them up into lots with his employer's worthless stock of fly-blown tin skimmers and shop-worn pie-pans, had advertised a prize for everybody, sold chances, and recovered equally the loss in money and in local reputation. Lotteries attracted him; he liked the jolts and surprises, the air of public excitement, the effect of pulling off unaccountable feats. He soon went into the lottery business on a considerable scale, with agencies in the villages round about, and became a kind of peripatetic auctioneer, crying his new and unstable wares from town to town and along country roads, flinging broadcast a profusion of posters and advertising with staring capitals and marks of wonder in the slender weekly papers of the region. "As the curious letters of 'Joe Strickland' were highly popular at this time I advertised my office as being under the special favor and protection of Dr. Peter Strickland, own blood cousin to the renowned Joe Strickland. In my bills and advertisements I rang all the possible changes upon the renowned name —'The Ever Lucky Dr. Strickland,' 'Five More Capital Prizes Sold by Dr. Strickland,' 'A Fortune for a Dollar—apply to Fortune's Favorite, Dr. Strickland,' 'Another Mammoth Prize!—Huzza for Dr. Strickland.'

"Customers who bought their tickets and found them blanks, were told that their only wise plan was to 'look for money where they had lost it'—'it was a long lane that never turned'—'such bad luck could not continue long.' . . ."

Connecticut had at first innocently sanctioned lotteries, even using them as a means of raising money for churches and public works; but as they had grown in wild popularity the public conscience was sharply pricked. In truth, the business was scarcely reputable when Barnum embarked upon it. Suddenly his new and chequered enterprise was prohibited by law. The measure was a mesh through which the supple could slip, and young Barnum lacked nothing in flexibility, but he now found himself frankly and noisily ranged—where he had tacitly been before—against the stricter tenets of his community. Soon, through a quarrel with his uncle, Alanson Taylor, he plunged into battle. The exact cause of the dispute remains obscure; perhaps young Barnum played upon him too gross a practical joke; certainly his uncle proved to be a more solid citizen, a more rigorous Presbyterian than Barnum had supposed; and their differences quickly became set deep in the matrix of the ancient political and religious conflict. Alanson Taylor was as furiously stung to expression as was Barnum. Each promptly launched a newspaper and carried on a running fusillade of hot-headed personalities and arguments which made other Connecticut journals of the time look like academic ghosts. With a warm flourish Barnum gave to his paper the waving name of the *Herald of Freedom*. Freedom was his battle-cry; he attacked Calvinism, its ministers, indeed the entire Standing Order—as it was still fitly called—in the name of Freedom, insisting that a conspiracy was afoot to restore the old alliance of church and state in Connecticut, which would in the end abolish personal liberty. In this charge Barnum was evoking an empty bogey. The effort of the Puritans to keep the seat of government in Connecticut was long since over. Nearly fifteen years before, when Barnum was a boy of nine, the Standing Order had been swept away by the effectual means of a new constitution. Even Lyman Beecher, one of its best known leaders, had acknowledged the wisdom of its destruction, and was now, in the early thirties, off to the West with the light of a dozen new momentous issues before him. But Barnum kept up his attack, filling it with wind and fury, inflating it as if the mere act of blowing up a monstrous balloon were his pleasure. Shouting for freedom, he now upheld the scarcely respectable faith of Universalism, which abundantly offered hope and happiness for all, and had been a thorn in the Puritan side for twenty years. When Barnum's adoption of Universalism took place is not apparent; but in Bethel, at least, there was only one church, the Presbyterian; and his acknowledgment of a buoyant creed placed him in further antagonism to the older elements of his community. Likewise, in the midst of a growing Whiggery he cried up the hated Democracy, harking back to what he called the principles of the Republic.

Mixed and virulent as was his platform, some of these issues ran deep; with the onrush of the Jacksonian era was developing the first heady liberalism of the age. His paper was no mean achievement for a young man of twenty-two with the smallest education. Not its least features were reports of the important speeches in the campaign of 1832, and of the proceedings of the Connecticut legislature; and Barnum included a column of foreign news. But after all, what amused him most was the parry and thrust of personal attack; and at last he strained the patience of his respectable orthodox opponents. During the three years of his editorship, from 1831 to 1834, Barnum was three times arrested for libel. Once he was fined; once he succeeded in having the case against him dismissed. The third time, having accused an orthodox church officer in Bethel of extortion from an orphan, he was made to feel the accumulated wrath of the entrenched opposition. He was sentenced to pay a fine of one hundred dollars and to serve a term of sixty days in the Danbury jail.

Freedom! Again he shouted freedom! With a perfect adaptability and an easy stretch of terms, Barnum made the issue one of freedom of speech, and found an ally in the Reverend Theophilus Fisk, editor of the *Watch Tower of Freedom* at New Haven, a rampant speaker who was adding to the swelling note of early American oratory catchwords which had been the watchwords of the Revolution. Fisk was voluble; the pronouncement of the word liberty alone could stimulate him to salvo after salvo of praise, indignation, or melancholy, as the case might require. "Is it possible," queried the Reverend Theophilus in an open letter to Barnum, "an American—a Freeman—a Husband—has been torn from his family hearthstone, and by the strong arm of oppression has been incarcerated within the gloomy walls of a Common Jail!!! An American Citizen!! By the iron hand of power shut out from the glorious sunlight—and that too *for no crime! ! !* . . . Amid the death struggles of prejudice, bigotry, and error to regain their palsying influence over the minds of men, the late desperate attempt to muzzle your press will be remembered when minor persecutions have been forgotten. The imprisonment of our friend and fellow-citizen involves more momentous consequences than that of any event within my recollection. . . . It tells us that the clouds which are thickening upon our borders are the fearful harbingers of an approaching storm! It tells us there is a demon rearing its hydra head in the midst of our peaceful valleys that has drenched the earth with gore! We must be up and doing. The deep silence, the hush, the awful stillness which pervades the moral atmosphere warns of approaching doom! Will men who love liberty—who prize our hallowed institutions, become, and continue to remain, the willing dupes of ecclesiastical domination? No. Let them, one and all, show to the world that they were not born with saddles on their backs for priests to ride. . . . Let them arise in the majesty of truth, and blow the trumpet of Zion!"

Barnum became a martyr. "The same spirit governs my enemies that imprisoned Sellick Osborn and burnt to death Michael Servetus by order of John Calvin," he wrote to Gideon Welles from jail in an impassioned letter. "The excitement in this and neighboring towns is very great, and it will have a grand effect." The grand effect he kept steadily in view; and though he seems not to have borrowed even the semblance of a fagot from the sad case of Michael Servetus, he took over intact the ritual which had attended Sellick Osborn, when, twenty years before, he had been released from the Litchfield jail. It was Osborn, from Danbury, who had invaded Litchfield in the desperate years when the foundations of the older Connecticut were first being shaken; the answer to his Democratic and anti-Puritan paper had been the cool one of imprisonment. The case had become famous up and down the land; Osborn had been made the very symbol of rebellion against the New England domination; and when he was released, a few noisy rebels had contrived a parade along the stately eminence of Litchfield Hill. Accordingly, at sunrise of the day on which Barnum's term was ended, the national flag was hoisted over a small gathering place. At the actual moment of his release the national salute was fired. The services, for so he expressly denominated them, were begun by the singing of an ode composed for the occasion. *Strike the Cymbal* was also sung, and a patriotic carol called *Jefferson and Liberty;* and the Reverend Theophilus Fisk, appropriately in the foreground, delivered a stirring oration on the freedom of the press in which he ascended to even higher flights of praise and denunciation than in his letter. After a feast, Barnum solemnly took his place in a coach. Drawn by six horses, preceded by forty men on horseback with a marshal bearing a flag, to the booming roar of cannon, and followed— so he said—by sixty carriages, he drove in state from Danbury the six miles to Bethel, where with his young wife he lived over the yellow store.

His account of this gala performance was entitled *The Triumph of the People.* Indeed, from the Reverend Theophilus Fisk—or from a sudden native spring of fancy—Barnum had learned the easy values of the baldly patriotic appeal. Thenceforward in his paper he sounded a national note. But in vain. The sentence for libel had left a deeper stigma than he ever was willing to admit; and in communities as small as Bethel and Danbury personal feeling was sharply militant. He was obliged to move *The Herald of Freedom* to Norwalk, and then to sell it; the paper never had been a paying venture. His store failed. He had continued his lotteries; but in 1834 lotteries were at last effectively prohibited; and the blue laws were being affirmed and enforced. If in the matter of government the Standing Order had gone down, the Puritan mode of conduct was now defined with increasing sharpness. Respectability and Puritanism were more than ever closely intertwined. Barnum had engaged in a reckless running warfare against the only society he knew; and he had lost. His defeat was unmistakable; he was ousted from employments which were greatly to his liking; and he was badly out of pocket. Money in itself he perhaps cared for very little; he was lavish; from the first there was nothing niggardly in his composition; in his simple scale of moral values hoarding was evil. He was one of those Americans of whom Harriet Martineau spoke, for whom the miser was "an antique classical kind of personage, pictured forth as having a high cap, a long gown, and sitting in a vaulted chamber, amidst money-bags." If Barnum had coin, he liked to feel it slipping through his fingers with a fillip of excitement; he enjoyed his adventures less for the returns they yielded than for their variety, or for the advantage they gave him over other people. Here was another rub. In small Connecticut communities thrift was a staple virtue, joined with the sterner moralities. At every point, it seemed, young Barnum had been reduced to ignominy. Small wonder that his high moment of conquest, that of the triumphal procession, should remain a flowing pattern in his mind! So it seemed; with his lusty ache for power, that forced and straggling episode took on enchantment; its outlines were to invite him in a hundred ways through many a long year, indeed, throughout his lifetime. Barnum went to New York with certain elementary conclusions which he never forgot; but penniless though he was, and something of an outcast, with a family to support, he apparently remained irrepressible; his spirits still bounded; and after a few mistrials he found an enterprise precisely fitted to his hand.

TWO • *In any sort of exhibit Barnum was always to find pleasure;* there was the happy combination of a public appearance and of pulling off a feat—in most cases a joke—of producing some preposterous object for public wonder or acclaim. But for his maiden effort in what he was invariably to call the show business he could have looked far without finding an object so well calculated to offer him a timely sense of triumph as the one he soon hit upon: this was the ancient negress named Joice Heth, who was said to be one hundred and sixty-one years old, and the nurse of George Washington. He bought the repulsive living mummy—thus becoming a slave-owner—placed her on exhibit at Niblo's Gardens, and easily and gayly strummed the patriotic note. But Joice Heth was something more than a means of extorting the sentiment of patriotism; indeed, her discourses on religion and her singing of hymns were the larger part of her program. Watching the simple solemn folk who came reverently to listen and observe, he achieved a primitive backslap at the organized religionists with whom he had done battle in Bethel and Danbury. When at last popular attention began to lag, a letter by a supposed visitor in one of the public prints declared that Joice Heth was an ingenious contraption of rubber, whalebones, and springs, that the proprietor was a ventriloquist, and and that "all conversations held with the ancient lady are purely imaginary." This bouncing inversion and quick slide into burlesque Barnum enjoyed to the full; the cry of fraud was one which he was to raise against his own exhibits throughout most of his long career. It not only provided advertisement, but an effect of a contest which Barnum seemed to relish. Now, as later, the device was successful; many serious persons came for a second look, and to pass a wise judgement. When this new inquiry had run its course Barnum took the ancient creature to Boston, Philadelphia, and Albany; and when the American Institute was opened in New York—that early ambitious organization for the promotion of American industry and science—he arranged to be on hand once more with his exhibit, this time presenting Joice Heth in the guise of a physical curio, thus by chance, knowledge, or intuition hitting upon one of his surest claims for public attention—the scientific claim. Though the creature survived the sessions of the Institute, she was not immortal; she died soon afterward; and Barnum, still cultivating science, still tireless and unhurried, stimulated a prolonged controversy as to the question of her age, in which a few men of scientific pretensions took part, and Bennett of the *Herald* was twice hoodwinked. This was sheer gratuitous sport, as Barnum's own name was not brought into play; and he was not then before the New York public.

Again he was without an occupation. During a visit in Washington he had interviewed Anne Royall, that picturesque early female journalist, lobbyist, editor, and thorough-going terror of national legislators, whom John Quincy Adams described as going about "like a virago-errant in enchanted armor, redeeming herself from the cramps of indigence by the notoriety of her eccentricities and the forced currency they gave to her publication." A bitter anti-Calvinist, Anne Royall had her sharp opinions about the powerful in Connecticut, indeed the powerful in all the New England states, where she had traveled some years before gathering material for her piquant *Black Books*. She became the editor of a little sheet appropriately called *Paul Pry*. It was proof of his continued absorption in the anti-Puritan rebellion that Barnum now tried to persuade her to lecture under his direction on the principles of government. In the early thirties the lecture platform was still a rough scaffolding in this country; the lyceums had just begun; but their power was already manifest. Barnum, with his easy assimilation, was trenching upon a movement of a signal importance. However, Anne Royall was strongly attached to the pastime of stamping through the halls of the Capitol with her huge umbrella; in spite of Barnum's blandishments she declined to leave Washington, and for many years continued to torment the nation's servants.

At his wit's end Barnum engaged an Italian plate-spinner and stilt-walker, and boldly set out to conquer Connecticut. He failed; the shadow of the blue laws still lay thick. He traveled through other New England states, and dipped into New Jersey, but with meager returns. In Philadelphia he trumped up a rival performer to walk stilts and spin plates for a wager against his own man; and the scene grew tumultuous, the profits were large, the sly effect of doubling much to Barnum's taste; but elsewhere he seemed unable to contrive similar matches. Presently he transferred the plate-spinner, whom he had christened Vivalla, to Aaron Turner's small traveling circus, joined the company himself as ticket-seller, treasurer, and part owner, and again entered Connecticut. Shabby and insignificant as it was, the little troupe received an ample volume of attack there and in Massachusetts; bitter invectives were flung from the pulpit; and to the pulpit Barnum ascended one Sunday morning at Lenox, pushing his way thither with bland effrontery, and delivering a defense of circuses from the sacred elevation. He repeated these tactics. Once an enraged minister shouted throughout Barnum's discourse, commanding his people to leave. Yet even with Barnum's cross-fire the circus failed to prosper; and the company traveled south. It was a rough life, crammed to the brim with hardships, enlivened in the main by practical jokes—which were often cruel—played by all members of the company singly or in groups against the others. Barnum apparently liked the whole haphazard journey, opposition and all, perhaps because he still was captivated by the hint of rebellion, possibly because he found a faint effect of the triumphal march in the poor little procession. Undaunted by slight rewards and hard fare, in North Carolina he resolved to create a circus of his own. By what sleight of hand he paid Turner is not clear; but he took Vivalla, a fiddler, a clown, and a negro breakdown dancer from the original company, and equipped with a single wagon and a small tent, proceeded further south, calling his assemblage a Scientific Theater. The roads were bad, the distances long; Puritanism was not without its outposts in the South. As he made a slow and tortuous way through Alabama and Mississippi and northward through Kentucky and Tennessee into that mid-country which was still called the West, his audiences were drawn from the roughs and tag-ends of every community through which he passed; at the same time he was obliged to avoid their boisterous attentions. Perhaps these inclined to mount as his Yankee birth became apparent; in the wake of the Yankee peddler every travel-ing Yankee was fair game. Barnum was muscular enough for defense when necessary, and sharp enough to use his wits instead of his fists whenever possible. If he could begin the performance he could usually win his audience; a fiddler was wickedly enchanting, a breakdown dancer the host of a hundred forbidden antics. Finally, by good luck, Barnum was joined by Henry Hawley, a sleight of hand performer who left his audiences gaping with astonishment, and proved to be a companion well adapted to run the gauntlet of rough travel. Hawley was a prodigious teller of tall tales.

Suddenly the tall tale was everywhere, a beanstalk growth which had shot up almost without warning all over the land. In the middle twen-ties, indeed, something of the sort had been decorously imprisoned by covers, in such an uproarious satire as Paulding's *John Bull in America;* but for the most part the native talent had become an affair of im-provisation by word of mouth or of occasional journalistic enterprise. Hoaxes of all sorts were the mode. The Moon Hoax had been perpe-trated by the New York *Sun* in a series of articles which purported to delineate the inhabitants of the moon as discovered by Herschel at the Cape of Good Hope. A little earlier Poe had published his *Hans Pfaall,* fabricated upon the same basis. "Humbug" was a word now in sudden common use, as if it denoted a discovery. But perhaps the most extensive application of the novel faculty appeared in casual tales told in remote regions, of the kind which was to appear thirty years later with so un-likely an effect of novelty in *The Celebrated Jumping Frog of Calaveras County.* In the backwoods the simple tale of adventure was growing elongated, was ascending, becoming preposterous—and was accepted. In the realm of supposed hazards anything was believed, not, perhaps, because life itself was so strange, but because it was not strange enough, because in those unsettled regions, once the risks of the first pioneering were over, men were bored. Out of an immense isolation came an equal lassitude; any jolt was welcome; and to match credulity a solemn, im-perturbable narration was developed which became as closely masked as the face of danger.

In later years, though Hawley dropped from sight like dozens of others briefly attached to his train, and though Barnum showed no more inter-est in his career than in that of the rest, he would repeat Hawley's tales with relish, and with a life-like touch was able to evoke him as an artist of the time and place. A young man, prematurely gray, Hawley possessed a quiet, formal dignity; he would take his place in the village bar-room with no particular insistence, and would gradually draw his hearers by strange tales which were known to be true. Step by mild deliberate step he proceeded to his preposterous heights. "Gentlemen," asked Hawley, "have any of you ever visited the Rocky Mountains?" They had not. "I have been there frequently," he continued; and he narrated his adventures in a region where all the trappers and hunters met to celebrate the Fourth of July, making an excellent ice-punch, the ice being obtained in cart-loads from a nearby cavern where the supply was perennial. On one occasion a couple of Irishmen who had been sent for a second load returned in terror, having come upon a pair of boots with legs in them. Through the efforts of the party, a little antiquated man was exhumed who wore short breeches and knee-buckles, an old-fashioned coat and a cocked hat, and who looked so life-like that many of the old trappers insisted that he must be merely dormant. Truly enough, by the aid of brandy, a hot bath, and woolen blankets, the quaint creature was brought to life and proved to be an officer of King George, sent on a mission to some Indian tribes during the Revolutionary War; he had tripped in the cave, and knew nothing more until rescued by the trappers seeking ice for their punch fifty years later, on the Fourth of July.

Hawley went on to tell of another phenomenon in the same region, an area some twenty miles square where the air was so pure that people never died, unless by accident. "Never died!" exclaimed several of his listeners. "No, gentlemen, it was quite impossible. The rare purity of the air prevented it. When persons got too old to be useful they would sometimes be blown away, and once outside the charmed circle they were lost." A literal member of his audience still raised a doubt. "A fact, upon my honor," declared Hawley. "Indeed, some years ago several philanthropic gentlemen erected a museum at that place, where persons who became too old for usefulness were put in sacks, labeled, registered at the office, and hung up. If at any subsequent period their friends wished to converse with them, for a fee of fifty cents the old friend would be taken down, placed in a kettle of tepid water, and would soon be enabled to hold a conversation of half an hour, when he would be taken out, wiped off and hung up again." Hawley himself had found an uncle there who had gone to the Rocky Mountains thirty years before and had not been heard of since; he proved to be the contents of Sack No. 367; he was taken down, conversed weakly, and was able to tell his nephew of the whereabouts of a large gun he had once owned. Hawley declared that he found the gun on the identical crossbeam which his uncle had described, a monstrous large weapon which required a pound of powder and four pounds of shot for loading, and with which he subsequently went hunting pigeons in a buckwheat field. He threw a stick to arouse the pigeons, and they arose as a single mass; but unfortunately he fired half a second too late, and succeeded only in shooting off the legs of the flock; he picked up four bushels and a half of feet and legs.

"That's a lie, by thunder!" exclaimed one of his audience. Possibly even in the thirties the tricks of a gargantuan fabrication were well known. Such tales had already been constructed around episodes in the lives of heroes like Davy Crockett and a dozen others whose heroism and skill are now lost to view. But if Hawley's audience was sophisticated in the matter of monstrous guns, it was intrigued by the discovery of King George's messenger and by the museum of rarefied old men; Barnum declared that several members of one group solemnly wrote down the number of the sack that contained Hawley's uncle. Whether or not they in turn were acting a tall tale, there was no doubt of their lust for magnitude; it was as if that sense of scale which was presently to overwhelm the American imagination in so many forms were now germinating obscurely in these scant and barren recesses of the backwoods. Again and again Hawley pulled his resilient long bow, and won the momentary pleased attention of many a little crowd as the circus moved on its precarious way. But alas! when the small caravan circled into the Ohio Valley even this device failed. Here once more was the New England public, if anything more deeply rooted in its standards, prejudices, and prepossessions than on its native soil. Stragglers and idlers and careless pleasure-seekers existed in plenty, truly enough; young Henry Ward Beecher, then beginning his career in southern Indiana, knew them well; perhaps Barnum's Grand Musical and Scientific Theater drifted through Lawrenceburg, and was enjoyed by a heedless little throng there. But in the main Barnum encountered that rigorous opposition of which young Beecher himself was soon to become the spokesman in his *Lectures to Young Men.*

Barnum tried his last resort, the direct attack, and began delivering a defense of the circus in the shape of religious or moral lectures of his own, in groves, in open fields, from the tail of his wagon. Never, even in the most exuberant moments of later years did he refer to these ventures with anything but a vague and tepid allusion, not—surely—because he was ashamed of them, but because they were unsuccessful. The dint which he made upon the surface of this half-formulated small society was exceedingly slight; he was defeated in the second New England of the West. He was obliged to leave a wagon in one village, a horse in the next, a watch elsewhere, in order to pay his bills. Other ill luck pursued him. Vivalla departed without warning; the negro dancer was drowned; once Barnum was obliged to disband his company altogether. Contriving to assemble another small troupe, he started down the Mississippi; but even in the small hamlets along the great river the circus was fair game; the rough gangs that haunted the river-front tormented the players and threatened to break up the performances; on one occasion Barnum was run out of town at the point of pistols. At New Orleans he wheeled about, and returned to New York. "I was thoroughly disgusted with the life of the itinerant showman," he declared. Yet in a few months he was traveling into the South and West once more with another crude little circus, enduring the same hardships, meeting the same resistance; round and round over these long and arduous circuits he made his way: these early tours covered four or five years, persisting with enormous endurance, with the incredible stability of madness or genius, as if either in the crude surprises of his own little performances or in the small gaping audiences which viewed them he found an irresistible attraction. With other scattered showmen and the race of Yankee peddlers and a few revivalists Barnum belonged to the pioneer travelers of the time and place, and learned an obscure lore whose value even then he may well have apprehended. In his own manner he girdled and possessed the new country.

When he reached New Orleans early in 1841 Barnum retrieved his fortunes in part by arranging a dancing match between his own breakdown dancer and another, much after the fashion of the duel of the plate-spinners and stilt-walkers which he had contrived in Philadelphia; but by a series of mishaps he lost most of his profits on the journey to New York. For a brief time he turned to the project of selling illustrated Bibles. "I thus made another effort to quit the life of a showman altogether, and settle down into a respectable calling." He became, as he said, a "Bible-man." But at the same moment he was moved to lease the Vauxhall saloon, where he conducted semi-theatrical performances throughout the summer. The double rôle was not successful, though in it may have been contained the pattern of a plan to keep one hand upon solid recommendations and the other upon a lively adventure. Barnum was at the end of a long and slippery rope when he learned that Scudder's Museum was for sale, at the corner of Ann Street and Broadway, half a block from the small printing shop where Horace Greeley had launched the *Tribune* earlier in the year.

With one of those sudden decisions which represented what he called "tact," he decided to acquire the Museum. He was always to entertain a number of ambitions at a single moment, tossing them up juggler-wise and keeping them in rapid motion until they seemed a single chain. He wanted Scudder's for all reasons. Museums were respectable, though circuses and theaters were not. Nearly sixty years before at Yale College a quaint little collection of relics had been gathered by Dr. Ezra Stiles in the name of science, history, and the classics; Peale in Philadelphia, an odd and gentle genius, had long since created his huge mixed aggregation of exquisite portraits, historical records, anatomical specimens, and amazing rubbish. Even in the strict and simple West few cities of any pretensions lacked a museum; Cincinnati possessed two. At first these institutions had been mere abiding places for the spoils of time and adventure, handy repositories for the queer trophies of travelers, explorers, sea captains; but gradually they had assumed scientific pretensions. Scudder's itself had won its earliest repute by means of a monster tortoise which had been exhibited as a marvel of nature and also as a patriotic emblem, since the creature had been nurtured and caught on American shores. Of late, from the scientific interest had come an easy transition to an absorption in the grotesque. A passion for the morbidly strange, perhaps always languidly sleeping in the human mind, suddenly had become devouring. Poe had written his *Tale of the Grotesque and Arabesque* at the end of the thirties; he was even now offering spectral chambers, other-worldly abysses, and shuddering catastrophes to hundreds of eager readers. In a more immediate world the legend perhaps was plainer; freaks and monsters of all kinds were a fashion; it was a poor museum which did not boast a Chamber of Horrors with a magnetic shock. Aberrations from the normal in anatomical specimens were shown everywhere, with teeth and bones or even more gruesome relics which evoked the scenes of Indian slaughter, or the hint of monstrous heathen rites.

Perhaps because the element of pleasure was successfully inverted, or heavily disguised, museums had remained respectable. In New York, moreover, there was at least a hint of moral latitudes which Barnum had not discovered in his endless travels in the West; New York had long since been called Gotham. And the enterprise of Scudder's was a gamble; for several years money had been lost there. Barnum's liking for any lottery remained; he believed that by sleight of hand of his own the place could be made to yield a golden stream. He succeeded in discrediting other prospective purchasers of the Museum. Lacking a penny, he aroused the owner of the building to buy the collection for him, giving him a lease and an option of purchase, and settled at once to a program of cold lunches and severe self-denial in order to meet his obligations. But his period of discipline was short; nor was he able to maintain his original intention of investing all his surplus in advertising, except a small sum needed for his family. The feat proved impossible. His returns were far too large; the golden stream had become a flood.

THREE • *A small New York sprawled uncertainly into farms* along the rivers; but even in 1841 opulence was lavishly spread over the town. Broadway was bright and confused, with posters and placards hung from wooden pillars and cross-beams outside the shops. Gaudy tokens of wealth appeared in the gayly painted and expensively upholstered equipages which brushed by. Velvets and furs and multi-colored silks were worn by men as well as by women. In the midst of this effervescent thoroughfare Barnum's Museum promptly became the showiest place of all, with its pennants and flags streaming from the four-storied building, its paintings of birds, beasts, and reptiles in serried parallels between the windows, its flamboyant posters or brilliant transparencies. With his huge gas lights that blazed at night up and down the street Barnum created a flood of prophetic illumination. On a balcony he posted a brass band—Music for the Million—and blared forth the attractions of the Museum by sheer noise. On the Fourth of July, without asking permission he had flags strung from the Museum to St. Paul's church opposite, and when he was ordered to remove them, staged a timely and noisy bit of drama, with brawny men in shirt sleeves asking the vestrymen to take down the national emblem if they dared, and inquiring loudly whether the rector was a Britisher. Crowds were drawn by the strange ritual of a man who set down single bricks at given places in the street and within the building, without a word, and who changed them for other bricks; he was steadily followed —through the Museum—by a respectful throng. Other throngs came with babies, with dogs, with flowers, and poultry, to compete in the many shows advertised by Barnum as a prime feature of the Museum; they came for fame, and for the appropriate rewards of diplomas, medals, and money, paying their twenty-five cents—children half price—to enter the Museum.

Inside the gaudy painted box came a sudden shock; instead of the colored illumination visible on Broadway were dark vistas, dim recesses, and strange forms and figures, with an atmosphere of solemnity. The awed spectator could climb broad staircases which had semblance of grandeur: where else in New York in the early forties could be found the effect of scale in a public building? He could enjoy a vague sense of possession, and suddenly be startled out of it by hideous surprise as he rounded a corner at the top. On the walls or suspended in cases were freaks of nature, stuffed or in wax or in their skeletal bones, two-headed calves and two-headed chickens, the more terrifying natural specimens, snakes and the Gila monster, startling amphibians, and dangerous beasts of the jungle. Presently Barnum brought to the attention of the public a creature which outstripped any contemporary offering as a fantasy in the grotesque: the tiny wizened relic of fin and skin, varnish and bone, forever contorted into a posture of agony, which he dubbed the Feejee Mermaid. Assisted by the agent who had helped him display Joice Heth —another fantasy in the grotesque—he teased and jogged and jolted the public curiosity for weeks by a series of adroitly contrived newspaper notices: the mermaid came from Pernambuco, and had been procured for the Natural History Lyceum of London; then, in Philadelphia, a few persons had gazed upon the wonder; and at last, after many circumvolutions, changes, new hints, and proposals, the mermaid was advertised to appear for a short time at Concert Hall. With amplitude Barnum now played upon the scientific importance of the discovery—anonymously. With the mermaid were to be shown other strange creatures in the great chain of animated nature, like the Orintho-Rhyncus, the Proteus Anguinus, and the Paddle-Tail Snake. Barnum appealed to a memory of the classics, to the esthetic sense—and to what else? Full-blown mermaids combing their hair and disporting their charms in trios and groups and happy shoals figured on posters and transparencies. A newspaper woodcut showed a small sail-boat filled with a company of ascetic-looking men in tall hats and women in Shaker bonnets; their gaze was fixed upon a retreating mermaid while a clerical gentleman appeared to be delivering a harangue: yet strangely enough, with its bow headed toward safe horizons, the little vessel appeared to be following the siren. There was no question as to the unhallowed excitement which Barnum aroused in the fabulous and pagan race of sea nymphs, or as to his gusto, or his deliberate skill. When after this long prelude, and the promised appearance at the Concert Hall, and a further shower of posters, pamphlets, and transparencies, the problematical creature was at last shown at the American Museum under Barnum's own aegis, multitudes came; the mermaid crowded into the newspapers again; indeed, the fame of the creature, Barnum said, was "wafted" from one end of the country to the other. Later the small horrid relic was sent

P. T. BARNUM [293]

on tour, and remained in Boston for some years; the excitement seemed deathless; as late as 1855 Barnum was successfully exhibiting the mermaid at the Museum.

Here was a practical joke on a grand scale. If by a crude contrivance the spectator was not bumped downstairs, or tripped into humiliating posture after the manner of country-made practical jokes, mentally the same effect was achieved; he went to see a siren of fair proportions, and was confronted by a hideous little monster. From the sharp contrast between its gaudy exterior and the portentous gloom within, to the mixed and changing charlatanry of its exhibits, the whole Musuem constituted a practical joke. Its object was to reduce the beholder again and again to an abject bewilderment; he might be terrified or horrified, disappointed or in the end amused, but he was also submissive and beaten. Barnum had only to walk about the halls of his new domain to hear empty giggles and helpless laughter, to see the dropped jaw and the pointed finger. By luck or insight he had found that a great undeveloped audience awaited him, which was bored and dull and aimless, without standards of taste, cramped by its heritage yet willing to shift this to a convenient formalism, desiring liberation and laughter—if this was laughter—desiring above all, perhaps, a common enjoyment. That sheep-like docility, that inclination to follow the crowd which had been satirically noted by Poe as an American characteristic, had already had at least one sufficient demonstration in the popular festival of the Harrison campaign the year before Barnum had opened the Museum, when the country had gone mad with contagious imitation, when whole mobs had worn the same emblems, shouted the same songs, cried the same phrases in unison for the first time in American history. An aborted hope of union—of companionship—what indeed?—was abroad; it seemed necessary only to strike some quaint and common interest to have its slogans run like loud essential signals, and to draw the expectant crowd into a close knot or a throng.

With his eye upon far larger numbers than he could assemble in the Museum, Barnum presently ranged outside, seizing upon the growing consciousness of the pioneer West which had lately been materialized by the figure of General Harrison. He advertised a free buffalo hunt at Hoboken. There was no hunt; the buffaloes were timid yearlings; one man appeared in a western costume. The crowd got nothing—for nothing. Almost any prophet would have declared that they would grow frenzied with rage: but no, as the small thin young buffaloes trotted out and quickly huddled in a far corner, the big assemblage roared with mirth, roared at its own predicament, and went good-naturedly home, demanding to know the perpetrator of so excellent a hoax. After all, a hoax is an elaborate form of attention. Who indeed had taken the pains to delude them on so preposterous a scale before?

A few years later, when the western fever was at its height, Barnum turned to his own ends the romantic excitement which had centered about the figure of Colonel Frémont. "Colonel Frémont was lost among the trackless snows of the Rocky Mountains," he said afterward in half-hearted apology. "The public mind was excited. Serious apprehensions existed that the intrepid soldier and engineer had fallen a victim to the rigors of a severe winter. At last the mail brought intelligence of his saftey. The public heart beat quick with joy. I now saw a chance for the woolly horse"—a small horse covered with wool like a sheep, and lacking both mane and tail, which he had purchased in Cincinnati some time earlier, and had hidden away until the suitable moment for exhibition should arise. Immediately after the announcement that Frémont was safe, another item appeared in the New York newspapers. "The public appetite was craving something tangible from Colonel Frémont," said Barnum. "The community was absolutely famishing. They were ravenous. They could have swallowed anything, and like a good genius, I threw them, not a bone, but a regular titbit, a bonbon—and they swallowed it at a single gulp." The second dispatch declared that on the Gila river Frémont and his band had discovered an amazing nondescript which resembled a horse, but which was undoubtedly made up of the elephant, the deer, the horse, the buffalo, the camel, and the sheep. According to further information, the creature had been sent by Frémont to a United States Quartermaster, and was to be exhibited in New York for a few days before being sent to London. Handbills appeared showing a huge horse in full flight, and making a terrific leap over a chasm which embraced, as Barnum said, at least five miles, with Frémont's men in full pursuit. Pamphlets were circulated about the horse, written in the unhurried descriptive style which still prevailed in public writing. These announcements came in rapid succession; the horse was brought on for exhibit—in an empty store—at a swift climax. After all, Colonel Frémont would not remain in the trackless snows of the Rocky Mountains forever; and United States Quartermasters were not wholly obscure figures. Indeed, when the horse was sent to Washington on exhibit—"to see if the wool could be pulled over the eyes of politicians"—the hot-tempered father-in-law of Frémont, Colonel Benton, sued Barnum's agent: but the case was dismissed.

At the outset Barnum's name was absent from public information about the woolly horse; but he calmly announced it when the rich returns were in. The venture was on the whole a minor sally; yet it represented—as did the Buffalo Hunt—a brisk tendency in Barnum's exhibits; he was still engaged in hoaxes, but more and more frequently these tended to come alive. Sitting among his show-cases, at the end of corridors, or in appropriate corners, were living monstrosities, like giants, fat boys, albinos; to these were gradually added a sprinkling of Indians, Chinese, gypsies, and even a "live Yankee"—so the advertisement ran, though why he became an exhibit is not entirely clear, unless Barnum wished to pillory or exalt the type. Presently sprightlier surprises appeared, in occasional ventriloquists who disturbed the many by uncanny sounds from unlikely quarters, in a pair of jugglers, a sleight of hand performer, and even a troupe of rope-dancers. Here and there his stuffed specimens were replaced by living animals in cages. "If I have exhibited a questionable dead mermaid in my Museum it should not be overlooked that I have also exhibited camelopards, a rhinoceros, grizzly bears, orangoutangs, and great serpents, about which there could be no mistake because they were alive." Here, indeed, were the scattered features of that dubious entertainment, the circus: here was another hoax. Barnum never mentioned the word circus; he hedged his diversions round with what he called "a wilderness of realities"—knitting machines, glass-blowers, mummies, models of Dublin, Paris, Jerusalem, an anatomical Venus, numberless dissolving views, automatons, and an increasing quantity of strange mementoes from all parts of the world.

"Bless me, what have we here? The hand and part of an arm, as I'm alive," said one of the good little boys who figured in an illuminated pamphlet describing the Museum. "Yes," said Uncle Find-Out in reply, "that is the arm of the celebrated Tom Trouble, the pirate, who was taken after a severe action, in which he lost the forefinger of his hand. He died in prison, at St. Thomas, while under the sentence of death. He was afterward nailed to a plank, and exposed in the harbor, when, strange to say, his whole body became bleached and preserved, similar to this arm, which was cut off by an American seaman, and brought to New York. Here, also, is a human body, found in 1814, at Glasgow, in Kentucky, in a saltpetrous cave, nine feet under ground. A very curious specimen, and in fine condition."

"I suppose the saline properties preserved the body, sir," said the wise little nephew.

Despite such opportune instruction, the circus grew a little larger and a little brisker year by year; and an even more equivocal amusement was developed with an abundant energy. In truth, any wanderer through the halls of the Museum might have surmised that drama would somewhere prove a rightful climax; the dramatic was evoked at every turn, in the club that killed Captain Cook, in the panoramic diorama of the obsequies of Napoleon, in the wax models of famous murderers of the past and celebrated heroes of the present, all life-size and shown in the act of introducing themselves to the spectator. Naturally enough, then, in a little room upstairs the drama quickly bloomed. At first, as part of Scudder's, this place had been devoted to lectures on the more puzzling exhibits; and Barnum kept the covering name of Lecture Room to the end. He provided another eleborate mask. The *moral drama,* as he emphatically called it, was approached through an avenue of Biblical waxworks, or scenes in wax illustrating the miseries of intemperance. "We must fetch the public somehow. Cum the moral on 'em strong. If it's a temperance community tell 'em I sined the pledge fifteen minutes after I'se born," said Artemus Ward afterward, drawing his episode, it seems, from the career of Barnum himself. Actually, in the midst of these presentations Barnum did sign a total abstinence pledge, in 1847, shortly after the meeting of the first world's temperance congress in London; the movement had lately received an immense impetus from the lectures of Gough. And in Philadelphia, where he had acquired Peale's Museum, and where the temperance harvest was ripe, Barnum not only displayed the pledge in the box-office, where he said thousands signed it, but brought forth both temperance waxworks and a temperance drama. But in New York, where reform sentiment was less pronounced, he offered Biblical drama, including scenes from the life of the early Christians.

Deftly and casually, along with these offerings appeared one of the early high examples of the ten-twenty-thirty shows, which were not to exist in their entire extravagance for another generation. On holidays there were continuous performances; Artemus Ward said that Barnum's actors could be seen going to the Museum as early as seven o'clock with their tin dinner pails; and their number included many who later appeared on a broader stage, like Sothern, who took comedy parts at Barnum's in the early fifties, having failed to please Boston with tragedy. Under the large enveloping domino were presented imitations of some of the more celebrated actors and actresses then in New York: Macready, Forrest, the elder Booth, Kean, and Fanny Kemble. Here, in fact, was the very substance of the feared and hated theater. This perhaps was to underscore Barnum's joke, but it blared forth in any case with incredible resonance. He now offered such opulent productions as *Love, or the Countess and the Serf,* which little Henry and William James witnessed, with other plays of the same order, when they were permitted to spend their Saturday afternoons at the Museum. In this production appeared Miss Emily Mestayer, said Henry James long afterward, "large, red in the face, coifed in a tangle of small, fine, damp-looking curls and clad in a light blue garment edged with swansdown, shouting at the top of her voice that a 'pur-s-se of gold' would be the fair guerdon of the minion who should start on the spot to do her bidding at some desperate crisis which I now forget. . . . I forget everybody but Miss Mestayer. . . . She had a hooked nose, a great play of nostril, a vast protuberance of bosom, and always the crop of close, moist ringlets. . . . She had a rusty, rasping, heaving and tossing authority of which the bitterness is still in my ears."

In a superabundant measure Miss Mestayer seemed to possess precisely those brave seductions which made the theater an abomination. The little Jameses were enchanted; doubtless other young people enjoyed a similar wedge of dubious pleasure. The little Jameses, indeed, were restrained by no narrow axioms; the only irony which hemmed them round lay in the fact that the elder Henry James politely and exquisitely detested what he called "flagrant morality." Flagrant enough it was at Barnum's, the mere blazing word and the adroit admixture covering the uproarious fact. Simple as the fraud was, Barnum's mere insistence turned the trick. The drama was still shunned by the great respectable public; the ministry still denounced it with entire regularity. Henry Ward Beecher, who had lately come to Brooklyn, avoided the theater to the end of his life though it offered much that fitted his taste and temperament, saying that attendance would involve him in endless explanations. Yet Beecher commended Barnum's, and perhaps was present at some of the programs of the Lecture Room, for he certainly wandered through the maze of curiosities. In fact, the ministry fairly contended to praise the Museum; and Barnum himself looked almost clerical in his long black coat and tall black hat—the notorious "emblem of equality." His countenance was bland and unbetraying; but as the curious and gullible swarmed to the Lecture Room he collected their remarks as he collected other grotesque exhibits; he was vastly entertained by the rapid discursive explanations of a maiden lady from New England who announced her prejudice against all amusements, and asked when the services were to begin. Barnum called his audience the congregation; the number of his private jokes on the ministry multiplied. His sheaf of

Biblical quotations which played upon the word "pass"—"Thou shalt not pass"—was originally compiled as a neat and stabbing method of announcing to the clergy that henceforth, like other people, they would have to pay to enter his Museum.

His burlesque took on enormous proportions, and plumbed unsuspected depths. Perhaps more than any other single force or figure Barnum broke down the barriers which had long kept the American public from the theater; irresistibly his audience must have filtered into the unsanctioned playhouses. But if he opened a sluice, he also deepened a channel. Though his designation was a shell, and his drama itself a caricature, he magnified the notion that the play must teach a lesson. Barnum, the anti-Puritan, thus perpetuated the stringent influence. As if indeed he belonged to the concentrated opposition, he seemed bent upon diminishing all the arts, by ridicule, with a battering gusto. He burlesqued the dance, naming a monstrous orangoutang for the exquisite Fanny Elssler. As for his Music for the Million, "I took pains to select and maintain the poorest band I could find," he declared, "one whose discordant notes would drive the crowd into the Museum, out of earshot of my orchestra." In these years the romantic passion was abroad in forms both delicate and profound. A wish to explore other worlds, beyond the seas, beyond any earthly region, within strange or evil places of the human heart, was apparent even in crude and minor expression, and was flowering in the writings of Poe and Hawthorne and Melville. Clearly a wave of this absorption or its fainter ripples must have flowed through the Museum, in the absurd responses to the grotesque, and to the unlikely relics from far places so thickly crowded there. Even that loose impulse toward assemblage upon which Barnum so steadily drew may have contained the beginnings of an attitude which makes a plastic audience for all of the arts. Barnum turned the obscurer hopes of his time upside down, presented its finer pursuits with destructive grossness: the Museum was his palace and his temple, filled to the brim with contemporary wishes and frustrations. Triumph! not only over the ancient Puritan enemy but over a whole society: triumph was what he wanted. Other men lived with the public; Barnum vanquished the public. Something of an outcast, himself defeated or diminished at every turn in that long and halted progress out of Connecticut into the farther reaches of the mid-country, and back to the emporium of New York—he finally had become the great trickmaster. If once he had fancied the image of the procession and had tried to create it trailing through a barren land, now the procession passed him in review. It was Barnum who determined its pace and direction, its gestures and noises of astonishment; using his favorite arrangement of the match, he even played off one public against another, pitted one museum against another, quietly buying Peale's in New York, and offering in each of his two possessions burlesques of the other which kept the crowd racing to and fro. "You and I are like a pair of shears," his manager at Peale's said to Barnum. "We seem to cut each other, but we only cut what comes between."

When the match of the two museums had run its length Barnum announced the consolidation—two in one for the same price—and was able to drag a further multitude into his own flamboyant building. The public laughed at the device; they often laughed at his extravagant promises—after the event. "I should hope that a little clap-trap occasionally, in the way of transparencies, exaggerated pictures, and puffing advertisements, might find an offset in a wilderness of wonderful, instructive, and amusing realities," said Barnum in casual apology. "Indeed, I cannot doubt that the sort of clap-trap referred to is allowable, and that the public likes a little of it mixed up with the great realities which I provide." It was true: they seemed to like it. Somberly enough they wandered through his halls; foreign critics noticed the grave American countenance; perhaps in the American Museum this was another example of the impassive look of the pioneer in the face of danger—fearing —in search of what? But afterward they laughed, or joked about old Barnum. "There's Barnum! That's old Barnum!" He frequently overheard the whispered excitement. One man paid his admission, asked for Barnum, stared at the famous showman a moment, and threw down his ticket. "It's all right. I've got my money's worth," he exclaimed, and left the Museum. As they came and went, arriving at sunrise or before breakfast, looking at Barnum, looking at his preposterous conglomeration, who can say what they found? The imagination of the forties or the fifties, like that of youth, is difficult to recover; and Barnum's greatest exhibit, the public, left little trace of its conclusions. Perhaps if he was bent upon conquest, his spectators caught only his indestructible gusto; if the arts were destroyed before their eyes, they may have discovered the tangible good of a livelier existence. A public for whom violence was not far in the background, either from remembrance of the past or because of the perpetual advances of a rough pioneering, may have craved violence, may have found a rough liberation in those boisterous jolts which Barnum perpetually offered. Fifty years later Henry James declared that his afternoons at the Museum were "flushed with the very complexion of romance," and that in the "stuffed and dim little hall of audience" he "plucked somehow the very flower of the ideal." It may be that he found there among the trooping hundreds something of that inveterate and questing innocence which long seemed to him the essence of the American character.

FOUR •

"I myself relished a higher grade of amusement, and was a frequent attendant at the opera, first class concerts, lectures, and the like; but I worked for the million," said Barnum in later years. His labor for the million was not too severe. Against the background of his huge medley of exhibits he found time from the first to trace a few patterns that might have been created for sheer pleasure, like his fantasy with the midget Tom Thumb. Barnum's taste usually ran to magnitude, to excess: here was excess inverted, the extraordinary in diminution, exquisitely producing the favorite start of surprise. Barnum trained the child in monologues and dances, tricked him out in pretty costumes, and after a season at the Museum, hit upon the audacious notion of taking his tiny curiosity abroad. Though visitors of all tempers and temperaments had been interchanged between the old world and the new for half a century only a few foreign actors or singers or dancers had come to this country; and the notion of an American conquest of the old world in the realm of entertainment was unheard of. But hopefully enough, in 1844, Barnum started off with Tom Thumb, who was now widely proclaimed to be an American midget; and after the fewest obstacles, and a sufficient blaze of advertisement by a short exhibition in London, the two were established in a Grafton Street mansion, where notables came rolling up in carriages by the hundreds. Presently the Baroness Rothschild sent for the pair; and Barnum entered upon the thousand and one nights.

"We were received a half a dozen servants elegantly dressed in black coats and pantaloons, white vests and cravats, white kid gloves, and, in fact, wearing the *tout ensemble* of a gentleman. One old chap was dressed in livery—a heavy laced coat, breeches, a large, white powdered and curled wig, and everything else to match. The hall was brilliantly illuminated, and each side was graced with the most beautiful statuary. We were ushered up a broad flight of marble stairs, and our names announced at the door of the drawing-room by an elegantly dressed servant, who under other circumstances I might have supposed was a member of the noble family. As we entered the drawing-room, a glare of magnificence met my sight which it is impossible for me to describe. The Baroness was seated on a gorgeous couch covered with rich figured silk damask and several lords and ladies were seated in chairs elegantly carved and covered with gold, looking indeed like solid gold, except the bottoms, which were rich velvet. On each side of the mantelpiece were specimens of marble statuary—on the right of which stood glazed cabinets containing urns, vases, and a thousand other things of the most exquisite workmanship, made of gold, silver, diamonds, alabaster, pearl, etc. The center table, and several tables about the size and something like the shape of a pianoforte, all covered with gold, or made of ebony thickly inlaid with pearls of various hues, were loaded with *bijous* of every kind, surpassing in elegance anything I had ever dreamed of. The chairs at one end of the room were made of ebony, inlaid with pearl and gold, elegantly cushioned with damask. The walls were paneled and heavily gilt—the curtains and ornaments of the most costly kind. The immense chandeliers and candelabras exceeded all my powers of description. Here we spent about two hours. About twenty lords and ladies were present. On taking our leave, an elegant and well-filled purse was quietly slipped into my hand, and I felt that the golden shower was beginning to fall!"

Gold—gold—he saw the aureate metal everywhere, not only in moneybags but in royal appurtenances.

Through the impetus of a letter from Horace Greeley to Edward Everett, Barnum quickly found himself in the yellow drawing-room at Buckingham Palace, "a magnificent apartment, surpassing in splendor and gorgeousness anything of the kind I had ever seen. . . . It was hung with drapery of rich yellow satin damask, the couches, sofas, and chairs being covered with the same material. The vases, urns, and ornaments were all of modern patterns and the most exquisite workmanship. The room was paneled in gold, and the heavy cornices beautifully carved and gilt. The tables, pianos, etc., were mounted with gold, inlaid with pearl of various hues, and of the most elegant devices."

The young Queen Victoria—she was only twenty-five—received the tall showman and his tiny charge graciously, took Tom Thumb by the hand, introduced the little Princess Royal, and the smaller Prince of Wales, and at the end of the songs, dances and imitations, presented the midget with "an elegant and costly souvenir." A second audience was granted by the Queen, and a third. Queen Adelaide also requested a performance, at which the old Duke of Cambridge was present, and offered the sprightly little dwarf a pinch of snuff. "Dear little General," said the kind-hearted Queen, taking him in her lap, like a story-book queen, "I see you have got no watch. Will you permit me to present you with a watch and chain?" "I would like it very much," replied the General, his eyes glistening with joy as he spoke. "I will have them made expressly for you," responded the Queen Dowager; and she did. The Duke of Devonshire with quaint eighteenth century notions, gave him "an elegant little snuff-box mounted with turquoise," and there were many other "costly gifts from the nobility and gentry." For four months the midget (and Barnum) held levees in London at the Egyptian Hall. "I do not believe that a single nobleman in England failed to see Tom Thumb," said Barnum exultantly. In gilded triumph the two went to Paris, where equally royal scenes were enacted. "King Louis Philippe was minute in his inquiries about my country, and talked freely about his experiences when he wandered as an exile in America. He playfully alluded to the time when he earned his living as a tutor, and said he had roughed it generally and had even slept in Indian wigwams." At the end of two hours the King presented the little General with a large emerald brooch set with diamonds; and it was arranged that Tom Thumb's superb tiny carriage with four ponies and a powdered coachman and footman should appear at Longchamps in the midst of the avenue reserved for the court and the diplomatic corps. Paris was in a furor. Statuettes of *Tom Pouce* appeared in plaster and sugar and chocolate; the daily receipts at the exhibition hall were so heavy that Barnum was obliged to carry home bags of gold and silver at night.

Then began a posting tour through the provinces. Barnum, who less than half a dozen years before had made his precarious way through the rough American back-country, now traveled in a magnificent post chaise with a retinue. A large vehicle transported the General's four ponies and little carriage; another carried the "elegant little house and furniture set on the stage." There were outriders and postilions. From France they went to Belgium, and from Belgium back to England, where interest in the midget was by no means exhausted. They toured Scotland; and the little General learned the Scotch dialect and Scotch dances, and appeared in a kilt. The entire journey lasted three years, with Barnum making an occasional hasty trip to New York—as rapidly as he could go in a sailing-packet—and back again; and it included an effort to purchase Shakespeare's house and Mme. Tussaud's, and the positive acquisition of some Lancashire Bell-Ringers whom he promptly converted into Swiss, a Happy Family of unlikely birds and animals trained to dwell together in a single cage, and a myriad other new attractions for the Museum. But Barnum's richest gain was not these, nor the golden shower of which he perpetually talked, nor that contact with the nobility which he so deeply relished, but an idea—a dream of personal splendor.

After all, he had haunted palaces—why should he not possess one? The full bloom of the early American country house was not to begin for another dozen years or more; Barnum forecast it on a prodigious scale, creating an archetypal dwelling called "Iranistan," from which the myriad later jig-saw, cut-work, wooden cottages of the Hudson Valley and the Berkshires might have sprung. During his stay in England he had seen the Orientalized pavilion which George IV had built at Brighton; and in all his travels he found nothing which better suited his taste. He copied it, choosing for his sovereign residence the scene of his many battles—Connecticut; among its cities he decided upon Bridgeport, "because the town seemed destined to become the first in size and opulence," and he bought a sufficient tract of land overlooking the Sound. There the extravagant house—his homestead, he called it—arose, with serried balconies, wide wings, shining domes, spires, minarets, and a lacy fretwork wherever fretwork could be introduced, along the balconies, above the windows, at the cornices. Everything glittered; the edifice might have been washed with gold or silver; a huge fountain played outside; bronze deer appeared in clusters on the grounds; and beyond, lay the fair semblance of an English park. Within was the same luster and scale. Rooms already sufficiently large were magnified by paneled mirrors on every side; gilt and a gorgeous patterning shone on the walls, on the thick-piled carpets, on the paintings, the abundant statuary, the furniture. Was it the trickery of the mirrors which gave the sudden notion that Barnum's palace was another more glowing Museum? Or was it the wide walnut staircase which wound straight upward to the conservatory in the central dome, a goal not wholly different from the little roof-garden with a wilted palm or two which Barnum maintained on top of the Museum, and mentioned in later years with apology? The huge pavilion even contained a kind of glorified office, what an admirer called "the bijou apartment of the villa," or Mr. Barnum's private study, the most golden of all the rooms, the walls and ceilings of which were hung with the richest orange satin, and with furniture, rugs, and hangings luxuriously made to match. If the Museum boasted a pictorial saloon, Barnum also had one in his dwelling; at every turn were cabinets full of curios; instead of a few bedraggled Chinese men, he had a whole Chinese library whose walls were entirely covered by Chinese paintings in oil. Here and there the arts were glorified—as if he must inevitably range among them— by rich panels which represented Music, Painting, and Poetry, and by a large apartment set aside for music and dancing. And, when the palace was at last completed, over a thousand persons trooped in for the housewarming.

Here Barnum sat like a sultan with the somewhat somber Charity and his four children; or he roamed through the gorgeous upper stories to command the view. He declared that he meant to "withdraw from the whirlpool of excitement." A friend of Horace Greeley's, he now exalted the occupation of the farmer; he became a member of the Fairfield Agricultural Society, and began to buy Alderney cattle, Suffolk swine, and fine specimens of poultry. But even in the midst of these pastoral pursuits he was drawn by his native calling. Discovering that the attendance at the Fairfield county fair was falling off, he arranged to exhibit a live pickpocket who had been captured on the grounds, and had appropriate handbills printed and circulated. Indeed, within his dazzling tranquillity, Barnum grew restless. The Philadelphia Museum, like one in Baltimore, had proved a transient venture; and apparently the New York Museum moved by its own weight. Still young, hardly forty, with the conquest of Europe behind him, he looked about for new material upon which to exercise his talents, and found it in what he called "the Jenny Lind enterprise."

"Little did the public see the hand that indirectly pulled their heartstrings, preparatory to a relaxation of their purse-strings," he exultantly remarked. "I may as well state that although I relied prominently upon Jenny Lind's reputation as a great musical *artiste,* I also took largely into my estimate . . . her character for extraordinary benevolence and generosity. Without this peculiarity in her disposition, I never would have dared make the engagements which I did. . . ." Her charitable enterprises, indeed, were famous; she was known for her piety, and for her rigorous moral standards in the midst of a dubious European world of art; she had refused to sing in opera because opera—she reasoned—was only a glorified theater. She was an exquisite Puritan. With an accomplished talent Barnum shouted all these circumstances through the public prints. He used subtler means. Since Jenny Lind represented song, he surrounded her by lyrics, using the prime means of a prize competition, and then with this sufficient impetus a hundred other poems sprang into being.

> "Blest must their vocation be
> Who with tones of melody
> Charm the discord and the strife
> And the railroad rush of life,
> And with Orphean magic move
> Souls inert to life and love,
> But there's one that doth inherit
> Angel gifts and angel spirit—"

Thus sang Mrs. Sigourney, one of the veterans among the poetesses who were now commanding public attention. The chorus mounted; the fever spread; presently there were Jenny Lind gloves, handkerchiefs, veils, shawls, riding habits, robes, mantillas, chairs, sofas, beds, and pianos—all the paraphernalia of imitation once more. At a punctual moment tickets for the first concert were auctioned off, with Genin the hatter as the highest bidder; the sum which he paid, well over two hundred dollars, was considered fabulous; the tale ran like wild-fire through the country; and according to Eyre Crowe, Thackeray's friend and companion, an enormous hat-brim was suspended over Jenny Lind's private box at the concert at Castle Garden.

For the public, the hat, if it existed, would always have remained phantasmal. In white—she invariably wore white—Jenny Lind seemed indeed the exquisite embodiment of a feminine vision which had been floating into consciousness in this country for half a dozen years, and was to remain a regnant fashion for a dozen more. She was an epitome of innocence, she was willowy, she suggested tears. "Sweet, tearful Jenny!" exclaimed an admirer. Through green arbors she had walked when she landed in New York—by Barnum's contrivance; now, in the midst of arbors she sang; she looked a sublime country maiden, sharing the cool marvel of her voice without premeditation. Around her Barnum kept a prismatic radiance, in the rainbow lights which illuminated the great hall, in the colored wands carried by the ushers; and he maintained as well, in that first novel multitude, a stringent perfection of order. Small matter that her figure was not truly graceful, that her character was not pliant and sweet, but stubborn and dogmatic. Small matter that a few critics were unmoved by her voice. Perhaps its unbroken coolness was the quality which completed the airy vision; a chilly purity was essential in those fragile heroines who were already drifting into fiction in passionless serenity. Those persons whom Barnum called "the fashionables" remained aloof for a time, but they too were captivated. "It was with some difficulty that I prevented the fashionables from monopolizing her altogether, and thus, as I believed, sadly marring my interests by cutting her off from the warm sympathies which she had awakened among the masses." It was the masses to which he constantly appealed by every known device in his armory; and he drew them by the thousands in a long tour over the country. When "the campaign closed," as Barnum said, fortunes had been earned both for Jenny Lind and for himself: how large these were it remains impossible to tell, for with a not uncustomary recession of candor he gave Miss Lind's net returns and his own in gross. But there was no question as to the magnitude of his accomplishment. Though a few dancers had come from Europe—

Fanny Elssler foremost among them—Jenny Lind was the first of a long line of famous continental singers to conquer this continent. With that fascinated circling about the arts which Barnum seemed continually to maintain, he had broken down another prejudice, he had created the revolutionary notion that pleasure of the senses might be indulged without harm or danger and even with benefit. And since music was a luxury, by introducing that prim figure, he perhaps assisted in the birth of a new worldliness, and did so with his habitual skill at an opportune moment: at the brink of the ample fifties, when opulence was to have a riotous sway in a thousand new enjoyments which had long been denied.

If Barnum was aware of the effects of his tireless momentum he gave no sign except a single reference to the "most humanizing of all the arts." In all his voluminous commentary on Jenny Lind there is scarcely a line to suggest that he recognized her voice except as a means of making money; he spoke of her as "the greatest musical wonder in the world," as though she were an automatic singer and a museum exhibit. Indeed, during the two years consumed by his preparation for the concerts and the tour, he had become preoccupied with the plan of quite a different kind of circuit. In those months of leisure at his palace in Bridgeport he had had time for reflection; he may have gone back to his years of drudging failure with a tiny caravan in the West. Certainly the scheme of a new and monster circus might have been devised expressly to blot out the old memory of failure. Chartering a ship, he sent agents to Ceylon to procure at least a dozen living elephants and a herd of other wild animals; a crew of one hundred and sixty natives plunged into the jungle at his remote bidding; presently his elephants were parading up and down Broadway harnessed to chariots; and the circus was sent on tour, not yet acknowledged as a circus, however, but sonorously proclaimed as Barnum's Great Asiatic Caravan, Museum, and Menagerie. Whether he failed to supervise its progress closely, or whether the time was not yet ripe for circuses, he dropped the project at the end of four years, but insisted that it had yielded another fortune. As a symbol and a prophecy, he kept a single elephant on view near Bridgeport, with a keeper in an Oriental costume, on a tract of ground near the railroad to New York.

The elephant advertised the Museum; yet Barnum seemed to have forgotten that rich source of fortune; his efforts there had grown mechanical. He introduced new features, it is true; when *Uncle Tom's Cabin* made its momentous appearance, he appropriated the book, as did many others, and turned it into a play for his Lecture Room without compensation to Mrs. Stowe. But these were minor matters; again he was seeking an absorbing new scheme. With a few others he engaged in the enterprise of creating another Crystal Palace in New York, modeled after the great shell created by Prince Albert: but the project failed. He promoted the manufacture of a new fire annihilator, became part owner of a steamship, invested in a copper mine at Litchfield, became president of a Bridgeport bank, and launched a weekly paper called the *Illustrated News* with Rufus Griswold as the editor, and young Charles Godfrey Leland as an assistant, whose gypsy days were far in the future, and who had not yet published *Hans Breitmann's Ballads.* In the cramped quarters of their office Barnum spent hours, as though fascinated by the making of copy; he submitted jokes, and was enormously pleased with them. "I think I see him now, coming smiling in like a harvest moon, big with some new joke," said Leland long afterward, and recorded one of the few genial judgments on Barnum which remain from his contemporaries. He insisted that Barnum was "a brother of the same band" as Lincoln, expressing "vast problems, financial, intellectual, or natural, by the brief arithmetic of the joke. To engineer some grotesque and startling paradox into tremendous notoriety, to make something *immensely* puzzling with a stupendous *sell* as a postscript, was more of a motive with him than even the main chance," said Leland, and declared that of all the businessmen whom he met in those days Barnum was the freest from guile. Leland himself was a master of uproarious stories; the two apparently listened to each other's tales like children.

"Lewd did I live & evil did I dwel"—

Such simple inversions seemed to give Barnum prodigious pleasure. But for some reason a niggardly policy prevailed on the paper in the matter of money; and the *Illustrated News* hardly made an impression among the flourishing new journals in New York. Presently it was sold to another magazine. Barnum still kept a literary strain; he interviewed Thackeray, and afterward insisted that Thackeray often consulted him as to his American tour. Perhaps as result of his association with Jenny Lind he now moved in circles which might earlier have been closed to him. The Cary sisters had recently come to New York, and had established their cheerful *salon;* with Greeley, Leland, Griswold, Whittier, Mrs. Stanton, and many other writers and reformers, Barnum appeared there, and was cordially welcomed. In these years he too entered literature, and brought forth his autobiography. Leland said that Barnum asked him to write the book, and that he declined; he added that Griswold probably performed the task.

Rufus Wilmot Griswold, the transient friend of Horace Greeley and the lasting enemy of Poe, may well have written Barnum's first autobiography. He was an editor by vocation; he had always done an immense bulk of unacknowledged hack work; in these years, the few before his death, he was in the thick of financial difficulties; and not least, Griswold had a liking for the extravagant and bizarre which found little outlet in his usual occupations. Indeed, most if not all of Barnum's books seem to have been written by humble servitors; it was his pleasure, perhaps, to command a literary style like any other exhibit. A little pamphlet containing a New Year's address, published in 1851, was written by a newspaperman; his stories for children were composed by his press-agent. To discuss his many progenitors in *Humbugs of the World,* and to let the reader decide in what manner he had surpassed them—this project, with the liberal lacing of anecdotes, surely belonged to Barnum himself; but it is incredible that he should have assembled the closely packed information on Cornelius Agrippa, Cagliostro, Riza Bey, Joanna Southcott, and a dozen others, or that he should have offered allusions to Virgil, Erasmus, Gulliver, Peter Wilkins, and Dr. Faustus, even though he had a considerable aptitude for appropriating picturesque information.

No doubt the schemes for all his books sprang from Barnum's own fertile fancy. His broad, thick-fingered hand must have shaped their substance. Surely he talked—talked by the hour to his hired scribes: the accent of speech breaks through the many styles. In his first autobiography, certainly, his own high voice was sharply lifted. If they read it, the Cary sisters must have considered the book an odd production, though Phoebe, who was witty, may have liked the jokes, and Alice, who was religious, may have accepted at their face value Barnum's frequent assertions that religion had always been one of his main preoccupations. What the little company which frequently met at the Carys' thought of Joice Heth or the Feejee Mermaid might make a social document of superlative value, or their commentary on Barnum's unvarying insistence that his main purpose had been to make money. "My prime object has been to put money into my purse." In a dozen forms he fairly shouted the statement. But at the end, perhaps under the influence of the reformers, perhaps because he received the suggestion that his blatant insistence needed amelioration, at the end he discussed the grave American temperament.

"The great defect of our American civilization is a severe and drudging practicalness," he declared. "A practicalness which is not commendable, because it loses sight of the true aims of life, and concentrates itself upon dry and technical ideas of duty, and upon a sordid love of acquisition—leaving entirely out of view all those needful and proper relaxations and enjoyments which are interwoven through even the most humble conditions in other countries. . . .The consequence is, that with the most universal diffusion of the means of happiness ever known among any people, we are unhappy. . . . As a business man, undoubtedly, my prime object has been to put money in my purse. I succeeded beyond my most sanguine expectations, and am satisfied. But what I have here said, will prepare the reader for what I conceive to be a just and altogether reasonable claim, that I have been a public benefactor, to an extent seldom paralleled in the histories of professed and professional philanthropists. . . ."

FIVE • *This peroration had the sound of benediction or farewell.* In the bright parlors of the Cary sisters Barnum had found a happy goal; untethered or outcast for years, he now belonged to a society. He was pleased, he was immensely reverential: one can see him bending and smiling amid the sparkling Bohemian glass and the carved rosewood. And these were Universalist circles in the main: not only the Cary sisters but Greeley had accepted that broad and hopeful faith. His lines could scarcely have fallen in more agreeable places.

There was no doubt of his responsive gesture: but Barnum was making it with a slight sweep of his left hand; his real preoccupations ran far beyond the delights of literary conversation in the *salon* of two maiden ladies. He wanted more than a circle: he had conceived the idea of possessing a city, and had set out to create one east of Bridgeport, on a plateau which Timothy Dwight—whom he quoted—had long before called "a cheerful and elegant piece of ground." Securing more than two hundred acres, he laid out a park, lined the prospective streets with trees, had two bridges built across the river at a large cost, and began to sell alternate lots to workmen. A coach factory was built and leased to a company of coach makers; and Barnum moved a small clock factory from Litchfield to East Bridgeport, where business was begun under the style of Terry and Barnum. Clocks! Barnum could hardly have hit upon an industry more indigenous to Connecticut. Clocks had been peddled and exchanged in his early days in a country store; wooden clocks were a staple of the peddlers whose path he had crossed in the West and South. Chauncey Jerome, with whom Barnum presently became associated, admitted that wooden clocks were often classed with wooden nutmegs and wooden cucumber seeds. But through his small factory

Barnum had inherited the most honored name in the Connecticut clock industry and had joined it to his own; soon he proposed to magnify his project by an alliance with the Jerome Clock Company of New Haven. Jerome was also one of the early makers of wooden clocks; he had peddled them as a youth; he had contrived a bronze looking-glass clock which was six inches taller than Terry's clock, could be made for a dollar less and could sell for a dollar more. Later, with an eye upon the foreign trade, he had invented the one day brass clock: wooden clocks could not be transported overseas. In the middle fifties Jerome was still one of the best-known names in the clock industry.

The tale of Barnum's alliance with Chauncey Jerome is mixed; and the outcome remains obscure: but at least his entry into the mystery of clock-making proved disastrous. Jerome declared that in the end he was swindled by the huge failure which followed; and it was true that as an old man he was obliged to begin life again without a penny. Barnum said that the first advances for a merger of the two companies came from Jerome, and that he was tempted to advance the large sum required, something over a hundred thousand dollars, because of his desire to promote the new city of East Bridgeport: the Jerome Company was to be moved there. Perhaps beneath all these transactions ran confusion: Barnum, who could on occasion plan precisely, lost his head. With his lust for public conquest he may have had in dazzling view not so much a profitable commercial speculation as a dominating replica of an ancient situation. Long before he had fought his native battles amid a medley of clocks; perhaps combs or hats would have been more exact materials for a later triumph: but here at least was a part of the early conglomerate—the substance of a native industry. With his own clock factory in full blast in his own village he would repeat his youth and achieve a perfect ascendancy.

Some such fevered purpose must have run through Barnum's mind; a positive obsession must have compelled him, or he could hardly have taken the wildly incautious steps which followed. He plunged into the merger of the two companies with only the slightest knowledge of the financial condition of the Jerome Company; he was completely unaware of an outstanding debt that far exceeded the amount which he had promised to lend. At the end of three months the agent of the company requested twenty-five thousand dollars more. This Barnum declined to furnish except in exchange for canceled notes of his original loan. The canceled notes were shown him, he said; but why these should have been in the hands of the company's agent at cancellation rather than his own is not clear. In any case he renewed them; the uncertain procedure was frequently repeated, "till finally my confidence in the company became so established that I did not ask to see the notes that had been taken up, but furnished new accommodation paper as it was called for." He declared that he not only furnished the new notes without assurance that the old ones were canceled, but wrote them without dates, allowing the agents of the Jerome Company to fill these in; and he seems to have been totally unconcerned with a financial situation which could interminably require his large original endorsement. At last a rumor reached him that the banks had grown doubtful of his paper. Then came the revelation that he had endorsed to the amount of half a million dollars for the Jerome Company; and he failed in 1856. Apparently a huge burden of debts had been adroitly transferred from the company to Barnum; and the clock company had not been moved to Bridgeport.

Barnum's subsequent strategy is far from clear. He declared that he found means to pay off every personal claim against him, and then failed: but the fact remains that even after the failure he still kept "Iranistan," and though the tract of land for his city of East Bridgeport was put up at auction, he found means for its re-purchase. The building of the American Museum stood in his wife's name; and it was announced that the collection had been sold a year before to one of Barnum's agents. If a valid transfer had been made and Barnum was no longer in control of the Museum, he would have had in train no other enterprises except those of the clock company and the promotion of East Bridgeport. His lapse in shrewdness thus became colossal, if not all but incredible. Indeed, a question remains whether with timely dexterity he had not put the Museum out of legal reach. He was reviled; he was praised; the press rang with his failure. Benefits were offered him, by Tom Thumb, by Cornelius Vanderbilt; he went through a long and teasing process of examination and cross-examination as to his assets. At length he found himself installed for the summer with his family in a farmhouse at West Hampton on Long Island. The scene must have appeared to him almost unbearably quiet; the upper end of Long Island had changed but little since the years that Lyman Beecher had spent there. But Barnum's familiar genius followed him even to that sequestered place. Strolling along the beach one morning, he discovered a young black whale that had been washed ashore. He sent it to the Museum, where it was placed on exhibition in a refrigerator for several days, and yielded sufficient returns to pay his expenses and those of his family for the entire summer.

If Barnum had scanned the American horizon he might have seen a phantom whale across the sky like a sign of the zodiac. A few years earlier that symbol of a monstrous warring universe had silently slipped into a lasting place through the epic of *Moby Dick*. With the turn of the decade, in truth, sheer size—very like a whale—had captured the American imagination. Like living emblems Barnum's own train of elephants had marched over the land in a series of long processions. In a dream of magnitude a drove of camels had been sent across the desert to San Francisco as pathfinders for a new and spacious travel. In poetry, like incantations, the first rolling numbers of *Leaves of Grass* were now heard, mounting and accumulating. On all sides, in the rush of oratory, in the growing clash of great regional forces the same huge blast was ascending. Did Barnum hear it? Did he observe the gigantic tokens— of size, of inflation?

Whether or not he gazed in clairvoyant revery upon his small black whale—which may after all have been a porpoise—a signal change came over Barnum's intention. His first movement was astute; it was clear that whatever he earned would now promptly be swallowed up by the clock debts. He went abroad, lectured on *The Art of Money-Getting* in England, exhibited Tom Thumb and little Cordelia Howard on the continent—though his connection as manager was kept secret because of the debts—spent two years, and collected an enormous new stock of attractions for the Museum. In the meantime his agents had gradually been purchasing the clock notes at a discount. Nearly free of debt he returned from Europe and re-purchased the Museum. Blazing posters announced to the city, "Barnum himself again." Decorating the entire building with new flags, banners, and transparencies as for a holiday, he took the stage and received, as he said, an ovation which surpassed anything which he had ever witnessed in a public career of quarter of a century. And strangely enough, the Museum was hardly launched under his own management when he learned that a white whale had been captured at the mouth of the St. Lawrence. He promptly went to the little port, determined to secure two living white whales for the Museum. The attempt was preposterous, the result a miracle. Who had captured living whales and transshipped them? All that was necessary, after the whales were secured, was to place them in a box lined with sea-weed and partially filled with salt water, with an attendant at hand to keep their mouths and blow-holes moist. Barnum had arranged to have the progress of the car telegraphed from one station to the next, "creating a tremendous advertisement seven hundred miles long." Despatches as to the progress of the whales on their long journey were bulletined in front of the Museum every hour; the newspapers burst forth into dithy-rambic advertisements, with the assurance that Barnum had built a small ocean in the Museum, and had filled it from the briny deep, where

"THE TWO LIVING WHALES
THE TWO LIVING WHALES

measuring respectively fifteen and twenty feet in length, may be seen in their native element." The whales died, for despite the advertisement they were placed in fresh water: but Barnum had salt water piped from the bay, paid a thousand dollars to the aldermanic ring for the privilege, built a glass tank twenty-four feet square, and procured another pair of whales. Then came a hippopotamus, "the Sweating Behemoth of the Scriptures," living sharks, porpoises, sea horses, and tropical fish.

Barnum was back; and the great noise which was to last for thirty years—with how many long reverberations?—had begun. Gone were the earlier days of a sprightly fantasy and a precipitous humor. Gone were the sudden adventures into unknown regions, half a step ahead of the public enthusiasm. With a resistless sweep Barnum inaugurated a dozen clamorous public enterprises as a prelude or an accompaniment for an enormous intention. He entered the Connecticut legislature at the end of the war, fought the railroads in their endeavor to raise commuters' rates in Connecticut, and won opportunely, with the onset of the Erie scandal. He was on the popular side; and truly enough he believed in cheap rates, in expansion, in the million, and in East Bridgeport; diminished fares were an advantage for surburban residents. In the end he declared that he made a greater fortune out of his speculation in East Bridgeport than he had lost in the clock enterprise. His city grew by leaps and bounds, grew in the safe, precise pattern of the New England village, with small trim white houses with green blinds, under a regimen that would have delighted Lyman Beecher himself. He insisted that purchasers should sign and keep the temperance pledge, and forego the use of tobacco. He advertised the Puritan program; with increasing frequency and ardor he mounted the lecture platform in the temperance cause. There was an oppostition, to be sure; a young man named John Fiske issued a manifesto in 1868 entitled *Tobacco and Alcohol: The Coming Man* WILL *Smoke; The Coming Man* WILL *Drink*. But Barnum was greeted by immense audiences which apparently accepted his exhortations, or listened with equal zest to his *Art of Money-Getting*, the lecture with which he had addressed England after his failure.

Even in the realm of his personal life Barnum tried to prune his old exuberance. "Iranistan" had burned after the clock failure; his next home, "Lindencroft," was a smaller, conventional residence "with no attempt at ostentation," as he explicitly said. "Elegance, pure and simple, predominated and permeated everywhere." Then he declared that Mrs. Barnum, whose health was failing, could not manage even the less pretentious establishment; he built another residence in Bridgeport, "Waldemere," which he said was still smaller. Yet after all Barnum could not forego size. An English newspaperman observed that the new dwelling presented a front of one hundred and sixty feet. "On entering, one is pleasantly struck by the spaciousness of the hall and rooms. One can breathe as freely inside as out. Nothing is small or contracted." The house appears, indeed, to have been even larger than "Lindencroft," with more verandas, wings, and bay-windows than the earlier residence; it was described as "a curious but pleasant *mélange* of Gothic, Italian and French architecture and decoration," and it was as crowded with strange curios as his first palace; but it never reached the preposterous splendor of "Iranistan." Barnum seemed possessed by a mania of housebuilding; a few years later he erected still another dwelling, "Marina." Was he seeking to conform to a style? To discover precisely the right accent in all that growing wilderness of expensive and elaborate establishments which now were rising everywhere about him? He insisted upon the simplicity of all these dwellings: but he could not be simple, and he could not be still. He purchased a mansion in New York; with a view to posterity he gave a park to Bridgeport; he was deeply engaged in the project of a cemetery. While he was addressing the legislature on his proposed railroad bill, a telegram was handed him which announced that the Museum was in flames. With that unruffled calm in the face of catastrophe which he probably first learned in the midst of the practical jokes of Bethel and Danbury, he betrayed not the slightest emotion and continued his speech. Within eight months he had assembled curiosities from all over the world, had purchased several large collections and hundreds of small ones, had gathered together his old companies of actors, actresses, and living curiosities, and inaugurated a new museum higher up on Broadway. Within a year and half this Museum also burned. "During my whole life," he remarked, "I had been so much accustomed to operations of magnitude for or against my interests, that large losses or gains were not likely to disturb my equanimity." He found the ice-coated ruins by moonlight "sublime," and this time complacently announced that he would retire. But as he said afterward, "Every one knows the history of the Emperor Charles the Fifth. His ambition gratified to satiety in the conquest of kingdoms, and the firm

establishment of empire, he craved rest. He abdicated his throne. . . .
I want a royal illustration; and the history of Charles the Fifth, in particular in advocating rest, I find very pertinent to my own experience.
I took a formal, and as I then supposed, a last adieu of my readers on
my fifty-ninth birthday. I was, as I flattered myself, through with travel,
with adventure, and with business. . . ."

He had only begun. In 1871 he had created his first mammoth circus,
a Museum, Menagerie, Caravan, Hippodrome, and Circus in one—the
name came out at last—whose tents covered three acres of ground, and
could be filled by ten thousand spectators, and required five hundred
men and battalions of horses to transport it through the country. He
horrified his assistants by his extravagance. "Undaunted, I still expended
thousands of dollars, and ship after ship brought me rare and valuable
animals and works of art. . . . As no giraffe had ever lived two years in
America, all other managers had given up any attempt to import them,
but this only made me more determined to always have one on hand
at any cost." For a few years he was obsessed by the towering absurd
image of the giraffe. Indeed, Barnum, who cared nothing for animals,
who never mentioned with pleasure even a dog or a horse, who showed
not a quaver of interest when the many living creatures in his museum
had burned, now added hundreds from all parts of the globe. He sent
to Alaska to procure sea-lions and barking seals, and rejoiced that they
devoured from sixty to a hundred pounds of fresh fish daily. His Italian
goat had been taught to ride on horseback, leap through hoops and over
banners, alighting on his feet on the back of a horse while going at full
speed. He procured four wild Fiji cannibals, whom he declared to have
been ransomed at great cost from a royal enemy—surely royal!—who
was about to eat them. For the winter display he opened a Hippothea-
tron. Four weeks later the building burned; only two elephants and a
camel were rescued. Barnum, who was in New Orleans, telegraphed
for the purchase of new attractions for a larger circus, and went on eating his breakfast. By spring he had sent out on the road a circus which
required double the tent space of the earlier one. He went to Europe,
"to rest my over-worked brain, and see what could be picked up to in-
struct and edify my amusement patrons." He came back to establish a
Roman Hippodrome, Zoölogical Institute, Aquarium, and Museum, and
to inaugurate his "Congress of Nations, in a grand procession of gilded
chariots and triumphal cars, conveying Kings, Queens, Emperors, and
other potentates of the civilized world, costumed with historical cor-
rectness, royally surrounded, and accompanied and followed by their
respective courts and splendid retinues. . . . Never since the days of the

Caesars has there been so grand and so interesting a public spectacle."
He tried to purchase the right to exhibit Brigham Young.

In those black and bitter years which followed the war when men
struggled for wealth and power, Barnum wanted both, attained both,
and gave to his monstrous creation a fabulous air. Other men gambled
with railroads, or caught a local government in a huge net, or piled
fortunes into the millions. Barnum proved his magnitude by constantly
dragging a huge and orderly mass of living creatures—men, women,
birds, beasts, creatures of the wild and of the deep, in a triumphant procession round and round over the land with himself at the head. His
friend Horace Greeley went down to tragedy. Barnum was numbered
among his supporters; but otherwise he gave no sign. The Cary sisters
died. Some years earlier rooms at "Waldemere" had been named for
them, but did Barnum have a private or personal feeling? His life was
in the circus. He was forever there; he was part of the show, and knew
it. He made his own engagements even for performers in his side-shows,
supervised such details as the printing of handbills and the new editions
of his autobiographies, which now were sold at the gates; he employed
his own musicians. With that extreme narrowing of judgment which
often accompanies the achievement of enormous projects he grew sharply
penurious in small matters, wrote out passes on the cheapest kind of
paper, cut and saved at every tiny corner—and remained tirelessly extravagant in his large expenditures. Loss of life in his enormous companies hardly touched him; occasionally, in his old manner, he played
drastic practical jokes; but these were the merest flicker on the face of
his dream. Magnitude was piled on magnitude, conquest upon conquest.
As a minor witticism he succeeded in drawing the king of the Sandwich
Islands to his Hippodrome in New York, and then, by an adroit persuasion, drove him round the arena in a barouche while the crowd
cheered. Barnum introduced the firing of Zazel from a cannon; he contrived Roman games and chariot races. Instead of a single midget he
now had a company of midgets, with Tom Thumb still regnant, and
with his marriage at Grace Church to the tiny Lavinia Warren staged
as a huge public notice of Barnum's monster troupe. He blew a prodigious blast for the centennial year. By 1878 he was using the title the
Greatest Show on Earth for the first time; the consummation of the idea
was reached two years later by his union with Sanger's Great London
Circus, which had been purchased by Cooper, Bailey, and Hutchinson.
Rivalry had been intense, and reached its climax over the matter of a
baby elephant, born in the captivity of the opposite camp. Barnum
found his own failure to possess a baby elephant unendurable: and in

1880, after suitable negotiations, he obtained the creature, and joined the two great circuses. He secured Jumbo from the Royal Zoölogical Gardens in London, and stirred two nations to an abysmal excitement by the transaction. Jumbo—Jumbo: the resonant sound and the vast image were battered back and forth across the sea. A cartoon of Nast's showed Barnum and Jumbo cheek to cheek. Then Barnum wanted a white elephant, and obtained one, "whiter than King Theebaud's." The elephant had supplanted the whale; for after all elephants could comfortably travel overland, and so could camels, and giraffes, with the train of lesser animals.

Across the sea, over the land, around the world he went either by proxy or in person. The world was now a constant image in his speech. He tossed off a lecture on *The World and How to Live in It,* made new encirclements of the West, purchased a cattle ranch in Colorado, again traveled to the rim of the continent, collected sea-lions, returned for a reminiscent buffalo hunt on the plains of Kansas, and again sent out expeditions to the Orient, launching another and still larger circus, scattering handbills, lithographs, pictures of himself, and copies of his autobiography over the country by the ton. His music was now furnished by four brass bands, a calliope, chimes of bells, a steam organ, a squad of Scotch bagpipers, and a company of negro jubilee singers. Louder and louder rose his clangorous vociferation. Out of sheer noise—power! In that immense concourse, triumph—the triumph which tramples and obscures, tosses all things into abstractions of size and space.

There were brief interludes in this accumulated procession. Barnum became ill, then at length recovered and was welcomed back to New York by a vast torch-light parade which he said was witnessed by over half a million people, and pronounced the most brilliant display ever seen in America. He brought reporters in drawing-room cars from all the leading cities round about for the spectacle, lodged them at hotels, and sent them home the next day. As a minor conquest he at last went back to Bethel, upon invitation, discoursed on the blue laws, and presented the village with a fountain whose Triton could suggest what one chose—the whale, the hippopotamus, or even Barnum himself rising from the elements. Official recognition of his contributions to science was made by the Smithsonian Institution, whose directors asked for a life-mask from which to mold a bust; and Barnum helped to found a college, where at last the stuffed semblance of Jumbo was enshrined.

These, in the main, were minor excursions. By the union of the Barnum and Bailey companies the three-ring circus was at hand: with Calliope, the muse of eloquence and heroic poetry, to herald the epos with shrill and blasting whistles, with the inevitable huge creatures of the wild which made man seem small, with the caprioles of trick horses, the procession of clowns, tumblers, aërial acrobats, a gaudy pilgrim's progress. In the triple ring the single actor with his tiny skill was lost; everything must be bold, whirling, changing: no brilliancy of lights can quite illuminate that monstrous top: flying color, the inevitable magenta and sky blue and silver stars, the grin of clowns and the swift turn of the acts, revolve and pass, projected against a void. Here at last was wonder, though Barnum never spoke of it—beauty amid that showy aggregation, an exquisite precision which seemed aërial, and informed the whole long march, and even the faint high fretwork overhead. A final gayety Barnum never saw or celebrated, though this was his creation. He still dragged the whole huge affair at his heels, took it to London, was observed by celebrities, and returned for final triumphs in his own country. In 1877, when the Greatest Show was yet to come, Barnum calculated his audiences as aggregating over eighty million persons. He had conquered an empire; and before the end he doubled it. Over and over his huge displays drew that friend—or enemy—to whom he had never capitulated, the public. Towns, cities, counties, the entire country poured into his huge tents. In his later years he heard that earnest if tepid satire on American tendencies called *Numbers,* and gave the hospitality of a night in Bridgeport to its author. Afterwards Arnold mentioned Barnum's remark that he meant to belong to the remnant; but Barnum perhaps knew as well as another that he had swallowed the remnant. Even in his own long, cumulative self-portrait scarcely a small and individualized quality appears. In that spreading design he comes forth with magnitude, energy, and an air of leisure: with all his nimbleness, which was often like that of a trapeze performer, apparently Barnum never hurried. These traits belong to the public: the crowd is also a reservoir of force, is large and slow-moving. With the bland and unbetraying smile which he seems to have kept to the end—a public smile—Barnum died in 1891, full of years, power, and unwitting romance. Fittingly enough, he has become a myth. His history grows into fable, mixed with the caprices of the time—not the great fable, perhaps, but a portion of what might be called the American legend.

Epilogue

TRAVELING *over the country on their large private* errands, seeking their personal goals, the popular spokesmen of the mid-century often seemed like the public which they addressed—young, defiant, noisy, unappeased: yet their rising voices mingled with more durable tones; they walked no immense distance from more splendid figures; they sometimes forecast emotions which greater men might use. Among many characters, great and small —and who perhaps was small, and who was great?—alliances existed, as if these groups had joined in purposes beyond their own.

Often enough their linked utterances were blown full of bombast. At the height of the mid-century and thereafter Barnum dedicated his autobiography to the "Universal Yankee Nation, of which I am proud to be one." The phrase had long been current; Emerson had used it in a mild query twenty years before. Boldly, easily, over many suasions and appeals was thrown the mask of the universal. "No dainty dolce affetuoso I," cried Whitman,

> "Bearded, sun-burnt, gray-neck'd, forbidding, I have arrived,
> To be wrestled with as I pass for the solid prizes of the
>   universe . . ."

In that long era the universe often seemed an American possession, its prizes within easy reach, with liberty for the race and for the individual as the simplest to grasp and hold. Even the sustained poetry and prophecy of the time offered only the framework of thought or a bold cartoon. As the task of possessing the continent grew monstrous and chaotic, who offered imperishable counsel? Not Emerson, or Whitman. No enduring reply was sounded as a crescendo of hatred arose beneath that great excess of faith. No organon appeared, or stable guidance. Even Lincoln was hesitant, gradually trying issues in company with the public mind. The far-flung utterances of that fateful period came forth mixed, uncertain, and often penetrated by a raw and gusty humor.

With a social equilibrium which was always changing, with a public always on the move, passing out of earshot, any consistent body of thought must have come slowly into existence, any enunciation must at times have grown blaring or thin. Of all modes of expression bombast is perhaps the most difficult to understand, because it uses contemporary metaphor, and may spring from both terror and exhilaration, and from heroic enterprise. If ideas in this era were often hardly ideas at all but emotions become dangerously diffused, surely this was in large part because the profoundest of human instincts had been shattered, a substantial human support torn away. That age-long sense of social solidarity upon which so many tranquillities depend was gone—the impalpable fabric which is called a society. Back even to the remaining numbers of the older communities rolled the rugged, inhuman force of migration, through numberless personal ties, through the stirrings of fancy. Yet, in the midst of upheaval, an ancient endeavor was being repeated: the purpose to shape a social identity was perhaps the great instinctive purpose urgent through all this period, crowding other efforts aside, blinding its sponsors to many a subtle pitfall and to dangerous other forces—itself the deep preoccupation of the time. Surely the intention was manifest in the easy coalescence of crowds, in the flood of language which was poured forth—as if to create a common intercourse—and again in those swift emotional acceptances which seemed a national trait—and which must perhaps exist in some form as a basis for a fundamental social unity. Even that return to the classic which runs through so many aspects of American thought in earlier years comes to us as a form of the same desire: the remembrance of those small, enshrined civilizations of the past seemed to bring the omen of peace. The movement of the pioneer toward established modes remains as part of the irony of his position—when all things were to be made new!—and part of the promise as well, for the reminiscence of a tradition may sometimes enclose a passionate wish, as well as a passionate sense of failure.

Primitive indeed were these many efforts to find the semblance of unity, or its shell. Often enough these endeavors were turned to a struggle for power: if a civilization did not exist, or a society, the more intrepid spirits could in some manner possess a crowd or an empire. For a widespread efflorescence of the humane spirit failure was ordained in this long era. Not only stability was missing, but that horded experience, that easy familiarity with the land and with the people, that "quickened earth," which seem a necessity for a great concerted expression. The marvel was the continuity of a blind but many-sided intention, the ease with which this took idyllic forms, and the tenacity with which large hopes—or illusions—were maintained for more than two generations. If not a body of thought, a substantial emotion was developed with courage and in rebellion.

Lyman Beecher gave an opening signal, as in the act of celebrating the Puritan canon he sounded an insurgent cry, at a moment when the western horizon was brightly gilded. New—new—with Lyman Beecher out of Revelations Emerson might have said, "Behold, I make all things new," chanting that miracle of fresh vision which was the center of his philosophy and of his temperament. Emerson's doctrine of intuitive self-trust—a pioneer virtue made crystalline—was repeated in the broad and careless arc drawn by Henry Ward Beecher with his faith in the individual and his stress upon the life of instinct. Liberty—a new, unbounded emotional life—the greatness of man—the perfect and complete and happy individual—the new Eden: how the consciousness of these arose during this time, beating against the barriers of many restraints, crowding through in spite of diverse intentions! Then, after the dark chasm of the Civil War, suddenly that essential era lay in a bright and hazy distance. In our perspective, its battles seem like old legendary wars; even Whitman has become an alien figure; we appear a full century away from his tenderness, his ecstasy of faith in love and democracy, his sense of the country as religion. Magnitude seems the single positive legacy of that forgotten time: magnitude which is upon us in a thousand rapid guises, with multiplied roaring sounds, with the greatest speed, the greatest numbers, with an infinitely expanding universe.

From that younger era shall we receive a warning, or a hope, or a challenge? Or a tradition? In those glances of retrospect which have become our habit we sometimes seem to be hunting for a tradition. For all our detachment occasionally we appear to be viewing the past with nostalgia, like the citizens of the mid-century as they gazed upon the classical heritage. Perhaps we may learn that we are not an altogether different people from our young ancestors of the forties and fifties. Surely we find ourselves in a predicament not unlike that by which they were confronted: we too must make a world out of a wilderness. In this endeavor traditions would offer a foothold, no doubt: but traditions are often hard to discover, requiring a long and equable scrutiny; they are hard to build, consuming an expanse of time which may pass beyond a few generations. Perhaps we cannot declare with precision whether that ample middle period of our history was the last of a whirlwind, or whether we are now fulfilling its purposes after the prolonged confusion which followed the Civil War. Yet certain clear emblems remain out of the past, for times of hesitation. Magnitude, which to us often seems deadening and terrifying and meaningless, held something else for that smaller world—a hope and a promise, a token of new eternities, a sense of wonder, even among the blind and restless numbers hurrying so carelessly together, hastening with such infinite trouble into strange territories and toward baffling encounters. Considering the past, we may remember that sense of wonder, and regain the belief that magnitude can inhere in human intentions. Largeness belonged to the leading figures of that day—belonged to its popular spokesmen. In their pursuit of liberty, laughter, composure, or even power, they seemed to move toward a periphery which exceeded simple boundaries, as though their errands were in truth great errands of the human spirit.

A Note on Sources

BIBLIOGRAPHIES are sometimes offered as an avowal of labor, or a pledge of good faith. Yet most readers seem to give the courtesy of confidence to the variable clan of writers unless the boundaries of honesty are palpably transcended; and to end a book with a display of the machinery by which it has been assembled is to stress to toil which has gone into its making, not the pleasure. No formal list can truly represent a lively aggregation of sources, or suggest the luster with which these have been touched in moments of discovery. Nor, in the present instance, would a complete bibliography serve useful ends. To enumerate the printed words of Mrs. Stowe or Henry Ward Beecher or Horace Greeley or Barnum would be to fill pages with items which any student may find in almost any good library, or discover with a minimum of research. As it happens, the pamphlet writings of Lyman Beecher are more difficult to come upon, but even these can be found by comparatively simple exertions, while the large mass of periodical material and ephemeral publications which in one way or another bear upon the lives of all these characters can be unearthed, if not with ease, at least with only a moderate amount of skill and patience. Naturally as other men and women have come within the range of view their letters, memoirs, biographies, and autobiographies have been considered in turn, as well as many of their published writings; indeed, one of the delights of this task has been the number of such excursions. If these have often been willful and long, perhaps they have helped to stimulate conclusions as to the general stress and tone and color of the period.

None the less certain special debts remain. However divergent the point of view of these studies from that of others which have gone before, this book could hardly have existed without a group of earlier biographies and memoirs. The writer gratefully acknowledges the use of material drawn from *The Autobiography and Correspondence of*

Lyman Beecher, edited by Charles Beecher; *The Life and Letters of Harriet Beecher Stowe*, by Charles E. Stowe; *Harriet Beecher Stowe: The Story of her Life*, by Charles E. Stowe and Lyman Beecher Stowe; *Harriet Beecher Stowe*, by Annie Fields; *A Biography of Henry Ward Beecher*, by William C. Beecher and Samuel Scoville; and *The Life of Horace Greeley*, by James Parton. Each of these books has offered many contributions to the present volume. Another group has provided essential material which could hardly have been obtained from miscellaneous sources. The following studies have put the writer under heavy but most agreeable obligations: *The Great Revival in the West, 1795-1805*, by Catherine C. Cleveland; *A Documentary History of American Industrial Society*, edited by John R. Commons; *A History of the Woman's Rights Movement for Twenty Years*, by Paulina Wright Davis; *Student Life at Yale College Under the First President Dwight*, by Franklin B. Dexter; *The Puritan Age*, by G. E. Ellis; *Discussions in History and Theology*, by G. P. Fisher; *A Genetic History of the New England Theology*, by F. H. Foster; *The Development of Religious Liberty in Connecticut*, by M. Louise Greene; *Lincoln and Herndon*, by Joseph Fort Newton; *Connecticut in Transition, 1775-1818*, by Richard J. Purcell; *A History of Woman Suffrage*, by Elizabeth Cady Stanton and Susan B. Anthony; *Economic and Social History of New England*, by William B. Weeden. A minor personal triumph may perhaps be mentioned in the discovery of copies of Barnum's *Herald of Freedom* in the Library of the American Antiquarian Society, as in the Library of Congress, when the descent into oblivion of this interesting journal had been noted; and it is a duty to state that letters of Lyman Beecher in the possession of the Congregational Society in Boston have been drawn upon, as have letters of Horace Greeley in the Library of the New York Historical Society.

In the end one is tempted to add a list of books which have offered a large enjoyment beyond their immediate contributions. Some of these have already been mentioned; such a study as Dr. Newton's *Lincoln and Herndon* has not only recorded important circumstances in the career of Horace Greeley, but provides a new understanding of the character of Lincoln, and a substantial portrait of that generous and high-minded iconoclast, Theodore Parker. R. H. Gabriel's colorful *Evolution of Long Island* would belong in such a list, and Ridelia Brisbane's *Albert Brisbane, A Mental Biography*, Parke Godwin's *Popular Views of the Doctrines of Fourier*, Noah Webster's *Letters to a Young Gentleman on Commencing his Education*, and a singular little work entitled *Letters on the Origin and Progress of the New Haven Theology*, anonymously printed, but apparently composed by Dr. Bennet Tyler. This small volume might properly have found a place among the books which have offered material not to be discovered easily elsewhere; indeed, one might look far and wide before finding so racy a revelation of the human character in so small a compass. A compendious delight has been furnished by *Elizabeth Cady Stanton as Revealed in her Letters, Diary and Reminiscences,* edited by Theodore Stanton and Harriot Stanton Blatch. It may be reckless to include the *Autobiography and Correspondence of Lyman Beecher* at this point when other similar records must remain without further comment; but Lyman Beecher himself possessed the happy virtue of incaution. This rich compilation remains as one of the freshest and strongest of the many writings which have given an impetus to the making of this book. Doubtless it would be wisdom to declare no other preferences; yet one more personal record must be included in the growing list, which is likewise the mirror of an incautious mind, *The Literary Diary of Ezra Stiles;* and since the figure of its author appeared early in the present book, so let it close with this word of distant recognition, and the hope that the passion by which Dr. Stiles was animated has not been altogether absent from these pages.

Index

Bryant, William Cullen, 194, 195, 250, 264

Byron, Lady, 88-89, 94, 102-07

Byron, Lord, 19, 23, 68, 88, 89, 102-05, 108, 109, 119, 184

Bullard, Eunice. See under Beecher

Calhoun, John C., 132

Calvinism, Calvinists, 5, 11, 29, 30, 33, 49, 54, 59, 61, 69, 73, 87, 88, 91, 95, 115, 185, 200, 221, 278, 281; Old School, 32, 33, 47, 50, 53, 54, 55, 58, 60, 65, 116; New School, 32, 33, 50, 55, 56, 66

Carlyle, Thomas, 178, 213, 214

Carson, Kit, 225

Cary sisters, Alice and Phoebe, 147, 232, 233, 253, 257, 308-10, 317

Cass, Lewis, 223

Ceresco Community, 221

Channing, W. H., 206, 207, 214, 221

Chappaqua, 233, 234, 235, 242, 254, 255, 256, 258, 262, 265, 270, 272, 274

Cheney, Mary. See under Greeley

Child, Lydia Maria, 38

Civil War, 93, 99, 111, 136, 170, 175, 224

Claflin, Tennessee, 149

Clap, Thomas, 5, 6

Clarke, Bayard, 241

Clay, Henry, 132, 185, 190, 198, 208, 209, 215, 223, 228, 236; American System, 185, 227; Compromise of 1850, 236

Clay Tribune. See Tribune

Cleveland, Cecilia, 270-72, 275

Cleveland, Mrs. Esther (Horace Greeley's sister), 270, 272-75

Cleveland, Grover, 175, 176

Cleveland, Marguerite, 270, 271

Colfax, Schuyler, 223, 246, 258, 268, 269

Columbian Orator, 182, 183, 188, 198

Come-Outers, 200

Comstock, Anthony, 156, 157, 158

Congregational, Congregationalists, 15, 53, 55, 122, 160, 231

Cooper, James Fenimore, 198; Homeward Bound, 198; Home as Found, 200

Corinne: Influence on Harriet Beecher Stowe, 70-72, 86, 100; Margaret Fuller as the American Corinne, 215

Cosmo-Political Party, 152

Courier and Enquirer, New York, 195, 212, 219

Cranch, Christopher, 206

Crowe, Eyre, 306

Crystal Palace Exhibition, 228, 308

Curtis, George William, 230, 233, 253, 264

Daily Whig, 190, 191, 193

Dana, Charles A., 214, 230, 235, 241, 249, 261

Dartmouth College, 38, 71

D'Arusmont, Fanny Wright, 145

Davis, Jefferson, 250, 252

Davis, Paulina Wright, 149, 153, 154

De Frees, 209, 246

Democracy: Jacksonian, 24, 185, 189, 190, 191, 195, 196, 281; Jeffersonian, 8, 16, 21, 278; Democratic Party, 261

Dewey, Dr. Orville, 215, 218, 232

Dial, 201

Dickens, Charles, 85, 91

Dickinson, Anna, 144

Douglas, Stephen A., 242-45, 265

Dred, 86, 101

Dwight, Timothy, 9-12, 16, 18, 20, 21, 30, 33, 64, 95, 120, 181, 278, 310

Edgeworth, Maria, 18, 19

Edwards, Jonathan, 10, 25, 27, 33, 90, 102

Edwards, Pierrepont, 278

Eggleston, Edward, 144, 152, 257

Eliot, George, 90

Ellet, Elizabeth, 215

Elssler, Fanny, 119, 120, 299, 307

Emancipation Proclamation, 138, 249

Emerson, Ralph Waldo, 131, 200, 203, 206, 213, 216, 221, 320, 322

English, Dr. Thomas Dunn, 194

Erie Canal, 184

Erie Gamble, 141

Evans, George Henry, 211, 222

Evarts, W. M., 246

Evening Post, New York, 195

Marietta College, 57
Martineau, Harriet, 284
McElrath, Thomas, 197, 239
Meeker, Nathan C., 256, 258, 265
Melville, Herman, 299; *Moby Dick,* 313
Mercier, 250
Methodism, 8, 114
Mexican War, 225-26
Millerites, 200, 221
Moody, Dwight L., 173
Moore, Thomas, 104-05, 119
Moral Society. *See* Society for the Prevention of Vice and the Promotion of Good Morals
Mormons, Mormon Church, Book of Mormon, 146, 186, 203, 225
Mott, Lucretia, 144, 149, 154
Moulton, Francis, 159, 162-67, 169
Muggletonians, 200

Nast, Thomas, 264-66, 267, 269, 318
Nation, New York, 263
National Manual Labor Society, 43
National Reformers. *See* Workingmen's Party
New England Society, 25
New Lights, 50
New World, 193
New Yorker, 187, 188, 190, 193, 194, 195, 197
North American Phalanx, 203, 207, 221-22, 231-32
Noyes, John Humphrey, 48-49, 158

Oakes-Smith, Elizabeth, 147, 215
Oberlin College, 46-47, 58
Oneida Community, 158, 203
Osborn, Sellick, 16, 283
Osgood, Francis S., 215
Owen, Robert, 41, 51, 147-48, 232, 253

Paine, Thomas, 7
Parker, Theodore, 128, 131-32, 135, 141, 206, 244, 257
Parton, James, 232, 235
Peace Union Settlement, 203
Phillips, Wendell, 83, 106, 131, 135, 138, 141, 148, 263
Plan of Union, Congregational and

Presbyterian Churches, 15, 39, 55
Plymouth Church, Brooklyn, 122, 123, 128-30, 134, 135-37, 142, 161, 168, 169, 174, 175
Poe, Edgar Allan, 187-88, 203, 213, 215, 234, 287, 291, 294, 299, 309
Polk, James K., 209
Porter, Harriet. *See under* Beecher
Porter, Noah, 29-30, 32-33, 55
Prescott, Harriet. *See* Spofford
Presbyterian Church, Presbyterians, 15, 47-48, 56, 122, 281; of Cincinnati, 47; of East Hampton, 12; division into Old and New Schools, 55-56; General Assembly, 53, 55, 65; Home Mission Board, 114; Cincinnati Presbytery, 49-50, 52, 53; New York Presbytery, 48. *See also* Plan of Union
Princeton College, 51, 52
Puritan, Puritanism, 5, 8, 11, 17, 19-21, 23-24, 60-61, 72, 90, 95, 108, 114, 120, 145, 157, 166, 181, 204, 278, 281, 283-84, 299, 305, 314. *See also* Anti-Puritan

Rainbow, 158
Rappites, 41
Raymond, Henry J., 193-95, 201, 212, 219-21, 236, 237-38, 239-40, 246-47, 263
Reeve, Tapping, 16, 18
Reid, Mayne, 274
Reid, Whitelaw, 257, 260, 261, 269, 272
Republican Party, 65, 137, 142, 175, 237, 240-41, 242-45, 246, 251, 258-59, 261, 268
Republican, Springfield, 261
Revivals: By Timothy Dwight at Yale, 9-11; Scotch-Irish, 33-34; of 1831, 36; Forest Camp-meetings, 121; of 1857, 91; during the Civil War, 140. *See* Great Awakening
Revolution, 149
Ripley, George, 206, 214, 230, 257
Rousseau, Jean Jacques, 8
Royall, Anne, 285-86
Rynders Mob, 135

A 3
B 4
C 5
D 6
E 7
F 8
G 9
H 0
I   1
J   2